MEDITERRANEAN GARDENING

A Waterwise Approach

MEDITERRANEAN GARDENING

A Waterwise Approach

Heidi Gildemeister

350 photographs by the author

Foreword by Christopher Brickell

University of California Press   Berkeley   Los Angeles   London

University of California Press
Berkeley and Los Angeles, California

University of California Press, Ltd.
London, England

© 1995 by Heidi Gildemeister
First California Edition, 2002

Library of Congress Cataloging-in-Publication Data

Gildemeister, Heidi.
   Mediterranean gardening: a waterwise approach /
Heidi Gildemeister ; foreword by Christopher
Brickell.—1st Calif. ed.
      p.   cm.
   Includes bibliographical references
(p.) and index.
   ISBN 0-520-23603-3 (cloth : alk. paper)—
ISBN 0-520-23647-5 (pbk. : alk. paper)
   1. Landscape gardening—Water conservation—
Mediterranean Region. 2. Drought-tolerant
plants—Mediterranean Region.   I. Title.

SB475.83.G56 2002
635.9'525—dc21   2002022335

Manufactured in Italy

10 09 08 07 06 05 04 03 02
10 9 8 7 6 5 4 3 2 1

Half-title page: A belvedere overlooks the Mediterranean
Frontispiece: Magnificent palms together with two lions
guard the access to a well-established waterwise garden

p.   6 In the author's garden
p. 10 *Nerium oleander*
p. 32 *Clivia miniata*
p. 60 *Hebe speciosa* hybrid
p. 92 *Passiflora* hybrid, possibly derived from *P. manicata*

Contents

FOREWORD by CHRISTOPHER BRICKELL   7

INTRODUCTION and ACKNOWLEDGEMENTS   8

Chapter One   THE ENVIRONMENT   10

THE MEDITERRANEAN CLIMATE   12
A Review of the Background

THE DOMINANT FORCES   16
Assets and Challenges

MEDITERRANEAN PLANT COMMUNITIES   20
Plant Life through the Seasons

NATIVE DROUGHT-TOLERANT PLANTS   24
How they Function and Survive

THE SOIL   28
Its Structure, Life and Care

**Chapter Two   WATERWISE GARDEN PLANNING
                AND DESIGN**   32

THE WAY AHEAD
Water-saving Gardening in Eight Steps   34

Step 1 - PLANNING YOUR GARDEN   36

Step 2 - CREATING PLANT COVER AND SHADE   40

Step 3 - USING DROUGHT-TOLERANT PLANTS   44

Step 4 - REDUCING THE LAWN, ALTERNATIVES   46

Step 5 - GROUPING PLANTS FOR WATER NEEDS   52

Step 6 - PLANNING WATER MANAGEMENT   54

Step 7 - USING WATER-SAVING PRACTICES   56

Step 8 - A WATERWISE GARDEN FOR ALL SEASONS   58

Chapter Three   WATERWISE GARDENCRAFT   60

PLANTING or The Happiness of Roots   62

MULCH. The Gardener's Ally   66

WATER. Its Wise Use   70

NUTRITION. Soil, the Primary Source   74

HEALTH. How to Prevent an early Death   78

PRUNING for Health, Growth and Flowering   82

WEEDS. Friend or Foe?   84

PROPAGATION. Simple Ways   86

MAINTENANCE   90

Chapter Four   PLANT SELECTION   92

HOW TO CHOOSE DROUGHT-TOLERANT PLANTS   94

PLANT LISTS FOR SPECIFIC USES   96

1000 DROUGHT-TOLERANT PLANTS   100

GLOSSARY   196

USEFUL ADDRESSES   197

BIBLIOGRAPHY   199

INDEX   201

Foreword

Although a few useful and informative books have been published in relatively recent years on gardening in Mediterranean climates, none has considered in any detail the vital need to assess accurately the relative water requirements for plants to grow successfully in regions where water availability is seasonally very limited.

In this book Heidi Gildemeister has drawn on her own very considerable experience over 20 years to fill this important vacuum and provides Mediterranean gardeners with an admirable account, not only of how to be successful, but the reasons why that success can be achieved if the practices of what the author terms 'water-wise gardening' are followed and implemented. In addition to advocating a range of water-saving practices and using a sensible organically-based approach to cultivation, (with particular emphasis on the importance of mulching and mulching materials), the author also takes into consideration the environmental aspects and consequences of growing plants in Mediterranean climates. She puts forward well thought out explanations for the gardening practices which she recommends from her own knowledge of what does and does not succeed. The descriptions of, and cultivation techniques for, over a thousand plants that the author grows, or has grown, in her garden in Spain and elsewhere (ornamentals, fruit and vegetables), will inspire anyone wanting to establish a garden in a Mediterranean climate, as well as those already gardening under similar conditions, to achieve similar results to those shown in the excellent photographs of her garden which illustrate Heidi Gildemeister's ideas. It is, in particular, the personal experience of success, and inevitably some failures, that will be invaluable to gardeners, not only in countries around the Mediterranean, but to other areas of the world where similar climatic and environmental conditions occur (California, Chile, South Africa, Australia) and where the principles and practices set out by the author are equally applicable.

The recommendations for integrating water-saving practices and related horticultural techniques with the environmental conditions that occur in dry regions, combined with the long personal knowledge and experience of the author, for whom this book has been a labour of love for more than 4 years, will undoubtedly provide inspiration for those in Mediterranean climates to succeed in producing gardens of beauty, not just in water-rich months, but throughout the year.

The Camber, April 1995   Christopher Brickell

Introduction

When I came to live in and love the Mediterranean lands, I brought with me, as probably most gardeners, memories of gardens I had tended elsewhere. A tropical jungle, a white bloom standing out against exotic foliage, exquisite scent pervading the air, was on my mind.

Pursuing this dream, I gardened all winter long and spring was exuberant. Later, the ardent summer sun burned for weeks over a rainless countryside. When the lawn turned brown and five inches of water were left in our tank, I awoke to reality.

The characteristics of the Mediterranean climate were new to me. What plants would tolerate such prolonged heat and dryness? Where to find them, how to make the right choice and care for them? How could water be saved?

After 'drought tolerance' became the main goal of my gardening efforts, I could find no books on the subject. Yet when I wrote to Botanic Gardens in Mediterranean type climates asking for information on drought tolerance, my gardening life changed. Experienced institutions were wonderfully willing to help, sending pamphlets on the subject, plant lists or even seed. One step led to the other while I discovered the long list of plants that do like dry summers.*

It was exciting to see that more often than not they had beautiful flowers and evergreen foliage. Some already grew in my garden, but were being watered unnecessarily. Discarding all unrealistic dreams, my choice of plants was now made on the basis of a reliable performance in Mediterranean summer drought, a well-defined plant structure and attractive blooms. Compact drought-tolerant evergreens were given high priority as their protective cover fulfils the needs of soil and humidity retention and harmonizes with the surrounding countryside. Easy maintenance and quick propagation were further characteristics looked for. Later, curiosity led me to include plants from the other four Mediterranean type regions. I considered hundreds to find those suitable for the many different niches on my ten acres.

When I did not know how to deal with new plants,

trial and error, supplemented by careful observation, had to replace written guidance. Plants do talk if we listen to them. Gradually I discovered that the 'dappled shade' of tall open tree canopies, wind shelter, generous mulching and excellent drainage were key factors in Mediterranean gardens and would keep most plants happy. 'Let winter rain do it' became one of my maxims together with respect for plants' summer dormancy. Choice of position needed more research, but provenance gave some guidance. For example giving plants from the South African Western Cape full sun would almost always work. The extremely dry 1994 summer taught me which plants stand up best to acute stress. Besides the rare 'problem child' for which I have not yet found the right approach, plants thrive.

It took me years to try out and assemble the Plant Selection for Mediterranean gardeners. Showing the vast plant potential of the Mediterranean climate, it includes over 1000 mostly drought-tolerant plants from nearly 500 genera, primarily Mediterranean natives, but also plants from other Mediterranean climates, such as bulbs from South Africa, ground cover shrubs from the California chaparral, *Acacia* from Australia, *Hebe* from New Zealand and little-known Chilean plants. A further choice (Asia, Argentina, Mexico) is perfectly suited to Mediterranean gardening. Little-used plants have been included whenever I felt they would serve gardeners well. The reader may wish to explore and experiment and thus widen the choice. Not every plant mentioned is easily obtained. I have tested their garden worthiness over years and believe that nurseries will offer them widely once gardeners ask for them. It would be a happy thought if this book contributed to that end.

Thanks to meteorological data kept by my husband since 1972, I know that in winter our garden (occasionally snow-covered) may experience zero degrees Celsius. Yet many plants that I grow are believed to need higher minimum temperatures or to depend on greenhouses, even heated ones. The Index thus provides a valuable up-to-date list of '0° Celsius tolerance'.

The use of the information in this book in places drier than the Mediterranean, where rain even in winter is scarce, is possible. Water-conserving practices are the same, the plant choice sometimes being iden-

---

* Plants that are invasive and therefore not recommended for use in the U.S. (California in particular) are identified in the list of drought-tolerant plants with •

tical to Mediterranean climates. Equally, horticultural practices as described suit all climates which experience drought.

Photographs aimed at giving botanical information, often showing plants in natural surroundings, will, it is hoped, delight the reader. I found much happiness while taking them.

Written for keen gardeners, professional horticulturists and landscape architects, this book also caters for beginners who require easy plants and plant enthusiasts who seek rare jewels. I have tried to make it easy for all to use, hoping it will help my fellow gardeners with modest but effective methods to create their evergreen paradise. To fit it all in, it is written in a rather didactic style.

Acknowledgements

I should regret it if a name was omitted as my gratitude goes to all who helped.

I am most appreciative of valuable information on drought from the East Bay Municipal District San Francisco, the Saratoga Horticultural Foundation, Dr. Sherwin Carlquist, the Los Angeles City Hall (Xeriscape Project), Jon Keeley, Department of Biology Occidental College, Los Angeles and in South Africa from the National Botanical Institute.

I gratefully acknowledge permission to quote from guidelines on drought published by the California Department of Water Resources and am indebted to Prof. Peter Raven for his generous permission to quote from 'Biology of Plants', to John Brookes to quote from his text and to Prof. F. di Castri for kindly allowing me to reproduce the map on page 13.

I express special gratitude to Christopher Brickell who all along has supported this book and who – between plant hunting trips to China – found time to write the foreword. I especially thank Dr. Michael Avishai who first recognized the need for a Mediterranean gardening book, for his encouragement and invaluable advice.

For their generous assistance I am indebted to the directors, curators and staff of the Botanical Gardens of Adelaide, Basel, Berlin, Bonn, Brissago, Canberra, Duesseldorf, Frankfurt, Geneva, Hamburg, Jerusalem, Kew, Kirstenbosch, Montpellier, Munich, Perth, Santa Ana, Santa Barbara, Soller, Villa Thuret and Wisley.

Seed exchange such as with the Indigenous Bulb Growers Association of South Africa, sometimes more unilateral than I should have wished, gave appreciated and stimulating new ideas.

Adrian Whiteley at Wisley helped with nomenclature. Jaume Garcias made the drawings. Elspeth Napier carefully edited the text before Francesc Moll, my publisher, took the project into his hands. I am grateful that I had a free hand with the design. It is to their courtesy I am greatly indebted.

'We' throughout the book refers to old Lorenzo, expert at setting stones or young Wil digging the best planting holes. I am grateful to them for never hesitating to go on when summer sun burned down on us, nor when winter winds brought showers of icy rain. Neither the garden nor the book could have been achieved without their unfailing help.

I plead forgiveness from family and friends who may have felt neglected while this book was in the making and thank them for their understanding and encouragement. Not least, my acknowledgements go to the garden for all it taught me and for its patience during the times when it could only be given scant attention.

My husband's faith in my ability to complete what I had begun made the book possible and it is to him that I dedicate it.

PHOTOGRAPHIC ACKNOWLEDGEMENTS

The following owners' kind permission to photograph their gardens, often involving considerable time, has been much appreciated: Señores de Arrom, Mrs Diandra Douglas, Condes de España, Mr and Mrs George Fischer, Señores de Garcia Ruiz, Señora von Haeften, Señor Bartolomé March, Señora Carmen March, Mme de Margerie, Señores de Obrador, M and Mme Pfitzner, Señores de Truyols, Señores de Zaforteza.

The following sent slides from their regions which I gratefully include in this book: Nancy Hardesty page 54; Ernst van Jaarsveld, Kirstenbosch 42, 112/bottom right; Montecito Water District, California 34; National Botanic Institute, Kirstenbosch (the late Prof. Rycroft 13, Liesl van der Walt 109/top, 132/bottom left); Walter Wisura, Santa Ana Botanic Garden 22, 77, 126/top, 137/top left, 141/top, 169/centre. Don Murray took the photograph on page 89 and Robin Saker 160. Rosemarie Brenneisen photographed the author.

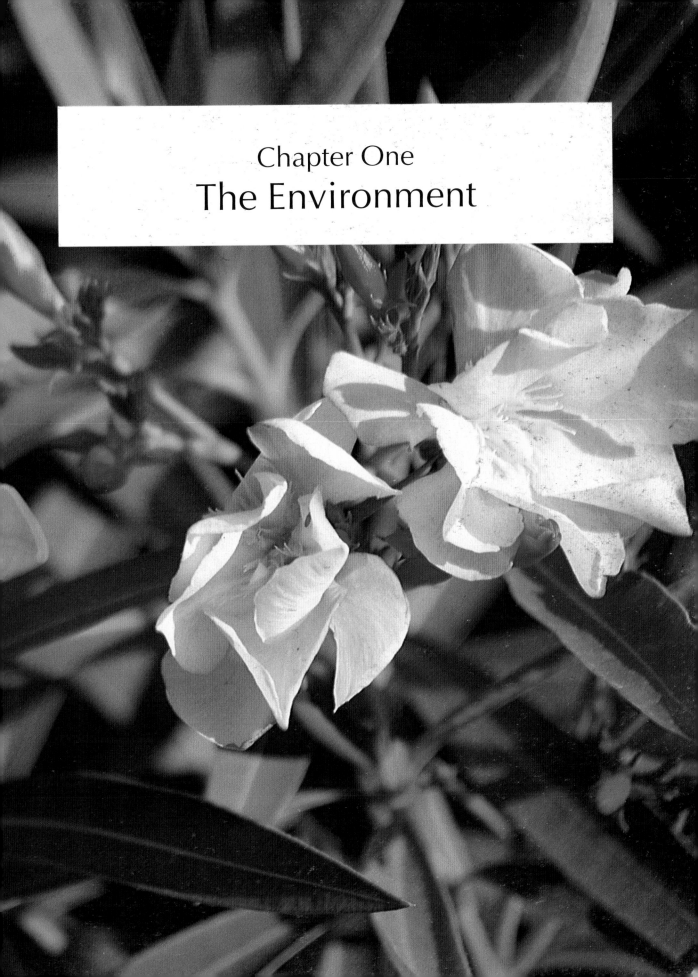

Chapter One
The Environment

The Mediterranean Climate
A Review of the Background

The Mediterranean climate takes its name from the sea which is one of its dominant traits. Its outstanding features are its hot and dry summers with mild winters bringing variable amounts of rain. A short spring and lengthy autumn are transition seasons. The predominant rainfall occurs during the cooler part of the year which gives rise to the appropriate term of 'winter rainfall' climate.

However, these factors, common to all Mediterranean type regions, still allow for a wide climatic diversity. For example in one region annual rainfall may amount to more than 1000mm, in another one 250mm is possibly all a thirsty soil will get.* Figures fluctuate considerably from year to year as was demonstrated by the 1994 drought.

The same variations occur with temperatures. Thus, depending on your region, you may describe winters as 'mild and humid', 'cool and moist' or even 'cold and wet'. But summers are always referred to as 'long, hot and dry'. Wherever you live in the world, if your climate corresponds to these characteristics, you will know that you garden in a Mediterranean climate.

The map illustrates the regions that have a Mediterranean climate: the winter rainfall belt of South Africa's Cape, central and southern coastal California, central Chile as well as southern and southwestern Australia. These five recognized Mediterranean ecosystems are located around 30-45° latitude in the northern and 30-40° latitude in the southern hemisphere and originate in global climate patterns. However, many regions in New Zealand and large stretches of coastal England, Ireland and Scotland, influenced by the Gulf Stream, qualify as well.

Romneya coulteri, a magnificent California native.

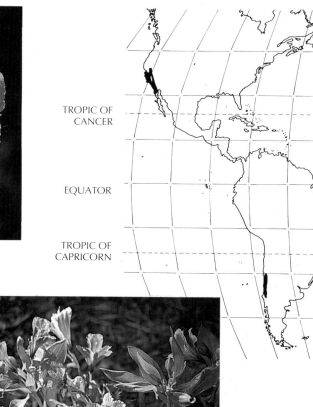

TROPIC OF
CANCER

EQUATOR

TROPIC OF
CAPRICORN

Right: *Alstroemeria,* one of the glories of Central Chile.

The map: di Castri,
Ecosystems of the World,
Amsterdam 1981.

A superb example of the Mediterranean *Chamaerops humilis,* framed
by a variety of other palms, thrives in the protected climate.

Acacia dealbata, an Australian gift to Mediterranean gardens.

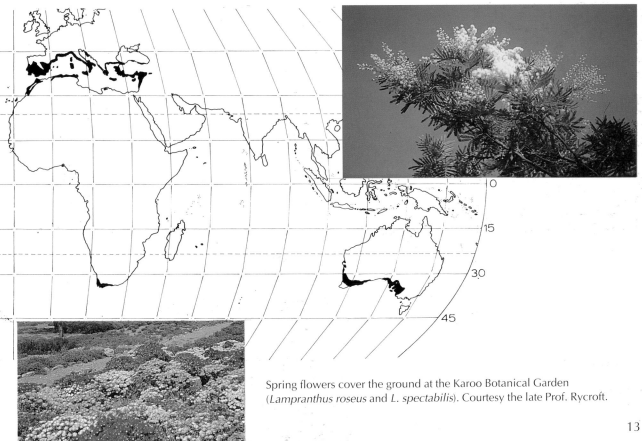

Spring flowers cover the ground at the Karoo Botanical Garden
(*Lampranthus roseus* and *L. spectabilis*). Courtesy the late Prof. Rycroft.

13

WHAT A MEDITERRANEAN SUN BESTOWS

Mean summer temperatures range from 22-27° Celsius while Seville (in one of the hottest Mediterranean regions) experiences 40°C throughout August.* During the 1987 July heat wave, in Athens temperatures rose to 45°C for days. Extremes are also endured in Lebanon, Malta, southern Turkey.*

Mean temperatures in January (the Mediterranean mean coldest month) range mostly from 5-10°C, but may drop to freezing and below. Coldest regions include former Yugoslavia (Split), northern Turkey, Israel.*

However, the Mediterranean basin is a reservoir for warmth. Locations near the sea (also near rivers or lakes) reduce the range between lowest and highest temperatures, particularly true for islands. Thus gardens enjoy more temperate climates the nearer they are to the sea; summers are not as hot as a few miles inland and winters are spared several degrees of cold. On a smaller scale, swimming pools or water tanks have a similar effect.

The characteristic blue Mediterranean skies give these regions the highest solar radiation and light intensities on earth. Almost all are more than the plants need and thus challenge plants' survival. Mean monthly hours of sunshine in January average 151, in July 366 hours. In winter, Almeria, Cyprus, Israel and Malta seem particularly favoured.*

The land and its shape (topography) strongly influence the climate, and altitude affects temperatures. Generally speaking, the Mediterranean-type countryside is either represented by low, often narrow coastal plains to an elevation of 350m (frequently protected by high mountain ranges) or by higher hilly areas, usually below 1000m above sealevel. There frost and snow may be experienced. Both are rare in coastal regions where the sea tempers climatic conditions.

The Riviera, protected from the north by the Maritime or Ligurian Alps, shows the influence of topography. Where mountains do not act as a protective shield, winter temperatures may drop below freezing (Rhône valley). Similar relief patterns exist in the other four Mediterranean-type regions, strongly affecting the local climate and creating many ecological niches which support a rich, extremely diverse, indigenous flora.

The Aleppo pine (*Pinus halepensis*) is one of the most drought-tolerant trees.

The Mediterranean basin is a reservoir for warmth. In summer, such clouds on a Mediterranean sky rarely bring rain.

RAINFALL

Mean annual rainfall ranges from Almeria/Spain 226mm to Antalya/Turkey 1028mm (Messina/Italy 974mm). Highest amounts are expected in December and January, lowest in August.*

Rain, rare in summer, generally begins around early autumn and continues into winter and spring, alternating with light drizzle. Occasionally, torrential rain may drop 100mm in 24 hours.

Note: If your garden were a basin, its water level would then rise by 10cm or, in other words, the entire garden would be covered by a water blanket 10cm thick!

Snow, hail or frost may occur in mountains or frost pockets. However, periods of drought with sunshine occur during what is considered the rainy winter season. They support growth and cell differentiation, crucial for control of flowering. Gradually, the rainy season tapers off into spring, followed by the dry summer, week after week of clear blue sky, clouds gathering only to disperse again. When the clouds finally burst, there may be little rain, not enough to wash the leaves.

Air humidity rises with proximity to the sea. Many coastal areas are frequently foggy (San Francisco). These 'grey days', without significant amounts of rain, have a powerful impact on growth. Bristles or hairs, which densely cover many Mediterranean plants, catch the moisture in the air, directing it to their roots either as drops or moisture flow along the stems. Such plants are virtually water-drenched after foggy days. This is an important factor, especially in those regions where fog hits sea-facing rock and water accumulates at its foot.

Note: Low fog, common during spring or autumn, allows watering (where carried out) to be postponed by several days.

* World Meteorological Organization, Geneva 1995

The Dominant Forces
Assets and Challenges

For the gardener, the Mediterranean climate, which is often believed to be merely 'warmer and sunnier' than a continental one, nevertheless differs in basic facts. Summer dormancy and winter bloom are among the prominent ones. Some characteristics can be considered benefits, others constitute challenges. A few, such as vegetative growth starting in autumn (via spring) triggered by the first cool nights, may elude classification. All must be taken into account to take full advantage of the Mediterranean climate potential.

THE MEDITERRANEAN GARDEN'S BENEFITS

In a Mediterranean climate, you have many assets in your hands. Their importance may vary depending on your region or personal criteria, but all contribute in making Mediterranean gardening an enjoyable occupation for all seasons.

– The foremost asset is winter rain which is guaranteed, though not its quantity. It lets plants thrive for months until they prepare for dry summers. However low, it will always provide sufficient humidity for the year *if* plants are chosen according to the region's average rainfall.

Basically, Mediterranean gardening is a simple affair: let winter rain do it. Freed of watering chores, you make good use of rain which is delivered to your garden, free of charge! The trick: use drought-tolerant natives, designed to grow and thrive with winter rain. Planted in early autumn, they fill up with water and become established over the mild winter. Although in the first summer they may need attention, with mulching most are on their way in the second year. Over the hot summer months bulbous plants go dormant, annuals die down.

– Next in line, mild, often sunny winters bring a wealth of flowers for gardeners to enjoy in their Eden. During this vital season plants grow and many garden activities take place. The garden is planned accordingly with walks, sheltered corners, winter-flowering evergreens.

– In a Mediterranean climate the unfavourable period for plant life is relatively short (summer drought and the ensuing dormancy), a quarter, maybe a third of the year. In contrast, the continental gardeners' unfavourable period (winter) may be long and frustrating when for months gardens are only seen from the house. The 'unfavourable' summer period is balanced by choosing plants with decorative survival strategies such as glossy, thick leaves and grey felt.

– Plants of a Mediterranean climate, mostly evergreen, provide year-round cover and interest. When well-planned, Mediterranean gardens have no 'dead season'.

– Mediterranean climates favour an exceptionally wide plant range, the so-called 'natives'. They allow you to choose plants best suited to each garden corner.

– Mediterranean climate vegetation is basically healthy. In the region where you garden, drought-tolerant natives grow wild and need no pesticides. With the liberal use of natives, your garden is lush yet you are saved many troubles. Remarkably carefree gardens result.

– Where the above assets are well understood, cost (water, chemicals) and labour savings (watering, fertilizing, spraying) are considerable.

Winter rain takes care of the evergreen lentisc shrubs (*Pistacia lentiscus*) and *Melianthus major* (back). Well-established bulbs provide splendid colour until summer drought forces them underground into rest.

Evergreen foliage, a main characteristic of the Mediterranean native plant world, is one of its great attractions.

Pistacia lentiscus (left) and *Ficus elastıca* (right) are among the best to stand long, hot and dry summers.

THE MEDITERRANEAN GARDEN'S CHALLENGES

With such solid benefits, a few challenges go hand in hand.

— The dominant forces of the Mediterranean climate's sun and light intensities and the seasonal character of its rainfall turn summer into an unfavourable interval for plants. Mediterranean plants cope with this period by becoming dormant, then resuming growth with first autumn rains.

— Wind, which in other climates is not always a liability, in Mediterranean regions can be a disadvantage. Hot dry winds from arid regions (Sahara sirocco) affect the moisture content of the air and desiccate delicate plant tissues (hard-leaved natives cope better). Cold moist winds primarily cause physical damage by ripping leaves. Winds from the sea carry saltwater drops which 'burn' vegetation, especially when tender spring growth has just come out. However, winds' beneficial effect is to harden tissues against drought or the weight of snow. Windbreaks constitute an important part of early garden planning.

— Dwindling water resources. When emerald green lawns became the fashion around the turn of the century, watering was applied to all plants whether required or not. Exotics were the novelty of the time. The 'English garden' with lawns, roses or recently introduced tropical trees was a forceful influence on the first gardens on the Riviera, made possible by ample labour and water. Although plant choice was not particularly suited to a Mediterranean climate, results were often magnificent where well carried out. Thus it was commonly believed that water was essential for splendid gardens. Where farmers formerly raised dry crops (olive, almond, carob, fig, wheat), today home owners envision swimming pools and green lawns. But neither unlimited water nor ample labour are available today. Dramatically rising demands, the result of increasing population and changing life styles, outstrip over-exploited sources. Brackish water penetrates over-abused wells while ancient cisterns bring little relief. And prices soar. Yet waterwise gardens are well possible, as you will see.

— Man's disruptive influence. Not only a shortage of water affects Mediterranean gardeners' lives, it is mankind's own doings they have to contend with. In former times, the Mediterranean countryside was covered by trees, giving shelter to man and protection from invading pirates. Most woods were lost early. Solomon gave Hiraj an army to cut down cedars in Lebanon to build temple and palace, followed by the Assyrian kings and Cyrus. Crusaders brought wood to Europe. Shipbuilding in the wake of New World discovery consumed more. Where large trees were venerated as gods, prophets ordered them to be cut to do away with competing gods (in Morocco, a few sacred groves still exist). To such mostly grandiose enterprises add the daily needs of the Mediterranean man and his animals which both took what they needed. Once the protective plant cover was removed, the fertile soil was washed into the sea.

Note: Woods covered early Greece to 60 %. Today 5 out of 100 trees remain (5 %). While you read this, of the five, not all may still be there.

Erosion is a constant threat in all Mediterranean environments. Bulldozers uproot trees, natural growth is destroyed, often replaced by unsuitable material. Uprooted vegetation, when dry, becomes a fire hazard. Stripped ground allows accelerated erosion. Unprotected, exposed to sun, wind and rain, soil is blown and washed away. New plantings seldom justify such violent action.

Fire. Man uses fire to open up woodlands, to renew plant growth or to increase land's pasture value (fire as a recycling power frees nutrients, returned to the soil as ashes). Badlands ravaged by erosion result, replacing established woodlands or a unique conifer forest. Invaded by short-lived weedy plants, they constitute a tremendous set back.

Lately humanity has created for itself an additional problem: waste, building up at an ever accelerating speed. While inorganic waste such as plastic is more difficult to dispose of, organic waste is recycled readily via mulch and compost.

The Air. Solar radiation, partly unchecked by the destruction of the ozone layer, may soon not only become too powerful for humans but also for plants. Replanting and greening the land, at every gardener's disposal, is a unique means to reduce CO_2 sent into the air. Research discloses that plants with prominent survival strategies best tolerate an impaired ozone layer.

Yet destruction is not necessary, as experience has shown me.

Although summer-dormant, *Euphorbia dendroides* (fore-ground) still looks attractive. This natural planting creates a perfect link with the surrounding countryside.

Almonds (*Prunus dulcis*) are a prominent dry crop, but many fields today have been converted into gardens with high water demands.

In this well-designed garden with wind-protected walks and carefully clipped *Quercus ilex* and *Rhamnus alaternus,* garden life in winter is ongoing. Such evergreen gardens thrive on winter rain and, of all year interest, have no dead season.

Mediterranean Plant Communities
Plant Life through the Seasons

MEDITERRANEAN PLANT COMMUNITIES

The Mediterranean region was once covered by trees, mainly oak, and in undisturbed areas woodlands may still cover larger tracts. The undisturbed, evergreen oak forest with holm oak (*Quercus ilex*) in the western and kermes oak (*Q. coccifera*) in the eastern Mediterranean, has a rich undergrowth of *Arbutus, Cistus, Erica arborea,*

Phillyrea, Rhamnus and *Viburnum tinus* while honeysuckle and clematis climb trees and shrubs.

Pines are legion. The Italian parasol pine (*Pinus pinea*) casts deep shade where grown in dense stands. Isolated on sandy western shores, with a rich undergrowth (*Juniperus phoenicea, Pistacia lentiscus, Spartium junceum*), its outline is impressive. On siliceous rock (French Riviera) the maritime pine (*Pinus pinaster* or *maritima*) grows in almost pure stands. The Aleppo pine (*Pinus halepensis*), usually not as large, likes a calcareous soil and much heat. As each prefers a distinct area, they rarely mingle. In open stands, these woods are undergrown by *Cistus salviifolius, C. monspeliensis, Erica multiflora, Myrtus communis.*

Ancient olive and carob grow in large stands on terraced land. In the eastern Mediterranean you may locate a few isolated laurel woods or scattered cypress. Deciduous trees (ash, chestnut) replace evergreen forests at higher altitudes and still higher are in turn replaced by conifers (fir, cedar). In Greece, secluded *Abies cephalonica* woods persist, occasionally accompanied by *Pinus nigra* (Huxley & Taylor, 1984).

Once trees are felled or burned, the woods degenerate into maquis, the Italian macchia. Dense, often spiny thickets predominate (*Calicotome*). Evergreen lentisc, Spanish broom and juniper, wild olive, rock rose, rosemary and lavender often accompany tree heaths. Maquis can also be seen as a potential forest, crippled by uncontrolled grazing. The lack of fencing, a relic of nomadic usage, prevents young trees from emerging and makes recovery difficult.

When over-exploited and more soil is washed away, maquis deteriorates further into a thin plant cover on rock, called garrigue. Low and shrubby, frequently impenetrable plant communities are dominated by the

Olive trees may grow from sheer rock and their twisted trunks are forever a dramatic sight.

holly-leaved shrubby oak (*Quercus coccifera*, actually a much grazed tree) and by *Euphorbia, Hypericum, Phlomis*, juniper or aromatic herbs. Thorny species such as the golden-flowered *Ulex parviflorus*, defend themselves against grazing. Among open rock, they grow with a rich range of often showy bulbous and annual plants in a massive spring display (*Allium, Anemone, Crocus, Gladiolus, Narcissus, Orchis, Ornithogalum, Scilla*). As you travel towards the dry inland, shrublands often open up and perennial grasses constitute an important ground cover.

Where sandy shores give way to rock, often dropping steeply into the sea, you find a vast range of indigenous cushion plants (white-felted *Anthyllis, Centaurea*). Often spectacular, they cling to cliffs, their shape protecting them against salt-laden winds (*Globularia*). Cliffs, often a last refuge for plants which formerly grew in fields, are botanists' cherished studying ground.

In a characteristic woody plant cover, *Clematis flammula* climbs over *Pistacia lentiscus* reaching for a sturdy oak (*Quercus ilex*).

The barren garrigue, almost soilless, still produces in autumn such glories as the delicate *Merendera filifolia*.

The Mediterranean is rich in endemics, plants whose distribution is confined to restricted areas, possibly to an acre or much less and which do not occur elsewhere. Greece has 559 species with probably more to be discovered.

Besides the natives, which amount to thousands, over the centuries a great number of exotics have been introduced. Some have adapted so well and been used so widely that today they often are considered to be natives. *Citrus medica*, known in Mesopotamia in 4000 BC, was the first citrus fruit to be introduced. And who would believe that palms (except *Chamaerops humilis*) are not native? Today, together with mimosa, they make up the Mediterranean landscape.

The Mediterranean maquis and garrigue have an equivalent in the other four Mediterranean type regions, in South Africa referred to as fynbos, chaparral in California, matorral in Chile, heathlands in Australia. A glance at the Plant Selection reveals their tremendously rich vegetation.

The flora of the western Cape is tolerant of the poor soils of the area (similar to Australia). An extremely rich flora (24,000 species in South Africa, 10 % of the world total), unsurpassed elsewhere, has a high proportion of endemism. An important component is the particularly rich geophyte flora, commonly called 'Cape bulbs'.

Californian native plants are sometimes defined as those the native Americans knew before the arrival of the European colonists. Ironically, English gardeners discovered this flora before most Californians did, and Americans visiting British gardens are often surprised to see so many Californian natives. The same seems to happen to Mediterranean gardeners who see more Mediterranean natives grown in England than in their own gardens.

A rich undergrowth of *Cistus albidus* graces many woods. In our garden, a wild stand was put to good use in the natural garden, a 'tended wilderness'.

The magnificent *Yucca whipplei* ssp. *parishii* grows wild in the chaparral-covered hillsides of the San Gabriel Mountains in California. Courtesy Santa Ana Botanic Garden.

MEDITERRANEAN PLANT LIFE THROUGH THE SEASONS

The seasonality of the Mediterranean climate profoundly differs from that of more northern or southern latitudes. A distinctive rhythm of growth and sprouting, flowering and summer dormancy is the main feature of the Mediterranean-type climate. Day length varies between seasons and serves as signal for many plants to start or end their life cycle.

When long, hot and dry summers draw to an end, the cool of the night comes and steers new life into dormant buds. Autumn, often referred to as 'little spring', actually starts with the first cool night towards summer's end. In the wild, a herald for rains approaching, the sea squill's milk white spires push up from giant half-buried bulbs, followed by shiny leaves (*Urginea maritima*). Once first rains fall, the strain of the heat is relieved and plants start to grow again. Meadows turn green once more and birds sing in champagne-like air. Delicate white bloom of *Abelia* and pink clouds of *Anemone hupehensis* var. *japonica* light up shaded corners. *Pistacia* puts forth brilliant reddish shoots while dainty flowers cover *Pavonia hastata*. *Yucca* grow slender stems with pendent creamy bells. *Euphorbia dendroides*, leaves shed with summer drought, recover green, spring-like foliage. Succulent *Aeonium* pull the sap back into their leaves.

Autumn brings also a first taste of spring splendour with flowering bulbs, many leafless (*Colchicum, Crocus, Merendera*). Out of nowhere, not minding the stoniest site, appears the lovely yolk-coloured *Sternbergia lutea*.
Note: You have cut back spent bloom in time and now enjoy a new flush (*Coreopsis, Felicia, Salvia*).

In this 'second spring' plants grow for many weeks, barely influenced by shortening days, occasional lower temperatures, wind or rain. But a week of adverse conditions makes itself felt.

While in cooler temperate climates winter with frozen or snow-covered ground brings garden life virtually to a stop, in mild Mediterranean winters rain alternates with periods of warm sunshine. This is the season of growth and bud formation to burst forth in a colourful spring display, unparalleled in other climates. Thanks to mild weather, flowers are out through the winter. A list made up at year's end would include dozens (see p. 97). *Euryops pectinatus*'s yellow stars accompany *Leonotis leonurus,* orange-coloured spikes standing high. *Freylinia lanceolata* with exquisite scent calls from afar, while *Hebe* from New Zealand enhances gardens over months. A few weeks later, in a field of fresh light green leaves, the first calla lily (*Zantedeschia aethiopica*) stands out. *Abutilon* bells droop gracefully against a light blue sky, *Buddleja madagascariensis* pushes forth soft yellow spikes while many *Acacia* follow each other over weeks. On a grey day, rosemary's bluest bloom stops you in your path.

In spring, annuals such as the yellow *Chrysanthemum coronarium* or the glorious poppy paint fields to the horizon.

Evergreens retain their leaves through the mild winter when they use the ample moisture and the high light intensity of sunny intervals to continue assimilating and building up their vegetative mass, compensating for the drought-induced summer dormancy.

Lowest temperatures are registered during January or February and it is during these two months that snow, if ever, can be expected. In the Balearic Islands, the quiet sunny days of January are called 'calmas de enero'. February has many faces. If by the end of that month snow has not fallen, its likelihood for the year is over and spring is on its way.

It is in spring that the Mediterranean native flora is seen at its best. With plenty of light, rising temperatures induce a burst of growth and flowering which carpets the land with colour to the horizon. In the garden, each week brings more bloom. *Crocus*, *Leucojum aestivum*, *Muscari* and *Narcissus* accompany South African *Babiana*, *Bulbinella*, *Hesperantha* and *Moraea*. Suddenly cyclamen are everywhere.

In many Mediterranean regions hot and dry winds plus rising temperatures often bring this splendid spring display to an abrupt end, causing seed to ripen and disperse. For many plants native to this area (*Euphorbia dendroides*), the first sign of water stress is a signal to stop their exuberant growth and enter summer dormancy, while annuals hurry to set seed. With moisture in the topsoil depleted and temperatures in the mid-twenties or thirties, the long, hot and dry summer arrives. As life subsides (garden work too), leaves use characteristic adaptations which allow natives to go without water for months (see Survival Strategies). Many bulbous plants (most Cape bulbs, bulbous or rhizomatous irises, *Ornithogalum*, *Pancratium*) bake in the hot ground. This summer dormancy is vital for flower formation and crucial for their health.

When fields turn golden and seeds rest in the dry ground, summer skies may be dramatic sights.

In a burst of vitality an almond tree (*Prunus dulcis*) in late winter is an early promise for rich, colourful spring bloom.

Yet, amid summer drought, *Amaryllis belladonna* pushes up pink, sweetly scented bloom in such hurry that leaves are left behind. For weeks glorious *Crinum* bridge this period of rest.

LIFE CYCLES

Annuals' life cycle originates in autumn, using the winter months to build up vegetative volume and burst into colourful mass-flowering in spring.

Bulbous plants have two different patterns. Most start their life cycle with first autumn rains, build up foliage over winter and burst forth with bloom during late winter or spring. Others (often still leafless) are autumn-flowering.

Evergreen trees start their life cycle in spring with a new flush of growth, deciduous ones with a deluge of flowers (almond, redbud, styrax).

23

Native Drought-Tolerant Plants
How they Function and Survive

No life on earth would be possible without oxygen. Plants are a vital link in the carbon and oxygen cycle in nature

Water is taken up by roots and is transpired via leaves as vapour into the air. Plants' water exchange with their surroundings is a colossal activity, widely responsible for rain and vital for life on our planet.

Water, 90 % or more of total plant weight, is essential for plant operations. A continuous water column extends from root hairs to leaf pores, taking root-absorbed nutrients to the upper plant body. In the other direction it transports sugars, produced in above ground sections, to roots. The water column's upward movement occurs when water pressure in the plant body exceeds its holding capacity and water vapour transpires via minute leaf openings (stomata). Under water stress when transpiration exceeds root-absorbed water, water-conserving plants close these openings, whereafter the plant ceases to transpire. It then produces no more sugars as closed stomata cannot take up carbon dioxide. Desert plants, transpiring little, reduce water exchange to a minimum and survive long life spans in dormancy.

Note: Water 'tightens' the channels which are responsible for plants' holding up. S. Carlquist (1985), Research Botanist, Santa Barbara Botanic Garden, discovered with many dry habitat plants a specific cellular arrangement which guarantees their remaining rigid even with lack of water. Thus wood structure may predict drought tolerance in plants.

Thousands of microscopic stomata, generally open only during the day, allow the entry of carbon dioxide from which, together with soil water, the green leaf cells photosynthesize sugars and provide them to all non-green parts, releasing oxygen as a 'waste product' into the air. Chlorophyll, the green pigment in leaves, is essential in this process for which sunlight provides the energy. Too high light intensities destroy chlorophyll, eventually scorching the foliage. When plants under drought can take up only little water, food production is reduced and plants live on their reserves.

Strong solar radiation with high light intensities results in increased evaporation from soil and transpiration from plants (evapo-transpiration). While temperate climate plants need good supplies to cool surfaces, Mediterranean natives maintain their water balance through their own combinations of adaptive qualities. By reduced transpiration they can survive with little or no water other than rainfall, storing it too. Their efficient adaptations to a low supply of water, soil and nutrients, (called 'survival strategies') are ingenious and fascinating to observe.

Drought tolerance, greatly affected by soil and microclimates, varies with site and species. In response to the continuous stress under which plants evolve, annual growth increment is small. The result is uniform size and shape. Compact growth and cushion form is characteristic. Consider for example the oak. Not usually tall, the trunk and branches are massive, storing water in tissues under a thick bark (cork oak). A dense canopy shades a secluded world against the brilliance beyond (holm oak).

Evergreen (sclerophyllous) leaves, often hard and spiny to touch, are characteristic not only of oak but of many Mediterranean plant families; they reduce water loss by a choice of adaptations. These include active control mechanisms (closing stomata, stomata sinking into cracks in the epidermis) as much as passive ones. A thick cuticle is often combined with light-reflecting waxy coating. Microscopic scales give plants a whitish or greyish tint, highly effective in reflecting light and heat. Once stomata are closed, leaves cannot continue photosynthesis to prepare food. Yet their evergreen character permits them to do so over mild winters. These leaves usually last several years before being discarded which saves precious water, nutrients and energy.

Careful leaf-positioning, another feature, creates within the plant a favourable shade centre. It may also, in contrast, avoid leaf exposure to sun (many legumes close up leaves during the day, *Cneorum* holds them

Verbascum with its felty leaves copes well with drought.

Euphorbia dendroides is a master in coping with drought. Spring foliage grows into the typical rounded shape. With summer drought, leaves dry up and fall off. The plant survives summer in a leafless state. Buds resume growth with autumn rains.

Above: Wax-covered succulence protects *Agave attenuata* from drying out.

Silvery leaves, here reduced to narrow lances, reflect light effectively.

vertically). Mutual leaf-shading is evident with *Ajania pacifica*. After planting, optimum drought-tolerance is only reached once leaves have repositioned themselves into their characteristic pattern!

Leaf reduction is common, achieved by scales in all sizes and shapes, but also by narrow leaves (rosemary, many *Hakea*). Often blade surface is limited to bits of tissue along needle-like leaves. Such 'needles', encountered in a wide plant range, cover the whole spectrum from perennials (*Asparagus*) to conifers (*Juniperus*).

Many species feature dissected blades (*Argyranthemum, Artemisia, Melianthus*).

Leaf protection is achieved by adaptations which cool the surface. The secretion of a water-repellent, gazeous layer (ethereal oils), well-known to one who walks lavender fields, conserves water vapour pressure on leaf surfaces. Similar patterns exist with South African *Atha-*

Below: Multiple survival strategies predestine *Ajania pacifica* for drought-tolerant gardens. White, felty leaf undersides inhibit drying out on hot summer sand (coastal gardens). This 'felt' covers also leaf edges (silver-lined appearance). Fine silvery hairs on leaves' upper side reflect light. Mutual leaf-shading and dissected leaf blades of compact rosettes are further features.

nasia or Californian composites. To retain water vapour pressure, an astonishing number of plants have protuberances on their leaves (felt, woolliness, dense spiny covers or their combination). When silvery, they also act as reflectors of light.

Doing without leaves. Many plants, including bulbs, have evolved life cycles that include summer deciduousness and dormancy. Others, in a summer-dormant, green yet leafless state, confine photosynthesis to stems (*Retama monosperma, Spartium junceum*). This is often combined with the conversion of the branch tips into protective spines.

When fields turn golden dry, countless annuals, in an 'avoidance reaction' to drought, complete their life cycle by seed dispersal. Mechanisms such as chemical inhibitors, in for example legumes, prevent germination in unfavourable conditions. Sprouting follows when conditions are favourable (rain, warmth). So-called ephemeral plants, surviving drought as dormant seed, respond to irregular rain periods (sometimes after years) by sprouting, flowering and setting seed with incredible speed.

Efficient water storage is widely used by succulents which store water in thickened stems, leaves and/or roots and harden the skin to seal it in (waxy covers).

Plants from different families such as Euphorbiaceae and Cactaceae, sometimes adopt similar survival strategies, looking almost alike. This so-called convergence is also found with *Fatsia* and *Ricinus*.

Numerous tropical families (bromeliads, orchids) or subtropical succulents (Crassulaceae) take in vital carbon dioxide only over night when water loss from stomata is lowest. Known as CAM, crassulacean acid metabolism is an efficient use of water.

Below the soil surface, multiple root adaptations are found, frequently combined (see The Soil). Contrary to common belief that all drought-tolerant plants search for ground water, in regions with one brief, often torrential annual rainfall the surface roots absorb water before it runs off quick-drying ground.

Through one or more of these adaptations plants cope with dry summers. In the fight for survival every species chooses its 'tricks and weapons'. But whatever method they use, the result is to retain precious water and *survive.*

Left: *Ricinus officinalis* (above) and *Fatsia japonica* (below) use similarly dissected palmate leaves as a survival strategy and show well the so-called convergence.

Right: Natives from Mediterranean climates such as *Pelargonium, Argyranthemum* and lavender against a background of olive trees create a drought-tolerant, low-maintenance plant assemblage.

The Soil
Its Structure, Life and Care

The soil, its life and care and the plant (also its nutrition) are interdependent. Understanding the soil and also plants' functions and needs enables us to grow healthy plants well able to withstand stress.

SOIL STRUCTURE

Soils consist of solid particles which are, depending on their shape, surrounded by smaller or larger open spaces filled with water and air. Ideal soils contain 50 % solid matter. The remaining open-spaced 50 %, divided equally between water and air, allow oxygen and carbon dioxide to circulate freely, provide vital drainage and retain water and nutrients. In Mediterranean climates, the following soil types (or any mixture of these) are found:

Particles seen by the naked eye constitute well-aerated, easily-worked sandy soils. High quartz contents build up healthy structures and warm the soil. However, sandy soils, threatened by wind erosion, have poor moisture retention. Predominant along coasts, often alkaline, the few nutrients they may hold are quickly washed out. Water retention, most favourably influenced by organic matter, is helped by adding humus, mulch and loam.

Microscopic particles constitute compact clay which tends to crack deeply when drying. Its low volume of air and water curbs life within it. Mineral content is usually high and contributes to healthy growth. Organic matter (compost, mulch) improves such soils which are heavy to work and slow to warm up.

Loamy soil is an intermediate type. Easily worked, warming up readily, its high humus content stores water, air and nutrients. Such favourable conditions are maintained by mulching and adding compost.

SOIL LIFE OR SOIL INHABITANTS

Ideal soils contain an active, microscopic life, living in well-defined layers with specific activities.

Most activity occurs in the top strata (a few centimetres deep, immediately below a mulch) which contains much organic material dead and alive. Here billions of microbes, myriads of minute bacteria, algae and fungi (organic material's principal decomposers, only seen with a powerful microscope) effect solids' first disintegration. Beetles and worms, working just under the surface, decompose fallen leaves, woody chips, decaying animal corpses. As will be seen with compost, soil life performs best in aerated, humid warmth.

The earthworm illustrates soil life's vital function. It works in the top layer but its tunnels go through all soil strata, contributing to aeration and water-holding capacity. Soils, rich in earthworms, produce yearly tons of casts per hectare. Such casts, pure humus of the finest nutritional value, contain 5x nitrogen, 7x phosphorus, 11x potassium, 3x magnesium, 2x calcium than surrounding soils (Raven 1986, p.523).

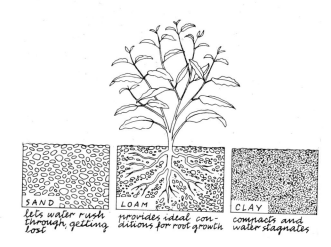

SAND
lets water rush through, getting lost

LOAM
provides ideal conditions for root growth

CLAY
compacts and water stagnates

In the second strata, immediately below the 'cutting up' horizon, decomposing plants and animals and weathered rock (ample trace elements, depending on stones' composition) are deposited. Different but equally specific microbes convert the top layer's cut up materials into nutrient solutions available to plants, the resulting material called humus. Humus contains a dynamic life, constantly building up or decomposing materials. Rich in carbon dioxide and nitrogen (fixed partly in the soil), it stores water and nutrients, phosphoric acid and potash from the remains of dead microbes. Porous, well aerated humus warms up quickly. The fine roots of most plants grow into this layer which rarely reaches 10-30cm deep and is at the base of the nutritional cycle between soil, plants, animals and human beings.

Below the second (humus) layer, roots find the third (mineral) layer which may reach a long way down, where soil life decreases steadily. Here, broken up rock provides plants with nutritional elements and stored water. Further down, roots encounter solid rock. In Mediterranean regions, rock belonging 'way down', is often seen at the surface.

Humus is the treasure of wise gardeners who tend and increase it so it will nurture and support their plants. They assist its microscopic life which, free of cost, works the soil and feeds plants. They follow the example seen in light mixed woods, where fallen leaves protect the ground. Carefully lifting the upper cover, one discovers a dark, aerated humusy soil, teeming with life, a beetle running for cover, worms retreating into the dark, ants carrying materials. Knowing little of this minute animal world, often associated with 'pests', we may not realize that it is an integral part of 'soil life' which steadily decomposes a light leaf layer and small animal corpses, enriching the soil for the growth of new organisms. Such forest soil stores nutrients and holds rainwater for a long time. In perfect equilibrium between resources and output, no fertilizing is needed. What has been taken from the earth is returned to it. This is an on-going process, if not interfered with by man.

Note: Forest soils conserve nutrients efficiently. When cleared of vegetation, calcium and potassium losses amount to around twenty-fold, nitrogen loss is even higher while the run-off quadruples in comparison with the previous forest. (Hubbard Brook Test USA, 1965/6),

Ideal living conditions (aerated humid soil, mild temperatures) assist this finely-woven soil life which scientists call edaphon. Careful gardeners refrain from disturbing it (i.e. by digging). Easily asphyxiated in a clogged winter soil or washed away by erosion, an uncovered ground exposes it to burning. Strong chemicals are uncongenial and due to a greatly increased public awareness, gardeners search for alternatives.

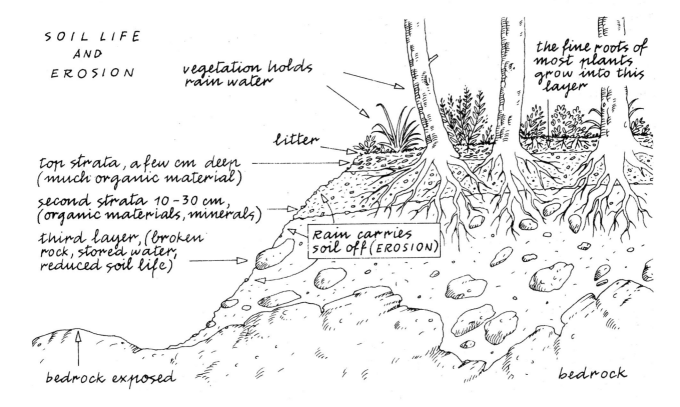

SOIL LIFE AND EROSION

vegetation holds rain water

the fine roots of most plants grow into this layer

litter

top strata, a few cm deep (much organic material)

second strata 10-30 cm, (organic materials, minerals)

third layer, (broken rock, stored water, reduced soil life)

Rain carries soil off (EROSION)

bedrock exposed

bedrock

Where winter rainfall's erosive forces have done away with most soil, rock is now seen at the surface, yet belongs 'way down'. In the foreground, a few wild olive (*Olea europaea* var. *oleaster*), grazed over the centuries, carve out a meagre living. Fenced, they would turn into trees (p.164).

Once the land is fenced, a few sturdy plants will gradually find a hold on rock and slowly build up soil, a first step towards covering the ground. Sturdy *Spartium junceum* and *Phillyrea angustifolia* (at the back) combine beautifully with a blue Mediterranean sky.

SOIL CARE: AMENDMENTS AND CORRECTIONS

Mediterranean soils, where exposed to erosion by winter rainfall, are poor in organic matter. Upper humus layers are usually lacking and rarely reach the required 5 % of soil volume. Due also to high solar radiation, organic materials break down rapidly. Soil-leaching is significant; nitrogen is washed out and is frequently absent in dry soils (careless summer irrigation has a similar effect).

High evaporation rates encourage salt accumulation in the topsoil from subsurface layers, inhibiting many ornamental, salt-sensitive plants (Ericaceae, certain Myrtaceae). Sandy saline soils, especially in low-lying coastal areas, may need flushing of salt by 'sweet' water.

As a general rule, soils in Mediterranean low-rainfall regions tend to be alkaline. Alkalinity affects the nutrient uptake of plants and where pronounced, may reduce nutrient availability. Iron deficiency for example induces symptoms of chlorosis and die-back and is bettered by organic matter. A pH of 6.8 seems to suit most plants.

Plants such as *Hibiscus* or *Camellia* demand acid soils. Sawdust and pine needle mulches acidify soils but as they are poor in nutrients, compete with plants for soil nitrogen while decomposing (see Organic Mulches).

Poor parched soils are ameliorated by slow-acting organic food such as mature manure or well-combined green mulches. They prevent the loss of nitrogen by leaching, provide well-aerated soils and thus activate soil life which in turn helps nitrogen absorption. But a balanced compost, rich in humus and microorganisms, is the best slow-release nitrogen source and ideally constitutes 5 % of soil volume.

Compost recycles vegetative substances, the same recycling which today is on everybody's mind. Compost holds the key to water retention and fertility and is an excellent alternative to peat. It is easily prepared while peat develops over thousands of years and is a non-renewable resource. Compost transforms garden refuse (spent flowers, cut branches, old reed baskets) into gardeners' fertile, nutrient-rich 'brown gold'. Do not shy away from adding fish bones. Animal manure and kitchen garbage can be mixed in too, but use woody materials sparingly and aim for variety. Choose a shaded area. Hot sun, deep shade, wind and paving are to be avoided. But even if not built as advocated by organic gardening books, such a compost heap is better than none.

Microbes decompose and transform the dead materials. Maximum surface area of the materials, achieved by shredding, supports their work. Aerated humid warmth results in a successful (aerobic) process; (an anaerobic slimy putrition, resulting from cold compacted layers, produces harmful products). In the process, other microorganisms replace the first ones whose dead bodies enrich the compost (a spade-full of compost contains more living material than human beings are on earth). Microbes generate heat (up to 70°C.) which, well-managed, destroys most weed seeds.

It is the aim of the gardener to encourage this transformation where dead materials promote life. Having achieved that delicate balance, plants grow in optimum conditions, faring for themselves, as in nature.

ROOTS

Drought-tolerant plants' survival is
largely dependent on roots' well-being.

A garden's visible feature depends on its hidden underground life: the roots sprout, store nutrients and are interrelated with soil life. In a constant, very complex interaction, soil life and roots live on each others' assimilation products. In Mediterranean gardens distinctive root systems (from northern, Mediterranean and tropical regions) exist:

Tree roots of the first two groups maintain wide-branching roots, tightly interwoven with soil life. Numerous species from Mediterranean-type environments (heather, oak, pine, Proteaceae) have evolved a mutually beneficial relationship between their roots and soil-borne fungi (mycorrhizae), important in water uptake, nutrition and establishment. Soil fungi penetrate (or cover) root tips and grow on root-provided nutrients until they are gradually destroyed by the roots which then feed on their components. Mycorrhizae supply nutrients (e.g. phosphorus) to plants which are otherwise unavailable.

A similar symbiosis between soil bacteria and root cells occurs in root nodules (especially legumes). Specialized soil bacteria use elements provided by the plant to fix nitrogen on which the plant can draw. Plants profit from this supply. Later, decomposing plant remains in the soil are a readily available fertilizer.

Additionally, Mediterranean woody plants' deep or wide-branching roots not only penetrate narrow crevices but also (in close association with soil organisms) absorb nutrients from what seems to us solid rock (*Genista, Pistacia*). Their secondary, superficial roots, easily damaged by horticultural malpractice (digging, ploughing) are directed towards rapid water absorption.

Smaller plants (grasses, perennials) with active and dormant stages rebuild roots seasonally, exploiting nutrients and moisture in varying depths at different seasons.

Bulbous plants have two root systems. Fleshy bulbs from cool temperate regions or mountain areas (*Colchicum, Crocus, Tulipa*) grow annual roots which die down in summer. Dryer rhizomes, tubers and bulbs from the warmer Mediterranean (*Asphodelus, Cyclamen, Paeonia*) or the southern hemisphere (*Alstroemeria, Nerine, Scadoxus*) have perennial roots which live 3-4 years. Annual rooted ones survive prolonged periods of drought which would set back perennial roots. Yet both require summer-baking in dry soil where undisturbed roots are dormant but functional. Irrigation at this time may cause rotting.

The roots of tropical plants (*Hedychium, Ficus*) are active all year and reflect the favourable native environment.

Root growth occurs mostly near root tips. Dense, fine hairs sense where to find nutrients, humidity or microbes, choosing among the supply those elements which suit the plant best. Feeder roots flourish in soil layers rich in organic matter. This can mean a shallow 15cm. While the new root hairs absorb nutrients, the older (woody) roots, in an impeccable labour division, anchor the plant.

Total root surface usually balances the above ground plant mass. Roots are often densest where leaves' drip line provides most water, while others abound around stems to where leaves direct humidity. During prolonged dry seasons, you may find root action as deep as 5m.

Tanacetum parthenium (left), the bulbous *Allium triquetrum* (right)
and in the centre a weed from the fields display widely different roots.

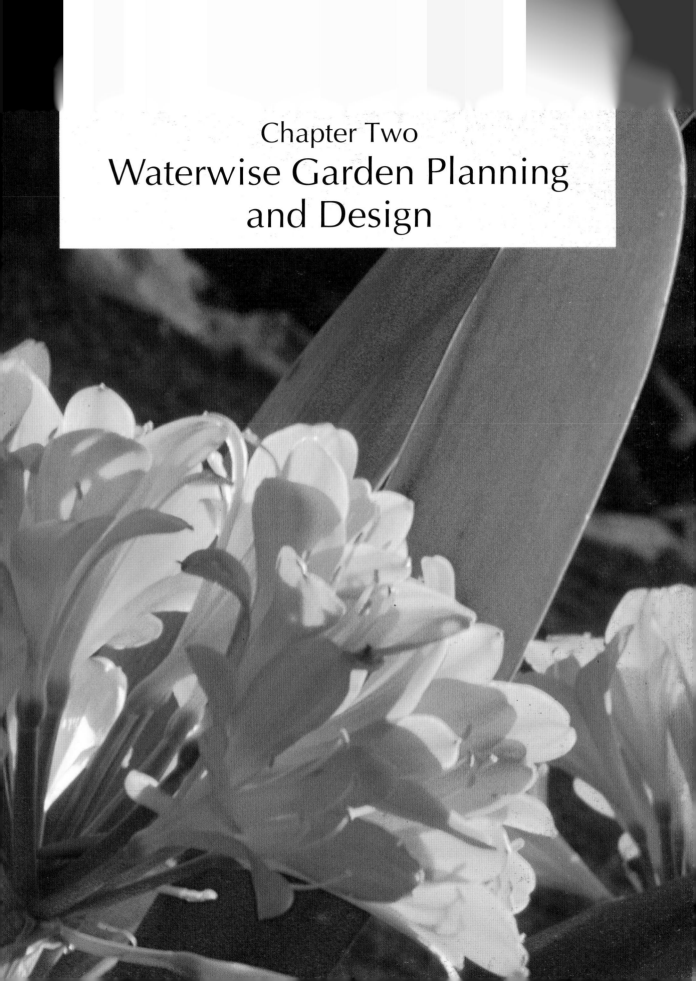

Chapter Two
Waterwise Garden Planning and Design

The Way Ahead
Water-Saving Gardening in Eight Steps

Water on earth is a stable resource and cannot be replaced.

Should you be new to gardening in a Mediterranean climate, you may wonder how to compensate for hot, dry summers and their intense light, made worse by wind's desiccating force, how to cover bare ground where winter rains have carried most soil away, expos- ing bare rock. You may wonder how to garden where water is short at the time when you feel that you need it most. How, you will ask, can I create the green Eden I dream about?

In the same way as plants have evolved their survival strategies, devise those for your garden. Balance the Mediterranean climate's unfavourable aspects by taking advantage of the favourable ones. The following guide lines will be the survival strategies of your garden and your prime concern. If you are prepared to follow a few simple steps, with little water, expense and labour, an evergreen flowering garden throughout the year will be yours, in harmony with its surroundings.

Many gardeners living in a Mediterranean-type climate, particularly California and Israel, use water-

saving methods. Apparently, it is not difficult to reduce water use by 50 %.

There is no need to sacrifice beauty for the sake of wa- ter conservation. Contrary to the popular image of a water- saving landscape consisting solely of cacti in a dusty area of rocks and pebbles, drought-tolerant Mediterra- nean natives are very attractive. They fit every landscape and offer the same variety of shape, texture and colour as the water-demanding plants. Such gardens will gain in radiance as drought-tolerant plants stand up to dry sum- mers and, when well-chosen, look as good in midsum- mer as in spring. Many colourful plants in existing gar- dens (glorious wisteria, heady jasmine) are drought- tolerant.

Waterwise gardens are attractive yet do not demand constant attention. Reduced maintenance is matched by significant savings in expenditure (water, fertilizer, labour). And such gardens promote health as plants respond vigorously to practices which copy their native habitats.

A change to a low-water-requiring garden is often quite easy and it is not always necessary to design from the beginning again. You are already on your way *if* you use plants of low water requirements, reduce the lawn, change watering from a time schedule to a need sched- ule and if you apply water carefully to avoid runoff. Success is assured by careful planning. Consider the Eight Steps.

Above: Water-conservering planting can be cheerful. No need to sacrifice beauty for the sake of water conservation. Courtesy Montecito Water District, California.

Drought-tolerant cypress and lentisc *(Pistacia lentiscus)* are the principal elements in this waterwise garden which harmonizes with its surroundings. *Alstroemeria, Penstemon, Gladiolus* and *Gazania* provide seasonal colour.

Step 1
Planning your Garden

GETTING ACQUAINTED

The success of your garden as a self-sustaining, water-saving landscape depends on your exploration of all its aspects, taking full advantage of them. Previous chapters have described overall realities. Now it is for you to explore your personal ones. Don't hesitate to start by taking time to understand the basics.

Analyse your garden's climate, its topography and above all the water available. Study exposure and prevailing wind direction. Observe the sun's position in summer *and* winter. Investigate microclimates. Note prevailing temperatures. Minimum temperatures above 6-8 °C allow the cultivation of a wide plant range from warmer regions (Canaries). With low temperature, one night of frost is a different matter from a month of snow and ice.

Tip: Cold air flows down, warm air goes up. On frosty mornings I go out early, look for frost, try to remember where it settled to recognize my garden's coldest spots, ideal for cold-requiring species such as lilacs.

Before rushing to nurseries to buy a flowering field, take time to discover your soil's characteristics. A soil testing kit is cheap. Soil types may change: the earth beneath pine or oak is known to be slightly acid while nearby alkaline rock may be uncovered. How deep is the soil? Has it underlying rock (solid or cracked) or isolated stones? Did you discover under a thin soil layer hurriedly buried building rubble? Don't hesitate to dig at one or two spots to see for yourself.

How much water is available? Is there a spring and how much water comes from it? August is the moment of truth. There may then not be a drop although on a balmy spring day an enthusiastic property agent pointed out a gushing stream. Do you pull cool water up from a well? Are you connected to old rights, water being allotted once or twice a week (also in summer?). Or you may have none of these, having bought your land for the peaceful countryside around and planning to buy water from a cistern coming by every now and again, expensive and also unreliable in summer when everybody wants it too.

Consider rainfall, perhaps collected via the traditional flat roofs and connecting pipes leading to a subterranean water tank? It is not only quantity that matters, but *when* rain falls and how often. In deserts, the annual amount may mean one deluge, hardly allowing the soil and plants to absorb the precious liquid. In other regions, the same amount may fall in more manageable portions: a slow country rain is infinitely beneficial.

Having assessed the availability of water, you can go on to decide on the plants. Ask what grows in adjoining gardens, streets or the open countryside, native and cultivated, especially trees. Consult neighbours. Plants in abandoned gardens or along motorways indicate drought tolerance or potential weediness. Certain plants serve as important indicators of hardiness. Where

Hibiscus, brilliant red-flowering *Bougainvillea* and bananas flourish, you are in the Mediterranean's warmest part. Where cedar, deciduous oak, apples and lilac dominate, beware planting tender, frost-sensitive species. All are indicators for your garden's future. By knowing your garden and plants' needs, you can match the right plant to the right site.

Think too of the visual environment, buildings, walls and sights you like or wish they weren't there. Look for the character of your site, its historical background. Where large rocks abound, they serve as architectural elements, anchoring a garden to the ground. There may be apparent difficulties, but often the problem site turns out the most successful. That is what this book is about, helping to meet challenging conditions.

STRUCTURING THE LAND

Whatever your garden is intended for, give it structure and backbone. In a Mediterranean climate the garden is a significant living space where one may spend most of one's time. Do you want to work in it or rest, collect plants or acquaint children with nature? Service areas planned as carefully as the garden, allotting each function its place, turn into attractive sites. Locate the compost pile, a place for mulch preparation, a sand pit for children to play. Anchor your house to its grounds, balance the garden with its mass. While using simple elements in design, the composition has to be right.

In northern winters, when leaves drop and herbaceous plants die down, the garden's structure is clearly seen. Yet evergreen Mediterranean gardens are best designed in late autumn when no riots of colour distract from a faulty design. Have you, on a moonlit night, walked through your garden in 'black and white'?

The well-known landscape designer John Brookes states: 'Flowering is seductive but fleeting - it's the plant's profile, stem, leaf shape and colour that you have to live with year-round. Good planting plans begin by siting the largest key plants so that they form a link with neighbouring planting and architecture. Next, plant evergreens for year-round bulk and screening, then add decorative shrubs. 'Small fry' (perennials, bulbs, annuals) come last. Impatient for colour and bloom, we start the reverse.'

Whether converting a water-drinking into a water-saving garden or planning anew, it helps to draw a map. Locate permanent elements (buildings, terraces, walks, large trees) and determine which plants need water. There may be not more than a few in an otherwise drought-tolerant area. And write down ideas you may like to pursue. The full coordination of the design, the areas with varying water demands and possible irrigation may need time. One year is ideal to get acquainted with all seasons. But who has the patience to wait for a year?

Left page: Do you pull up cool water from a well?

This area is planned carefully for family enjoyment. Its horizontal lines avoid erosion. Courtesy Mrs Diandra Douglas.

PREVENTING EROSION, SHELTER FROM WIND

A well-planned garden, large or small, has pronounced horizontal lines. They give structure to the garden, define its areas, improve the precious rainwater's infiltration and above all: prevent erosion. The horizontal backbone (patio, terrace, wall, path) often requires stonework. Retention walls hold up soil, providing soil depth. While formerly extensive terracing was done to this effect, on a small scale a levelled trail might do. A similar result can sometimes be achieved by plantings. Hard-surfaced 'horizontals' can substitute the controversial lawn and render gardens more user-friendly, permitting garden pleasures and tasks to continue once rain stops (see also Lawn Alternatives).

It may surprise you that paths are mentioned before planting. It is usually the right order. Try to visualize where paths will be most useful and how best they can be incorporated into the surroundings. While earth-moving equipment is still around, a path can be dug with little expense and may make all the difference. Keep it as horizontal as possible, for wheelbarrow, lawn mower and old age (not necessarily one's own). Steep paths trodden by sheep or washed-out gullies impose themselves as walks and are of no use. Winter rains will turn them into river beds, carrying precious soil away.

Paths also have an aesthetic purpose, creating perspectives, moving in harmonious curves (wherever straight lines do not impose themselves). A well-thought out tracing requires care.

An inclinometer helps, cheap to buy and easy to handle (even for beginners). A roll of string checks on even grading, a garden hose traces the lay-out. Three dimensions need coordinating, one easily is forgotten. 'Seams' need special attention to avoid harsh transitions. It helps to survey from a distance, return for corrections, adjusting lines until one finds them absolutely right, best on a sunny spring day when one feels creative and has time at hand. A faulty tracing is there, forever to be regretted.

When deciding on width, visualize the path's purpose. For walking with a companion give double width (150cm), but in many areas a narrow trail for yourself or a few stepping stones facilitating garden tasks, may be all that is needed.

Pebble-inlaid surfaces, in past times artfully designed, are best located where only looked at. Walking on them is usually uneasy, sweeping time-consuming. Paths with smooth, even surfaces are easy to tread and transport materials, giving less chance for weeds. Often harmony is achieved with materials used for house building (left-overs). Locally available paving (stone slabs, brick, sandstone) may be economical. Gravel is an alternative. It allows succulents to thrive, small bulbs push through, softening harsh borderlines. However, gravel acts as a mulch for vigorous weeds.

Iris germanica and *Pistacia lentiscus* accompany a walk which was laid with sandstone slabs.

Walks create perspectives. Harmonious curves with a carefully thought-out tracing make all the difference.

A mature planting with palms, cypresses and climbers shelters the garden from wind.

Below: Beautiful old steps lead from the mystery of darkness up into light.

Steps modulate garden areas, are part of the horizontals and thus retain precious soil. Large sandstone slabs 40 × 80cm are quick to lay, as long as their weight is manageable. 15cm height is comfortable for steps. Tight-fitting joints prevent weeds. Laid on sand, they last forever, looking ancient in a year. Railway sleepers are good among pine. Needles smother weeds while *Cneorum tricoccon, Convolvulus cneorum, Digitalis, Erica, Helleborus, Hypericum, Trachelium* add bloom. The arrangement feels natural in its simplicity.

Tip : While working, leave a string beneath the slab in case you wish to lift it for correction.

While paths and terraces (the so-called hard landscapes) are being created, planting schemes may evolve by themselves. Consider winds and their drying out effect and find out where protection is essential. Start planting trees to provide backbone and backdrop for more fragile specimens. Vigorous plants, even rather common ones, well-kept, will give shelter and on sandy coasts, they will prevent soil from being blown away.

Gardening can start during house building. Fencing off space not needed for construction activities prevents the removal of topsoil and damage to tree roots. A symbolic rope will do. Plan the completion of the garden framework before the winter rains; wet soil will compact, losing its value as growth medium for years. Consider rubble, left over from house building, and its use for fill. At first, little grows in it. Later, small cypresses, annuals or bulbs will come up, thriving in its excellent drainage.

Step 2
Creating Plant Cover and Shade

COVERING THE GROUND

While British gardeners ponder about shape, texture or variegated leaves, 'covering the ground' is at the forefront on Mediterranean gardeners' mind. Evergreen vegetation retains soil, protecting it year-round from dehydration. The resulting soil humidity encourages a flourishing soil life which in turn stimulates vigorous growth. A lush plant cover suppresses competing weeds. It cools the atmosphere and plants, also the gardener! Where under a blazing noon sun the air stands still, a single tree on a lawn or paving creates a refreshing breeze. Midsummer days (or nights) are never unbearably hot if trees and climbers surround the house. By establishing a lush plant cover, you create a better environment and simple beauty.

21 % oxygen (Raven 1986) in the earth's atmosphere makes life possible on earth. Vegetation generates oxygen, releasing it into the air. As forests, its producers, are burned, let us consider planting as each gardener's modest contribution towards restoring a favourable percentage.

With even, steady strokes the old man sweeps the ground – clean. His work finished, not a leaf covers the polished 'floor'. Countless town squares are given over to this time-honoured practice. Are there other ways?

Scientists (Lawrence Berkeley Laboratories, California) estimate that, nationwide, 100 million trees planted around buildings and along roads could cut air conditioning in half, reducing the carbon pumped yearly into the air by 20 million tons. (Power plants needed to

A few wild olive trees, found on location, cast dappled shade. *Fatsia japonica* and *Hedychium gardnerianum* effectively cover the ground. Further back, a wild *Rhamnus alaternus* has been made use of and was clipped into a rounded shape, completing the harmonious picture.

Naturally-growing oak *(Quercus ilex)* and lentisc *(Pistacia lentiscus)* have been carefully retained and tended. Complemented by quickgrowing pioneer plants *(Myoporum)* and a few lilies *(Lilium candidum)*, their dappled shade and tall, windbreaking canopies encourage plant growth.

Podranea ricasoliana is a wonderful helper in covering vast expanses.
A cypress successfully frames the picture.

generate the energy saved by these trees, cost 10x as much as trees themselves). As well as saving energy, trees take up carbon dioxide, save water (surviving on subsurface humidity from rainfall), shade landscapes, reduce irrigation, cut down winds, absorb pollution and dust. Summer temperatures in residential areas with mature trees are 5-10°C lower than in unplanted ones. ('Trees Save Energy' San Francisco Chronicle, Jan. 8, 1989).

After centuries of stripping, let us pull again a protective coat over the earth as nature does if we let her. A deteriorated site should not discourage us. Nature quickly regains lost territories, cloaking stone and rock. Weeds come up (often spreading flat, ground-hugging) as nature's first step to cover the soil. Hers are multiple ways, but from our point of view we may interpret them as follows.

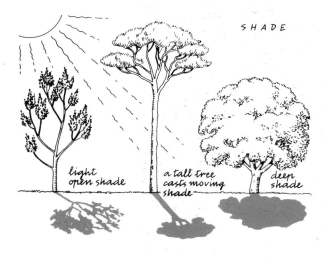

mer all shade, even if only light, provokes a gentle breeze to refresh plants and all living things.

Note: Photosynthesis is unimpaired as plants in Mediterranean shade are usually exposed to higher light intensities than under continental sun.

Each plant throws its characteristic shade. Tall or low, dense or light, summer long or year-round, shade is of different types. *Acacia* (actually many Australian trees) cast light shade while darkness creeps in under oak. Tall, open tree canopies' moving shade suits the basically sun-demanding Mediterranean vegetation. Filtered, dappled, intermittent or broken, a few hours daily over midday or hottest afternoons, it benefits most plants. Shade can also be created by structures (pergola, lath house, arbour). Whatever rises above the ground cools plants.

In winter, vegetation such as trees protects from frost which settles first where not obstructed by plant growth, but it also lowers temperatures. Sun-loving plants, intolerant of cold shade, attract health problems (fungus-prone *Viburnum tinus*). As plants grow, initial shade and sun patterns change and require a yearly reassessment.

Note: A deciduous tree with bare branches lets you take the cherished winter sun while you yearn for cool shade during summer, a tree to hang a hammock.

ESTABLISHING SHADE

A major way towards successful Mediterranean gardening is the moving shade of tall trees and where missing, is the first priority. Shade is nature's way of keeping down leaves' transpiration. Shade attenuates sun reflection, decreases evaporation from the soil, protects soil life, retains air humidity - and it refreshes the air! In sum-

A rich cover of *Osteospermum fruticosum* protects the ground from drying out, cools the air and provides over months a colourful display. Courtesy E. van Jaarsveld, Kirstenbosch, South Africa.

This carefully designed pergola casts cool shade during hot summer months. Openings let in light for sun-demanding *Bougainvillea*.

As you intend to establish the plant cover quickly, study the local situation. Whether clearing newly acquired ground, reshaping an existing garden or restoring an overgrown one: only take away what does not belong. Don't take out everything! Save native plants and naturally growing trees whenever possible, especially oak. Trees not only protect vegetation and shade plantings at early stages, they also stop the dehydrating effect of wind and break the force of rain, encouraging water absorption into the soil (remember the forest floor?). A forest diminishes temperature contrasts in the same way as the Mediterranean sea does, maintaining within itself an equalized climate.

Before deciding on anything and in order to see clearly, tidy up the land. Cutting out dead branches, eliminating brambles, removing waste may turn an ugly duckling into a presentable shrub or uncover a landscape with potential.

Should you want new plants, replace the plants already there gradually. As planned growth progresses, discard them slowly, always leaving the ground covered. This practice may puzzle you, but you will soon notice how well it works (see Weeding).

Lonicera, one of our best pioneer plants, for years covered difficult to plant shallow soil. By the time it became invasive and required removal, the new permanent vegetation had matured.

For a vegetative cover, choose evergreen or evergrey natives from Mediterranean climates, making a sturdy framework for a water-saving garden. Use ground covers, shrubs, climbers or trees in several tiers. Simple effects are often best: fields of periwinkle in light tree shade. Or lavender covering the ground, a few almond trees standing out among their solid mass.

In Mediterranean conditions, new plantings are often slow. When isolated, they hardly want to grow and only shoot up once the soil is covered and mulched, soil life established and crowding sets in. A well-planned garden initially includes quick-growing 'pioneer' plants, the permanent plantings following on. Not all may belong to well-established Mediterranean gardens, but they serve an important function during establishment. Use *Gazania, Tropaeolum majus* and annuals for a quick, low cover. *Bupleurum fruticosum, Coronilla, Phlomis fruticosa, Teucrium fruticans* are for intermediate stages. *Elaeagnus, myrtus, Phillyrea, Punica, Pittosporum* represent bulk. *Eucalyptus, Fraxinus, Jacaranda, Tipuana tipu* give overhead shade. Consult the list on page 96.

As gardens mature, the vigorous growth of pioneer plants requires control which results in ample 'green waste'. Its beneficial side effect is that it can be used in shredded mulch, a vital soil covering in itself (see Mulch).

Step 3
Using Drought-Tolerant Plants

Where water is scarce, look to native Mediterranean climate plants for help. A wonderful group, ideal for water-saving gardens, they live on natural winter rain. Over the hot summer months they look after themselves while the gardener retires to the cool of a terrace, to emerge again when summer is over. Mostly evergreen, Mediterranean natives have attractive flowers (see p.12 and the Plant Selection). The fragrance of many lingers in the air all summer long. As with all plants, they look best with occasional trimming.

An understanding of how native plants function under stress contributes to their evaluation. The careful use of native and introduced plants with drought-tolerant characters is the main theme, based on nature's way of coping with Mediterranean climates. Plants which have adapted to these conditions can and should provide the backbone of Mediterranean gardens.

Correctly planted and maintained, once established (after a year or two), Mediterranean natives do with the natural winter rain in response to their yearly, prolonged dry season, going dormant when (with summer heat and drought) the climate turns unfavourable. Bulbous plants play a prominent role among them and are in line with waterwise, low-maintenance gardening. Natives mostly resent irrigation to the point that summer water shortens the life of *Dendromecon, Fremontodendron, Heteromeles, Romneya* or *Trichostema*. *Pelargonium*, an early introduction from South Africa, once fully established, is summer-watered unnecessarily as it gets no watering in its native land.

Mediterranean natives are suited to all garden situations as long as you remember their climatic and horticultural needs and duplicate their native habitat as closely as possible. Their prolific choice makes it easy to

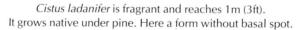

Cistus ladanifer is fragrant and reaches 1m (3ft).
It grows native under pine. Here a form without basal spot.

This well-established garden takes advantage of the wide range of drought-tolerant evergreens
and is highlighted by giant *Euphorbia candelabrum*, *Phoenix canariensis* and a glorious sky.

find suitable plants for each site. In contrast to wild land-scapes, a careful plant selection, grouped according to sound landscaping rules and regularly maintained by deadheading and cutting out old wood, allows natives to develop their full potential.

Plants from other areas of the world with a Mediterranean climate may be satisfactorily grown together with the Mediterranean natives. They include drought-tolerant trees, shrubs and bulbs from the California cha-parral, the South African fynbos or the Australian heath-lands and grow in the same climate we garden in. These plants, often referred to as exotics, are natives too – in their homeland. *Carpenteria*, one of the most beautiful flowers and given a choice site in English gardens, in California is considered a weed from the wild. The same is true of South Africa where such lovely bulbs as *Ixia*,

Sparaxis, *Watsonia* are on the verge of being lost to con-struction sites, while *Westringia*, one of the most useful plants for Mediterranean gardens, would turn nobody's head in its native Australia.

Many drought-tolerant plants in this book, chosen for their dependable ways, may already be known to you (*Ceanothus*, *Penstemon* from California, *Agapanthus*, *Euryops* from the Cape, *Acacia*, *Melaleuca* from Australia, *Cytisus*, *Cyclamen* from the Mediterranean). Do explore them further to find those best suited to your garden.

Once you have carefully observed this flora which not only survives but also grows successfully in difficult conditions, yours will be an attractive, evergreen flower garden, easy to care for. By designing and working with nature, such gardens save natives from extinction, feed and shelter wildlife and establish a link with the natural world outside.

Step 4
Reducing the Lawn, Alternatives

It is commonly accepted that lawns use up to 3x more water than most other plantings.

As one of the key ingredients of water-saving gardens is minimal lawn area, lawns need reassessment of their place in water-conscious gardens. A main element of temperate gardening, grass areas are often automatically used in Mediterranean climates where they are the most water and labour intensive landscape element around, a luxury justified only where essential in outdoor living. Mostly intolerant of prolonged exposure to sun, lawns are fragile and need more water than most other plants likely to be grown. Of the water applied to most gardens, lawns use more than 70 % (information kindly provided by the East Bay Municipal Utility District, San Francisco CA.).

English garden books occasionally read 'To save labour after the war, the owner abandoned complicated plantings, putting all down to lawn'. Even in Mediterranean climates, that thought may be tempting. But reasonably well-kept lawns are hard work. Only dense grass will suppress the multiple weeds which are ready to compete from spring to autumn. If labour is on your mind, the lawn should be replaced.

Study the function of a lawn. Distinguish for example between the horizontal spaces described in Step 1 and the empty space to set off your plantings. Level ground is also required to sit, eat, play. Lawns often provide that floor and should be placed where families spend their time, in areas used frequently – or omitted altogether. Too often, lawns cover ground where nothing more imaginative has been thought about.

THE REDUCED LAWN

Should you decide that you do need a lawn after having considered all alternatives (do you have water at summer's height?), a labour-intensive, thus costly lawn is possible. Look for new, tougher grass varieties, slow-growing, deep-rooting, with low water needs. Lawns inland must stand dry air and changing temperatures and so are best planted with a mixture. Most warm-climate grasses perform well over summer but are winter-dormant; winter-green grasses turn yellow in summer (mostly recuperating in autumn). During their dormant periods multiple weeds become established. Nurseries and golf courses will advise on the grasses suitable for your region.

Well-designed box and a graceful fountain replace successfully a lawn.

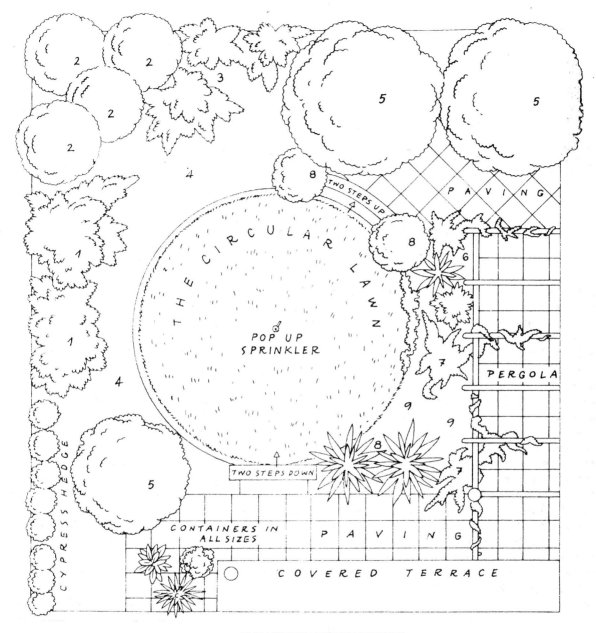

THE UNDERLYING THOUGHTS:

This garden project includes both the reduced lawn and lawn alternatives, well covered by plants of various heights.

– One (pop up) sprinkler, only for the lawn, once a week. The reach of the sprinkler determines the size of the lawn.

– Ample hard surface, shaded by trees, borderlines softened by plants. A pergola with scented climbers provides a shaded walk.

– Undemanding drought-tolerant planting for the rest. Plants are chosen for cheerful bloom. Ultimate height is considered to reduce maintenance (cutting back).

1. *Argyranthemum frutescens, Euryops pectinatus, Lavandula, Pelargonium, Phylica ericoides, Rosmarinus officinalis.*
2. *Nerium oleander, Ligustrum lucidum, Tamarix, Viburnum tinus.*
3. *Westringia fruticosa, Eriocephalus africanus.*
4. Flowering ground cover in sun: *Gazania*, ice plants, thyme, *Tropaeolum majus.*
5. Deciduous flowering trees for summer shade.
6. Flowering ground cover in shade: *Iris foetidissima, I. japonica, I. unguicularis, Vinca.*
7. Flowering climbers: scented jasmine, *Solanum jasminoides, Tecomaria capensis, Wisteria.*
8. For accent: artichoke, *Phormium tenax, Yucca.*
9. For yearlong delight: many bulbs.

Simple lawn shapes are easiest to irrigate. Consider for example full or half circles, allowing yourself *one* submersible (pop up) sprinkler in the centre to water evenly the entire surface (once a week for well-chosen varieties). Consider also rectangles served by another sprinkler type. Narrow strips are inefficient.

Mixing lawns with other plants complicates mowing and also irrigation as lawns need more than twice the water than most other plantings which makes it logical that lawns are watered on a separate line. Planning irrigation and placing equipment before planting is essential, also coordinating sprinkler reach with the lawn area.

Exploit applied water: plant lawn borders with water-thrifty vegetation, terrain beyond sprinkler reach with plants that require air humidity, further out with drought-tolerant plants. Or let water reach somewhat beyond the lawn for water-requiring species.

Often the best site for a lawn is under tall trees' moving shade. Well-prepared sites (organic matter), turf aeration and weed removal ensure effective water use. Mowing height greatly influences water retained. Let the grass grow taller as heat increases. Sharp blades allow wounds to heal quickly. The same applies to lawn replacements such as *Erigeron karvinskianus, Hypericum, Lantana montevidensis.* In California, water-stressed gardeners are advised to let lawns go before trees or shrubs. They often recover when rain returns.

Above: Colourful island beds soften hard surfaces. A similar effect can be achieved by containers.

Above: Mounding volumes of drought-tolerant *Argyranthemum frutescens* invade an attractive paving, softening harsh borders.

Below: This apple green 'lawn' is actually tightly planted *Carpobrotus edulis*. Stepping stones facilitate walking.

Below: Paving, interplanted with grass, is less water-demanding than a lawn, but requires a bit of maintenance. Roots keep cool under the slabs.

P A V I N G

C O V E R E D

T E R R A C E

S E C R E T
G A R D E N

E L E V A T I O N → A   B

THE UNDERLYING THOUGHTS:

Ample paving replaces the labour-intensive lawn and in summer is shaded by trees. This garden may copy a village square with benches and promises easy maintenance.

– Arches with climbers cool and beautify the area. They may frame a cherished view.

– The open ground to the right is planted with any waterwise plant you may fancy. A single species is best for easy maintenance.

– A small secret garden behind the house takes advantage of the protected environment and may house cherished pots which are easily watered by hand. The list for containers proposes a wide choice of plants (p. 99).

1. Deciduous flowering trees for summer shade *(Cercis siliquastrum)*, also tall palms.

2. *Bougainvillea, Campsis radicans,* honeysuckle, jasmine, *Trachelospermum,* a grape vine.

3. *Euonymus japonicus, Laurus nobilis, Rhamnus alaternus* or *R. ludovici-salvatoris* shape easily into decorative volumes.

4. The lists on p. 96 propose choices for your specific needs.

5. Evergreen, drought-tolerant plants such as *Agapanthus* give cover all year. Scented-leaved *Pelargonium* will invade the paving or tumble over a wall, breaking hard lines. Or use scented herbs.

Colourful plantings replace a lawn.

LAWN ALTERNATIVES

Should you opt for drought-tolerant alternatives to grass, evergreen low-lying foliage plants (single species in large patches) achieve the tranquil effect lawns provide. Yet open spaces do not necessarily require treatment as lawns. Broken up by ground-covering vines, shrubs of varying heights, low walls, paths or such constructions as pergolas, they offer diversion. Take time out to search for inspiration or seek professional advice.

Paving, even extensive, is an excellent lawn alternative and may double as patio, courtyard or terrace. Materials similar to those used for house building give wider scope (avoid unfriendly cement). Open, sunny stretches heat up, but a tree together with arbour or pergola gives cooling shade. Such an arrangement may suggest a village square with trees, benches, potted flowers, easy to maintain, suiting family life. Do you crave for more greenery? Interrupt pavings with drought-tolerant, flowering *Dimorphotheca, Grevillea, Lantana,* oleander, *Plumbago,* to name a few. Many herbs qualify. *Helichrysum,* juniper or scented lavender cover fast bordering banks. *Tropaeolum majus,* tucked into a crevice, spreads miles with cheerful bloom.

Wooden decks, bordered by bench-railings, are Californian alternatives. Adjoining chaparral or maquis vegetation is improved by selective pruning or trimming.

Gravel, another non-vegetative lawn alternative, requires maintenance and is not really satisfactory. Weeds grow in it while the gravel in its turn invades plantings.

Vegetation offers the most attractive options and drought-tolerant evergreens are best. Besides the low-growing ones, use any drought-tolerant plant you fancy. There is no end to vegetation which gives cover with less attention, water and fertilizer than required by a lawn. And a lawn does not flower while most suggested plants do. For larger expanses it may be economical to choose plants which are easy to propagate.

To cover level spaces, use compact-growing, 'flat-as-grass' plants. All thrive spreading over gravel, mounds or sloping ground (avoid hollows where winter rain collects), some should occasionally be mown. Not all can be walked on (the juicy ones). Some tolerate occasional treading, delightful when giving off scent (thyme). However, stepping-stones may line out a path.

In sun carpets of ground-hugging succulents are colourful lawn alternatives (*Aptenia cordifolia, Carpobrotus edulis, Crassula, Sedum*). Suitable for moderate foot traffic: *Achillea millefolium, Arctotheca calendula* (invasive), *Fragaria chiloensis* (California beach strawberry), *Gazania*, *Grevillea rosmarinifolia* 'Prostrata' (lovely winter flowers), *Phyla nodiflora* (winter-deciduous, attractive white summer buttons, difficult to eradicate), *Verbena peruviana* (flattest, weekly water). Sun and shade: *Coprosma* x *kirkii* (tough), *Duchesnea indica* (mimics strawberry), *Fragaria vesca* (fraises des bois*)*, *Polygonum capitatum* (vigorous). Shade: *Ajuga reptans* (weekly water), *Vinca minor, Viola*.

Not as flat as grass, but still low to about 20cm, spreading into dense patches: *Achillea tomentosa, Baccharis pilularis, Felicia amelloides, Helianthemum nummularium, Hypericum calycinum, Iris japonica* (shade), *Lantana montevidensis, Lithodora diffusa* (weekly watering), *Osteospermum fruticosum, Pelargonium tomentosum* (or other scented ones), *Teucrium chamaedrys*.

Cushion shapes in full sun need excellent drainage, do well among gravel, stones, paving: *Aurinia saxatilis, Ballota, Cerastium tomentosum, Dianthus deltoides, Erigeron karvinskianus, Iberis saxatilis, I. sempervirens,*

Lavandula, Phylica ericoides, Rosmarinus officinalis 'Prostratus', *Santolina*. Very drought-tolerant: *Verbena tenuisecta*.

Upright growth habit, sun or half shade, easily divided for ever-expanding patches: *Agapanthus, Iris unguicularis, Liriope spicata* (creeping lily turf, no mowing), *Ophiopogon japonicus* (mondo grass), *Ruscus aculeatus, R. hypoglossum* (larger-leaved*)*, *Sisyrinchium bellum* (Californian blue-eyed grass, slow propagation). Warmest locations, full sun: *Arctotis venusta*.

Shrubby fast-growing 20-40cm, extending to 2-3m: *Arctostaphylos hookeri* 'Monterey Carpet' (rooting branch tips), *Ceanothus thyrsiflorus* var. *repens, Cotoneaster dammeri* 'Lowfast', *Juniperus*.

Vines, lending themselves for flattish looks, cover large expanses. Full sun: *Doxantha unguis-cati, Hardenbergia violacea, Pelargonium peltatum, Trachelospermum, Tropaeolum majus*. Sun or shade: *Vinca difformis*. Shade: X *Fatshedera lizei*. Invasive pioneers: *Hedera, Lonicera*.

To replace a small lawn, a path was laid and edges planted with water-conserving plants. Today, maintenance is minimal.

Step 5
Grouping Plants for Water Needs

You will achieve important savings in water (and labour!) if you divide your garden into areas with high, medium and low water requirements, according to the specific needs of the plants.

Winter rain takes care of Mediterranean climate plants and generally carries them through summer without further attention (*Halimium, Helichrysum, Hypericum, Mespilus, Platanus, Punica, Ruta*). These plants qualify for low-water regions, such as the natural garden, and make up the non-irrigated area.

Yet many plants you may want to grow do not come from a Mediterranean climate and show improved performance with weekly watering in summer (*Abutilon, Fatsia, Hebe, Phygelius*). Closely planted and generously mulched, a lush picture will be obtained in this second group.

Species from tropical or summer rain regions require ample supplies (*Begonia, Camellia, Canna, Hibiscus rosa-sinensis, Hydrangea macrophylla*). Planted near the house or for example beside a small lawn and watered together with this, they constitute the water-intensive area.

Containers are a group apart. In a courtyard or patio, or assembled under a tall tree canopy, they are easily watered according to their individual needs.

When you divide your plantings into these areas, remember that certain good-humoured plants tolerate life in high or low-watering zones alike, *if* planted according to their requirements (i.e. *Abelia* and *Escallonia* in dappled shade). Seek also inspiration from Step 4.

In hot summers, especially if long, additional applications may be needed at the peak of the season or after drying winds. Spot-watering of those in need will keep your garden thriving.

Grouped pots highlight drought-tolerant
evergreens and are easily watered.

Anisodontea, Agave and *Senecio glastifolius* (front to back) thrive in this unwatered South African setting.

Clipped myrtle (left), *Chamaerops, Pelargonium peltatum* and *Myoporum* frame a gate to a waterwise hotel garden.

Weekly watering carries well-chosen roses in this otherwise drought-tolerant Provence setting through summer.

Among closely planted lavender, *Pelargonium* and *Chamaerops,* only *Hibiscus* at the back requires weekly watering.

Water-intensive 'exotics' such as *Alocasia macrorrhiza* (right) or *Begonia* and *Canna indica* (above) require adequate water

supplies. Closely planted, thus conserving soil humidity, twice or three times weekly may suffice.

Step 6
Planning Water Management

In this California country garden, a carefully planned flow control foresees where winter rains will rush along, followed by suitable planting as a second step. Courtesy Nancy Hardesty.

Right page: A tap to a distant corner of this natural Spanish scene *(Cistus, Quercus ilex)* helps the establishment of new plants. A path guides the rainflow.

RAINWATER FLOW CONTROL

Plan water distribution and
its means before planting

Rain, absent over long periods, is nevertheless an important element in planning for water-saving gardening. While blue summer skies are overhead, try to foresee where winter downpours may make a stream. You may not see real rain for years, but when it comes, it can be destructive, washing away your garden's fertile soil.

Your best strategy is avoidance. Evade situations where precious water is a curse, not a blessing. Observe the amount of water which flows over your land during and after downpours, best observed while they happen! Survey slope grading and existing drainage courses and identify problems to take precautionary measures.

Rainwater, if retained and stored on your land, brings relief in dry periods, providing the best water, free of charge. So-called ground water recharge is achieved by natural drainage. It is improved by the soil's water retention, by soil-protecting vegetation and mulch. Reduce the water, flowing along a drive or steep path, by diverting it over the widest possible area. Surface drains, gravel-filled ditches, terracing in all its aspects filter rainwater, avoiding erosion and wasteful run-off. Cisterns store rainwater from roofs and terraces. A reservoir behind a retention wall doubles as terrace and replaces costly fill. A tank or pond, planned with neighbours, brings relief for all.

Note: Mini dams or 'wattling', erosion control methods reintroduced by Hardesty (Hardesty 1984), disperse the force of the water, trap eroding soil by turning water channels into stairways of living plants. Tie cuttings 30-50cm long into bundles and place them secured by rocks where you intend to break water's force. Planting is unnecessary as selected plants root, by summer growing into notable specimens *(Populus, Salix, Sambucus, Spiraea douglasii, Symphoricarpos)*. Temporarily, place branches over surfaces which are susceptible to erosion.

PLANNING WATER DISTRIBUTION

> Most of the following can be avoided
> by the use of drought-tolerant plants.

In Mediterranean climates, natural rain replaces irrigation efficiently. But even drought-tolerant or waterwise gardens need a tap while plants become established. It is easy to lay a pipe to a distant corner.

Hoses are not aesthetic and are best put underground (laid below paths, they will be safe from the pickaxe). Expense is matched by saving in time. You will be thankful in the future if today you mark on your garden plan the position of the pipes and junctions.

When considering irrigation, use efficient equipment. This may mean single sprinklers for small lawns as much as sophisticated apparatus which is improving all the time. However the subject has its pitfalls; where for example a sprinkler originally provided an even flow, a quick-growing shrub now deflects water from plants behind it.

Sprinklers supply water over large areas, convenient for low-growing ground cover. With drought-tolerant plants they may encourage fungus disease and surface-rooting. Old-fashioned sprinklers often emit more water than dry summer soils absorb (soil-clogging, asphyxiation) while low-output sprinklers allow water to infiltrate gradually. Drip systems, often placed too near stems, achieve up to 50 % savings in water supply.

When planning for new equipment, test its performance *before* final installation. Water pressure determines water distribution and is difficult to calculate. The amounts applied are influenced by sloping terrain, sprinkler quality or a light breeze. With all the equipment installed, a trial run indicates reliably how much (or little) the water covers. Well-maintained equipment and a separate garden water meter save water. Measure and record; you will be surprised how much you save.
Tip : Distribute goblets in irrigated zones, checking the amount each catches.

Install all equipment before planting. This shows you the water's actual extent and also dry regions beyond. Based on these findings, the planting plans can be revised.

Planting is always the second step. Frequently planting is done first, later followed by thoughts of water requirements. The result is usually unsatisfactory, as I learned. Water applied is not related that closely to plant needs and may be wasteful (overlapping, reaching unplanted sections, a terrace, the street). Such details, catering to the plants' needs, lead to successful waterwise gardens.

CHANGE IRRIGATION FROM A TIME TO A NEED SCHEDULE

Automatic equipment irrigates gardens without assistance. One only sets the time – once and for all, one tends to believe. But as the requirement varies from month to month, from rainy to dry weeks, from sunny to cloudy days, remember to adjust the timing. A moisture sensor will help you to get the feel, resulting in significant savings of water. However, few Mediterranean natives require routine irrigation.

CONSIDER 'GREY WATER'

When there is a water crisis, gardeners use 'grey water' (not authorized everywhere) by which they understand used water (dish-washing, not sewage).

Step 7
Using Water-Saving Practices

Favourable growing conditions replace many a water ration.

The closer one can cater for plants' requirements, the better they are equipped to withstand drought and the less water they will need. Recapitulating what is said elsewhere, such requirements include:

– Water loss through leaves is reduced by choosing suitable sites. Keep shade plants in the shade, water-loving ones at the bottom of slopes or adjacent to lawns. Exacting sites (midday and afternoon sun) are reserved for sturdy plants. Separate thirsty plants from those with low water needs.

– Many colourful native plants grow in infertile, rocky soils with poor water-holding capacity (Mediterranean *Hypericum balearicum*, South African *Eriocephalus*), yet excellent drainage is essential for all (waterlogged roots lack soil oxygen and rot).

– Grouping plants close together creates micro-environments for moisture retention, shades the ground, protects small plants from wind, discourages water-stealing weeds.

– Deep root runs for those demanding it, keep roots cool.

– Give careful attention to mulch, one of the pillars of low-water gardening.

– When planted in early autumn, root systems adjust over humid mild winters and plants often enter the summer drought period already well-established. Plants from 2-4 liter containers establish best. If smaller, they need too much coddling over harsh summers.

Right page: In this Spanish garden of ancient origin *Plumbago* and *Bougainvillea* thrive, wind-protected by evergreen oak *(Quercus ilex).* Their close planting keeps evaporation down. A reservoir in times past gave inspiration for a glorious terrace.

Lantana camara intermingling with *Euryops pectinatus,* shades the soil and takes advantage of a cool root run below paving. Such well-matched plants and sites reduce water loss.

Extra good drainage on top of a well-made dry wall protects the roots of this succulent from rotting. Good aeration lets it thrive.

Step 8
A Waterwise Garden for all Seasons

Although water may be scarce, enjoy vigorous greenery and flowers all year round by planning your garden for the four seasons (see also Mediterranean Plant Communities).

Cooler nights and the first autumn rains awaken the plants from summer dormancy and trigger off new growth. Take advantage of autumn-flowering bulbs (X *Amarine, Colchicum, Sternbergia, Urginea*) and climbers (*Bignonia, Passiflora, Plumbago, Solanum jasminoides*) to grace your garden.

Winter bloom is the great benefit of Mediterranean gardening. Exploit it, for so much is in bloom at this period. White flower clusters after Christmas cover laurustinus *(Viburnum tinus),* a Mediterranean basic plant. Carob's *(Ceratonia siliqua)* young, lemon-green foliage looks from afar like *Acacia*, ready to bloom. *Chasmanthe*'s sword-like leaves look as unruffled by wind as if grown in a conservatory and the tall flowers last for weeks, while *Aeonium* lights dull areas with yellow radiant flowerheads.

Golden *Sternbergia lutea* after summer drought pop up with first autumn rains and naturalize readily. A wall fulfils their demands for perfect drainage.

In late winter, the wild *Prunus spinosa* throws a white veil over its leafless branches, a haven for bees. Annual shaping makes it garden-worthy.

Aloe arborescens can be counted on for a colourful mid-winter display.

Create sunshine by planting to lighten a wet day's dreariness. Grow mimosa (*Acacia*), a few *Euryops virgineus*, *Coronilla* in masses; their yellow bloom gives an illusion of sunshine. While yellow achieves the sunniest effect, any mixture succeeds. White unifies many shades or brightens the picture to spring-like radiance. Plant white, yellow and pink marguerites in billowing masses (*Argyranthemum frutescens*), while *Leonotis leonurus'* orange-coloured spikes stand out against the sky.

Spring gardens thrive on winter rain, when native vegetation is usually seen at its best. Exuberant flowering is breathtaking and many trees (*Cercis siliquastrum, Crataegus, Styrax officinale*) and shrubs (lilac, spiraea) are covered with bloom. Choose early-flowering ones (the wide range of *Prunus*), growing spring bulbs beneath (crocus, cyclamen, fritillary, muscari, tulips).

After flowering, let your evergreen garden rest under hot summer skies while you retire to cool shade. Pines' resinous scent or rock roses' ethereal oils will greet you. Drought-tolerant evergreen foliage prevents a dried up midsummer look (box, lentisc, myrtle, oak, *Grevillea, Taxus, Thuja, Westringia*). Also enjoy the summer flowers. With little or no water bloom *Agapanthus, Amaryllis belladonna, Crinum*, accompanied by *Coreopsis, Gaillardia* and climbing *Bignonia*. Cream, yellow or apricot flower shades complement attractively a straw-coloured summer countryside when many shrubs take on a rusty tint.

The delicate but sturdy rose 'New Dawn', backed by drought-tolerant evergreens, is hundred times worth the weekly summer water it demands.

Vivid *Bougainvillea,* structural cypresses and shady palms are mainstays of low-maintenance and waterwise summer gardens. Few are their demands on the gardener.

Chapter Three
Waterwise Gardencraft

Planting
or The Happiness of Roots

CHOOSING PLANTING SITES

We may be under the impression that where water, fertilizer and pesticides are used generously, gardens will thrive. Not so in Mediterranean climates. Nobody waters, fertilizes or sprays plants in nature and how beautiful are they – on their own. Smaller maybe, but also sturdier, better equipped to withstand stress such as drought or wind. Yet there is something we can and *should* do for our garden: seek the best possible site for each plant, above ground (position) and below (soil). Drought-tolerant plants do need carefully chosen sites, planting time and watering until established. With careful attention to planting, less water is required.

Hylotelephium telephium (Sedum t.) has found a comfortable bed in a rock crevice where its roots keep cool while the succulent foliage remains dry on the rock.

ABOVE-GROUND CONDITIONS, POSITION

More than in temperate regions, position affects plant growth. A characteristic of Mediterranean summers is strong solar radiation when dry air absorbs humidity from both soil and plant surfaces (the air in coastal gardens is moister than in inland ones). Even on the smallest plot, there are widely different sites, each with a specific character: heat on sun-facing walls, cooler sites under tree shade, permanently windy spots. Plants themselves create sheltered microhabitats. Understanding a garden's microclimates is crucial for choosing the right planting sites. The more these are exploited, the better a garden will be.

Match sites carefully with the shade or sun demands of a particular plant. As plants under heat stress are wasteful of water, use overhead protection. Tall, moving shade reduces leaf transpiration and suits those plants which need light and sun, but not intense heat. Afternoon sun taxes plants most and can be mitigated by planting to the east of existing trees or shrubs. This can result in fewer flowers as light stimulates flower production, shade leaf growth. Not to be avoided, north-facing slopes and walls with little winter sun offer a cool root run (box, erica, hellebore, peony). In frosty gardens, morning shade ensures gradual thawing before sun reaches delicate plants. Reserve hottest locations for Cape plants – they love it.

Temporary shade at times of stress favours establishment. 'Roofs' depend on material available. Twiglets, firmly stuck into ground and covered lightly with dry grass, will help small plants. Branches will serve temporarily before drying leaves fall off. Several palm leaves tied in 'Indian hut style', leaf bases pushed well into the ground, are an elegant solution. At the end of summer, remove roofs and check the plants.
Note: Southern hemisphere gardeners will remember that their 'south' for us means 'north'.

Open tree shade protects plants from hottest noon sun

BELOW-GROUND CONDITIONS

Below-ground conditions and water needs are closely related. Good below-ground conditions encourage strong roots for efficient uptake of water and nutrients, helping plants to withstand heat stress. Plants survive with less water where roots find a cool run, for example under nearby rock (p. 67). Humidity is preserved longer in places protected from drying out by vegetation, shade, a northern position or lying in hollows, swampy in winter. In these places plants carry on well into summer.

Wherever possible, dig a generous planting hole. If required, incorporate compost, sand, place meals at the bottom, mixing well with the local soil to help the roots to penetrate new soil. Holes, watered before planting, supply moisture for a good start. If after an hour water has not fully drained, choose plants which do not need perfect drainage or continue to probe with the crowbar.

Around the Mediterranean, more likely than not, you find thin soil layers over solid rock, indicated by rocky outcrops. Visiting a famed garden on the Côte after its owner's death, I learned how initially soil was brought in by the truckload, men with rush baskets all winter carrying soil until terracing resulted in the best. Your own terrain may be inaccessible, you may not find the half dozen men, nor may you want to pay for such luxuries. Don't despair. Although sacrifices benefitting soil are never wasted, there are also other ways to go about it.

Knowing your garden well, you will find places with just a bit more earth, such as cracked bedrock, for roots to discover a way down. Where holes cannot be dug, mulch gradually builds up soil which is continually exploited by growing roots. When bringing in additional soil and to save on expense, start out with well-draining fill (broken pots), finishing off with soil to required depth.

Succulents in this carefully planned garden enjoy perfect drainage and maximum sun exposure on raised beds while a path controls winter rain flow.

On bedrock, soil dries quickly, drainage is poor, growth is slow (in my garden *Melia azederach*, normally a vigorous tree, remained a healthy bonsai). Choose superficially-rooting plants, undemanding succulents or the so-called chasmophytes whose roots do the digging for you. They adjust to cracks, store water and nutrients in thickened (often carrot-like) roots. For woodlands use *Arbutus unedo*, oak, pine, *Umbellularia californica*. Shrubs include *Arctostaphylos, Baccharis, Heteromeles arbutifolia, Prunus ilicifolia, Rhamnus* or scrub oak.

SOIL QUALITY, DRAINAGE

Water retentive soils benefit plants where water is short. Sandy soils drain quickly and water disappears before being absorbed. Unless planning for dune vegetation, compost assists water retention. Good loams (adding organic matter, sand) let air and water circulate. Polymers store 800x their volume in water and, placed premoistened below roots, keep plants going into summer. Heavy soils necessitate preparation; however, gardeners today try out alternatives for peat. Green manure enriches poor soils. But as long as plants are chosen carefully, it may not be necessary to change soil properties.

Perfect drainage is crucial for drought-tolerant plants. Is the soil permeable and the underlying rock cracked to allow water to drain off? Roots require well-aerated soils (oxygen) to breathe and to absorb water, extending among soil particles to nutrient-rich fields. Wet soil is compacted if walked on. Containers require special care (a layer of gravel or shards at the bottom).

Terraces, ideal for drainage-demanding plants, are a common Mediterranean feature. Among their rubble water circulates freely. At the back, trees or shrubs in search of cool dampness send their roots beneath upper terraces. Towards edges, bulbs, cushion plants or succulents find perfect drainage (is there sufficient soil besides fill?). Crevices (open at the bottom), raised beds or gravelly soil on sloping ground give similar results.

Where drainage is poor, water stagnates, expelling air from the soil. Roots become asphyxiated. Weakly-functioning or inoperational roots succumb first (recent transplants, cuttings in over-sized pots). Summer-dormant roots, especially sensitive, object to a sudden rush of water (*Ceanothus, Eucalyptus*). Thus I lost a lovely *Pimelea* after an untimely summer rain. Poor drainage shortens the life of bay (*Laurus nobilis*), redbud (*Cercis siliquastrum*), strawberry tree (*Arbutus unedo*), manzanita (*Arctostaphylos*) and flannel bush (*Fremontodendron*). *Lavandula dentata* is more tolerant than *L. angustifolia*. On the other hand, poor drainage (pockets where winter rain gathers) suits those bulbous plants which like soggy winter roots followed by summer-baking (*Leucojum aestivum, Zantedeschia aethiopica*).

MULCHING

See the next section.

PLANTING PERIOD

Mediterranean climates have two main growing seasons when root growth is active: autumn and spring. Mediterranean plants should be in the ground as soon as summer heat is over, the moment the first autumn rains start and still-warm soils favour root growth. Plants will settle down during the mild winter. The same is true for bulbs which later will summer-bake and naturalize. Tropicals are put out in early spring when the soil is warming up. In winter, their inoperational roots may rot. Theoretically, potted plants could be transplanted throughout the year, but watch plants closely until established. Planting before departure leaves plants to an uncertain fate; planted upon arrival they can be watched.

Note: Get yearlings growing before cold sets in as ground level temperatures in winter are 3-4° C lower than further up.

STAKING, MARKING SITES

Winds dislocate roots of newly planted top-heavy plants, particularly after heavy rains. *Ceanothus* is especially sensitive. Such plants need careful staking and tying to about medium height with upper parts free to move.

Mark small plants, easily stepped on, with canes or encircle with stones. Gravel indicates bulb positions.

TRANSPLANTING

Dig the new planting hole *before* lifting and prepare plants: cut out dead wood, shorten branches by a third to decrease leaf transpiration, balancing shoot with root volume. Well-balanced plants cope better. Conserve fine feeder roots when lifting, taking some original soil with them (mycorrhiza). Protect roots from drying out with a cloth. Firm plants into the soil, so that the roots are in close contact with surrounding ground (watering in). Temporary protection from wind and damping the foliage revives plants under stress, foliar feeding helps those with non-functional roots.

Tip: After severing all roots, a crowbar hoists heavy root balls.

The Mediterranean is host to countless legumes which are difficult to transplant whichever way it is done (smallest plants sometimes succeed). *Thryptomene* (Myrtaceae), *Coleonema* (Rutaceae) or *Ceanothus* and *Bougainvillea* have a similar reaction. Most Proteaceae and Ericaceae dislike root disturbance. Others can be transplanted at any time of year (*Argyranthemum, Pelargonium*). Many hard-leaved plants (*Carissa, Elaeagnus, Laurus, Sarcococca*) promise success.

Tip: The strongest root pointing into the direction of the prevailing wind anchors the plant best.

ESTABLISHMENT

Establishment means adapting to new living conditions. Drought tolerant or not, roots adjust to new soils, pushing down or extending into moister regions, seeking interaction with soil life. Leaves, often protecting each other, re-establish their species' characteristic positioning towards light (large or soft leaves are particularly sensitive towards disturbance). Adjustment may take 1-2 years, depending on soil quality, moisture and the site. Once they settle down in new surroundings, plants are 'established', faring for themselves.

Between well-set steps, waterwise perennials reach into cool soil flowering almost through the year. Design Chaltin & Chardin, Antibes.

Mulch
The Gardener's Ally

Protective gravel suits *Arum pictum* and soil life.

A layer of organic matter is a characteristic feature of undisturbed Mediterranean shrublands, but conventional horticultural practices (sweeping, turning over the ground) have altered this situation. Results such as soils drying out and erosion are incompatible with modern ecological thought: plants' well-being is strongly influenced by nature's way of recycling resources by natural mulching. Think of a forest floor, layer upon layer of decaying leaves covering soft friable ground. Mulching consists of the intentional return of organic material.

Most gardeners use mulch for improved looks, for keeping weeds under control or for water conservation. While these are some of its benefits, not everybody is aware of many others obtained from its use. Those involved with the plants' basic well-being, the crucial underground conditions, are often overlooked.

The greatest significance of mulch is the restoration of the usually damaged humus content in Mediterranean-type soils. Though only 5 % of the soil volume, its prime importance is in water retention and nutrient content, especially of microelements.

Mulch creates a temperature range in the soil which encourages the microfauna and microflora. On a hot day the surface temperature of an unmulched sand soon climbs to 50° C., while that in mulched soil stays in a 17-25° range. The effect of this on soil moisture is obvious. Less well-known is the fact that the break-down of important trace elements by microorganisms and their absorption from the soil solution is much more effective in a moderate temperature range.

Bacterial action decomposing organic substances only occurs freely in upper soil layers (15-20cm). There, during the humid season, most soluble plant food is absorbed by root hairs, the main feeding source for soil nutrients. Mulch protects these fine surface roots from cultivation and its damaging action. Even weeds should be removed with the least soil disturbance.

Mulch affects soil life in many ways. It activates and feeds the soil life which works the ground, thus mixing the upper soil layer into lower ones, providing the necessary aeration and a better soil structure. Gradually decomposing into humus, mulch acts as a weak fertilizer.

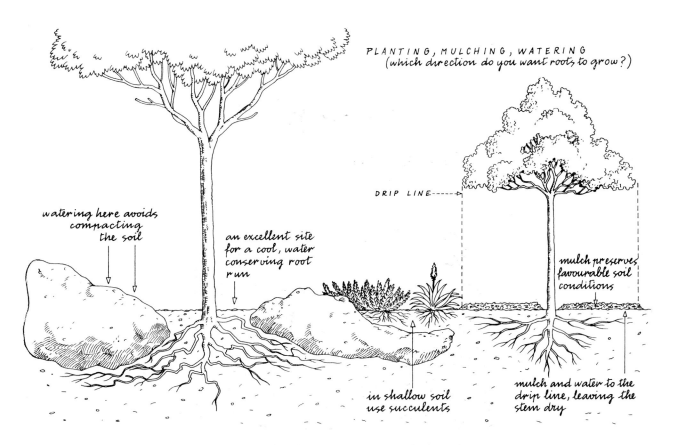

PLANTING, MULCHING, WATERING
(which direction do you want roots to grow?)

watering here avoids compacting the soil

an excellent site for a cool, water conserving root run

DRIP LINE

mulch preserves favourable soil conditions

in shallow soil use succulents

mulch and water to the drip line, leaving the stem dry

Mulched ground absorbs rain readily and winter rains accumulate as a considerable water reserve in the sub-soil. Mulch maintains this reservoir for a long time by reducing surface evaporation.

Note: 24 hours after a cloudburst, 150mm of rain were measured (a 15cm 'blanket' covering the countryside), the year's total for many Mediterranean countries! Café-au-lait coloured lagoons covered the fields, flowing off towards the sea - the fertile topsoil lost forever! Little run-off and erosion occurred in forests where leaves cover the ground, their continual decay creating the permeable soil beneath. Such ground readily absorbs downpours while hard-baked soil on open fields takes hours to absorb the deluge.

Bedrock with little soil is a frequent feature around the Mediterranean. Over the years, mulch builds up topsoil, turning into an ever thicker root cover. Where access to terraced or steep terrain is difficult, mulch, lighter than soil and easily carried in bags, may replace soil.

The economic benefit of mulch is not the least. Weed-suppressing mulches save labour. Savings on feeding or 'plant protection' are significant as mulched plants tend to be stronger and healthier, also less dependent on the gardener. A mulched garden can be left on its own for longer than one would risk otherwise.

CHOOSING MULCHING MATERIALS

There is no need to use identical mulches throughout the garden. Each mulch, chosen according to plant needs, has advantages or drawbacks. Light-coloured mulches absorb less heat than dark ones. Consider looks, using finer materials in the foreground, coarser ones at the back. Your choice depends on suitability and your taste. Consider also cost.

The faithful shredder during the winter cleanup. Seldom the pile is that high. A second processing provides finer texture.

Organic materials. During dry summers, green, juicy mulches encourage plant growth, acting as weak, slow-release fertilizers. To avoid sogginess, coarse, drier and well-ventilated mulches are appropriate in winter. During decomposition which varies in length, all woody materials (including straw) consume nitrogen. They compete for it with plants, unless nitrogen such as dried blood or hoof and horn is added and are best used with restraint.

In every garden, especially in older ones, lawn clippings, weeds, discarded plants, cut branches accumulate. These are the basic materials for one of the best mulches. I aim for variety and also include a sprinkling of wood ashes for their wealth of trace elements. The idea is similar to composting. Shredders and chippers process this 'green waste', together with kitchen refuse and other organic leftovers to a required size (double-process for finer texture). Choosing shredders demands careful deliberation. Usually a larger model than initially planned is needed. Hammer mills avoid knive-sharpening. Sharing one with neighbours reduces cost.

Depending on nearby agriculture or industries, count on almond and other nut shells, cottonseed or rice hulls, grape pomace, mushroom compost or ground corncobs; all qualify. Spent hops may heat up and are best kept away from the base of the plant. Lawn clippings and soft-textured leaves tend to mat, so combine them with coarser materials for good aeration. Fresh or dried herbage and hay are excellent mulches but may introduce weed seeds (cut before going into seed). Baled straw is weed-free and cheap. Bark chips are coarse, durable, neat-looking, suitable also for paths. Or secure wood shavings and sawdust from your carpenter. Pine needles, while slow to break down and consuming nitrogen in the process (as all woody materials), are used where a long-lasting, neat appearance and soil acidification are desired.

Materials for mulching are no longer collected from the wild. Plants need fallen leaves as protective ground cover. For centuries, farmers drove their mule carts to the beach to load seaweed ('Algumin' at Garden Centres), but seaweed stabilizes shorelines and collecting is now discouraged.

These *Zantedeschia aethiopica* flower in early spring where rock for years lay bare. A few years ago, they were planted in early autumn in barely enough soil but covered lavishly with a vegetative mulch (10-15cm). Renewed whenever available, mulch gradually built up nutrient-rich soil. With winter rain, plants grow vigorously, flower early, in summer dry up. At first, a few health hazards occurred. Today, all factors seem to have balanced out.

The Sea Squill (*Urginea maritima*) flowers from naturally mulched ground. Leaves come up later.

Crinum bulbispermum 'Album' enjoys its rich mulch.

Living mulches, the so-called green manures (alfalfa, clover), possess similar benefits to the aforementioned. When mature, they are cut and left lying (compare with Nutrition, Green Manures). Ground covers (see lawn replacements) or pioneer plants give a few comparable advantages.

Inorganic mulches provide a few benefits but do not feed soil life nor do they convert into humus. In summer pebbles or gravel protect roots from drying out. In winter they keep weeds under control and foliage dry (grey felty leaves). Not all stones lying on the ground need clearing away; they mulch the soil and keep fine soil particles from blowing away. Many cacti and other succulents appreciate the heat they reflect. Gravel is also in line with their low nutrient requirements and an often negative response to excessive nitrogen.

Note: *Aptenia cordifolia* seemed right for a sun exposed site but by midwinter lay lifeless on sodden ground. Coarse gravel, generously spread, raised it from its miserable bed and soon plants spread.

CORRECT MULCHING PROCEDURES

Success depends largely on quantities applied.

Apply mulch generously, a layer of 10-15cm is generally considered adequate. Mulches, decomposing into humus, need to be replenished whenever available, at least annually. This could be theoretical when little is within reach. Still, a handful is better than nothing.

The ideal spread reaches to plants' dripline (the width occupied by roots), preferably somewhat further (see drawing p. 67). Place mulches, especially juicy green ones, away from rot-sensitive root crowns and, instead, surround by a handful of gravel. Beware small plants which are easily smothered.

Well-placed mulches, compact enough to keep soils from drying out, allow the air to circulate (soil life needs oxygen). Ideally applied after the rainy season when soil water content is maximal, make sure the weeded soil is thoroughly moist. Later rain (or irrigation) would moisten the mulch, leaving underlying soil dry.

Water
Its Wise Use

In years to come the ultimate in gardening will be 'independence from irrigation'.

Plants absorb water through their roots and lose it through the openings in the leaf surface. Water-saving plants release less water from their leaves, grow more slowly in hot weather and have a wider-spreading or deeper root system than thirstier plants. Watering aims at making good the water that plants have transpired through their leaves, yet watering is only *one* means of maintaining a favourable water balance within a plant. Others are optimum growth conditions such as dappled shade and wind protection.

Although you may have larger areas of your garden planted with drought-tolerant plants or planned for a completely drought-tolerant garden, you may still use *some* water to irrigate a few vegetables, water a choice subtropical fruit tree or containers – and establish new specimens. How go to do this?

RESPONDING TO NEED

Watering in Mediterranean climates is simple: rely on winter rain. Mediterranean plants are used to this. The usual quantities are sufficient to carry them through the year. Roots 'sense' water. Allowing them to search for moisture develops a stronger root system and prepares plants for finding water during summer.

Irrigation should be limited to plants that, without it, would not survive as garden-worthy. It is difficult to accept this, as the idea that only watering makes our gardens thrive is so firmly rooted in our minds. Plants which become dormant in summer should be allowed to do so. Many Mediterranean climate plants resent summer water which may drown their dormant, inactive roots. They are incompatible with the watering of a sown lawn, reacting to irrigation with decreased vitality. However, others are quite resistant to irrigation (*Osteo-*

spermum, palms). Where plants *must* take summer water without requiring it, give them superdrainage.

'Plants require most water during hot dry months', we read occasionally. But this is not so. Plants require most water when in active growth. Bulbs for example grow over humid winters, flower in spring and, protected by their dried up leaves, become dormant in hot dry months (even *need* this summer-baking). Such bulbs, the same as all Mediterranean climate plants, require ample water in winter, the time of natural Mediterranean rainfall. In an exceptionally dry spring, late-flowering bulbs may require one or two artificial waterings. Should watering become necessary during prolonged winter droughts, apply it early to allow water to disappear into the soil before midday sun evaporates it. Late afternoon-watering gives conditions encouraging fungus disease (moisture remaining on foliage overnight). In winter remember to open watering basins to avoid rot-inducing moisture to collect around stems.

Early in the year, hot sunny days after a dull period cause stress to the plants. Leaf-spraying often restores affected ones. Check all recently planted or tender specimens immediately after strong winds. An extra ration of water offsets their drying out effect.

Should your garden require watering in summer, give deep night irrigation rather than shallow, frequent day irrigation. It encourages deeper roots and saves water. Watering at midday is wasteful (high evaporation) and droplets in sun burn plants, acting like magnifying glasses. Always water when the air is still.

Right: Many cacti such as the tall *Echinopsis candicans* and other succulents thrive in dry air and may attract health hazards where a sprinkler reaches them regularly. Whichever water they are meant to receive is best applied directly to the soil, away from the stem.

Although palms and cycads do with little summer water and, well-established, survive drought for years, they are irrigation-tolerant on lawns *(Phoenix canariensis* and *Cycas revoluta).*

CORRECT QUANTITIES

Avoid the thought 'the more the better'.

Water-saving plants require less water than other plants. They need extra water until established, but then less and less as they mature.

In the period after planting until plants are well-rooted in the surrounding soil (established), water-saving plants must be watered in the same way as other vegetation. At that stage they depend upon water supplied directly to the root ball as little water moves there from the surrounding soil. The water required varies between species and sites and is affected by subsoil conditions and the care taken at planting. Plant size at planting time also plays its part. A healthy, well-set specimen, generously mulched, may survive with weekly applications while another plant with wrong exposure, careless planting in wrong soil and roots heating up, may droop a few hours after planting. Such factors largely determine the plants' water needs or drought tolerance and careful observation replaces rigid rules. However, it is generally accepted that in the first year after planting, drought-tolerant plants require 1-4 monthly waterings and could be established by year's end. During the second season and thereafter some will need a thorough watering once a month (driest summer months), while others already can do without.

When established, a range of near drought-tolerant plants needs occasional deep soakings. Generally speaking, few are overwatered in well-drained soils by watering once a month while a weekly supply may carry water-demanding plants a long way. Gradually reduce watering to ripen wood, preparing plants to endure winter cold.

Overwatering seems to be a common practice. Apparently, California lawns receive twice the amount of water even the thirstiest grass may need ('Horticulture', California's Drought, l991). Waterlogging forces the air out of the soil and overwatered rootstocks rot. Many plants suggested in this book may succumb to soil-borne diseases. *Coronilla, Cupressus, Teucrium* seed in cracks, away from wet soil. After planting, water once and allow to dry moderately before watering again.

Established, well-tended plants look after themselves and survive on less water than might be expected. Watch the leaves: if they lose their gloss or turn limp, if top growth folds over, water is needed (see also p. 81). But keep calm in midsummer when drought-tolerant plants discard older leaves in favour of growth tips (this is a survival strategy). The leaves return with autumn rains.

When converting a water-consuming into a water-saving garden, accustom the drought-tolerant plants which are used to ample water but can do without, to the new schedule gradually. For example cut down to twice and later to once a week, being generous again over hottest periods.

HOW?

One tends to think that any child knows how to water a plant. Watering, carried out correctly, maintains water-retaining soil conditions, avoids leaching, reduces pest and disease incidence and saves water! Consider five all-important aspects which should be well-described to unskilled help.

This plant folds up its leaves, clearly showing water need *(Olearia insignis).* Compare with the specimen on p.164.

Water thoroughly. Drought-tolerant plants cope with scarce water either by deep roots or by widespreading ones which are quick to catch a bit of rain (desert plants). Infrequent, deep or extensive irrigation fulfils these plants' needs. Soils should become moderately dry between applications to encourage roots to search for moisture. In time, roots may do without supplementary watering.

Doing a little watering is pleasing to eye and mind, giving the erroneous impression that the garden is well looked after. Yet surface water evaporates quickly, resulting in considerable water loss.

Note: Autumn rain had gathered in puddles. The garden looked well-watered and I meant to cancel its weekly quota. Instead, a hole was dug revealing barely 1cm of humid topsoil. Surface water had nearly fooled me.

Water slowly. Dry soil is reluctant to absorb. Giving time for the water to penetrate avoids run-off and leaching. Premoisten the soil once or twice. After the first water has been absorbed, do the real watering. For example allow a sprinkler to run for 10 minutes, shut off for 30 minutes or so before the real run. Containers require particularly slow applications. When dry, their soil cracks and water percolates, going straight through.

Basins, ditches, terraces. After planting, leave a shallow basin over the root area to the drip line. Filling this twice allows water to infiltrate slowly. Once plants are established, fill the basin with soil. For water-demanding ones dig instead a ring beyond the canopy's periphery, taking the entire root extension into account. Rings encourage outward root growth, leaving stems dry. Rings should be widened annually in accordance with root growth.

This attractive container in an evergreen, waterwise scene requires extra care as roots may heat up in sun.

Terracing keeps water from running off and a few well-placed stones will help plants on slopes. Where a dense tree canopy shields plants from rain ('rain shadow'), ditches bring rainwater from open terrain.

Watering by hand. Roots move to the direction where they 'sense' water. A low-pressure hose, moving in circles around plants, attracts roots towards the periphery. Watering simultaneously neighbouring plants several times, allows water to infiltrate.

Mulch, replaced where disappearing, avoids soil compaction.

On sloping ground, water only above the plant; the run-off takes care of areas below.

Water plants near a rock via the rock surface. Its run-off moistens the ground more evenly than a splashing hose and encourages roots to grow beneath cool rock (see drawing p. 67). While changing to dry-gardening, i.e. separating water-saving from water-consuming plants, be prepared to water at first by hand.

Avoid wetting the leaves and stems of drought-tolerant plants. Hairy or velvety leaf surfaces (survival strategies) cannot function when soggy, and wet trunks may encourage root crown rot. Both are a problem with sprinklers.

However, plants from climates other than Mediterranean ones, may require increased air humidity and leaf-wetting (dowsing, turning a sprinkler on and off several times daily or exploiting raised air humidity near sprinklers).

Plants with hairy or felty surfaces prefer dry leaves and are often best watered by hand beneath the leaves.

Plant Nutrition
Soil, the Primary Source

Sufficient nutrients are usually present in all well-aerated soils with a high organic content and an active soil life.

Plants manufacture their food by photosynthesis, which means taking up carbon dioxide from the air, water from the soil and using the energy for this process from the sun. The sugars produced are used as building material, as stored food within the plant or as energy for further turn overs. Nutrients made available by soil bacteria and absorbed by the plant, help in this process as well as in plants' growth and development.

Soil microorganisms receive energy for their operations from 'burning' (decomposing) organic matter which provides them with oxygen. Carbon dioxide is released in the process (the same carbon dioxide used by plants for photosynthesis). A continuous interaction results between the atmosphere, soil and plants (see also Soil Life).

NUTRIENTS

Besides carbon dioxide from the air and water from soil, plants need three vital elements: nitrogen, phosphorus, potassium.

Nitrogen in the soil stimulates vigorous vegetative growth, resulting in a healthy green colour. Nitrogen is a major component of the air we breathe but plants cannot draw directly from this vast supply. Specialized soil bacteria fix nitrogen from the air in the soil (root nodules). Plants have also a second supply store. Microorganisms break down decaying vegetative matter to make it available to plants. Thirdly, rainfall brings nitrogen in small quantities (around 7kg ammonia per ha).

If nitrogen is deficient, new (pale) leaves draw nitrogen from older tissues. Thus watch for abnormal yellowing and leaf-drop furthest away from new growth. Nitrogen deficiency is remedied by hoof and horn (slow nitrogen release) or dried blood (quick). Mixing them lightly with topsoil or mulch before the growing season encourages plant growth.

High nitrogen fertilizers favour foliage at flowers' expense. An excess results in spindly weak growth, bulbs' decay, retarded flowering or fruiting, susceptibility to disease or stress.

Phosphorus encourages flowering and reproduction, ripens tissues, increases hardiness. Roots find phosphorus in the soil. Derived from decomposing rock or organic matter, phosphorus is slowly given up to soil solutions from which roots draw when needed. This is prevented in strongly acid soils. Although they may contain adequate phosphorus, it may not be available to plants (phosphorus fixation, i.e. phosphorus ions combining with other elements). Once other elements are fixed, phosphate becomes available.

Plants deficient in phosphorus have dull green leaves with a purple hue and/or stunted growth. Roots are poorly developed with few fruits. Phosphorus is transported slowly and is best applied where roots are feeding. Bone meal, slaked lime (high calcium content) or powdered rock phosphate, well-mixed with the surrounding soil at planting time, release the nutrient slowly (first broken up by microorganisms).

Excess phosphorous inhibits plant development. Potassium and phosphate levels, commonly encountered in Mediterranean alkaline soils, are much higher than southern hemisphere plants are used to (Proteaceae, originating from leached sandy soils). This interferes with their micronutrient uptake and leads to phosphate excess, indicated by chlorosis, die-back and eventual death. Avoid feeding such plants with fertilizers rich in potassium or phosphate.

Potassium enhances drought tolerance, promoting root growth and thicker cell walls. It regulates the opening and closing of the stomata, helps nutrient distribution in plant tissues, improves disease resistance, encourages bud formation (bulbs) and seed production (fruits). Potassium is present in most soils, deriving mainly from soil minerals and organic matter, independent from microorganisms. Plants feed heavily on the so-called 'exchangeable potassium' but cannot absorb 'insoluble potassium', by far the larger percentage. However soils, unless very light, usually contain sufficient quantities.

Potassium deficiency inhibits plant growth. Leaf edges and tips first turn yellow (necrosis), later dry up similar to drought symptoms. Growth retardance or death follow. Wood ashes are excellent providers of potassium providing they are derived from young wood and have not been leached by rain. Spreading them thinly avoids compaction. Use also bone meal, animal manures, liquid seaweed.

Excess potassium results in poor growth and may also provoke magnesium and calcium deficiencies.

Other nutrients required in smaller quantities are:

Calcium, present in limestone or alkaline soils, enhances cell and root growth. As lime, calcium reduces soil acidity. Excess of lime (above 7 pH) locks in iron and potassium which thus become unavailable to plants.

Magnesium is a chlorophyll builder. Interveinal chlorosis (green leaf veins standing out, premature leaf-dropping), starting on older leaves, indicates magnesium deficiency, a consequence of excess nitrogen or potassium. It may also be a result of a poor root system during periods of rapid growth.

Iron is usually present in sufficient amounts in the soil. However, iron is strongly dependent on other nutrients. Not only their deficiency but also their excess may result in iron deficiency (interveinal chlorosis beginning with young leaves). Deficiency occurs mostly in high pH soils and is controlled by reduced soil alkalinity (acid mulches) and well-aerated soils with ample organic matter.

Note: Yellowing of older leaves indicates poor drainage. So these plants need better drainage, not iron.

Plants also need the seven **trace elements** (boron, chlorine, copper, manganese, molybdenum, zinc, plus the above mentioned iron). These are usually supplied in sufficient quantities by a well-mulched soil rich in organic matter, but one or the other may be deficient in compacted, extremely acid or alkaline soils. Possibly, additional trace elements and their vital function in plant life have as yet to be uncovered. So how do we feed plants accordingly?

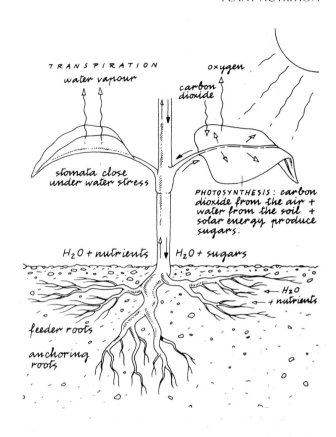

Healthy green colour reveals adequate nitrogen in the soil and results from careful soil management.

Hydrangea macrophylla, not a Mediterranean climate native, does require a fertile soil (humus, mulch) and summer water to achieve this glorious performance.

ORGANIC PLANT FOOD

Organic plant food derives from living or dead organisms (animal, plant). Some nutrients are only available to plants via soil life and correct nutrition means feeding plants via the soil, not directly. Myriads of microorganisms populate well-mulched garden soil and steadily provide plants with such nutrients as nitrogen, phosphorus, potassium or all-important trace elements. Roots take up their current requirements. Nature's way reduces the risk of leaving out necessary elements and suits the gardener. To keep this process going, build a fertile soil with organic matter (compost, organic mulch, green manures) and feed soil life with varied mulches. Healthy plants result from such knowledgeable gardening (see also Soil Life).

Vegetative manures

Compost, well-composed and matured, contains all trace elements plants may require. Although low in nitrogen, phosphorus and potassium, compost, while decomposing in the soil, is a continuous slow-release nutrient supplier.

Note: "As waters become increasingly polluted with fertilizer run-off and organic wastes, composting is an increasingly attractive alternative" (Raven 1986 p.537).

Organic mulches are mild fertilizers. While 'mono-mulches' are useful, mixed mulches feed soil life better. Consider the carbon-nitrogen ratio. Woody mulches (sawdust, ground bark, also straw) have a high carbon (cellulose) content. To break this down, soil bacteria take nitrogen from the soil, competing for it with plants. So add nitrogen-rich hoof and horn, dried blood or use so-called 'fortified' organic mulches.

Grapepomace (high in nitrogen, phosphate, potash), is an excellent soil conditioner and alternative to meals.

Wood ashes (phosphoric acid, much potash and calcium, particularly rich in trace elements) best from young wood. Collect chemically untreated wood ashes as soon as cooled, lest potassium leaches into the soil.

Green manures improve soil fertility. Their deeply penetrating roots aerate the soil and add vegetative matter. Easy and fast, controlling weeds, they are useful to get gardens off to a good start after building rubble has been cleared. Buckwheat (*Polygonum fagopyrum,* poor soils) improves soil structure. Legumes enrich soil with nitrogen (nitrogen fixation). For light soils use trefoil (*Medicago lupulina,* tolerating dry shade); crimson clover (*Trifolium incarnatum*); fenugreek (*Trigonella foenum-graecum,* very fast, medicinal, culinary) or bitter lupin (*Lupinus angustifolius,* slightly acid soils). For heavier soils use broad bean (*Vicia faba*) or spring vetch (*Vicia sativa*).

Animal manures

Matured animal manures, depending on animal feed, have superior qualities. Among them are dried cowdung (potassium-rich), horse manure (excellent combined with the above), hog (mostly potassium), sheep (alkaline), goat and rabbit (nitrogen-rich), chicken, pigeon, guano (much phosphorus, calcium, ample trace elements, suiting alkaline soils). Cats and canary birds may contribute too. These potent manures should mature with the compost pile. Applied fresh, they burn plants and may bring about health risks.

Fish (wide mixture of all basic elements, including microelements), similar to guano.

Dried and powdered meat (nitrogen-rich, ample trace elements, iron). Slow, long-lasting nitrogen conversion for vigorous plant growth. Use when planting or during plant growth, to control chlorosis. Dried and powdered blood is relatively fast-acting.

Bone meal (phosphorus- and calcium-rich) encourages strong roots, flowers and fruits. Slow-release, it can be used throughout the growing season. Place where roots can get at it as it does not move. In planting holes, well-mixed with the surrounding soil, it acts as a good starter. Withhold bone meal (pH around 10) from acid soil loving plants.

Hoof and horn (much nitrogen, some phosphate, minor elements). Feather (also hair, fur) is similar to horn. Beware: Use only properly sterilized meals!

Note: Andean people under Inca rule, corn-growing experts, interred a small fish with each maize kernel. Children bury cut fingernails and hair (human or the dog's) near a best-loved plant.

Proper dispersal is vital. Choose a cool day before rain to spread plant food on humid ground, or water immediately. Use the above also in liquid form. Soak 24 hours in sufficient water until tea-coloured, apply on humid ground. Delicate plants profit from lower, more frequent applications. Reduced roots (recent transplants) respond to foliar feeding.

Note: Chemical fertilizers, water-soluble synthetic salts, quickly release minerals. Their ease of use made them a favourite. Applied directly to the plant, roots take them up. However overfeeding may result or they may lack vital trace elements. Plants are sensitive to excess or deficiencies. And salts burn soil life. They may show as 'white bloom' on unmulched soils when evaporation is strong.

Heathers and Proteaceae develop extremely branched nutrient roots, their considerable surface area permeated by fungi and soil organisms. Improper feeding may harm these delicate roots, resulting in quick collapse. Overapplication of organic nutrients can cause similar problems.

The leaching of quick-release nitrogen and the washing out of excess inorganic nutrients into deeper soil layers is well-known.

This magnificent *Ceanothus leucodermis* grows wild in the chaparral of the Santa Ana Mountains. It clearly requires no additional food. Courtesy Santa Ana Botanic Garden California

TO FEED OR NOT TO FEED

To feed or not to feed as much as 'when and what' are crucial issues for plants' well-being. The indigenous Mediterranean flora (lavender, myrtle, thyme), adapted to its living conditions, needs no feeding. The same goes for the California chaparral *(Carpenteria, Mimulus)*. Shrubs from South Africa's Cape and southern Australia's sandy soils are no exception. When *should* I feed? you may inquire. We rarely open a book without being told to feed every week and the gardener dutifully complies. Expense and labour may be high while the result could be adverse. You have done your share: you have carefully planted and mulched. Why not wait and see? Nature is often best when left alone.

Feed if you have reason to do so. Ecologically oriented feeding (as watering) is adjusted to plants' growth rhythm and is justified when it supplies their requirements during periods of rapid, active growth.

Consider the time factor of nutrient release. When plants enter into their preflowering phase, approximately 6-8 weeks before flowering, slow-release fertilizers may be useful. Phosphate-rich dressings, for example, encourage flower- and fruit-setting (bone meal for bulbous plants). Trees, shrubs and annuals appreciate mature manure. Basic dressings sustain planting, providing a good start for plant development.

Yet there is a second feeding season. When first autumn rains set in, you may apply well-balanced food to support plants over several weeks of growing until cooler days persist.

Stop feeding native Mediterranean plants (*if* you intend to feed) 6-8 weeks before they start to show stress (late spring when summer drought approaches, autumn when winter cold nears). Woody plants, left to mature, enter into winter in a well-ripened state. Hardened wood copes better. Feeding at the wrong time affects plants unfavourably. The ability of dormant plants to absorb food is minimal.

Avoid overfeeding *any* plant at *any* time of the year. It is tempting to give a generous helping of plant food for quicker growth, larger flowers or heavier crops. But plants with largest flowers or quickest growth are not necessarily the strongest. Soft sappy growth exposes *Acacia,* for example, to wind breakage. And pests or diseases are quick to colonize on forced growth; sturdy plants are less susceptible.

Plants from other environments frequently occupy a prominent place in Mediterranean gardens (*Brugmansia, Canna, Hydrangea*). Their different needs demand feeding (and watering) in order to thrive.

Heat-requiring plants (*Beaumontia, Hibiscus rosa-sinensis*) do not need autumn-feeding as with such tender plants winter begins early.

Plant Health
How to Prevent an Early Death

Searching for plant afflictions' cause, frequently cured with simple means, is the right measure.

Pests and diseases are not normally a problem in gardens of Mediterranean climates. They are attracted to plants which are under stress and are important indicators of weak plants which are the first ones to show symptoms of disorders. The incidence of pests and diseases tells us that something has gone wrong.

Crises in health are generally a result of mistakes in cultivation. However, adverse local conditions, for example high temperatures coinciding with high humidity (fog), may also favour them. Eelworms (nematodes) occur mostly in light sandy soils during high temperatures and frequent irrigation. The same atmospheric conditions encourage whitefly.

In dry air, many pests and diseases, especially fungal ones, have a limited effect. Where planting and cultivation is carried out with care, vigorous growth will withstand problems more easily.

Gardeners today are reluctant to use pesticides which decimate soil life and destroy our best helper, the 'pest' which signals weakened plants. Having observed tits tirelessly picking insects off branchlets, one hesitates to poison their food.

Raven reads (1986, p.660 shortened): 'Approximately half a billion metric tons of pesticides and herbicides are produced annually for application to crops in the US only. Of this enormous total only around 1 % reaches the target organisms. Most of the remainder either reaches soil, water or non-target organisms in the same ecosystem or spreads into neighbouring ones. When it does so, it may have important detrimental effects on their functioning such as elimination of certain species which may affect the functioning of the system as a whole or lead indirectly to the elimination of other species. Important decomposers, such as earthworms and other soil organisms, may be greatly reduced by pesticides, so that the ecosystem as a whole ceases to function properly. The intensity of such effects depends on chemicals' toxicity and on their persistence in the environment. ... some chemical pollutants tend to be concentrated as they pass up through food chains, reaching highest concentrations in the top predators. In addition, many strains of insects, bacteria and fungi have evolved that are resistant to the pesticides designed to control them. Of the estimated 2000 major insect pest species, about 1/4 have already evolved strains that are resistant to one or more insecticides. Other effects are less direct. Important predators which naturally control pest populations, may be eliminated by pesticide poisoning, leading to outbreaks of the very pest organisms that the pesticides were employed to control. Scientists are searching for less damaging substitutes.''

In the meantime, we have simple, inexpensive and natural remedies at hand: observation, water and secateurs being foremost. Prevention and hygiene are excellent control measures, being most successful at early stages. Not all pests and diseases may become a problem, many disappear after a season!

It is the wise gardener's goal to create favourable conditions for the many relationships between plants, animals and their surroundings which are more complex than often believed. If one link is interfered with, the whole balance may be upset.

LEAVE IT TO NATURE

Protect birds and natural predators (frogs, snakes, salamanders, spiders, wasps) who control the pests. Duck swallow every slug or snail in sight.

Raven (1986, p.660) reads: 'When oak are defoliated by certain moths, new leaves develop within days which contain more tannin and are therefore less palatable to the moth, interfering with its digestion.' The wild olive, when grazed, develops new shoots which are smaller, woodier, spinier – less palatable.

Unpalatable plants (felt, spines, hard leaves) are an
efficient alternative to tempting, juicy growth.

PHYSICAL CONTROL OR REMOVAL

Where, early in the year, white 'nests' appear in trees
(mostly pine), these are procession caterpillars
(*Thaumetopoea pityocampa*) in their early stages. They
feed on new tree growth and can become epidemic,
causing severe damage if not tackled in time. Cut off the
colonies within reach, using a ladder. Avoid standing
underneath while doing this, as poisonous hairs induce
skin rashes. Burn 'nests'. Many gardeners destroy higher
nests with a shotgun which requires care.

Bacteria occasionally infect cacti (soft white patches
increasing rapidly in size), finally destroying plants. Cut
out all diseased tissue, dust with flowers of sulphur,
move to well-aerated and lighted areas.

Spartium, disfigured by witches'-broom (usually
caused by parasitic fungi), benefits by being cut to the
ground. *Impatiens walleriana*, attacked by aphids,
benefits from cutting back.

Where pests hide, cut out dead wood, eliminate
infested growth, remove affected leaves (leaving
enough for photosynthesis), and give the remainder a
thorough hosing. Often new vigorous growth follows.
Also check newly acquired plants for pests, cutting out all
dead, infected or 'unnecessary' growth, making sure no
unwanted slug is harboured. Burn all diseased material.

Summer-baking may suppress virus infections
(isolated, irregularly patterned chlorotic cell patches,
transmitted by sucking insects), occasionally encountered on bulbous plants (Iridaceae, Liliaceae). Control
aphids and burn affected specimens.

Slugs and snails feed on tender juicy growth, especially
that of *Crinum, Hippeastrum, Scadoxus*. Snails can be
kept at bay by surrounding plants with ash (renew after
rain), by hand-picking or baiting overnight. Or grow
plants in a container on a terrace and destroy any hiding
places.

Tip: Follow the time-honoured practice of picking larger snails
after rain. Village friends will gratefully acknowledge your
harvest, eating them spiced with garlic.

If larger animals (rabbit, deer) are a pest, fencing may
be required. Hares mostly investigate newly planted
vegetation, so protect with wire baskets. Fumigate with
bitter tea made from *Artemisia absinthium* from your
garden or consult literature on biological pest control.
Also consider planting unpalatable vegetation such as
Artemisia, Ballota, lavender, rock roses.

Although spiny succulence is unpalatable, close planting to a wall may attract health hazards (*Yucca elephantipes*).

Disorders may be due to excessive heat. Allow heat-stressed plants to recover in shade.

Removal of shelter trees may cause sun damage (discoloured, dull greyish upper leaf surfaces, later turning into dead brown patches). With cold, similar symptoms may be seen. Cut back damaged parts.

Discoloured leaf margins may indicate low air humidity during periods of high temperature.

CAREFUL CULTIVATION

Aeration is vital in Mediterranean climates. Poorly aerated positions (too near walls, under an overhang, overcrowding) encourage diseases, but can often be remedied by a change of location or light pruning. Self-seeded plants seem to resist health problems best.

Watering at the wrong time favours two fungal infections common in Mediterranean regions. *Armillaria mellea* (honey or oak-root fungus) affects mostly oak which is irrigated during hot summer months and can become an important scourge of established oak woods. Control by excellent drainage and avoid summer irrigation where *Armillaria* occurs. Resistant species include *Carya illinoensis, Castanea sativa, Diospyros kaki, Ginkgo biloba, Ilex aquifolium, Jacaranda mimosifolia, Maclura pomifera, Magnolia grandiflora, Mahonia aquifolium, Psidium littorale, Sophora japonica, Vitex agnus-castus.*

Phytophthora cinnamomi affects many plants. It becomes active in warm, wet, disturbed conditions where the natural soil ecology goes haywire, and is usually discovered too late. Dying root systems and rotting root crowns are followed by a rapid collapse. Control is difficult. The best means are excellent drainage and no

summer watering. Removing affected tissues may save partly diseased plants (burn dead material, disinfect tools). Fungicides, a short-term remedy, may kill the beneficial soil fungi together with pathogens.

Summer watering endangers *Artemisia schmidtiana, Fremontodendron* or those bulbs which require summer-baking.

Poor drainage results in waterlogged roots which drown. Allow soil to dry moderately before resuming routine watering.

Allow wood to ripen before the cold of winter sets in.

The common practice of soil cultivation damages surface roots. Best protect by mulch.

Poor plant care (nutrient deficiencies) is indicated by disorders such as die-back, reddish shading of new growth or dark green veins on discoloured light green leaves. A good dressing of compost is like feeding with vitamins. The wider the range of materials included, the more likely it provides the necessary elements. Control may also include applications of acidifying mulches, wood ashes or foliar sprays rich in microelements, resulting in healthy new growth (consult Nutrition).

Drought-tolerant plantings (*Viburnum tinus*) are right where fungus in established oak woods is a threat.

CAREFUL PLANT CHOICE

Healthy plants raised in the open in conditions similar to those of your garden, survive best. Greenhouse plants need attention when first put out.

Choose plants unpalatable to insects. Thick cuticles protect leaves from insect stings, hairy surfaces are unappetising to sucking insects. Select those with aromatic or ethereal resins and oils, a bitter flavour, spiny succulence.

Where air pollution is a problem, choose almond, calendula, citrus, fig, grape, petunia, zinnia.

Monotonous mass-plantings of single species encourage pest attacks. Whitefly flourishes in row upon row of its favourite dish (tomato, beans) and populations rapidly become bigger where chemicals have destroyed natural enemies. Reduce the pest's food by mixed plantings and rotation of crops. Best avoid very susceptible plants.

Observation: Such 'favourites' in my garden often belonged to the Solanaceae or Malvaceae family, now mostly excluded. A wide choice replaces plants for which, over the years, no way of producing healthy growth could be found.

Zinnia help out where air pollution is a problem and thus better the air we breathe.

Healthy plants produce vigorous tip growth.

THE 'ROOT-TO-CROWN CHECK'

Since treatments are always preceded by careful diagnoses, use the Root-to-Crown-Check. Bare roots, for example, are susceptible to many problems. Once soil has been added, plants recuperate readily. As strong roots are clearly at the basis of healthy plant growth, check on soil conditions:

– Are roots properly covered?
– Are they well-anchored (wind)?
– Are roots waterlogged (poorly-drained pots)?
– Is the root crown set too deep?
– Is soil depth inadequate (underlying rock)?

Next, examine the stem:
– strangled by a wire or string, rubbed by a stake?
– gnawed by an animal, scratched by a vehicle?

Followed by leaf examination: Shoot growth is an excellent indicator of the plant's well-being. Smaller-than-normal spring leaves are a sign of low reserves or inability to absorb nutrients (brought about by pest-reduced foliage or root damage).

– Is tip growth wilting (lack of water)?
– Are leaves yellowing, spotted (nutrient deficiencies)?
– Are leaves eaten (pests)?
– Are pests or diseases hiding on the undersides?

After inspecting the plant, check on growing conditions.

Finding the right treatment demands observation and care for the one entrusted to us. We occasionally forget that plants are living things. Let us cater to their needs and listen when they cry for help. They will repay us with healthy growth. Nothing replaces the gardener's loving care, often called 'green fingers'.

Pruning
for Health, Growth and Flowering

Pruning in Mediterranean climate regions follows similar principles as elsewhere.

PRUNING FOR PLANT HEALTH

Pruning for plant health aims to establish and maintain a strong, healthy framework by pruning out dead, damaged, diseased, weak, twiggy or inward-growing shoots and branches. Well-kept plants are less susceptible to health problems or wind damage while neglected plants provide hide outs for pests. Savings in water and improved landscape appearance are additional benefits.

Air circulation around or within plants during summer heat is vital to Mediterranean vegetation, be it shrublet or tree. Find the right balance between branches shading the ground and allowing air to circulate (see drawing).

Multi-stemmed trees make a dense crown, requiring substantial pruning. Taking out stems at ground level lets air circulate. The same applies to suckering shrubs (*Hydrangea quercifolia, Euonymus japonicus*). Where crowns interfere with neighbouring plants, it is better to take out a whole branch rather than snipping here and there. Each cut makes a wound, but one large cut is considered preferable to many small ones. Prune with close, clean cuts as stubs attract rot, predisposing trees to wind break. Plants which need constant training deteriorate as the years pass, being the wrong plants in the right place or vice versa.

Conifers can be left to themselves, but thin out dense groups for adequate light. As *Ceratonia siliqua's* wood is tender best whitewash previously shaded trunks.

Note: No gardener should feel obliged to prune without a reason. Excellent books advise the beginner. Mediterranean people observe moon cycles. Fenceposts, cut with the waning moon, are said to last forever. The same moon suits pruning of grape vines. Watch sap drip when cut with the rising moon.

PRUNING FOR FLOWER AND FRUIT

Pruning for flower and fruit aims to improve plant performance. It takes into account the season in which flower buds form. Many drought-tolerant plants set buds on autumn growth, flower early (almonds, apricots) and are pruned immediately after flowering. If pruned too late, all bloom is lost. Redbud (*Cercis siliquastrum*) requires restraint as after New Year the first buds swell.

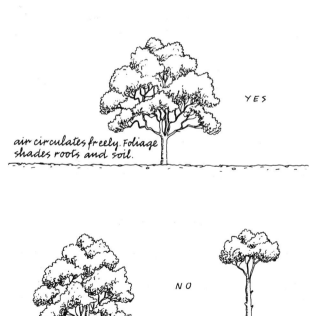

air circulates freely. Foliage shades roots and soil.

YES

air cannot circulate pests find a hiding place

little foliage left for photosynthesis. weakened plants result

NO

Carefully trimmed lentisc *(Pistacia lentiscus)* mimics box.

Spring pruning encourages branching in late-flowering perennials (*Salvia leucantha, S. azurea*). Cutting them back after summer heat gives a second flowering.

Tip: Cut material can be used for propagation.

Pruning avocado (*Persea americana*) induces water shoots, which means more pruning. But cut out weak or dead shoots, and lift lower branches (and fruit) a bit off the ground.

Select the main framework of vines before pruning. Two or three buds on flowering branches may suffice. *Podranea* and *Tecomaria* (Bignoniaceae), when winter-pruned, flower at the tip of current season's growth. The evergreen, winter- and summer-flowering *Solandra maxima* reaches out with long shoots which produce few flowers if left to themselves. So cut back periodically. *Wisteria* bloom looks best on long arching shoots, well-spaced, free-hanging. In spring, cut *Plumbago capensis* to ground. In Portugal, *Bougainvillea*, jasmine and banksiae roses are espaliered close to the wall and, after much labour involved, produce glorious sights.

AESTHETIC ENDS

Shaping of tree, shrub or perennial is fascinating work where, as often, less is more. A single well-shaped tree, a work of art, can make a garden. Judicious thinning, cutting out badly-placed branches, shows good proportions and an attractive appearance.

Tip: Easily carried away, I go about slowly, occasionally stepping back to take the overall view, considering (even for weeks) whether or where to cut a branch. Badly damaged trees (wind, snow, old age), with annual shaping regain harmonious shapes.

Clipping keeps plants well-groomed, prevents them falling apart. Many maquis plants and natives of other Mediterranean regions, clipped immediately after flowering, develop attractive compact growth (*Barleria, Boronia, Coleonema, Eremophila,* many *Senecio*). When animals feed on wild bay, germander, lentisc or olive, pine and oak, these are pruned naturally into rounded masses.

Clipped *Callitris, Cupressus* and *Tetraclinis* produce denser growth. Keep narrower at the top to let light reach low branches. Pinching back individual branch tips often corrects appearance.

THE ANNUAL CLEANUP

Once the first autumn rains come and cover the parched countryside, vigorous growth resumes and continues week after week under clear blue skies. It is time for a preliminary tidy up: during summer robust pioneer plants overtook small treasures which they were meant to protect, rugged vines half-covered windows while tall salvias overwhelmed young plants. Pinching, light shaping and corrective clipping restore plant structure and direct future growth. Olive trees sucker from base and removal is routine.

A garden changes constantly. Plants grow in unexpected directions, seldom stay within assigned boundaries. Over the usually short winter, decide which plant has precedence over the other, evaluate horizontals and verticals. Taking back one plant to allow another to expand is continuous. Giving each sufficient space is one of the aims of a winter cleanup.

Weeds
Friend or Foe?

Weeds are quick to spread on uncovered ground, they part easily from mulched ground.

Nature will always cover bare soil and to this end uses plants we call weeds. Ground-hugging, wide-spreading, the more the soil is disturbed the tougher they are. Often the most pernicious weeds, whether annuals or trees, are pioneers in colonizing devastated land. Replacing them with other plants that cover the soil similarly, means getting rid of weeds in an ecologically correct way. Mostly, weeds constitute a temporary phase in the sequence of plant associations, eventually being replaced by plants best adapted to certain sites.

WEEDS ARE OUR FRIEND

Weeds prevent erosion and drying out of soils, protect soil life and decompose into humus. They give valuable information on soil type. Sorrel for example, grows on heavy, compacted ground and disappears when soil turns into fertile humus. Nettles indicate a nitrogen-rich soil and, with time, may be overtaken by gross feeders. Thistles choose disturbed ground. Their deeply penetrating roots loosen the soil when foraging for minerals. Thistles will disappear from a mulched, humus-enriched ground. Meanwhile, these 'weeds' give the soil vital elements. Many weeds are even attractive, behaving only moderately aggressive. Why not enjoy them until new plantings come up?

Note: Our weeds may be another gardener's cherished possession.

OR OUR FOE

They are our foe when they disturb our planting plans and compete with planned vegetation for water, nutrients and space.

This pretty little weed returns each year
(*Blackstonia perfoliata*).

HOW TO CONTROL THEM

Around the Mediterranean, there are sites so dry that no weed will grow. But seeds of countless weeds lie dormant in the soil, sprouting when conditions are right. Rainfall (or irrigation) stimulate weeds, especially at the start of the two active growth seasons (spring, autumn). Preventing weeds from seeding is an obvious measure. Hedge shears control smaller, brush cutters larger weed expanses. A hoe's well-aimed stroke removes deep-rooted asphodels for good. Brambles or *Smilax* often root among rock. Repeated cutting back exhausts most.

Weeds that have seeded are best burnt or made up in a separate compost pile and turned over (several times) as soon as seed germinates.

Solarization, a new highly efficient method, gets rid of soil-borne weed seeds. During hottest months cover well-watered soil with transparent non-perforated plastic sheets, burying the margins. Let the sun work for 4-5 weeks. Seeds rot at soil level in contact with oxygen (fine microlife seeks refuge further down). Plant up immediately. Afterwards do no more deep digging or drilling, not to turn up more weeds.

In open ground, weeds are quick to colonize. While you decide on plantings, a quick-growing living mulch (see Mulch), green manure (see Nutrition) or ground cover (see Lawn Replacements) suppresses weeds.

Mulched ground is easy to weed as it preserves soil moisture and soft topsoil structure. A common practice weeds the soil between plants, leaving plants themselves untended. However weeding plants' root area and close around them, leaving soil elsewhere undisturbed, is the right treatment (drawing). At the rate that plants grow, the space occupied by weeds will shrink, finally giving way to planted specimens. Fairly close planting accelerates this process. When using a tool, choose a sharp one that works on the surface (scuffle hoe), sparing delicate surface roots.

But weeding is only one answer. Perennial weeds are often a problem to eradicate (bindweed, cinquefoil, *Oxalis*). Withholding light kills many plants and black plastic sheeting, tiles or stones on an infested area will often be effective. If nothing (really nothing!) works, carefully apply Roundup.

Further reading: *Weeds How to Control and Love Them* by Jo Readman (see Bibliography).

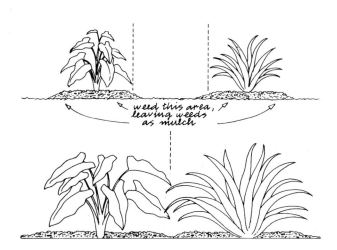

weed this area, leaving weeds as mulch

INVASIVES TO BE WATCHED

The difference between a weed and a cultivated plant becoming a weed is often startling. Many man-introduced 'invasive aliens' escaped from gardens. The long list extends from *Hakea suaveolens* (introduced as hedge plant to South Africa), *Opuntia* (as drought-tolerant fruiting plant to Australia), *Chrysanthemoides monilifera* (as dune stabiliser to Australian coasts) to *Spartium junceum* (a relatively recent garden escape in California).

Mediterranean climate environments are liable to alien invasion. Each region has its own invasive plants. Although the Mediterranean basin seems less exposed, the South African Cape is particularly vulnerable. A Cape Town University study ('Veld & Flora', June 1993) mentions *Acacia* (many), *Eucalyptus*, *Lantana camara*, *Myoporum serratum*, *Nerium oleander*, *Pennisetum clandestinum* (Kikuyu grass), many pines, *Pittosporum undulatum*, *Quercus robur* (the common English oak).

The limiting factor which turns a brilliant introduction from a blessing into a curse is one of the following or their combination: a high seed-set, efficient dispersal mechanisms (wind and birds), coincidence of seedling establishment and rainfall, no natural enemies. Bird- and wind-dispersed plants can also find a convenient 'invasion beach' in a nearby moist habitat such as a brook. Still, all conditions have to be favourable before plants become invasive. For responsible and ecologically considerate guidance inquire in your neighbourhood.

In Mediterranean gardens, suitable growing conditions may turn the following into weeds, often seed-distributed: *Acanthus* (also root fragments), *Ailanthus*, *Albizia lophantha*, *Arctotheca calendula* (runners), *Centranthus*, *Cytisus scoparius*, *Duchesnea indica* (also runners), *Genista monspessulana*, *Hedera helix* and *Lonicera* (also rooting branch tips), *Nicotiana glauca*, *Robinia pseudoacacia* (suckers), *Spartium junceum*, *Tamarix aphylla*, *Tanacetum parthenium* (pretty, easily pulled out), *Ulex europaeus*, *Wigandia*. Beware of abundant bulblets (*Allium*, *Ornithogalum longibracteatum*, *Oxalis pes-caprae*) and runners (couch-grass).

Note: Should you be tempted by thistles, praised in UK catalogues, understand that, once at home in Mediterranean gardens, they will stay.

Control invasive plants by altering their living conditions. In my garden *Amorpha fruticosa* seeded itself with abandon. Yet I liked its discreet but elegant flower spikes. By transplanting it to a little-watered spot, few seedlings germinated.

Propagation
Simple Ways

From a handful to a forest.

In a Mediterranean climate, long periods of mild weather favour propagation. To master the art may lead to an inspiring garden at little expense. A few seed packets are cheap. Seed gathered in the wild or distributed free to garden club members, cuttings given by friends or material exchanged among neighbours may well form the basis of one of those passionately loved gardens which, by exploiting propagation to the hilt, invariably attract attention and stimulate admiration. Plants prepared in advance come in handy to enliven drab corners, cover barren patches or reciprocate gifts. Propagating rare natives and distributing them widely helps conservation.

Propagation is helpful for other reasons than increasing stock. Plants from the protection of a hothouse may not always cope with a new environ-

Cold-stratification benefits *Paeonia cambessedesii* seeds.

ment, but cuttings may survive in time. *Pandorea jasminoides* looked sickly on arrival with me. Taking cuttings insured against its loss. The next generation became rampant climbers. The same was true for *Tropaeolum majus* which today, raised from seed, is exuberant.

Setting aside an area for propagation is a good idea. Recycled cartons or berry trays substitute for expensive containers. Compost saves on potting mixtures. But be prepared to involve some time and patience.

SEED

Seed allow you to grow run-of-the-mill and also rare plants (see Addresses). Seed-raised plants protect gardens from unwanted travellers which may be introduced in pots (pests, weeds). Seed from your garden may be stored in tight-fitting glass jars in the refrigerator. It is worth experimenting, even if only half comes up.

Small seed of native plants from Mediterranean-type regions are sown before the first autumn rains. Fluctuating temperatures in winter promote germination.

Short-lived seed (oak, chestnut), sown as soon as ripe, germinate with the first rains. They develop a root first, taking up to three months to emerge above ground. Those seeds which are rich in endosperm (*Amaryllis, Clivia, Crinum, Haemanthus*) germinate as soon as they touch the ground but take several years to flower. Press in lightly but do not cover with soil.

Species evolved in tropical conditions need warmth. With many Leguminosae members (*Caesalpinia, Erythrina, Hardenbergia, Senna*) and a number of other genera (*Rhus, Romneya*) various seed structures inhibit germination. To get rid of these and the chemicals supporting their activity, give the seeds 'heat stratification'. Pour boiling water over seed, allow them to cool and soak for

Amaryllis belladonna readily comes up from fresh seed. Here it flowers among neighbouring foliage.

24 hours, sow the viable (swollen) ones that sink to bottom, and discard the water! Alternatively, simulate a wildfire; cover the seedbox with dry pine needles and burn over.

'Cold stratification', the best germination treatment for species of temperate origin *(Buxus, Elaeagnus, Fraxinus, Mahonia, Paeonia,* Rosaceae) and plants from high altitudes, simulates short, cold winter days, similar to those in northern climates. Sow into moist soil, seal pots into plastic bags, refrigerate for up to three months at 3-4°C. Check periodically for germination. In gardens with cold winters sow outdoors.

Annuals are started in the last days of summer warmth and grow well till the end of autumn. When pricked out, they are strong enough to survive cool winters.

Ericaceae, Leguminosae, Proteaceae and many annuals, among the most beautiful natives of Mediterranean regions, cannot regenerate damaged roots. Sow direct in the garden or into individual containers where, undisturbed, they can develop good root balls. Discard weaklings by thinning. When potting on, leave roots undisturbed, adding mix round the edge and at the bottom of the pot.

Prick out natives when they are large enough to handle. When done in early spring, the risk of damping off is avoided, more likely in warmer periods. Provide good drainage, selecting a suitable pot size. If too large, a major part of the soil remains humid, without roots to absorb water, and this is especially damaging in cold winters. After transplanting, shade for a week. Gradually harden conservatory-grown seedlings outdoors.

Water seeds, cuttings or divisions of drought-tolerant plants sparingly. They rot if watered generously. Repeat initial watering when the topsoil feels dry.

EASY: *Anemone coronaria, Aquilegia, Arthropodium, Bupleurum fruticosum, Calendula, Chamaerops, Cistus, Coronilla, Cupressus, Cyclamen, Digitalis, Echium, Fatsia, Koelreuteria, Melaleuca armillaris, Mirabilis, Nigella, Olea, Pinus, Quercus ilex, Rhamnus, Ruta, Tulbaghia, Viburnum tinus.* Iridaceae sown in late summer germinate with first autumn rains *(Aristea, Belamcanda, Chasmanthe, Crocosmia, Dietes, Freesia, Libertia, Sisyrinchium).* Lilies tend to be temperamental and either come up like grass or not at all. From a single seedpod you may get more bulbs than you have room for. Pot several together, grow on for two years.

Nerium oleander strikes readily from cuttings and flowers within the first year.

CUTTINGS

Cuttings of a wide range of trees, shrubs and climbers can succeed. Succulents are particularly easy. In principle, cuttings should be handled by type, soft ones in spring, woody ones in autumn. Each plant has its own optimum season. Take *Cistus* for example in very early spring while deciduous woody plants (*Prunus, Spiraea*) are best with ripe, woody late winter cuttings. But try them also at other periods (snipping off a broken branchlet). Faced with the risk of losing a plant, I take cuttings even at the 'wrong' season.

Kalanchoe beharensis grows roots at the end of a leaf stalk which has fallen onto ground. New plants are ready within months.

Cuttings from most Mediterranean climate plants do well in the open. Choose a protected, free-draining site with maximum light, but not direct sun. Incorporate sand and leaf mould (a mild, slow-release fertilizer). Cut sections or pull off sideshoots 10cm long with a heel. Insert half – at least one bud above, one below ground. Space evergreen cuttings so they barely touch each other, letting air circulate. Individual pots hold many and are easily moved around, so ensuring that each species has its favourite growth condition.

A conservatory will protect tender cuttings at first. Mist would be nice but neither is essential. If you have time, cover pots with plastic bags which keep in humidity. Initial watering settles the cuttings and lasts for a long time. Weekly checks allow in fresh air and the removal of dead leaves.

Fuchsia, Impatiens, Nerium oleander, Pelargonium, Tradescantia strike roots in water. So do *Streptocarpus* leaves (also in soil).

Many succulents (*Aeonium, Crassula, Kalanchoe, Sedum*) grow new plants from a single leaf. Allow cuts to dry before inserting shallowly into soil. Aerial roots develop at the stem end of a fallen *Kalanchoe beharensis* leaf, reaching for the ground (p. 88).

Cuttings of drought-tolerant plants prefer drier surroundings. Grey felted leaves rot easily. Water sparingly, leave in good light but shaded from the sun until signs of growth show. Later gradually move into sun.

After taking out *Acanthus* or *Anemone hupehensis* plants, roots which have been left behind will develop into plants. Detach also *Yucca*'s offshoots; many are found in established pots.

EASY: *Abutilon, Anisodontea, Argyranthemum, Artemisia, Ballota, Buddleja, Cerastium, Choisya, Dimorphotheca, Eriocephalus, Euonymus, Euryops, Felicia, Hebe, Jasminum, Lavandula, Lotus, Myoporum, Myrsine, Myrtus, Nerium, Pelargonium, Phlomis, Pittosporum, Plectranthus, Plumbago, Polygala, Prunus laurocerasus, Rosmarinus, Salvia, Solandra, Solanum, Tamarix, Teucrium, Thymus, Westringia,* succulents.

Your own easy ones:

Division is promising with *Iris germanica*. After a few years, your ample supplies may line a walk.

DIVISIONS

Divisions profit from the warmth of a Mediterranean climate. Divided roots develop best in spring. Not ideal, sturdy plants can be divided at any time (*Agapanthus, Coreopsis*). Pull apart where they part naturally. Cut back leaves and damaged roots before replanting. Unless you need large supplies and are patient, keep clumps generous-sized. Initially shaded and protected from the wind, divisions that are moderately watered recuperate best. Separate also crowded clumps of bulbous plants (*Allium, Freesia, Hippeastrum, Homeria*), divide scales (*Lilium*), cut up tubers (*Canna*) or rhizomes (*Iris germanica*), detach offsets (*Sempervivum*). The field is wide open.

EASY: *Abelia, Agapanthus, Aspidistra, Clivia, Dietes, Escallonia, Gazania, Haemanthus, Hemerocallis, Iris, Kniphofia, Liriope, Ophiopogon, Phormium, Ruscus.*

Your own easy ones:

LAYERING

Several jasmines, *Lonicera, Rosmarinus* or *Vinca* layer naturally. *Solandra* and the climbing rose 'Mermaid' root on the roof onto which they climb. Peg down *Viburnum tinus'* branches, later cut off rooted sections.

Further Reading:
The Gardening from Which? Guide to Successful Propagation by Ajres.
Seed Propagation of Native California Plants by Dara Emery. See Bibliography.

Lilies increase also from scales

Maintenance

Careful pruning at the right time maintains this glorious *Wisteria*.

While gardening in rhythm with the Mediterranean winter rain cycle, maintenance of a waterwise, well-planned, carefully planted and amply mulched garden can be minimal. There may not be more than corrective pruning, spreading mulch, pulling out a few obtrusive weeds, but above all checking closely the plants, individuals with individual demands, coming to their help should they ask for it. A bucket of water brought when needed, an ill-placed branchlet cut in time, a health problem attended to when first seen, will all correct minor problems before they get out of hand. Such continuous attention to the needs of plants allows them to thrive. Although it is important to choose the right period for each work, caring for one's garden counts most. With less time involved a better result may be achieved. The ill-effects of occasionally transplanting in summer are balanced by extra care when carrying this out. To *care* is often more important than to be lavish with time.

Maintenance means paths swept and secateurs sharpened, but also corrective assessment of the garden's structure and balance, the continuous readjustment of spaces allotted to each plant. Growth in maturing gardens is vigorous. Freeing space for one plant means taking it from the neighbouring one, until one day one decides to take the latter out altogether. Although this is part of the winter clean-up, I am readjusting all the time. Too easily, an overbearing neighbour smothers a choice plant, rescued almost too late.

AUTUMN WORK

With summer gone, the first rain brings a sigh of relief. Have you:
– cut-back branches which have dried out over summer?
– freed choice plants from invading branches?
– planted new bulbs before first rains?
– divided *Iris germanica*?
– taken hardwood cuttings and sowed seeds?
– finished planting and transplanting to allow plants to become established over winter?
– spread ample mulch?
– given maximum light to the conservatory?
– started preliminary winter tidying while climbers are still in leaf?
– done a bit of weeding so everything looks neat?
– stopped in your path to enjoy the renaissance of your garden after the dry summer?

WINTER CLEANUP

Winter cleanup is a serious affair and follows preliminary tidying. Time is always short as new growth starts early in the year. Cut back specimens growing too densely, producing tons of 'green waste' and making mulch.

From my garden diary: 30th January, sun is out, buds start swelling, bulbs get ready to burst into bloom. Can we still interfere?

SPRING ATTENTIONS

– Water all recently planted or shallow rooted plants which show signs of needing it. If the usual rainfall is absent, irrigate.
– Mulch generously with a thick layer of vegetative matter, sealing humidity into the ground ahead of summer drought.
– Cut off dead flowerheads.
– A strimmer controls vigorous spring weeds. Do some hand-weeding if you have time (see Weeds).
– Harvest nettles for medicinal teas (for plants).

SUMMER HELP

Help to withstand drought more easily. 'Drought-tolerant' does not mean that once planted, plants can be forgotten. When summer is over, one would find a dried up branchlet, tag attached, giving the dead specimen's name. The first hot summer days come as a shock to plants, still geared to 'grow', not yet to 'survive'. Seek out those which need help, allow others to fare for themselves. Summer wind, hot and dusty, can be bad for the sturdiest plant. Check closely on all. Cover those in distress with a temporary roof. Shade from the hot western sun. Reduce foliage volume, prune out dead or damaged portions.

And watering? I hear you ask. Little need for those who carefully planned their water-saving garden. Generous mulch (10-15cm) keeps moisture in the soil. But water new plantings once a week (those tolerant of summer water), containers 2-3 times, tropicals as required. If no rain has fallen for months, check plants individually for water needs. Larger sunny areas heat up at midday, yet a sprinkler turned on for a minute several times a day generates a breeze which cools the air. Humidify leaves but not the furry ones. If you like to be active, weed a bit once the sun sets.

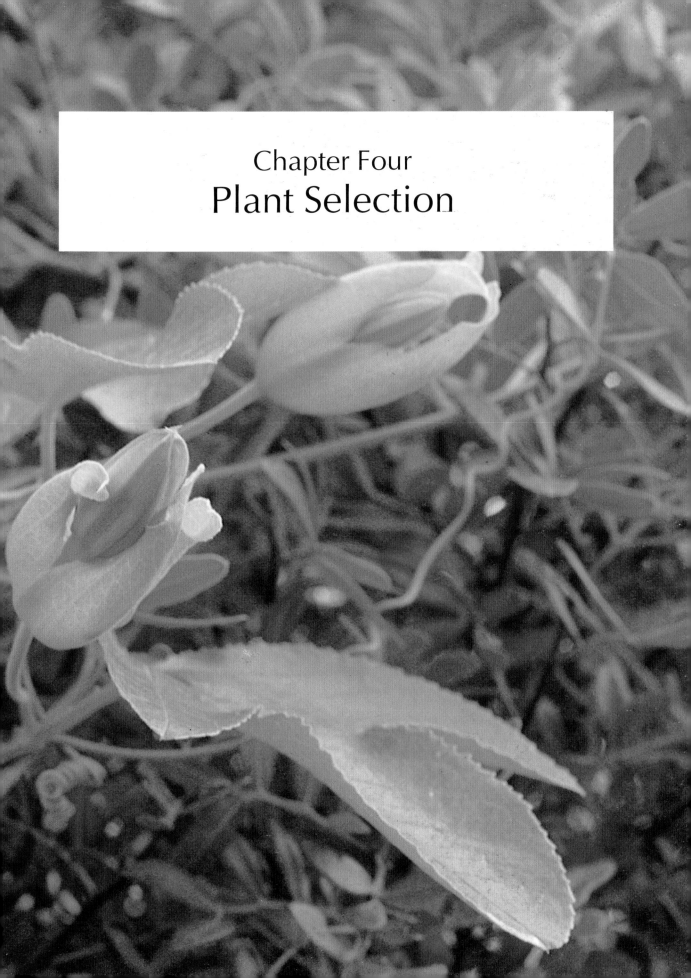

Chapter Four
Plant Selection

How to Choose
Drought-Tolerant Plants

Choosing plants for gardens in a Mediterranean climate is the same as for all gardens: it requires careful consideration. Choose plants for shape, texture, colour, consider size, evergreen foliage or edible fruit. What are the plants meant to achieve: to cover the soil (large or small areas?), provide colourful bloom (when?), protect (against wind, unpleasant views?). Consider house style, relaxed and natural, or more formal with clipped evergreens? Study the site (sun or shade, soil quality, prevailing winds?).

Drought-tolerant plants are highly specialized and the position chosen should suit their needs. Allow for future increase in size. And always such practicalities as plant health, maintenance and availability come into the picture. Plant selection also depends on what grows in your area and your readiness to blend into the local setting and the surrounding lands. There are plants for all sites and the task is to find the most suitable ones.

Watch leaves closely. Where dappled shade in woodlands reduces transpiration, larger, leathery leaves occur (*Laurus nobilis*). Smaller, firm leaves grow in sun (olive). Desert plants may discard leaves altogether. Grey foliage in full sun turns whitish-grey while foliage within the plant is only greenish-grey (*Artemisia*).

Spines indicate highly drought-tolerant plants (*Aloe, Opuntia*) and also a situation where animals threatened plant survival over thousands of years. The wild olive (*Olea europaea* var. *oleaster*) has a compact habit and spiny growth in response to difficult living conditions. Once these become more favourable (fencing), plants grow taller, leaves larger and defensive characteristics gradually disappear.

The ability of plants to establish themselves in harsh living conditions represents only part of our considerations. The principles behind suitable plant selections for water-saving gardens include the overall evaluation of their landscaping potential.

AESTHETIC MERIT

Aesthetic merit relates to plants' structural and flowering features. *Arbutus unedo*'s well-built canopy, shiny evergreen foliage and reddish new leaves, its profusion of white, bell-shaped flowers in dense inflorescences and brilliant autumn harvest of red fruit is a perfect example. The same goes for palms or *Eriobotrya* with their all-year attraction.

Attractive foliage deserves high priority. Leathery leaves, waxy covers, silvery hair avoid a dried up midsummer look. Proficient midsummer performers are hard-leaved box, carob, bay, myrtle, oleander, tough *Myrica pensylvanica*, also *Choisya, Cussonia, Grevillea, Myrsine, Rhamnus, Westringia*, climbing *Macfadyena, Pandorea, Podranea* and *Trachelospermum*. Few beat the humble *Pistacia lentiscus*. When most plants seem unable to stand another rainless day, lentiscs come into their own under the burning sun with brilliant apple-green 'spring leaves'. Few drought-tolerant plants achieve this, yet yellowing summer leaves should not alarm you. Although one longs for green during dry summers, dried up plants often have a special attraction. All they need is the right company: warm-coloured apricot, burnt orange or rich salmon flowers enhance golden oat fields.

Evergreens receive priority but deciduous plants may be chosen for special features such as exuberant flowering (*Philadelphus, Spiraea, Syringa*) or their 'shade in summer' and 'sun in winter' (*Celtis, Robinia*). Summer-deciduous *Euphorbia* looks spectacular all year; their leaf-dropping avoids loss of water and growth resumes with first autumn rains.

Shape is fundamental. Neat cushion shapes, helped by corrective clipping, retain humidity and please the eye.

A courtyard in southern France is enlivened by drought-tolerant *Nerium oleander* which does not mind the stony site. Striking oleander is readily available and easily increased.

ENVIRONMENTAL TOLERANCE

Environmental tolerance is essential for successful adaptation. A plant must be able to tolerate the challenges of a Mediterranean climate and still maintain aesthetic and functional merits.

The prime requirement is drought-tolerance since water is the most seriously limiting factor. Next comes the ability to withstand heat. Among those able to stand hottest sun for long periods are Mediterranean redbud and rock roses (*Cercis, Cistus*), Californian summer lilac (*Ceanothus*), Australian bottle brushes and emu bushes (*Callistemon, Eremophila*) and South African honey flowers (*Melianthus*).

Wind, another site factor, tears large leaves apart (*Sparmannia, Musa*), while firm waxy leaves, together with rounded plant shapes, are most resistant. Where animals graze, *Phoenix canariensis* with formidable thorns is the right choice. Small-leaved ice plants withstand light treading. *Hebe* is tolerant of shade which encroaches over the years. *Rhus lancea* thrives in brackish soil, while water-conserving succulents are miracle performers on shallow soil in hottest sun. All tolerate unfavourable conditions.

Match the plant with the site for which it is intended and in Mediterranean climates choose the so-called 'winter rainfall plants'. If healthy trees are growing on neighbouring lands, use them as borrowed landscaping. Avoid unnatural plant/site combinations such as cacti at water's edge.

Select plants that thrive in your soils. If your garden features '10cm soil on bedrock', you may be advised to import soil. Plants with shallow, wide-spreading roots, well-chosen sites (using cracks and exploiting dappled shade), together with careful planting and mulching, can create an evergreen flowering world, adapted to shortage of labour and water. On the coast, choose plants accustomed to sea breezes (p. 98).

AVAILABILITY AND HORTICULTURAL KNOW-HOW

Mediterranean regions are characterized by a tremendous plant diversity. Each contains thousands of trees, shrubs, perennials. Finding the chosen plant is often challenging. Many *Ceanothus* varieties have been selected, but only a few are available outside California. The same applies to the Mediterranean where the widely useful *Myrtus* or *Phlomis* may be absent from local nurseries. Yet nurseries will stock native drought-tolerant plants following customers' demand! The Plant Selection (p.101) suggests alternatives. Furthermore, plant exchange between gardeners fills gaps. Many garden journals run a readers' section which offers surplus plants and lists desiderata.

THE FUNCTIONAL MERIT

The functional merit of the above *Arbutus* lies in its wide range of garden uses: as a specimen tree, a hedge or container plant, or as an element in woodlands.

The proper assessment of such merits reflects above all an intimate knowledge of plant aspects. Plants with high rooting frequency along widely-spreading branches have obvious merits as ground covers, efficient slope stabilizers or erosion control (*Arctostaphylos* and *Arctotheca* in sun, *Ribes viburnifolium* under oak shade). If time is your limiting factor, choose a reliable plant. Many plants fill several functions; besides its aesthetic merits, the dense canopy of *Euryops pectinatus* for example smothers weeds, conserves humidity, assists beginners.

In addition, horticultural expertise dictates the choice. Many plants do surprisingly well in adverse conditions. One scratches the soil, tucks in the well-known *Aloe arborescens* and forgets about it. Growth will resume shortly after. Not all are so easy. Most members of the *Protea* family, not a first choice for beginners, are demanding. Palms, otherwise easy, still need expertise in transplanting.

CONSERVATION

As exploitation has significantly decreased the Mediterranean's most beautiful and useful plants, conservation minded gardeners devote their efforts to the region's vegetation. Well-tended, these plants provide excellent ground cover or background. Arranged in natural life zones, they suit the environment into which they are planted. As in nature, group for example oak with *Cneorum, Myrtus, Pistacia, Rhamnus, Viburnum tinus*, underplanted with *Iris unguicularis*, or pine with *Arbutus, Cistus, Cytisus, Erica*, underplanted with *Cyclamen* – truly splendid choices.

Of all endemic Mediterranean plants, over 50% are threatened or rare (Gómez-Campo 1985). Although cultivated forms exist in the trade, many native bulbs are on the list of threatened plants (*Calochortus, Cyclamen, Freesia*). Rescuing plants from locations where their survival is at risk (road-building) and planting them in the garden, gives them a new lease on life. Later, they may even be restored to nature. However, digging up wild populations is strongly discouraged.

LOW INFLAMMABILITY

Plants serve many functions. They are able to resist or retard burning. Where surrounding vegetation is ravaged, countless juicy, water-retaining succulents or hard-leaved bay, box and buckthorn, low on inflammable contents (turpentines, resins) help limit fire hazards (see list p.98). Oaks resprout from stumps.

Gardeners need time to adapt to new gardens. So do plants. Assess their performance once they seem at home. Even careful choices do not always fulfil expectations and may require further experiments. Often a left-over, tucked in as an afterthought, proves a wonderful surprise. Be flexible in the early stages of your garden, allow for a learning period, and you will be rewarded.

Plant Lists for Specific Uses

Plants listed are described in the Plant Selection.
An exclamation mark signals a particularly good choice.

Plants that are invasive and therefore not recommended for use in the U.S.
(California in particular) are identified in the list of drought-tolerant plants with •

EXUBERANT FOLIAGE

Plants were chosen for compact growth and attractive, often large foliage. A careful choice will impart a lush, mature look. Add Agavaceae and large-leaved succulents (*Kalanchoe beharensis*) for striking accents.

Trees and Shrubs
Ceratonia siliqua
Choisya ternata
Eriobotrya japonica
Fatsia japonica !
Ficus
Griselinia lucida
Hebe, large-leaved
Laurus nobilis
Magnolia grandiflora !

Melianthus major !
Myoporum, most
Myrtus communis
Palms!
Pittosporum tobira !
Prunus lusitanica
Rhamnus alaternus
Ricinus communis !
Schefflera actinophylla
Viburnum suspensum

Vines
Beaumontia grandiflora
Solandra maxima
Trachelospermum

**Ground Cover and
Bulbous Plants**
Acanthus mollis !
Agapanthus
Alocasia macrorrhiza !

Arum italicum
Aspidistra elatior
Bergenia
Canna indica !
Clivia miniata
Crinum × powellii
Cynara scolymus
X Fatshedera lizei
Ferns
Haemanthus albiflos

Hedychium, all
Iris japonica
Limonium perezii
Pelargonium, most
Phormium tenax !
Ruscus hypoglossum
Strelitzia reginae !
Vinca difformis
Zantedeschia

COLOURFUL MIDWINTER BLOOM

The generous Mediterranean climate delights the gardener with bloom through winter. The plants mentioned below may bloom abundantly or produce a few flowers, depending on location.

Trees and Shrubs
Abutilon
Anisodonthea
Argyranthemum frutescens
Buddleja officinalis !
Callistemon !
Cassia tomentosa !
Citrus
Coronilla !
Elaeagnus × ebbingei
Erica 'White Perfection'
Eriocephalus africanus !
Euonymus, berries !
Eupatorium ligustrinum
Euryops pectinatus !
Fatsia japonica
Freylinia lanceolata !
Grevillea, all
Hakea, many
Hebe, many
Jasminum, many
Osteospermum fruticosum
Polygala myrtifolia
Prunus dulcis !
Pyracantha, berries !
Rosmarinus !
Senecio linearifolius !
Syringa microphylla
Templetonia retusa
Teucrium fruticans
Viburnum tinus !
Westringia fruticosa

Vines
Clematis cirrhosa !
Passiflora, many
Solandra maxima !
Thunbergia gregorii !

Ground Cover and Bulbous Plants
Aloe arborescens
Clivia nobilis !
Erigeron karvinskianus
Felicia amelloides
Gazania
Gladiolus dalenii !
Haemanthus albiflos
Helleborus
Iris unguicularis !
Narcissus tazetta
Nerine sarniensis
Pelargonium peltatum
Salvia microphylla
Vinca difformis !

SCENT

Mediterranean maquis plants give off scent under hot midday sun. Many subtropical flowers perfume the evening air. Culinary herbs release their scent when leaves are crushed. Not everybody appreciates Coronilla's scent.

Trees and Shrubs
Acacia, many ! •
Argyrocytisus battandieri
Boronia heterophylla !
Brugmansia, most
Carissa grandiflora
Carpenteria californica
Cestrum nocturnum !
Choisya ternata !
Citrus, all !
Coronilla !
Cytisus × praecox •
Elaeagnus, all !
Genista aetnensis •
Laurus nobilis (leaves) !
Lavandula
Lonicera fragrantissima !
Osmanthus heterophyllus
Philadelphus, most !
Pittosporum, many !
Robinia pseudoacacia
Rosmarinus
Spartium junceum •
Syringa microphylla !
Viburnum, many !

Vines
Beaumontia grandiflora !
Clematis armandii !
Jasminum, most !
Lonicera !
Mandevilla laxa !
Solandra maxima
Trachelospermum !
Wisteria sinensis !

Ground Cover and Bulbous Plants
Freesia !
Hedychium coronarium !
Iris unguicularis !
Narcissus, many !
Pelargonium (leaves) !
Tulbaghia fragrans
Viola odorata !

POOL PLANTINGS

Pools are usually located in full sun, ideal for heat-loving plants. Succulents thrive on heat-reflecting paving. Sword-leaved plants provide accents. Beware of plants which are untidy, carry thorns, have invasive roots or later will overshadow the pool. The following will not impose on water resources.

Trees, Shrubs, Palms
Acca sellowiana
Anisodontea capensis
Bupleurum fruticosum
Callistemon citrinus !
Chamaerops humilis !
Citrus, all !
Coleonema pulchrum
Cordyline australis !
Cussonia !
Eriobotrya deflexa !
Euryops pectinatus
Griselinia lucida !
Hakea laurina
Heteromeles arbutifolia
Hibiscus, most
Lagerstroemia indica
Laurus nobilis
Leptospermum laevigatum
Myrsine africana !
Myrtus communis !
Nerium oleander !
Phoenix canariensis !
Psidium
Rhaphiolepis indica !
Rhus lancea
Schinus terebinthifolius
Umbellularia californica
Westringia fruticosa

Vines
Beaumontia grandiflora !
Gelsemium sempervirens
Jasminum, many
Solandra maxima !
Thunbergia gregorii

Ground Cover and Bulbous Plants
Agapanthus praecox !
Arctotis, all
Canna indica !
Cerastium tomentosum
Crinum, many !
Cynara scolymus
Dietes, all !
Dimorphotheca, all
Echium, most !
Felicia amelloides
Gazania
Gerbera jamesonii !
Hedychium, all
Kniphofia uvaria
Lantana camara
Liriope !
Neomarica gracilis
Ophiopogon
Pelargonium
Strelitzia reginae !
Yucca gloriosa !

WINDBREAKS

Although they may not tolerate salt spray (for which see Coastal Gardens), these plants moderate the wind and its harmful dessicating action. To be effective, they should be planted in several rows, spaced at 3-5m. The outer belt is preferably planted with dense, low shrubs. The next belts gradually increase in height, so the wind is lifted upwards. Loose planting is more effective in breaking the wind's force than a dense barrier.

Trees and Shrubs
Acacia melanoxylon ! •
Aesculus californica
Callistemon citrinus !
Calocedrus decurrens !
Casuarina, most
Cedrus deodara !
Cupressus arizonica !
Dodonaea viscosa !
Elaeagnus !
Escallonia
Eucalyptus, many !
Griselinia littoralis
Juniperus !
Lagunaria patersonii !
Laurus nobilis
Ligustrum lucidum !
Melaleuca !
Myoporum laetum !
Nerium oleander !
Pinus, many !
Pittosporum, most !
Pyracantha
Quercus ilex
Rhamnus alaternus
Rhus ovata !
Schinus molle !
Sophora secundiflora !
Tamarix •
Taxus baccata

COASTAL GARDENS

Common to all is the coastal humidity and its salt content. A shelter belt protects the garden from drying winds. *Arctostaphylos'* roots soon become established in sandy soil, quickly covering large areas. Colourful annuals are unrivalled for shallow soils. Many palms or sword-leaved plants tolerate an occasional flooding. Often succulents survive the best. All fulfil an important stabilization function.

Trees, Shrubs, Palms
Acacia, many •
Acca sellowiana
Arbutus unedo !
Atriplex !
Aucuba japonica
Buddleja davidii
Bupleurum fruticosum
Callistemon, all
Chamaerops humilis
Choisya ternata
Cistus, all !
Coprosma repens !
Cordyline australis !
Corokia, all !
Cotoneaster, many
Cupressus macrocarpa !
Cytisus ! •

Elaeagnus, all !
Escallonia rubra !
Eucalyptus ficifolia !
Euonymus japonicus !
Genista, most ! •
Grevillea robusta
Griselinia littoralis !
Hippophaë rhamnoides !
Juniperus
Lagunaria patersonii !
Laurus nobilis
Lavandula angustifolia !
Lavatera maritima
Leptospermum
Melaleuca, most
Melia azederach
Metrosideros excelsa !
Myoporum laetum !

Phoenix canariensis
Pinus, many
Pittosporum, several !
Populus alba
Pyracantha coccinea
Quercus ilex !
Rhaphiolepis indica
Rhamnus alaternus !
Rhus integrifolia !
Rosmarinus officinalis !
Santolina chamaecyparissus
Schotia afra
Tamarix, all ! •
Teucrium fruticans
Tipuana tipu
Viburnum tinus
Westringia fruticosa !

Vines
Campsis radicans
Lonicera, most
Parthenocissus tricuspidata
Tecomaria capensis !

Ground Cover and Bulbous Plants
Aloe arborescens !
Anemone, all
Arctostaphylos, various !
Argyranthemum
Armeria maritima
Aurinia saxatilis !
Calendula officinalis
Ceanothus, several
Centaurea cineraria !

Cerastium tomentosum !
Erigeron karvinskianus
Eriogonum, many !
Eschscholzia californica !
Euryops pectinatus !
Felicia amelloides !
Freesia refracta
Gazania
Kniphofia
Limonium perezii !
Osteospermum !
Pancratium maritimum
Penstemon heterophyllus
Phormium tenax !
Sparaxis tricolor
Succulents, many !
Urginea maritima

EROSION CONTROL

Soil is kept in place by a carefully chosen ground cover composed of variously sized plants and their well-developed root system. Large patches of a single species, quickly-expanding, are beautifully set off by deep rooted trees.

Trees and Shrubs
Acacia, many •
Aesculus californica !
Atriplex !
Ceanothus, many !
Celtis
Ceratonia siliqua
Cercis
Cistus !
Coronilla !
Cotoneaster dammeri !

Eriocephalus africanus
Eriogonum fasciculatum !
Fraxinus
Juglans
Juniperus, prostrate !
Koelreuteria paniculata
Lantana camara !
Lavandula
Morus nigra
Myoporum
Myrsine africana

Nerium oleander
Pinus
Pistacia chinensis
Pyracantha
Rhamnus !
Rhus integrifolia !
Rhus lancea
Ribes viburnifolium !
Rosa rugosa !
Rosmarinus officinalis !
Santolina

Vines
Bougainvillea
Hedera !
Jasminum, many
Lonicera japonica !
Rosa banksiae !
Solandra maxima
Tecomaria capensis
Tetrastigma voinierianum
Trachelospermum

Ground Cover
Aptenia cordifolia
Arctostaphylos uva-ursi
Arctotis
Baccharis pilularis
Coprosma × kirkii !
Cotoneaster congestus !
Gazania
Hypericum calycinum !
Osteospermum
Vinca !

FIRE RETARDANCE

Plants cannot stop fire but hazards are reduced by replacing combustible vegetation (cypress, eucalypts, juniper, pine) by plants with lowest fuel content. Water-retaining succulents have the greatest potential.

Trees and Shrubs
Atriplex semibaccata
Callistemon citrinus !
Callistemon viminalis !
Ceratonia siliqua !
Cercis occidentalis !
Cistus !
Citrus
Feijoa sellowiana
Heteromeles arbutifolia

Myoporum laetum !
Nerium oleander, low ones
Pittosporum tobira
Pyracantha 'Santa Cruz'
Quercus
Rhamnus alaternus !
Rhus integrifolia !
Schinus molle (watered)
Thevetia peruviana
Washingtonia

Vines
Campsis radicans !
Lonicera japonica
Solanum jasminoides !
Tecomaria capensis
Trachelospermum
Wisteria

Ground Cover
Achillea tomentosa !
Agave !
Aloe !

Arctotheca calendula !
Armeria maritima
Artemisia (low ones) !
Cerastium tomentosum
Convolvulus cneorum !
Dietes
Erigeron karvinskianus
Eschscholzia californica
Galvezia speciosa
Gazania !
Lantana montevidensis
Myoporum parvifolium

Osteospermum !
Pelargonium peltatum !
Phormium tenax
Punica granatum 'Nana'
Ribes viburnifolium
Salvia sonomensis
Santolina chamaecyparissus
Senecio cineraria !
Tulbaghia violacea
Verbena peruviana
Vinca, all
Yucca (trunkless species) !

BEGINNERS' PLANTS

These easy plants fit any occasion and always come to your rescue, delighting you with flower and scent. Use them for their quick growth, drought tolerance, sturdiness, low maintenance and easy propagation.

Trees, Shrubs, Palms
Abelia × grandiflora
Anisodontea capensis
Bupleurum fruticosum
Callistemon, many
Ceratonia siliqua
Chamaerops humilis
Cistus
Coprosma repens
Coronilla
Cupressus
Elaeagnus, most

Eriobotrya japonica
Eriocephalus africanus
Escallonia rubra
Euonymus japonicus
Euryops pectinatus
Fatsia japonica
Genista hispanica ●
Juniperus, most
Lantana
Laurus nobilis
Lavandula
Magnolia grandiflora

Myoporum
Myrsine africana
Nerium oleander
Pelargonium, most
Phlomis fruticosa
Pittosporum tobira
Rhamnus alaternus
Teucrium fruticans
Viburnum tinus
Westringia fruticosa
Yucca

Vines
Jasminum, most
Plumbago auriculata
Solanum jasminoides
Tecomaria capensis

Ground Cover
Agapanthus, evergreen
Aloe arborescens
Argyranthemum frutescens
Cerastium tomentosum
Clivia miniata

Dietes iridioides
Hemerocallis
Hypericum calycinum
Iris, most
Lonicera, most
Osteospermum
Plectranthus arabicus
Salvia officinalis
Succulents
Tropaeolum majus
Vinca difformis

QUICK RESULTS

The following have been chosen for their evergreen foliage and abundant flowering and grow fast under almost any condition. Cuttings from *Nerium oleander* flower the first summer. Cypresses structure a view quickly. Most annuals or bulbous plants in large clumps give a quick return. Palms and sword-leaved plants, though not fast, provide instant style.

Trees and Shrubs
Abelia × grandiflora
Abutilon !
Acacia, many ! ●
Buddleja, most
Casuarina !
Ceanothus arboreus
Cistus !
Coronilla
Cotoneaster, many
Cupressus !
Elaeagnus × ebbingei

Eriobotrya japonica !
Escallonia rubra
Eucalyptus, most !
Euryops pectinatus
Fraxinus, most
Hakea laurina !
Hebe, larger-leaved ones
Lantana camara
Ligustrum, most !
Melianthus major !
Morus alba
Myoporum, most !

Nerium oleander !
Pinus, many !
Populus nigra !
Prunus lusitanica
Ricinus communis !
Rhamnus alaternus !
Robinia pseudoacacia !
Schinus molle !
Sparmannia africana !
Tamarix, most ! ●
Teucrium fruticans
Tipuana tipu !

Viburnum tinus
Westringia fruticosa

Vines
Campsis radicans
Lonicera, most
Parthenocissus tricuspidata
Podranea ricasoliana
Polygonum aubertii
Tecomaria capensis
Tetrastigma voinierianum

Ground Cover
Argyranthemum frutescens
Artemisia
Calendula officinalis
Coreopsis
Erigeron karvinskianus
Lantana montevidensis
Lavandula
Mirabilis jalapa
Salvia, most
Tropaeolum majus

CONTAINERS

Many shrubs, palms, annuals, sword-leaved and bulbous plants suit containers. Potted kitchen herbs find a place on every windowsill. Countless succulents tolerate neglect over weeks. Tubs confine invading roots (*Agave, Ailanthus*). Containers require aerated, well-drained soils and call for slow, patient watering. Plants which tolerate or prefer a restricted rootrun are marked*.

Trees and Shrubs
Abelia × grandiflora !
Abutilon !
Brugmansia
Buxus
Choisya ternata
Citrus !
Coprosma repens
Corynocarpus laevigata
Cotoneaster
Cupressus
Cytisus ●
Dombeya
Elaeagnus
Eriobotrya
Euonymus
Fatsia japonica
Ficus, most*

Griselinia
Hebe
Hibiscus
Juniperus
Lagerstroemia indica !
Laurus nobilis !
Lavandula
Metrosideros excelsa
Myrsine africana
Myrtus communis
Nerium oleander
Olea
Pittosporum, most
Prunus laurocerasus
Punica granatum !
Quercus ilex
Rhamnus, most
Rosmarinus

Salvia officinalis
Sparmannia
Thuja plicata
Viburnum tinus

Vines & Trailers
Antigonon leptopus
Bougainvillea*
Campsis radicans !
Convolvulus mauritanicus
Hedera helix !
Jasminum !
Lampranthus !
Lantana montevidensis !
Osteospermum fruticosum
Pandorea jasminoides
Pelargonium
Plectranthus

Polygonum, all !
Pyrostegia venusta
Tecomaria capensis
Thunbergia, all
Thymus
Trachelospermum, all
Tropaeolum majus
Vinca !

**Palms and
Sword-leaved Plants**
Brahea armata
Butia capitata
Chamaerops humilis !
Cycas*
Phoenix canariensis*
Phormium tenax*
Yucca*

Bulbous Plants
Agapanthus! *
Babiana
Canna
Clivia*
Crinum
Cyclamen !
Freesia
Haemanthus! *
Hippeastrum !
Kniphofia*
Lilium !
Nerine !*
Scadoxus !*
Sternbergia !*
Strelitzia !
Veltheimia !
Zantedeschia !

How to use the plant selection

The following lines may help you to get the most out of the Plant Selection.

Botanical names often reveal plant characteristics. *Lonicera fragrantissima* tells of the plant's strong fragrance. The same goes for popular names (BOXLEAF MYRTLE) which, however, may change from country to country. Only botanical names ensure that you get from nurseries what you want to order.

To gardeners' dismay, botanical names are sometimes changed. A plant that you have known all your life as *Datura,* is now correctly named *Brugmansia*. I have used the name valid at the time of printing (following the *RHS Index of Garden Plants,* 1994), but include widely used older names.

The **plant family** may help with unknown plants, giving, for example, guidance on cultural requirements. Members of the Leguminosae family dislike root disturbance which for the gardener means raising them in individual pots. One from the Iridaceae family can mean a bulbous plant, often easy from seed. The family Bignoniaceae indicates to me the possibility of very ornamental, drought-tolerant climbers or trees.

The **country of origin** sometimes helps to find supply sources and may give indication of water requirements. Natives from Mediterranean climates such as the south west coast of Africa, Australia and California are probably drought-tolerant,* while east coast plants (Florida or Natal) may characterize a more tropically humid climate. A wide-ranging origin suggests broad tolerances *(Schinus molle)*.

Native habitats give clues to growing requirements and facilitate the choice of suitable planting sites. There may also be some surprises. *Clivia miniata* grows in South Africa in moist shaded forest valleys. But this adaptable plant in gardens will tolerate moderately dry summers. Everybody waters geraniums daily – so did I. But when I realized that *Pelargonium* grows wild in South Africa's western Cape, I started experimenting with it in summer-dry areas.

Plant features which are shown in photographs are not described. However, the page where photographs appear is given. Consult also the Index.

Measurements cannot be more than approximate. *Laurus nobilis* is said to grow slowly to reach 3-15m. This wide range depends on position, soil type, water availability, maintenance and plant quality. In waterwise gardens plants tend to be more compact as a defence against moisture loss, adapting to the climate in which they live. Measurements given take this into account.

The same is true for flowering or fruiting periods or climatic tolerances which all depend on microclimates, soil type or horticultural expertise. Your own observations will often be your best guide. In difficult conditions experiment with several plants in various positions.

Watering. Most plants in the Plant Selection come from a winter rain climate (or will adapt to one) and, unless otherwise noted, are meant to receive such a regime. They are accustomed to dry summers (or will adapt to them) and, once fully established, may survive without additional summer watering. However, at the peak of a long hot summer watch for water demands. On the other hand, most Cape bulbs require summer-baking for bloom and plant health.

In dry desert regions, supply winter rain by whichever means are suitable.

Plants from climates other than the Mediterranean one *(Hydrangea)* require different schedules. Again, precise advice as to water amounts would be theoretical as many facts influence a plant's transpiration rate and thus the amount of water needed to replace it. Once more, your own observation (young leaves) may amend recommended quantities.

Drainage is essential for drought-tolerant plants whose roots during summer are mostly non-functional. In poor drainage, inactive roots remain soggy and may rot after a summer downpour, resulting in unexpected plant losses. The same may occasionally occur after first autumn rains, following a long hot summer.

Planting sites. Most Mediterranean climate natives require sun. In hot inland regions, coast plants may require some shade. A tall open tree canopy with moving shade seems to suit many plants and helps establishment.

Planting time. Most plants benefit from settling in over a mild, humid autumn and winter – long before the stress of summer. Winter rain bulbs should be in the ground before the first autumn rains stimulate their growth. Planting time is only mentioned when differing from this (tender exotics start active growth with spring warmth).

Planting bulbs. Place hood and horn and some sand beneath bulbs. Unless indicated otherwise, cover with soil twice the height of the bulbs and mark sites with gravel. Water to settle soil and then allow winter rain to take over. A range of bulbs has so-called contractile roots which pull the bulb down to the adequate depth *(Amaryllis)*. Others, among them many members of the Amaryllidaceae family *(Crinum)*, prefer their necks above ground.

Feeding. Natives usually do best without fertilizers as a mulch takes care of their needs. Plants which do require feeding are pointed out.

Invasive weeds. Use all plants from the fantastic floral heritage of the Mediterranean climate regions. For potential invasiveness see Weeds.

Propagation. Described are those ways which usually give easiest results in Mediterranean gardens.

Temperatures. Plants listed (unless otherwise stated) withstand short-term frost and a few days of snow.

The United States Department of Agriculture USDA has introduced zoning. Plants listed grow well in their zone 10 (average annual minimum temperatures –1 to 4°C.), many in zones 9 or 8 *(Viburnum tinus)* or even in zone 7 (–18 to –12, *Yucca gloriosa*). 0° Celsius = 32° Fahrenheit.

Cultivars which are offered vary from one region to the other. Consult local nurseries for the best ones.

Text length is unrelated to plants' suitability.

* Plants that are invasive and therefore not recommended for use in the U.S. (California in particular) are identified in the list of drought-tolerant plants with ●

Plant Selection
Plants which tolerate Drought
* Invasive, not recommended for planting in the USA

ABELIA   Caprifoliaceae
A. floribunda   México
The evergreen MEXICAN ABELIA (150-220cm), native to mountainous regions, has attractively arching branches with drooping purple flowers on previous year's growth. In hotter areas, provide dappled shade.

A. × grandiflora   E. Asia
A gracefully arching shrub, the evergreen glossy-leaved ABELIA (100-150cm) is a reliable asset to any garden. In colder climates, it is deciduous. Reddish-brown calyces follow white flowers, dyeing plants reddish for weeks. When well-established (once branches shoot up vigorously), abelias become quite drought-tolerant *if* planted in deep, well-worked soil, protected from hottest mid-day sun. Tolerant and healthy, always attractive, invaluable for long-lasting autumn bloom. Rejuvenate by cutting out oldest branches. Transplants readily (prune to half height). Propagation: late summer cuttings, division.   p.101

A. schumannii   W China
From dry river valleys, this deciduous shrub (150cm) is evergreen in warmer climates. Attractive pink summer to autumn flowers enhance dull leaves in dappled shade.

ABIES   Pinaceae
A. bracteata   SW California
Although most firs do best on mountain slopes, the SANTA LUCIA FIR (15-30m) thrives on dry, sunny rock, tolerating drought. Before planting, remember its height and natural environment.

A. cephalonica   S Greece
The GREEK FIR (20m-30m) still grows in isolated stands in southern mountains.

Abelia × grandiflora with *Clematis flammula* (left).

A. pinsapo   SW Spain
The slow, sombre SPANISH FIR (7m-25m) forms open stands in the Serranía de Ronda. It is closely related to var. **marocana** (Atlas mountains).

ABUTILON   Malvaceae
A. × hybridum
Grown widely in most temperate regions, but not sufficiently around the Mediterranean, the FLOWERING MAPLE (1-3m, depending on variety) is a deciduous to evergreen fast-growing open shrub, also pruned as small tree. Plant where graceful bells, best seen from below, stand out all year against a wall or the sky. Quite cold and heat hardy, *Abutilon* likes dappled shade, rich soil,

weekly watering in summer. Fine container plant, easily propagated by cuttings. Lower and slower are 'Cloth of Gold' yellow flowers, 'Boule de Neige' white.

A. megapotamicum ·   Brazil
Evergreen leggy growth (70-150cm) initially needs staking. Shape carefully. A dark green background contrasts well with the curiously shaped 'lanterns'. An accompanying *Tropaeolum majus* brings the dull foliage to life.

• **ACACIA**   Leguminosae/Mimosoïdeae
When evergreen MIMOSA flower in winter (their common name, but no *Mimosa*), your spring dreams seem to come true. Well-chosen among many sizes, they bloom abundantly for months. Requirements are a somewhat acid soil, perfect drainage, sunniest position. Soft growth, encouraged by over-watering or fertilizing, is liable to wind damage. Prune after flowering (even severely) for compact growth, or cut branches for vases. High soil phosphorus levels are harmful. Useful as rapid, soil-binding covers. They also suit containers, several attract bees. Propagation for species: seed.

Note: South African and Australian gardeners avoid potentially invasive species.

A. baileyana   SE Australia
Winter-flowering GOLDEN MIMOSA (4-8m), multi-trunked trees, adorn the French Côte d'Azur and Italian Riviera. Wind and frost resistant bank covers, they create debris with age, becoming invasive where watered.

Acacia longifolia

A. cultriformis　　　NSW, Australia
The soil-and wind-tolerant KNIFE-LEAF
WATTLE (3-4m), a showy grey winter-
flowering shrub, covers slopes, hides
unsightly views, shields you from the
street.

A. cyclops　　　　　S Australia
The billowy COASTAL WATTLE (3-4m) is
an extremely drought-tolerant highway
plant (negligible flowers). Invasive in
South Africa.

A. dealbata　　Tasmania, Australia
The florist's MIMOSA (10-15m, equal width)
rapidly covers river banks and creeks with
silvery foliage. Use where wide open
spaces need covering and a frost-tolerant,
suckering habit is an asset.　　　p.13

A. glaucoptera　　　W Australia
Choose the recently introduced CLAY
WATTLE (1-2m), a low, rounded shrub, for
its quaint glaucous foliage.

A. longifolia　　　　E Australia
The frost-and lime-tolerant SYDNEY
GOLDEN WATTLE (3-5m), a quick-growing,
spring-flowering shrub/tree, stabilizes
sandy beaches, screens salt spray and
wind. Easily propagated by seed, invasive in South Africa.　　　p.102

A. melanoxylon　　　　Australia
One of the toughest, the undemanding
BLACKWOOD (7-10m) rapidly covers
undesirable sights. A pleasant outline,
straw-coloured flowers and somewhat
messy seedpods relegate it to the background. Place where potential invasiveness is an asset.

A. podalyriifolia　　　NE Australia
The scented, winter-flowering QUEENS-
LAND SILVER WATTLE (3-4m) grows fast as

Acanthus mollis

a multi-trunked, short-lived shrub/tree
in wind-protected sites. Exquisite
foliage.

A. saligna (A. cyanophylla) W Australia
The quick-growing, suckering BLUE-
LEAVED WATTLE (3-5m) displays flower-
laden, drooping branches in spring.
Grows in poor, sandy, chalky soils,
tolerates coastal winds (invasive in
South Africa).

A. verticillata　　Tasmania, SE Australia
The widely tolerant PRICKLY MOSES
(3-5m), a rounded shrub, grows into a
sturdy hedge with lemon bloom in
spring.

ACANTHUS　　　　Acanthaceae
A. mollis　　　　　Mediterranean
The attractive leaves of summer-dormant
BEAR'S BREECHES appear with first autumn
rains and in fertile soil grow very large.
They thrive in any site, but prefer light
shade. A root fragment may develop into
a mature plant if conditions are right. To
avoid invasiveness, cut spectacular
flower spikes before seeds set, confine to
cracks or tubs and pull out unwanted
plants. Although challenging in small
gardens, they merit a place in natural
settings.　　　　　　　　p.102

ACCA　　　　　　Myrtaceae
A. sellowiana (Feijoa s.)　　Uruguay
Ornamental evergreen PINEAPPLE GUAVA
(3-5m), slow-growing multi-trunked
shrubs (small trees) have glossy leaves.
Pure white spring flowers with crimson
stamens attract bees. Egg-shaped green
fruits are eaten raw or as jelly. Tolerates
drought, irrigation, coastal conditions.
Easy in light well-drained and mulched
soil in warm, sheltered locations (inland
under tree shade). Plant several or
choose a self-fertile variety.

ACHILLEA　　　　Compositae
A. millefolium　　　Europe to Iran
The perennial and wide-spreading
YARROW likes hot, dry locations.

A. tomentosa　　　　S Europe
A flat spreading mat and excellent lawn
replacement.

ACOKANTHERA — Apocynaceae
A. oblongifolia (A. spectabilis) — Natal
The evergreen AFRICAN WINTERSWEET (2-3m) carries shiny foliage, scented white spring bloom, extremely poisonous olive-like fruit. It likes enriched, well-drained, sunny soil, watering monthly in summer and tolerates moderate freezing. Propagation: seed, cuttings. All parts yield arrow poison, a valuable possession which bushmen store on highest trees.

ACTINIDIA — Actinidiaceae
A. chinensis — China
The deciduous KIWI VINE requires protection from wind, fertile well-drained soil, nutrient-rich mulch, weekly watering in summer, a sturdy support. Judicious pruning controls exuberant growth. Vitamin-rich fruit are well-known; fruit production requires male and female plants.

ACTINOSTROBUS — Cupressaceae
A. pyramidalis — SW Australia
Closely related to *Callitris*, this low shrub (1-3m) has dense, erect branches. Widespread around Perth on winter-inundated sandy soil (salt-tolerant).

AEONIUM — Crassulaceae
Succulent *Aeonium* with sunny-yellow bloom are legion. Easy to grow, thriving in sun but tolerating shade, with frugal soil and water requirements, they cover large patches. To reduce transpiration over summer, leaves are partially shed and rosettes close, turning ever smaller as summer progresses. With first autumn rains, rosettes expand to presummer size. Easy propagation: cuttings (let cuts dry before inserting).

A. arboreum — Canary Is.
The most commonly grown, it carries yellow spring flowers (60-90cm). 'Atropurpureum' looks striking together with pale pink bulbs. p.103

A. canariense — Canary Is.
The CANARY ISLAND AEONIUM (30cm) has usually unbranched stems. Flowers on tall stems rise from giant rosettes 30-40cm across.

A. simsii — Canary Is.
Gradually spreads to a dense, low carpet.

AESCULUS — Hippocastanaceae
A. californica — California
From dry hill country, the deciduous, round-headed CALIFORNIA BUCKEYE reaches 3-6m (shrub or tree). Branch structure and pinkish, fragrant flowers offer spectacular spring displays, chiefly where looked down upon. Plant in sunny, well-drained soil where late leafing out and early leaf drop (delayed when watered) are advantages. Drought-tolerant once established.

Agapanthus hybrid

AGAPANTHUS — Liliaceae/Alliaceae
While deciduous species suit colder climates, it is clearly the evergreen AGAPANTHUS which provide year-round, labour-saving ground cover. Available in a bewildering range of cultivars (final naming subject to study), they mainly differ in size and compactness of flower umbels. You may prefer porcelain to deep gentian (or vice versa), still all are splendid, indispensable for waterwise gardens. Divide rootstocks after flowering. Cut back leaves by half, protect fleshy roots from drying out, water carefully after replanting and await active growth. Flowering resumes in 1-2 years. Free-germinating seeds take longer to flower. p.103

A. africanus — S Africa
Evergreen, low 50cm. Many cultivars, also a white form.

A. praecox — E Cape
Native to sunny South African rocky hillsides, in summer azure flower umbels stand high above evergreen strap-like leaves, sometimes exceeding 1m. Drought-tolerant once established, use as ground cover in large patches, also under tall trees or in containers. A few plants with time divide to cover a field. 'Plenus' has double flowers. ssp. **orientalis** 'Albus', lovely white flowers.

Aeonium arboreum

AGATHOSMA Rutaceae
A. foetidissima Cape
An evergreen heath-like shrub with tiny white flowers, BUCHU (30-60cm) is a reliable performer. It appreciates well-drained, sandy, slightly acid soil in full sun (inland dappled shade). After flowering, clip for compactness (unpleasant scent). Transplanting is risky. Propagation: cuttings (easy). p.104

A. ovata Cape
Evergreen aromatic leaves, clipped like box, make this low shrublet a useful garden subject.

Agave americana

Agathosma foetidissima

AGAVACEAE
Members of this drought-tolerant family, frequently the only survivors in abandoned gardens, are valuable subjects for carefree, waterwise plantings (sword-shaped leaves, spectacular flowers, easy propagation). See *Agave, Beschorneria, Cordyline, Dasylirion, Doryanthes, Dracaena, Furcraea, Phormium, Sansevieria, Yucca.*

AGAVE Agavaceae
A. americana Mexico
The CENTURY PLANT (100-180cm) with basal glaucous rosettes is an easy accent plant. After a century, it is said, a single flower stem shoots high up after which the plant dies. Multiple offsets take over and are easily transplanted. As it is difficult to eradicate, choose the site carefully. Tolerant of drought, irrigation,

snow, even of building rubble. Well-drained soil and sunny, airy locations prevent health problems. Negative aspects: leaf juice may induce blindness. Cut off fierce tips and warn children. p.104

A. attenuata Mexico
Altogether smaller and spineless, its tall flower racemes gradually fold over. Picturesque near pools. Requires a well-drained deep root run. p.25, 53

AGONIS Myrtaceae
A. flexuosa SW Australia
The neat WILLOW MYRTLE (4-6m) quickly forms a single-trunked, round-headed

Ailanthus altissima

tree. Slender drooping leaves are strongly scented of peppermint. White fragrant flower clusters cover the PEPPERMINT TREE (Californian common name), a delightful sight in early summer. Favours limestone, tolerates drought or irrigation, suits lawns or containers.

AILANTHUS Simaroubaceae
A. altissima (A. glandulosa) China
Exquisite large leaves and wide tolerances of soil, exposure and drought would make the fast-growing deciduous TREE OF HEAVEN (5-11m) an ideal proposition were it not for its evil-scented flowers, suckering habit and difficult control. Cutting it to the ground every year prevents seeding and stimulates tender summer foliage. Containers confine roots and adorn terraces or patios. p.104

AJANIA Compositae
A. pacifica (Dendranthema p.) Japan
This evergreen perennial (deciduous below freezing) grows wild on the sandy, well-drained shores of Honshu Island, exposed to summer heat, sea wind and drought. Yellow flowers (late summer to winter) are not spectacular, yet complement artfully the scented, silver-edged leaves. It is well-equipped to survive drought. White, felty leaf undersides prevent drying out on hot sand. This 'felt' covers also leaf edges, giving them a silver-lined appearance. Fine silvery hairs on leaves' upper side reflect sun light. Compact rosettes' mutual leaf-shading is a further feature. Plant in full sun in open situations. Control spreading rhizomes by pulling out and using for propagation (or prepare cuttings). p.25

Note: In Tokyo, the Washington National Arboretum's Chief Horticulturist spotted *Chrysanthemum pacificum*, as it was then called, among bonsai. Little-known in Europe, only recently introduced to the USA, *Ajania pacifica* has now found its way into an enthusiastic trade.

AJUGA Labiatae
A. reptans Europe to Transcaucasia
The excellent, ground-covering BUGLE, spreading freely, likes good garden soil in half shade, weekly watering in summer and tolerates moderate drought.

Allium roseum

ALBIZIA   Leguminosae/Mimosoideae
A. julibrissin   Asia
The delightful, deciduous SILK TREE
(4-6m) prefers light, sandy soils and long
hot summers, gradually becoming
drought-tolerant. A wide-reaching
canopy and pink flower 'puffs' among
fern-like leafage are best appreciated
from above. During establishment, the
condition of the foliage indicates how
often watering is required. Propagation:
seed, varieties by cuttings. 'Rosea' pink
with crimson stamens, smaller.

ALCEA   Malvaceae
A. rosea   Turkey
An architectural plant, HOLLYHOCK does
well in drier soils.

ALLIUM   Liliaceae/Alliaceae
Some *Allium* thrive in sun, *A. moly* and
A. triquetrum prefer shade. Mostly
native to stony hills or arid fields, they
flourish in garden soil and naturalize
readily. By taking advantage of all you
will get monthlong bloom.
A. caeruleum (A. azureum)   Near East
BLUE ALLIUM and GOLDEN GARLIC
(*A. moly*), of similar height, flower simultaneously.

A. cepa   Widespread
For a waterwise mini kitchen garden
grow onion and add leek (*A. porrum*),
garlic (*A. sativum*) and chives (*A. schoe-
noprasum*).

A. giganteum   Himalaya
Look eye-to-eye into the GIANT ALLIUM'S
lilac flower clusters.

A. haematochiton   California
The RED-SKINNED ONION naturalizes as a
flowering spring carpet, together with
other natives.   p.141

A. neapolitanum   Mediterranean
White clusters on 25-30cm stems which
naturalize freely. Best planted closely for
massed effects.

A. roseum   Mediterranean
Garlic-scented leaves are a disadvantage but are compensated for by delightful pale-pink flower heads. Native to
vineyards and the littoral. Use in coastal
gardens.   p.105

A. triquetrum   Mediterranean
White, nodding spring flowers, lasting
weeks in a vase, naturalize freely in light
shaded soil. If invasive, pull up in winter
when they part easily from the ground.
Leaves are edible.   p.31, 105

ALOCASIA   Araceae
A. macrorrhiza   India
The perennial ELEPHANT'S EAR is evergreen in warmest climates. Giant leaves,
gigantic where pampered, provide an
instant tropical look. When protected
from wind, GIANT TARO thrives in permeable well-mulched soil in sun or shade.
Native to tropical Asia, used to ample
water, nevertheless it can survive with
little. Edible tuberous roots may remain
in the ground to freezing. Easy to transplant. Outstanding in containers. Propagation: division, seed.   p.53

Allium triquetrum

Aloe ciliaris

ALOE   Liliaceae/Aloeaceae
Succulent, drought-tolerant ALOE is
among the least demanding plants
grown in Mediterranean climates, but
good drainage is essential. Practically
maintenance-free, aloes happily cover
difficult areas and also suit containers.
Offspring strike easily.   p.64,71

A. arborescens   Cape
Orange flowers contrast splendidly with
blue winter skies.   p.59

A. ciliaris   Cape
The CLIMBING ALOE pushes for 1-2m
through shrubs, inflorescences standing
out above their foliage.   p.105

A. ferox   Cape
Fierce and sizeable.

A. thraskii   Cape
Among the tallest (1-3m), it grows orange winter flowers on candle-like
spikes. Provide sandy soil.

A. variegata   Cape
The miniature white-marked TIGER ALOE
(10-15cm) has pink flowers.

A. vera   Trop. America, Mediterranean
This intercontinental distribution means
it has wide tolerances for covering difficult areas. The aloe's leaf juice treats
external inflammation.

ALOYSIA Verbenaceae
A. triphylla (Lippia citriodora) S America
Although threadbare while deciduous, the easy LEMON VERBENA has its place in all Mediterranean gardens as a kitchen herb.

ALSTROEMERIA Amaryllidaceae
Numerous species of the perennial LILIES OF THE INCAS live in regions from summer-dry sandy seashores to rocky dry banks at 3000m. Flowers are exquisite. Grow the fragile roots in pots (sometimes sold thread-like) until suckering clumps are formed. Plant 20cm deep in fertile, sandy loam in dappled shade, water every week until they die down. Experiment also in drier surroundings.

Note: I was advised to remove seed heads to avoid 'uncontrolled spreading' when I was still struggling to establish this beauty. p.12, 106

A. aurea (A. aurantiaca) Chile
'Dover Orange' and 'Lutea', taller than most species, carry delightful summer flowers.

A. ligtu Chile
Around 40cm, wind-tolerant.

ALYOGYNE Malvaceae
A. huegelii Australia
Evergreen LILAC HIBISCUS (150-250cm), spring-to autumn-flowering, favours drier, sunny locations. Propagation: seed.

Alstroemeria hybrid

X *Amarine tubergenii*

ALYSSUM Cruciferae
A. montanum Mediterranean
Of typical Mediterranean mounding habit, this scented yellow-flowered perennial is widely grown in sunny rock clefts.

A. wulfenianum Europe
Golden flowers in summer cover a carpet of small, grey oval leaves (lawn replacement).

X **AMARINE** Amaryllidaceae
X **A. tubergenii**
It was potted and carefully watered over years, but this startling South African bulb only flowered when finally planted out in my garden's hottest, driest spot. There it got what it needed: summer-baking. Flower stalks appear over weeks, the bulb has quintupled. p.106

AMARYLLIS Amaryllidaceae
A. belladonna S Africa
Native to sunny or half-shady slopes, the shiny leaves of the BELLADONNA LILY die back in early summer. Silvery pink, faintly scented summer flowers shoot up from leafless bulbs. Plant poisonous bulbs level with surrounding ground. They thrive on winter rain and need baking in summer. p.86

AMORPHA Fabaceae
A. californica S USA, Mexico
A dry chaparral native, the deciduous drought-tolerant INDIGOBUSH (2-3m) flowers with wispy, purple racemes above feathery foliage. It gives maintenance-free erosion control in sunny sites (wide rooting), but requires good drainage. Propagated by seed, it naturalizes if watered.

ANEMONE Ranunculaceae
A. blanda E Mediterranean
Small tuberous-rooted anemones, peeking out beneath deciduous shrubs, are first to greet spring.

A. coronaria Mediterranean
Together with **A. pavonina** (scarlet), these are basic plants for Mediterranean spring bloom, naturalizing well, both from your own seed.

A. hupehensis, var. **japonica** Japan
My garden could not do without the perennial tall JAPANESE ANEMONE's large leaves and massed pink bloom from late summer into autumn. Once established, fibrous roots spread. Silvery white 'Honorine Jobert' looks exquisite in dappled woodland shade.

ANIGOZANTHOS Haemodoraceae
Native to open *Eucalyptus* woods together with *Doryanthes*, the evergreen perennial KANGAROO PAW is an Australian fashion as tulips were in Europe in centuries past. Plant from containers into free-draining sandy soil in dappled shade. No water should reach sword-shaped leaves or woolly flowers in summer (initially hand-water). Divide fully-grown clumps into generous portions. Occasionally, *Anigozanthos* sell where least expected, acquainting plant collectors with this captivating species. p.107

A. flavidus W Australia
Striking red and yellow flower stems (1-2m).

A. viridis W Australia
50cm tall, flowers greenish to sulphur.

Anisodontea capensis

Anigozanthos 'Ruby Blaze'

ANISODONTEA Malvaceae
A. capensis Cape
This undemanding, healthy shrub (1×1m) flourishes in drought-tolerant Mediterranean gardens with fast wispy growth and pink mini-*Hibiscus* flowers. It can be allowed to grow uncontrolled, shaped as low evergreen hedge, pruned as standard or planted in containers. Easily increased by cuttings. p.53, 107

ANTIGONON Polygonaceae
A. leptopus Mexico
In hottest locations, the deciduous CORAL VINE (8-10m) shades roofs and covers undesirable sights quickly, climbing by tendrils. Evergreen in mildest winters. Tops, killed by drought or frost, recover from mulched roots.

ANTIRRHINUM Scrophulariaceae
A. majus Mediterranean
The perennial, well-known SNAPDRAGON naturalizes readily in cobbled or gravelled courtyards.

APTENIA Aizoaceae
A. cordifolia S Africa
This evergreen trailing succulent carries small purple flowers among glossy fleshy leaves. An outstanding ground cover for the hottest location, it is a large-scale lawn replacement on sloping ground. Easy propagation: cuttings. p.107

AQUILEGIA Ranunculaceae
The sturdy perennial COLUMBINE with finely cut leaves grows into ever wider clumps without much attention. Graceful spring to autumn flowers in delicate shades naturalize and hybridize freely. It dies down in autumn. Weed out unsuitable ones or transplant. Sow seed in boxes or *in situ* and thin later.

A. formosa USA
30-80cm, sets ample seed, naturalizes freely in woodlands. Red and yellow flowers.

A. vulgaris Mediterranean
Reaches 70cm in fertile, summer-watered gardens, half that in unwatered ones.

ARABIS Cruciferae
A. caucasica Mediterranean
Plant the reliable ROCKCRESS (a perennial 'cushion') for profuse white bloom on top of well-drained walls together with spring bulbs. Tolerates also colder regions.

Aptenia cordifolia

Arbutus unedo

ARBUTUS   Ericaceae

An undemanding tree with superb evergreen shiny foliage, the bark peeling to a rich terra cotta, ARBUTUS is one of the most desirable plants for Mediterranean gardens. Resistant to honey fungus. Transplanting is difficult.

A. andrachne   E Mediterranean
This outstanding tree (5-10m) bears creamy clustered bells among large leaves.

A. menziesii   California
The MADRONE (6-20m) has large leaves and abundant bloom. Plant in well-drained, non-alkaline, humus-rich soil and protect from extreme heat. Once established, do not water in summer with the thought of getting quicker growth. Group with evergreen woodland vegetation.

Arbutus unedo, fruit

A. unedo   W Mediterranean
The STRAWBERRY TREE (6-10m) is shrubby, but if grown as a tree, stems reveal ever more beauty. White, honey-scented flower clusters, sometimes together with last year's colourful fruit, complement shiny foliage. Plant in well-drained, humus-enriched soil (lime-tolerant) bordering sunny pine or oak woodlands. It needs an open site; crowding neighbours may encourage fungal diseases. Although irrigation is tolerated, it thrives on natural winter rain. Responds to pruning, not clipping. Excellent as specimen, hedge or coastal second row.

Note: Insipid fruit, a visual asset to fruit salads, turn tastier when dark red. Leaves are said to be astringent and antiseptic.   p.108

ARCTOSTAPHYLOS   Ericaceae

Evergreen MANZANITAS are Californian native shrubs that I wish I had known earlier. Attractive, leathery glossy foliage takes on red tints. Waxy bells in spring may develop the preceding year (take care when pruning). Manzanitas demand fast-draining, sandy, mulched ground, full sun for species from arid regions, half-shade for coastal ones. Water weekly first year, later monthly, depending on species and establishment. Overhead water may result in die-back, caused by fungus, which can be cut out. After fires, deep-rooting manzanitas sprout from the stumps while wide-spreading, shallow-rooted ones regenerate from seed. Of value as honey fungus-resistant ground cover, the larger ones have pleasing outlines, remarkable stem colouring, attract birds. Propagation: seed (pre-treated), cuttings (easy), rooted branch tips (quick).

Note: Indians ate small berries (try a clear jelly).

A. densiflora   California
All winter, profuse pink bloom covers 'Howard McMinn', a mounding shrub (1x1m or more).
'Emerald Carpet' (30×70cm) maintains dense summer foliage. In hot interior valleys water twice monthly.

A. edmundsii 'Carmel Sur'
A speedy ground cover (3×2m), tolerating heat, drought and garden conditions.

A. franciscana   San Francisco
Almost extinct. 1×2m in full sun, also inland. Dense foliage suggests formal clipping.

A. glandulosa   Oregon to California
Grey foliage, superb in landscaped chaparral gardens, resprouts after fire to 2×2m.

A. 'Green Sphere'
Has dense-foliaged, formal appearance (1×1m).

A. hookeri   S California
'Monterey Carpet' is an excellent lawn replacement of uncertain origin. 'Wayside' (60×300cm), dependable from coast to inland.

A. pumila   California
Dune Manzanitas spread 50×100cm, tip-rooting in coastal sand.

A. uva-ursi   USA, Eurasia
Common BEARBERRY reaches a flat, tip-rooting 3m. Prefers cold winters. Tolerant of salt spray, so use among coastal conifers. 'Point Reyes' is most drought-tolerant.

ARCTOTHECA   Compositae
A. calendula   Cape
The evergreen drought-tolerant CAPE WEED, not a choice plant, quickly covers poor soil with golden bloom (lawn replacement). Runners can be detached easily.

Arctotis acaulis, annual display at Kirstenbosch

ARCTOTIS   Compositae

Arctotis with furry leaf rosettes has contrasting flower centres which distinguish it from *Dimorphotheca* (annual, smooth leaves, mostly yellow flowers) and *Osteospermum* (perennial). Similar and not always correctly named, all are called AFRICAN DAISY. These vivid-flowering, quick-spreading ground covers to various heights are most desirable. They flower best on free-draining sunny slopes and tolerate light frost. Water until established. Easily propagated by cuttings, even *in situ.*

A. acaulis (A. scapigera)   Cape
Perennial, spreading, yellow flowers.
p.109

A. fastuosa (Venidium fastuosum)
S Africa
Quite frost-hardy, spectacular orange flowers rise above low leaf rosettes.

A. venusta   S Africa
The attractive BLUE-EYED AFRICAN DAISY (40-50cm), a rampant shrubby annual, bears white spring flowers.

ARGYRANTHEMUM   Compositae
A. frutescens (Chrysanthemum f.)
Canary Is.
This reliable, billowing subshrub (80-120cm), evergreen and winter-flowering in Mediterranean climates, enjoys well-drained sunny gardens. Ample mulch conserves water. Keep on dry side to promote compact growth and reduce health problems. Outstanding for instant colour, coastal gardens and impatient gardeners. Cuttings reach flowering size within months (beginner-friendly).   p.27; 48

ARGYROCYTISUS
Leguminosae/Papilionoideae
A. battandieri (Cytisus b.)   NW Africa
Native to oak and cedar forests with poor dry sandy soils, the pineapple-scented MOROCCAN BROOM is well-known to English gardeners for its silvery foliage. Cut back to base each year for best performance. Sow seed in individual pots.

ARISARUM   Araceae
A. vulgare   Mediterranean
The perennial FRIAR'S COWL, the calla lily's small brother, is native to woods on northern slopes. Heart-shaped leaves emerge with first autumn rains, followed by curious 'flowers'. Small tubers naturalize readily in leafmould-enriched soils; divide for easy propagation.p.109

ARISTEA   Iridaceae
Evergreen strap-like leaves grow from small creeping rhizomes into large clumps. In early spring, attractive blue flowers in lax clusters stand above the foliage, closing by midafternoon. Compost-enriched garden soil, semi-shade with morning sun (shade in air-dry inland areas) suit these reasonably hardy plants. When well-established after copious winter rains, they need only weekly summer soakings, possibly less (more in full sun). Best left undisturbed for years, immediately replant divisions. Use ample seed.

A. ecklonii   Cape
Cheerful BLUE STARS grow 70cm tall.

A. macrocarpa   Cape
Worth the effort to obtain, large pale blue flowers rise 1m in coastal sun.

A. major (A. capitata)   Cape
Inflorescences with deep blue clusters bloom naturally on stony coastal slopes, reaching almost 1.6m tall, leaves half the height.

ARMERIA   Plumbaginaceae
A. maritima   S Europe
In well-drained sunny gardens, evergreen perennial SEA PINK grows slowly into low, dense carpets, tolerating coastal conditions (lawn replacement on reduced scale). Propagation: division.

Arisarum vulgare

Artemisia arborescens

ARTEMISIA
Compositae

Its attractive, silvery often feathery foliage but insignificant flowers, suit drought-tolerant, water-saving gardens. Water sparingly until established; routine irrigation weakens plants. Unde-

Arthropodium cirrhatum

manding for soil, they require excellent drainage, full sun. Occasional clipping keeps them compact. Aromatic leaves have many uses, often medicinal. Propagation: summer cuttings. A fire risk, the inflammable *A. californica* is omitted.

A. abrotanum   Mediterranean
SOUTHERNWOOD (1-1.5m) has wide uses: low clipped hedges, moth repellent.

A. absinthium   Mediterranean
The very drought-tolerant COMMON WORMWOOD (60-100cm) has pungent leaves (cooking, preparation of absinth). Bio-gardeners prepare with fresh or dried leaves a bitter-tasting infusion to fumigate pest-infested plants.

A. arborescens   Mediterranean
This evergreen (or 'evergray'?) grows to 1m on rocky hills, preferably on poor, sunny but well-drained soils. Limestone-tolerant.   p.110

A. schmidtiana   Japan
The perennial, white woolly ANGEL'S HAIR eventually reaches 50cm, a mainstay of water-conserving gardens.

ARTHROPODIUM
Liliaceae/Anthericaceae
A. cirrhatum   New Zealand
Native to dry, rocky coasts, perennial evergreen ROCK LILIES are members of the appealing 'Australian Lilies' and reach 30-60cm with arching leaves and abundant flower sprays. Initially, tender foliage may attract pests, but it gradually grows more sturdy. RENGARENGA favour light, compost-enriched soil, protection from hottest sun, watering in summer until established. Jet-black seeds germinate readily. Also divide rhizomatous fibrous roots. Maoris ate roots after prolonged cooking.   p.110

ARUM
Araceae
Mediterranean climates suit perennial ARUM. From summer-dormant tuberous roots, shiny arrow-shaped leaves rise with first autumn rains. Bloom resembles small calla lilies. Best in shaded, permeable garden soil with winter rain. Propagation: seed (remove caustic pulp with gloves) or divide tubercles.

A. dioscoridis   E Mediterranean
Green, purple-blotched spathe, purple spadix.

A. italicum   Mediterranean
ITALIAN ARUM (30-40cm) has creamy spathes, attractive, long-lasting red berries, occasionally attractively marked leaves. Subspecies vary mostly in leaf and spathe colour. Cut up tubers become invasive in ploughed fields.   p.111

A. pictum   W Mediterranean
Purple spadix and spathe in autumn.
                    p.66

ASPARAGUS
Liliaceae/Asparagaceae
Mediterranean maquis and garrigue are rich in perennial *Asparagus*. Young tender shoots with inconspicuous, often scented bloom spring from hedges and are edible, not so ornamental berries. Grow where fleshy roots can spread and a gracefully arching or vigorously twining habit expand. Difficult to train, they have their own ways. They tolerate summer water, but survive without it. In winter, cut back old shoots.

A. acutifolius   Mediterranean
The WILD ASPARAGUS climbs and arches to 2m. Harvest edible, tender green spring shoots.

A. albus   W Mediterranean
Woody and arching to 80cm, its thorns (modified leaves) are vicious. Short-shooted asparagus include *A. maritimus*, *A. tenuifolius*.

ASPHODELINE
Liliaceae/Asphodelaceae
A. lutea   Mediterranean
YELLOW ASPHODEL, closely related to *Asphodelus* (see below).

ASPHODELUS
Liliaceae/Asphodelaceae
A. aestivus   Mediterranean
Beautiful ASPHODEL invade overgrazed, dry rocky sites as animals scorn sword-like, glaucous leaves. Enjoy their glorious flower stems but cut them off before seeding or grow in pots. Dying down over summer, ample seed and tuberous roots ensure survival.   p.111

A. fistulosus Mediterranean
distinguished from *A. aestivus* by narrow, hollow leaves but just as invasive, difficult to extract from cracks. Stems carry delightful starry flowers.

ASPIDISTRA Liliaceae/Convallariaceae
A. elatior China
Evergreen, perennial CAST-IRON PLANTS are seldom given locations which do their large polished leaves justice. Planted out, they are undemanding.

Note: I planted a divided clump in a shady woodland where leaves expand attractively.

ASTER Compositae
This much-used tolerant perennial colours late-summer gardens. Provide reasonably good soil and water occasionally.

A. amellus Widespread
Violet ITALIAN ASTER grows to 50cm.

Arum italicum

A. dumosus SE USA
Slightly taller BUSHY ASTER has blue or white flowers.

ASTERISCUS Compositae
A. maritimus Mediterranean
This grey-leaved, cushion-like shrublet, native to dry pastures or crevices on coastal rock, has calendula-like flowers.

ATRIPLEX Chenopodiaceae
The SALTBUSH, deciduous or evergreen, is an excellent choice for difficult sites (drought, erosion, coastal conditions). And it retards fire. Provide ample space. Cuttings strike well.

A. canescens California
This SALTBUSH reaches 1-2m with equal spread.

A. halimus Mediterranean
The silvery-white ORACH (2-3m) is native to sandy or rocky coastlines on salty soils but also thrives inland.

A. semibaccata Australia
The evergreen reliable AUSTRALIAN SALTBUSH (30cm) quickly covers the ground. Plant where its deep, expanding root system is an asset, such as for erosion control on dunes or banks.

AUBRIETA Cruciferae
A. deltoidea E Mediterranean
Perennial AUBRIETA qualify for rock gardens, among gravel and paving or as flat lawn replacement in full sun (inland shade). Propagation: cuttings.

AUCUBA Cornaceae
A. japonica Asia
The evergreen spreading AUCUBA (2-3m), although undemanding and drought-tolerant, still appreciates good garden soil. Small flowers are insignificant, red berries an asset (plant both sexes). Aucuba is among the best for dark dry shade or coastal conditions. Easily increased by cuttings.

AURINIA Cruciferae
A. saxatilis (Alyssum saxatile) S Europe
In California called BASKET-OF-GOLD, this

Asphodelus aestivus

perennial is a useful cushion plant. A crevice for roots to penetrate, some shade and occasional water are all it needs.

BABIANA Iridaceae
Attractive BABIANA had to stand difficult travelling conditions when first introduced to Europe. White, blue or purple spring flower spikes stand above low foliage which rises from a corm. Rich sandy soil in sun, well-drained, suits them. Although corms are small, plant 20cm deep, where winter rain soil moisture is maintained into late spring. Babianas naturalize readily, dying down in summer (summer-baking). Propagation: offsets, autumn-sown seed (keep shaded, moist and warm in deep containers until germination occurs).

B. stricta Cape
to 25cm, royal blue flowers.

B. villosa Cape
CRIMSON BABIANA (30cm) likes loamy soil.

111

Bauhinia variegata 'Candida'

BACCHARIS Asteraceae/Compositae
B. pilularis California
Native to dunes and coastal lands, the evergreen prostrate DWARF CHAPARRAL BROOM covers 20-60×100-400cm with insignificant flowers. Silky female seeds, after a fine display, fly about messily. In California called COYOTE BRUSH, it will grow in heavy to sandy soil, full sun to light shade, with little or no summer water (supplemented inland). Drought-stressed leaves are shed but resprout. Annual clipping and removing older woody and upright stems produces close ground covers. An extensive root system stabilizes slopes. Fire-retardant, unpalatable to deer. Propagation: quick-germinating seed, tip cuttings (male plants). 'Pigeon Point' grows quicker, 'Twin Peaks' hugs the ground more closely.

Ballota acetabulosa

BALLOTA Labiatae
B. acetabulosa Mediterranean
Evergreen spreading with delightful flowers, BALLOTA (40×70cm) does particularly well among rock or on walls. It is native to alkaline soil, but will tolerate an acid one. As with all felted, grey-leaved plants, only the best drainage is good enough and full sun is essential. Cut back after flowering for compact growth. Confined locations induce health problems. Easily propagated by cuttings. p.112

BANKSIA Proteaceae
This genus of around 50 Australian evergreen shrubs and trees, easily killed by kindness, needs a well-drained, lime-free, sandy soil on the poor side, a sheltered, sunny site and long, hot, dry summers. Nitrate- or phosphate-rich soils or waterlogging in summer are fatal. Mulch protects the shallow feeder roots from cultivation. Increased by seed (individual pots avoid root disturbance).

Note: I lost a well-established *Banksia* shortly after an untimely copious summer rain.

B. ericifolia E Australia
One of the easier of the genus, the HEATH-LEAVED BANKSIA (2-4m), a rounded shrub with amber flower candles through winter, is useful as an informal hedge or screen.

B. integrifolia E Australia
Widely grown COAST BANKSIAS, valued for their foliage, quickly reach 6-8m in favourable conditions. Greenish-yellow bottle brushes all year.

BARLERIA Acanthaceae
B. obtusa E Cape
Plant this twiggy, drought-tolerant shrublet (70-90cm) in free-draining soil, protected from midday sun and frost. Outstanding for pale purple winter flowers. Propagation: cuttings. p.112

BAROSMA see **AGATHOSMA**

BARTLETTINA Compositae
B. sordida (Eupatorium sordidum)
Mexico
The evergreen scented VIOLET MIST (60-190cm) is a welcome shrub for the winter garden. It demands little care other than moisture-retentive shaded soil.

BAUHINIA
Leguminosae/Caesalpinioideae
Closely related to *Cercis*, the evergreen to deciduous ORCHID TREE, naturally shrubby, flowers mostly towards summer's end. It can also be trained as a tree. Long taproots require deep, humus-enriched, fast-draining soils, amply mulched. Heat demands are high, yet afternoon shade is beneficial. Otherwise undemanding, *Bauhinia* likes occasional watering, in favourable sites can manage without. Easily raised from seed, but

Barleria obtusa.
Courtesy E. van Jaarsveld, Kirstenbosch

transplant early. Correct naming seems complex, but spectacular blooms make it desirable. The following can take a short period of frost.

B. galpinii (B. punctata)   S Africa
is a rambling, climbing shrub (2-3m), in South Africa called PRIDE OF DE KAAP. At the end of summer, brick red flower clusters appear on arching branch tips, not unlike *Bougainvillea*.

B. variegata   Tropical Asia
Rose purple flowers appear on this ORCHID TREE (5-7m) before leaves in spring, followed by somewhat messy seed pods. Remember this litter when choosing sites. 'Candida' has large white fragrant flowers.   p.112

BEAUMONTIA   Apocynaceae
B. grandiflora   E Himalaya
The evergreen HERALD'S TRUMPET (3-6m), a magnificent vigorous climber, bears spectacularly large, white scented trumpets on previous year's growth. Wind protection, much heat and light and an ample root run are required. Heavy pruning after flowering encourages next year's flowering.

BEGONIA   Begoniaceae
Given shade and water, most begonias (many South American species) stand well up to summer heat.   p.53

BELAMCANDA   Iridaceae
B. chinensis   Japan, China
Perennial LEOPARD LILY rises from rhizomes with fans of sword-like, elegantly arching leaves. Plant 5cm deep in light garden soil wherever graceful leaves are appreciated. Seed capsules follow spotted orange summer flowers and reveal shiny black beads used in dry flower arrangements. Easy to raise from seed.

BERGENIA   Saxifragaceae
Evergreen rounded leaves rise from a perennial rootstock, a perfect foil for long-lasting flower clusters. Although quite drought-tolerant once established, bergenias perform best with occasional

watering in light, shaded soil. Propagation: division.

B. ciliata   Asia
Late spring flowers 25cm tall (white and pink shades).

B. crassifolia   Asia
Pink midwinter bloom 40cm tall.

BESCHORNERIA   Agavaceae
B. yuccoides   Mexico
The sword-leaved, unbranched *Beschorneria* is grown like *Yucca*. Spectacular inflorescences and soft-tipped leaves suit pool gardens.   p.113

BIGNONIA   Bignoniaceae
Most TRUMPET VINES, formerly known as BIGNONIA, have been assigned new names (listed below). Unperturbed by name changes, all are successful climbers in Mediterranean climates. To be sure that you get what you want, buy plants in bloom. Where flowerless (labelled 'Bignonia'), ask what the colour is. If the plant purchased is not what you had in mind, you have still acquired an asset for your garden. I list trumpet vines under what are now considered their valid names.

B. capensis see ***Tecomaria c.***

B. capreolata (Doxantha c.)   SE USA
The CROSS VINE, suitable for cooler areas, retains its original name. Given a support or left to spill over walls, its ample foliage and purple-brown summer flower clusters cover areas to 10m, becoming bare at the base.

B. cherere see ***Distictis buccinatoria***

B. chinensis see ***Campsis grandiflora***

B. ignea see ***Pyrostegia venusta***

B. jasminoides see ***Pandorea j.***

B. Madame Galen see ***Campsis x tagliabuana*** 'Mme Galen'

B. radicans see ***Campsis r.***

B. speciosa see ***Clytostoma callistigioides***

B. tweediana see ***Macfadyena unguis-cati***

B. venusta see ***Pyrostegia v.***

Beschorneria yuccoides

BILLARDIERA   Pittosporaceae
B. longiflora   Australia
This evergreen (1-3m) rambles over shrubs or covers unsightly objects. Delicate greenish summer flowers are followed by plump purple 'berries'. Quite drought-tolerant, it likes well-drained forest soils and watering until established. Clip lightly to keep under control. Propagation: fresh seed, cuttings.

BLETILLA   Orchidaceae
B. striata   Japan, China
The winter-dormant CHINESE GROUND ORCHID (30-40cm) has sword-shaped, pleated leaves and magenta spring flowers. In time, it colonizes humusy forest soils in dappled shade. Divide dormant corms, replant immediately, water weekly in summer. No health problems. White-flowered forms exist.

BLOOMERIA   Liliaceae/Alliaceae
B. crocea   California
Native to dry sunny hillsides, golden stars flower in spring among sparse, dying foliage, stunning where massed among sun-loving Californian plants. They tolerate heavy soils. Seed bloom after four years.

BOLUSANTHUS
       Leguminosae/Papilionoideae
B. speciosus   S Africa, Transvaal
The graceful, widely-praised SOUTH AFRICAN WISTERIA TREE (4-10m) from afar resembles *Jacaranda*. Flowers sometimes appear before, but mostly with the deciduous foliage. Hardy and drought-resistant, with high heat requirements. Raising from seed is slow.

Bougainvillea cv.

BORONIA   Rutaceae
B. heterophylla   W Australia
The evergreen RED BORONIA (1-1.5m)
has erica-like foliage. Crimson flowers
delight us from winter to spring with
their heady, far-reaching scent. Easily
grown in lime-free, sandy, well-drained
soil, never completely dry, sheltered
from midday heat and wind. After flowering, prune lightly for compact
growth. Transplanting is difficult. Propagate in spring from fresh seed or try
autumn-cuttings, kept cool and shaded
over winter.

B. megastigma   W Australia
Scale insects may afflict the well-known,
scented BROWN BORONIA. 'Lutea' yellow
flowers.

BOUGAINVILLEA   Nyctaginaceae
This vigorous, mostly frost-tender
climber or bank cover will delight you
with its extravagant colour display.
BOUGAINVILLEA thrives on poor soil,
drought, general neglect, but abhors root
disturbance. Plant carefully from containers, stake well in windy areas. In hottest
regions, long spiny shoots cover a house
within the twinkling of an eye. Pruning
may be time-consuming, thus look for less
rampant cultivars. Severe pruning keeps
container plants within bounds.

B. glabra   Brazil
Rather intense purple bloom. More
cold-tolerant than other species (-7°C).
'Magnifica', a good choice.   p.43

B. spectabilis   Brazil
Cultivars come in all shades (white,
pink, yellow, orange, red) and hottest
locations bring out their brilliance. To
obtain the desired colour, choose while
bracts are out. Double forms' faded
bloom requires picking-off.
                                          p.57, 59, 114

BRACHYGLOTTIS   Compositae
B. greyi (Senecio g.)   New Zealand
Evergreen, drought-tolerant shrubs
(50-100cm) with attractive silver grey
foliage. Insignificant yellow flower clusters need tidying up. Any well-drained,
sandy soil in sun will do. Rarely in cultivation, most plants sold are the hybrid
'Sunshine'. Propagation: cuttings.

BRAHEA   Palmae
B. armata (Erythea a.)   Mexico
Creamy flowers in drooping clusters
make the BLUE FAN PALM (7-9m) an outstanding plant. Excellent in hot, dry,
windy areas.

B. edulis   Mexico
Light green leaves distinguish the
GUADALUPE PALM.

BRUGMANSIA   Solanaceae
Evergreen DATURA (2-8m) flower periodically through the year with exquisite,
often scented bloom. Deciduous and

more compact in colder regions. Allow
it to grow at will or train as small tree.
Best performance with generous compost and mulch under dappled shade,
also in containers. Annual careful pruning promotes vigorous growth. Well-
established plants in suitable locations
do not get whitefly, but some experi-
mentation may be required. Without
weekly summer watering, daturas become dormant, being revived by first
autumn rains. All parts are poisonous.
Easily propagated by cuttings, bearing
flowers in the first year. Many species
and cultivars in pale colours, seldom
correctly named. Whichever is chosen,
all are worthwhile.   p.115

B. arborea   Andes
ANGEL'S TRUMPETS have exquisite white
flowers, tips pointing upward.

B. aurea   Andes
Large, white to golden flowers, scent-
ed at night.   p.115

B. sanguinea   Colombia to Chile
Arborescent (2-4m) with a sturdier
'look'. Narrow, pendent orange-red
flowers are scentless.

B. suaveolens   Brazil
White, night-fragrant flowers (also yel-
low, pink) are veined with green. Leaves
are flannel-like. A double form exists.

BUDDLEJA   Buddlejaceae
Many species and cultivars with flowers
from delicate white to darkest purple.
Grow all and enjoy long-lasting flowering periods. Tolerant of stony ground,
these shrubs do best in garden soil with
occasional summer-watering. Cutting
back in spring stimulates growth and
flowering. Prune early ones after flowering. Propagation: cuttings.

Buddleja × weyeriana 'Sungold'

B. alternifolia   China
Native to dry slopes, this deciduous billowing mass (3-4m) demands space. Tangling, arching branches are covered early with a pale lilac veil. Use as hedge or shape as fountain-like small tree.

B. davidii   China
The deciduous BUTTERFLY BUSH enjoys coastal conditions.

B. madagascariensis   Madagascar
Somewhat rampant, climbs into nearby trees from where spill creamy yellow, winter-flowering panicles with far-reaching scent. Or prune close to a wall (labour-intensive).

B. officinalis   China
Well-branched to 2m. Scented winter flowers last for weeks.

B. x **weyeriana** 'Sungold'
Deciduous, particularly vigorous, outstanding for colder regions and its orange, scented bloom in early winter.
p.114

BULBINE   Liliaceae/Asphodelaceae
B. frutescens   S Africa
Succulent evergreen leaves grow into a quick and easy spring-flowering ground cover. Tuberous fleshy roots send out long runners, spreading into large clumps. Widespread in South Africa, totally undemanding, it endures drought, heat, poor soil, tolerates some shade but flowers best in sun. More drought-tolerant but less pretty than *Bulbinella*.

Brugmansia aurea

Brugmansia × candida 'Knightii'

BUPLEURUM   Umbelliferae
B. fruticosum   Mediterranean
An aromatic shrub (1.5-2m) with attractive, leathery leaves and discreet yellow flower umbels, *Bupleurum* grows wild in rocky garrigue, a useful evergreen. Good health, an undemanding character and easy propagation (seed, cuttings) are added advantages. However, excellent drainage is essential.   p.115

BUTIA   Palmae
B. capitata   Brazil, Argentina
Over the years, the desirable, slow-growing YATAY PALM (3-6m) becomes drought-tolerant. Suitable for containers.   p.13 left

Bulbinella floribunda

BULBINELLA Liliaceae/Asphodelaceae
B. cauda-felis   Cape
White flowers.

B. floribunda   SW coastal Africa
Spectacular golden spring flowers (30-50cm) last well in water. Narrow leaves sheath each other attractively. After flowering, bulbinellas die down. Plant the fibrous roots at soil level in sun (light shade in hottest areas), adding sand and compost. Roots rot in poor drainage or if summer dormancy is prevented by untimely watering. Several species grow in swamps which dry out in summer. Fresh seeds germinate quickly. Plant out the following year.
p.115

Bupleurum fruticosum

BUXUS — Buxaceae
The evergreen, well-behaved BOXWOOD is unrivalled for drought tolerance and formal shaping, compensating for slow growth. Lime-tolerant. Increased by cuttings.

B. balearica — W Mediterranean
The BALEARIC BOXWOOD can still be found on native mountain screes. But largest specimens (30cm trunk diameters) have long ago been carved into durable spoons. Shiny leaves are larger than common box. p.116

B. microphylla — Asia
Together with its many cultivars (60-150cm) it shares dense, thin-textured foliage, slow growth and tolerance towards hot Mediterranean summers. Protect from wind. p.46

B. sempervirens 'Suffruticosa' — Mediterranean
This dwarf form of the COMMON BOX (30-90cm) responds well to clipping when used as low edging in shade.

CAESALPINIA — Leguminosae/Caesalpinioideae
C. gilliesii — S America
A sight to behold, the fast-growing BIRD OF PARADISE (1.5-3m) is evergreen in warmest locations. Golden-petalled flowers with red stamens stand above feathery foliage. Plant in deep, well-drained soil. Propagation: seed. p.116

Buxus balearica

Caesalpinia gilliesii

C. pulcherrima (Poinciana p.) — West Indies
After a long summer under tropical heat, the spectacular somewhat taller BARBADOS PRIDE will be the glory of your garden. Spring pruning promotes bushy growth.

CALENDULA — Compositae
C. officinalis — Mediterranean
The good-natured, annual MARIGOLD, useful in new or in beginners' gardens, cheerfully flowers all year with little water in any sunny soil. In my garden, this pioneer performed best in virgin soil, before it was 'improved'.

CALLISTEMON — Myrtaceae
Evergreen, drought-tolerant BOTTLE-BRUSHES like well-drained, sandy soils in sun.

C. citrinus (C. lanceolatus) — SE Australia
The undemanding, widely grown CRIMSON BOTTLEBRUSH (3-4m) suits coastal gardens. Abundant late spring 'brushes' flower among narrow leaves, attract hummingbirds.

C. rigidus — E Australia
The STIFF BOTTLEBRUSH (4-6m) has deep red flowers. Attractive silky hairs cover young shoots. Its pointed leaves may harm passers by.

C. viminalis — SE Australia
The fast-growing WEEPING BOTTLEBRUSH (6-8m) has narrow pointed leaves. Bright red brushes are visible from afar. A neat, undemanding shrub for sheltered areas where roots in summer find a cool run.

CALLITRIS — Cupressaceae
Clip CYPRESS PINE for compact growth and enjoy easy maintenance.

C. columellaris — W Australia
The ornamental, dense COAST CYPRESS PINE in ideal conditions reaches 15m (often less). It thrives in sandiest soils in warm coastal areas.

C. preissii — Australia
Slender, usually much smaller, lime-tolerant.

CALOCEDRUS — Cupressaceae
C. decurrens (Libocedrus d.) — California
The evergreen INCENSE CEDAR, native to high elevation slopes, gradually reaches 25m. Tolerant of heat, poor soil and wind, it will also grow where honey fungus is a problem. Watered infrequently and deeply, plants become drought-tolerant.

CALOCHORTUS — Liliaceae/Calochortaceae
This delicate Californian 'lily' grows wild in open pine groves, under evergreen oak, on grassy slopes in dappled shade, flowering late spring to early

summer. All species require free-draining soils and summer-baking. Water in spring if nature does not.
From a wide choice, the Mediterranean gardener chooses:

C. albus   California
White 'lanterns' (30-50cm).

C. luteus   W USA
The long-flowering yellow MARIPOSA LILY (30-50cm) grows in Sierra Nevada foot-hills, also suits coastal gardens.

C. venustus   W USA
30cm tall, largest flowers (white, pink, purple, yellow).

CALONYCTION see **IPOMOEA**

CALOTHAMNUS   Myrtaceae
The evergreen NET BUSH, closely related to *Callistemon*, has leaves like pine needles. Mostly grown for the vividly coloured, one-sided 'brushes'. Annual trimming after flowering keeps shrubs compact. Tolerates most adverse conditions, but not poor drainage. Young specimens can be transplanted. Propagation: small cuttings.

C. quadrifidus   W Australia
1-2m, flowers with crimson stamens and yellow-tipped anthers.

C. villosus   W Australia
The SILKY NET BUSH (1m) bears brilliant red brushes among silvery green foliage.

CAMELLIA   Theaceae
C. japonica   Japan
Although not Mediterranean climate natives, evergreen and glossy-leaved

Campsis radicans

Camellia japonica hybrid

camellias (1-4m) thrive in patios and courtyards, protected from wind and hottest sun. Plant in free-draining humusy soil (the 'crown' above soil level!), mulch generously, above all never let them dry out. Cut out inward-growing shoots to allow air to circulate. Newer cultivars flower longer and discard spent flowers. Camellias suit containers.

p.117

CAMPANULA   Campanulaceae
Well-known, blue- or white-flowering BELLFLOWERS appreciate some water and dappled shade.

C. carpatica   mostly S Europe
Late spring flowers favour rock. Propagation: seed, division.

C. isophylla   N Italy
The perennial ITALIAN BELLFLOWER is an excellent flat ground cover on sloping ground.

C. rapunculoides   Europe
Sends up spike-like flower racemes to 1m. Helpful in poor soil, don't pamper as it could become invasive.

CAMPSIS   Bignoniaceae
A splash of colour from late summer to autumn on house walls or pergolas, the deciduous TRUMPET CREEPER is woody-stemmed, drought-tolerant and frost-hardy. Most are self-clinging. It appreciates free-draining soil in fullest sun. Wide-spreading roots, where watered, may become invasive and are confined by containers or rock pockets. Transplants well when young. No health problems. Pruning keeps this buoyant climber in its place. Propagation: seed, root suckers.

C. grandiflora (Bignonia g.)   Asia
The CHINESE TRUMPET CREEPER carries magnificent orange to scarlet flowers and with support quickly reaches 5-7m.

C. radicans (Bignonia r.)   E USA
This rampant vine (8-12m) has deep red or orange flowers. Aerial roots cling ivy-like onto walls, rocks or tree trunks (labour-saving). 'Flava' is rich yellow.

p.117

C. x tagliabuana 'Mme Galen'
The best-behaved with weakly developed aerial roots, yet vigorous. Salmon-red flowers.

Capparis spinosa

Capparis spinosa thrives on old city walls, a site difficult to match for most of us (but summed up into 'full sun and perfect drainage').

Carpenteria californica

CANNA   Cannaceae
C. indica   Asia, S America
Large leaves arise from tuberous rootstocks, followed by spectacular summer flowers (red, orange, yellow). This tropical and tropical-looking plant (many hybrids) needs rich, fertile soil, full sun, watering twice a week. Striking against dark-green backgrounds, successful in containers.   p.53, 75

CAPPARIS   Capparidaceae
C. spinosa   Mediterranean, Asia
The CAPER, a prostrate, spreading, spiny shrub, hangs from sun-drenched city walls, roots growing between stone. In summer, startling pinkish-white blossom lasts for weeks. Difficult to establish, try spreading seed in sites resembling their native ground, replacing the 'old city wall' with any dry wall. Initially watch closely without pampering.

Note: Pickle flower buds in vinegar (not the fruit).   p.118

CARAGANA
          Leguminosae/Papilionoideae
C. arborescens   Europe, Asia
The deciduous SIBERIAN PEA TREE grows steadily to 4-6m with equal spread and pea-like, yellow fragrant spring flowers. Entirely undemanding, guaranteed drought-tolerant, it grows in poorest soils in sun or half-shade. Prune to keep it to the size you want. Propagation: own ample seed in individual pots.

CARISSA   Apocynaceae
The CARISSA is an asset to every garden. Its evergreen foliage turns shinier the hotter and drier the air, while the fragrant flowers gleam silvery white on moonlit nights. The paired spines should not deter you. Tolerant of salt-laden winds and most soils, they need full sun to grow well and to mature edible fruit. Spiny branches mean they are often used as hedges. Somewhat slow to establish, so it is best to buy well-grown plants in gallon containers. If patience is one of your qualities, propagate by seed or cuttings.

C. bispinosa (C. acuminata)   S Africa
The HEDGE THORN, native to dry woodlands and coastal scrub, ultimately reaches 1-4m. Hazelnut-sized flowers and fruit.

C. macrocarpa   Eastern S Africa
Often labelled *C. grandiflora*, the NATAL PLUM (1-3m) from warm coastal regions has spreading growth with larger flowers

Carissa macrocarpa

and nut-sized fruit. Jam is excellent. 'Tuttlei' makes a dense ground cover.
                    p.118

CARPENTERIA   Hydrangeaceae
C. californica   California
Scented late spring flowers in clusters, resembling single white roses, cover dark evergreen foliage. The glorious, drought-tolerant BUSH ANEMONE (1-2m), a quite hardy but rare native to Sierra Nevada foothills, likes well-drained garden conditions with part-day (afternoon) shade, doing well near the sea. Water in summer until well-established; leaf edges go brown if too dry. Tolerant of irrigation in well-drained soils. Resistant to honey fungus. Before transplanting larger specimens, cut back by half. Propagation: cuttings, layering (seed will give variable flowers).

CARPOBROTUS   Aizoaceae
C. edulis   Cape
The rather coarsely foliaged, succulent HOTTENTOT FIG is often used as a large-scale ground cover on sandy banks, an excellent candidate for fire prevention. Attractive pinkish-yellow flowers are valuable, fruits are said to be edible. Will grow in poor dry soil (see also Ice Plants). Cuttings root easily.   p.48

Beware: The juicy, thus heavy foliage slips on steep banks.

CARYA   Juglandaceae
C. illinoinensis   S USA
The deciduous PECAN with attractive

autumn colour, grows into a large, fine-foliaged tree. It requires deep, well-drained soils and in hottest regions monthly summer watering. Nuts ripen best with mild winters and long summers. Unfavourable conditions such as coastal salinity result in health problems, but tolerant of honey fungus. Match varieties with your climate.

CARYOPTERIS Verbenaceae
C. x **clandonensis** E Asia
Grown in light well-drained alkaline soil in full sun, the aromatic BLUEBEARD (50×50cm), a deciduous dainty shrub, can put up with drought. Attractive seed heads follow blue feathery flower clusters. Planted among evergreens, plants disappear when leafless. Cut back hard each year to promote bloom. Cuttings will flower the following season.

CASSIA see **SENNA**

CASTANEA Fagaceae
C. sativa Mediterranean
The deciduous SPANISH CHESTNUT (9-25m), imposing when mature, grows in rich, acid, well-drained sunny soils with infrequent deep summer irrigation. Resistant to honey fungus. Transplants even when large but stake well. Readily propagated from edible chestnuts.

CASUARINA Casuarinaceae
The evergreen BEEFWOOD (SHE OAK) has pine-like branches and a broad crown. Tolerant of most conditions (dry or irrigated soil, heat, wind, salt spray, alkalinity), it survives in poor stony dry ground and thrives in sunny, well-drained, moisture-retentive soils. Transplants when young. Easily propagated by seeds. In a container, it shades open pavings or patios. A word of caution: Humid, light sandy soils on Florida coastlines turned *Casuarina* invasive.

C. cunninghamiana N and E Australia
The vigorous RIVER SHE OAK associates with *Grevillea* and *Eucalyptus*, reaching a stately 20m. Infrequent deep watering.

C. equisetifolia NE tropical Australia
Native on cliffs and dunes, the shallow-rooted HORSETAIL TREE (SOUTHSEA IRONWOOD) stabilizes sandy coasts.

Ceanothus rigidus 'Snow Flurries'

C. verticillata (Allocasuarina v.)
SE Australia
This moderately fast-growing BEEFWOOD (7-10m), broad-crowned and weeping, lends itself to clipping. Male trees with golden pollen are a lovely sight.

CATHA Celastraceae
C. edulis Tropical E Africa
Evergreen maintenance-free KHAT is a spreading shrub/tree (2-4m) of sturdy health. Shiny coppery red leaves are its chief attraction. Flowers and fruit are inconspicuous. Tolerates coastal wind and poor dry soil, requiring good drainage. Easily transplanted. Propagation: cuttings, division. Arabs use leaves for honey-sweetened infusions.

CATHARANTHUS Apocynaceae
C. roseus (Vinca rosea) Madagascar
MADAGASCAR PERIWINKLE, an undemanding perennial, flowers over long summer

Cataranthus roseus

months (white, pink) in sun or half-shade with little water. Medicinal properties.
p.119

CEANOTHUS Rhamnaceae
The mostly evergreen CALIFORNIA LILAC is an important chaparral plant. Around 50 species and countless cultivars make up a wide range of useful ground covers, shrubs and small trees, variable in size depending on growing conditions. Usually in spring, profuse white, lavender or blue flower panicles show above dark green, often glossy leaves. In hottest areas give afternoon shade. Although undemanding of soil, delicate roots require locations where they can become well-anchored. Carefully balance top growth with root volume. Dying back, caused by root breakage (wind!), is often wrongly supposed to be caused by disease. Roots are susceptible to rot, so give superdrainage and avoid planting near sprinklers. No transplanting, thus insert cuttings individually and pot on carefully. For hottest inland areas: 'Concha', 'Joyce Coulter', 'Ray Hartmann'.

C. arboreus California
The attractive CATALINA MOUNTAIN LILAC (2-5m) grows on scrub slopes, taller than most shrubs. Pale blue spring flowers.

C. 'Concha'
Densely-leaved shrub (2×2m), dark blue flowers, among the best. 'Frosty Blue' gradually reaches 2×2m. 'Joyce Coulter', a mounding shrub (1.5×3m), blue flowers. p.141

C. leucodermis California
An evergreen spring-flowering shrub, the CHAPARRAL WHITETHORN (2-4m) has rigid, wide-spreading branches. p.77

C. maritimus California
The variable MARITIME CEANOTHUS flowers in late winter.

C. 'Ray Hartmann'
A dependable, billowing shrub (4×4m), clear-blue bloom.

C. rigidus 'Snow Flurries'
exuberant (2×3m), white-flowering.
p.119

C. thyrsiflorus var. **repens** N California
The creeping BLUEBLOSSOM covers the ground on wooded coastal slopes with profuse early summer flowers (many blue shades).

Celtis australis

CEDRUS
Pinaceae
Undemanding cedars, well-suited to parks or reafforestation, need ample space. Deep-rooted, they are very drought-tolerant once established. Propagation: seed; cuttings retain growth forms.

C. deodara
Himalaya
The very drought-tolerant DEODAR grows fast to 25×10m.

C. libani
Lebanon
LEBANON CEDAR reaches 25m. ATLAS CEDAR ssp. **atlantica** grows slowly to great height and width and is still found in isolated forests. ssp. **brevifolia** is smaller, very slow, native to Cyprus.

CELTIS
Ulmaceae
Deciduous HACKBERRY, large, deep-rooting trees, tolerate alkaline soil. In hot dry conditions they are best with some shade or northern exposure. Cut back side branches before transplanting.

C. australis
Mediterranean
MEDITERRANEAN HACKBERRY (10-20m) has shiny grey bark and small, sweet and edible fruits, attractive to birds. Farmers bend young branches into sheep collars.
p.120

C. occidentalis
USA
Taller than the above, it resists honey fungus. Leaves appear late (suitable near houses). Berries attract birds.

CENTAUREA
Compositae
C. cineraria
Mediterranean
The grey-leaved, purple-flowered VELVET CENTAUREA (20-40cm) is a perennial mainstay of drought-tolerant gardens. Trim into shape, use pruned material as cuttings.

CENTRANTHUS
Valerianaceae
C. ruber (Valeriana rubra)
Mediterranean
The perennial RED VALERIAN'S graceful pink flowers (spring to autumn) are well-worth the risk of their becoming invasive. Very drought-tolerant, entirely undemanding of soil or position, they place themselves naturally to great advantage, combining elegantly with most flowers. Cutting back after flowering induces a second flowering. 'Albus', singly or in patches, gives instant style to dark corners.
p.120

Cerastium tomentosum

Caution: Established in gardens by a single plant, valerian increases by wind-distributed seed – unless spent flower heads are cut off (all!). Easily dug in open ground, difficult to eradicate amidst rootstocks, the fleshy roots swell in the tiniest crack.

CERASTIUM
Caryophyllaceae
C. tomentosum
Italy
A well-established SNOW-IN-SUMMER needs little summer watering and in the Mediterranean flowers in spring. Sunny rocks or gravel will keep winter foliage dry. Clipping into rounded shapes maintains compact cushion-like growth. Propagation: cuttings (easy).
p.120

CERATONIA
Leguminosae/Caesalpinioideae
C. siliqua
E Mediterranean
Native to stony regions, a beautiful shiny mass of foliage if left to grow naturally, the evergreen bushy CAROB (5-10m) may also be shaped as a tree. Wind moulds it lop-sided. Flowers are insignificant. Bean-like pods are an important crop (animal fooder, medicinal use). Children relish their high sugar content. Healthy, no particular soil requirements, drought-tolerant once established. Summer watering induces root crown rot. Maintenance means raking up the beans. Far-reaching roots may lift paving stones. Propagation: seed.
p.121

Centranthus ruber 'Albus

Ceratonia siliqua

CERATOSTIGMA Plumbaginaceae
Near drought-tolerant subshrubs (also irrigation-tolerant), coming back to life somewhat late in spring, are valued for their gentian-blue flowers from summer to autumn. No special soil requirements, they require full sun or half shade. With no health problems, maintenance means cutting back for compact growth. Transplanting requires care. Propagation: cuttings, division (*C. griffithii, C. plumbaginoides*).

C. griffithii Himalaya
Perennial (50×100cm).

C. plumbaginoides W China
In warm areas a perennial ground cover (15-20cm), spreading fast by underground runners in loose soil.

C. willmottianum China, Tibet
This deciduous shrub (1×1m) sprouts from the base in spring. More open growth than *C. griffithii*, larger flowers, better hardiness. p.121

C. occidentalis California
Native to California foothills, purple spring bloom covers the smaller WESTERN REDBUD for weeks. Winter cold improves flowering.

C. siliquastrum E Mediterranean
The larger JUDAS TREE is native to sunny, dry, rocky hills. Give excellent drainage. Tart flower buds adorn salads. Many cultivars from pale pink to magenta, 'Album' a fine sight. p.121

Ceratostigma willmottianum

CERCIS Leguminosae/Papilionoideae
The deciduous REDBUD is shrubby or grows into a middle-sized tree. Spectacular pink flowers cover branches, twigs and trunks before the leaves come out. Softly rounded leaves turn golden in autumn. Transplanting requires care. Avoid planting bare-rooted plants, shorten side-branches and stake well. The below are drought-tolerant, resistant to honey fungus, maintenance-free. Propagation: abundant seed.

Cercis siliquastrum

Chamaerops humilis, wild stand

CESTRUM   Solanaceae

Native to the tropical Americas. Mostly evergreen (1.5-4m), CESTRUM are quick-growing shrubs with rank, often graceful growth. They appreciate fertile, generously mulched soil in dappled shade and, once established, need little additional water (more in a sunny position). They recover if dried up or frozen. Prune for compactness, taking out old stems. Disguise bare stems by evergreens. Easy propagation: cuttings, suckers. Self-layered plants quickly gain in size. A wide choice is available: p.122

C. aurantiacum   Guatemala
Deciduous in colder climates. White berries follow orange late spring to summer flowers. Crushed leaves give off an unpleasant scent. Can be trained on a wall. 'Album' white-flowered.

Cestrum hybrid

C. elegans (C. purpureum)   Mexico
Among the tallest. Evergreen, downy growth, red to purple flower panicles from summer onwards, later poisonous purple berries. Quite drought-tolerant.

C. nocturnum   Caribbean
NIGHT JESSAMINE grows tallest. Long slender shoots carry greenish-yellow, strongly scented flowers.

C. parqui   Chile
Train the deciduous WILLOW-LEAVED JESSAMINE with a single trunk or as a shrub or cut back to ground every year for compactness. Greenish-yellow summer to autumn bloom.

CHAMAEROPS   Palmae
C. humilis   W Mediterranean
A maquis member, native to poor sandy or rocky soils in full sun or dappled shade from seashores to high altitudes, the western MEDITERRANEAN FAN PALM (PALMITO) tolerates snow. Single-trunked or in clumps, it slowly reaches 1-4m, in gardens occasionally more (irrigation-tolerant). Amber inedible fruits follow creamy spring inflorescences. Leaf petioles are spiny (beware near path or pool). Plant seed *in situ* or in pots. Virtually pest-free, this low-maintenance palm is a mainstay of waterwise gardens to which it gives, even when young, instant style. Use as accent plant or in formal groups. Larger specimens in containers shade terraces or paved areas. Fine leaf fibres fashion brooms or baskets.   p.13, 53, 122

CHASMANTHE   Iridaceae
C. floribunda   Cape
Over winter, long lance-shaped leaves (60-100cm) rise from corms and, together with the long-lasting winter flowers, are *Chasmanthe*'s attraction. Easy to grow, allow it to expand into ever lusher clumps until crowded. It likes dappled shade or full sun, a cool root run with plentiful compost and, in coldest regions, mulch protection. Propagation: seed; also remove dormant offsets which flower the second season. The rare var. **duckittii** has yellow flowers.   p.122

CHOISYA   Rutaceae
C. ternata   Mexico
The MEXICAN ORANGE (1-2.5m), native to semi-arid regions, is a rounded, shiny-leaved shrub, profusely covered from spring to autumn with white fragrant flower clusters. *Choisya* transplants well (but cut back) and can be clipped. Drought-tolerant, low-maintenance and pest-free, plant an evergreen mound or attractive hedge wherever you want i.e. under oak where no summer watering is done. Propagation: seed, autumn offshoots, cuttings.   p.123

CHORISIA   Bombacaceae
C. speciosa   S America
This spiny-trunked tree is a drought-tolerant, hardy addition to Mediterranean gardens. Pink orchid-like flowers

Chasmanthe floribunda var. *duckittii*

Cistus ladanifer

are a glorious sight. *Chorisia* accepts a wide range of soils and is pest-and maintenance-free. Propagation: seed in spring. Suitable where animals graze.

CHRYSANTHEMUM   Compositae
C. coronarium   Mediterranean
In spring, the annual CROWN DAISY carpets cultivated and uncultivated fields with golden bloom. It also spreads by seed in gardens.   p.22

C. frutescens see **Argyranthemum f.**

CINNAMOMUM   Lauraceae
C. camphora   China, Japan
The evergreen CAMPHOR TREE (8-15m) grows into a refined, spreading shade tree or tall screen. Lemon-green to rosy spring foliage is startling. Requires deep, well-drained (sandy) soils in warm, mulched positions and weekly summer watering (monthly once established). No health problems if well-planted. Propagation: cuttings or fresh seed. Spreading roots inhibit other growth beneath and nearby.

CISTUS   Cistaceae
The evergreen ROCK ROSE (30-200cm) is a maquis native. In sun, spring bloom covers rounded shrubs which thrive in adverse conditions of poor, stony soils in regions dry in summer. Fibrous shallow roots (good for erosion control) are in close relationship with soil microflora; thus drainage and mulch are vital. Pampered plants do not live long. For compact growth trim after bloom. Easy to raise from seed. Use quick-growing rock roses widely as pioneers for low-maintenance cover. The highly aromatic large-flowered species deserve special attention.   p.55

C. x aguilarii
Tall upright (120-150cm), becoming bare at base. Same lovely flowers as parent *C. ladanifer.*

C. albidus   W Mediterranean
This grey-leaved, felty rock rose (50-90cm) often covers bare rocky limestone areas. Crinkled, pink flowers.
                p.21

C. ladanifer   SW Mediterranean
Grow the tall fragrant LADANUM under pine. Large solitary white flowers, often blotched purple.   p.44, 123

C. laurifolius   SW Mediterranean
Resembles the former, but flowers with a yellow basal blotch are clustered among larger leaves.

C. monspeliensis   SW Mediterranean
This aromatic shrub, barely reaching 90cm, covers the garrigue with snow when small white flowers come out.

C. populifolius   W Europe
Spreading and straggly, carries bronze drooping buds and white yellow-centred flowers. It requires space to grow freely.

C. x purpureus
This tall rounded shrub (100-150cm) suits coastal areas. Pink flowers.

Citrus limon

C. salviifolius   Mediterranean
A flat cushion (50-70cm), soft sage-like leaves and smaller white flowers.

CITRUS   Rutaceae
Native mostly to China and the West Indies, half a dozen well-known crops are useful container plants (grapefruit, kumquat, lemon, lime, orange), valued for evergreen foliage, edible, ornamental fruits and exquisite scent. All require deep, well-mulched soils in warm, watered settings. – I grew from pips spiny shrubs which bear wrinkled 'lemon' of uncertain origin. What fruit lack in looks, these plants replace by sturdy growth and low water requirements.
                p.123

Choisya ternata

Clematis cirrhosa

CLEMATIS   Ranunculaceae
These slow-growing climbers require a
well-drained cool root run in sun or dappled shade. Amply mulched, they
entwine shrubs or cascade over
supports. *C. cirrhosa, C. flammula* and
C. texensis will grow in dry soils. Choice
cultivars prefer cooler regions with high
air humidity. Propagation: fresh seed,
root-cuttings in winter.

C. armandii   W China
Evergreen glossy leaves, covered profusely with white scented spring bloom,
make a truly beautiful sight. 4-6m once
established, it rambles over shrubs, railings or trees.

C. cirrhosa   Mediterranean
Native to woodlands among shrubs or in
rock crevices, holding onto any branchlet at hand. Shiny leaves die back in hottest summers but regrow with autumn
rains. Best near paths where creamy
winter bells can be appreciated from
nearby. This brave little plant, gradually
reaching 2m, can be kept at 50cm with
pruning. var. **balearica** has flowers pale
cream, purple-spotted or flecked within.
Pink forms are rare.   p.124

C. flammula   Mediterranean
Trusses of white, foamy summer bloom
grow up into trees or cover shrubs, their
fragrance pervading the air. If cut to

ground, growth resprouts vigorously.
Beautiful where trained on wire fences.
p.21, 101

C. montana   China
Plant where a new garden needs quick
colour, at the foot of open shrubs or
trees.

C. orientalis   Mediterranean, Asia
This drought-tolerant climber (4-5m),
deciduous foliage on slender shoots,
carries abundant yellow bells on new
season's growth. In winter cut by half.

C. texensis   Texas
Deciduous, semi-woody (2-3m) with
dense glaucous foliage and nodding
carmine flowers. Tie slender stems to a
support.

CLEOME   Capparidaceae
C. isomeris (Isomeris arborea)
California
Cherished for bright yellow flowers,
grows wild on coastal bluffs and sandy
desert washes (excellent drainage),
reaching 1m. Monthly watering in
summer improves looks. A reliable
plant for difficult places, it suits natural
gardens. Increased by seed.

CLIANTHUS
Leguminosae/Papilionoideae
C. puniceus   Australia
The spectacular PARROT'S BEAK with
brilliant red claw-like flowers, a usually
evergreen trailer from the desert, is an
excellent pest-free choice for hot, sandy
soils or any well-drained sunny site.
Pinch back for floriferous growth.
Autumn-sow *in situ* near terrace walls or
fences and allow it to grow with winter
rain. Hot water treatment accelerates
germination. Avoid root disturbance.

CLIVIA   Amaryllidaceae
C. miniata   Natal
This vigorous, pest-free perennial,
popular for shaded or semi-shaded
ground, flowers intermittently through
the year and provides evergreen cover in
problem sites. Roots prefer a confined
run (containers, crevices, shallow soil).
Plant tuber tops at soil level, mulching
well. Although used to summer rain in its

Cneorum tricoccon, wild stand

Cneorum tricoccon, wild stand

home, clivia adapts to Mediterranean winter rain plus monthly summer watering. Easy propagation: fresh seed (your own?), division. p.32

CLYTOSTOMA — Bignoniaceae
C. callistigioides (Bignonia speciosa) — Argentina

Another bignonia, the exuberant ARGENTINE TRUMPET VINE can climb a long way. An ideal plant to cover unsightly positions with yellow-purple bloom, but not in a restricted space. Tendrils need support. Prune in winter.

CNEORUM — Cneoraceae
C. tricoccon — W Mediterranean

The SPURGE OLIVE (50-90cm), an evergreen leathery-leaved shrub, flowers throughout the year except over hottest summer months. Pretty red berries follow suit. A so-called endemic, native to localized areas in dry stony soil, it grows together with oak, olive, carob, lentisc, juniper, *Chamaerops*, *Phillyrea angustifolia* and *Rhamnus*. *Cneorum* lives on winter rain but tolerates summer water (excellent drainage). It transplants reluctantly, but propagates easily (seed, cuttings). Clip for compact growth or allow it to grow as it will. A 'new' plant, reasonably quick, always tidy, it could well replace box. p.124

COLCHICUM — Liliaceae/Colchicaceae

Exquisite pale lavender to amethyst flowers come up from corms with first autumn rains. Basal leaves follow, dying down as summer arrives. Should you consider financial sacrifices, plant generously 'The Giant' single, or the flawless double 'Waterlily'.

C. cupanii — C Mediterranean

Star-shaped purple pink flowers, native to dry grassy fields.

C. longiflorum (C. neapolitanum) — W Mediterranean

Resembling **C. autumnale**, for dry sand (beach gardens).

C. stevenii — E Mediterranean

Bright purple pink flowers in dry rocky places.

COLEONEMA — Rutaceae
C. pulchrum — SW Cape

Also sold as *Diosma pulchra* it is a rounded, finely branched shrub (1-1.5m). Minute lavender-rose bloom covers the delicate foliage from winter to spring. It requires well-drained soil in full sun and occasional summer watering until established. Hot dry autumns ripen the wood best. May transplant when small. Easy propagation: cuttings, seed. Maintenance: a lazy gardener's dream! Always neat, with no health problems, a key plant for any garden. p.125

COLUTEA — Leguminosae/Papilionoideae
C. arborescens — Mediterranean

The deciduous BLADDER SENNA (2-3m) has delicate leaves and yellow bloom. An open shrub for poor, disturbed soils in hottest dry locations. Trim after flowering for bushiness. Propagation: autumn cuttings, spring sowing.

CONVOLVULUS — Convolvulaceae

Thrives in dry soil under hot sun. Several are troublesome weeds (field bindweed *C. arvensis*). Propagation of desirable species: seed *in situ* or cuttings. See also *Ipomoea*.

C. althaeoides ssp. tenuissimus — Mediterranean

Feathery light growth, delicate pink summer flowers on slender shoots. Control by growing in a container.

C. cneorum — Mediterranean

The non-invasive SILVERBUSH (50×50cm) has silken-grey leaves and white summer bloom. Plant on sunny, well-

Convolvulus sabatius

drained banks among rock as a fire-retardant cover. Frequent clipping keeps this drought-tolerant shrublet compact.

C. sabatius (C. mauritanicus) — Mediterranean

Use the evergreen, perennial GROUND MORNING GLORY where harsh growing conditions prevent it from becoming invasive. Gravel keeps foliage dry. p.125

COPROSMA — Rubiaceae

Grown for its glossy evergreen leaves and wide tolerance to seawind, drought, sun or shade, it takes kindly to pruning. Best in part-shade with weekly summer watering. Easily increased from cuttings.

C. x kirkii

covers banks with small-leaved, far-reaching growth.

C. lucida — New Zealand

Large lacquered leaves are superb.

C. repens — New Zealand

TAUPATA or MIRROR PLANT (2-5m) is an acclaimed fast-growing coastal windbreak, spreading and mat-forming but not creeping as its name suggests. p.125

Coprosma repens

Coleonema pulchrum

Coreopsis gigantea, wild stand at Point Dume, California

under oak, coastal exposure and, once established, grows with winter rain. Can be clipped to desired shape (box-like hedge). Health problems nil, minimal maintenance. Propagation: cuttings, seed.

C. buddleioides   New Zealand
Selective pruning suits its large leaves better than overall clipping.

C. cotoneaster   New Zealand
A densely branched rigid shrub, native to drier scrublands.

C. macrocarpa   New Zealand
Small tree, larger leaves, attractive flowers.

CORDYLINE   Agavaceae
C. australis   New Zealand
This evergreen rosette plant with sword-like leathery leaves and scented, creamy flower panicles in early summer, grows single-trunked to 2-3m from where branching starts. The undemanding CABBAGE TREE appreciates sunny locations, deep soil for carrot-like roots, ample mulch, summer water depending on locations. Pruning encourages multiple trunks (use sections as cuttings). Blue berries (spring-sown) multiply your stock. Use as coastal accent plant, near pools, in containers, wherever litter-free features are appreciated.

C. baueri   New Zealand
Dwarf, clump-forming with wider leaves.

COREOPSIS   Compositae
Useful, drought-tolerant annuals or evergreen perennials with summer to autumn bloom (mostly yellow). Cutting

down after bloom gives a second flush of flowering. These easily divided pioneer plants and colourful ground covers suit coastal gardens with well-drained light, sandy soil in full sun. No health problems.

C. gigantea   California
Perennial fleshy stems around 1m, short-lived.   p.126

C. maritima   California
The SEA DAHLIA (40-80cm) naturalizes freely. Tuberous taproots need adequate soil depth.

C. verticillata   USA
Perennial (60-90cm), maximum drought-tolerance.

COROKIA   Cornaceae
Known in England and the USA for some time, evergreen COROKIA (1-3m) are mostly compact, twiggy shrubs with shiny, leathery leaves. Attractive drupes follow starry, delicately scented yellow spring flowers. Tolerates dry shade

Coronilla valentina ssp. *glauca*

CORONILLA
          Leguminosae/Papilionoideae
Evergreen dense scraggy shrubs, CROWN VETCH (60-140cm) are native to open woodland or dry grassy scrub. Golden flowers scent the air from winter to spring. Plant in lean, well-drained calcareous soil on sunny slopes and enjoy their easy-going ways in the natural garden. Overhead irrigation results in premature death. Clip for compactness where plants fall apart. Propagation: autumn cuttings, seed. Small self-sown seedlings transplant.

C. emerus   Mediterranean
The SCORPION SENNA graces Riviera hillsides with fresh green foliage. 2-3 flowers per umbel.

C. valentina ssp. **glauca** Mediterranean
Native to coastal cliffs. Blue-green foliage, 4-12 flowers per umbel.   p.126

CORREA   Rutaceae
The AUSTRALIAN FUCHSIA, a small compact shrub from heathlands and sandy or rocky coasts, differs from the 'real' fuchsia by drought-tolerance and evergreen small rounded leathery leaves, felty beneath. Pendent flowers are most attractive. Easy to raise, required are free-draining soils (lime-free, sandy, humus-enriched) in a well-aerated but sheltered position in dappled shade. Mulch well and water until established. Tolerates short-term frost. Autumn cuttings in sand flower soon after rooting. Excellent health, maintenance-free. Plant as reli-

able shrubby ground cover in unwatered gardens, above a path to appreciate pendent bloom, also in containers.

C. alba S Australia
Arching growth (70-100cm) with waxy white summer bloom; use as coastal hedge, untouched by animals. 'Pinkie' has pale pink flowers.

C. backhousiana (C. backhouseana) Tasmania
A heat-tolerant hedge (1-2m) with greenish bells.

C. pulchella (C. neglecta) S Australia
Brittle prostrate shoots (60-100cm) with rosy-red flowers require wind-shelter. Cold-hardy.

C. reflexa (C. speciosa) S Australia
Considered the best ornamental species, bushy to 150-250cm, also prostrate. Small heart-shaped leaves and flowers in many colours are both variable. Few cultivars are named. Somewhat lime-tolerant. p.127

CORYNOCARPUS Corynocarpaceae
C. laevigata New Zealand
Evergreen glossy 20cm leaves are the chief attraction of the drought-tolerant NEW ZEALAND LAUREL (6-10m). Grow in well-mulched garden soil (full sun or half-shade) as slow-growing, low-maintenance shrub or tree. Poisonous, plum-like fruit contain readily germinating seed.

Cotoneaster franchetii (not listed)

Correa reflexa hybrid

COSMOS Compositae
This colourful drought-tolerant, self-sowing Mexican annual does well in Mediterranean regions.

COTINUS Anacardiaceae
C. coggygria (Rhus cotinus) S Europe, Asia
The deciduous SMOKE TREE (3-7m) grows into a large rounded shrub. Attractive feathery panicles follow faded flowers. It requires cold winters, dry summers and full sun on poor stony soil with excellent drainage. Transplant while dormant, even when older (but cut back). Use as a pleasing, dense background in the natural garden and clip for shape or for handsome young foliage. No health problems if cultural demands are fulfilled; resistant to honey fungus. Propagation: seed, 'Purpureus' by layering.

COTONEASTER Rosaceae
COTONEASTER carries gracefully arching or creeping branches which are covered with white or pink spring flower clusters and bright red berries for Christmas. It likes ample space in full sun and good drainage. Widely tolerant, it needs little attention once well-established. Occasional deep watering may be required in hottest regions. Selective pruning enhances plant structure (clipping results in stubby growth). Susceptible to several pests and diseases, sometimes host to these, so do not plant near oak or apple. Cut back overgrown or diseased plants hard. Use in dry gardens as undemand-

ing ground cover, background planting, hedge, erosion control or coastal windbreak. Bees are attracted by bloom, birds by berries. Propagation: cuttings in autumn. p.127

C. buxifolius India
Native to the Nilgiri Hills, this arching shrub (1-2m) suits rock gardens. Tiny leathery leaves.

C. congestus Himalaya
Mounding growth (1×2m), slowly spreading.

C. dammeri China
Prostrate, rooting branch tips creep fast along 3m, tolerating half shade. 'Low-fast' is flattest ground cover.

C. lacteus China
Larger leaves than most others on wide-reaching branches, 2-3m tall. Invasive, it is useful in adverse sites as a hedge.

C. microphyllus Himalaya
Very drought-tolerant and hardy.

COTYLEDON Crassulaceae
C. orbiculata S Africa
Succulent, shrubby (60×60cm) and drought-tolerant, native to hot, dry sand, large leaves store water. In summer, orange heads with pendent tubular flowers rise from leaf clusters. Where frost occurs, choose warmest locations. Low-maintenance in containers, litter-free near pools. Propagation: leaves, stem cuttings. p.127

Cotyledon orbiculata

Crinum moorei 'Roseum'

CRASSULA Crassulaceae

Succulent, drought-tolerant CRASSULA in many shapes and sizes carries white, pink or scarlet flowers. Health problems are virtually non-existent where well-grown which means sandy, compost-enriched, well-drained soil, full sun or part-shade, air circulation, wind protection, additional water in driest locations. It transplants and propagates well (leaf or stem cuttings, spring-sown seed). Low-maintenance, litter-free crassulas suit second homes, pools and containers or cover ground on a gravel bed.

C. coccinea Cape mountains
Neat 30-40cm, showy and lasting crimson summer bloom. Inland dappled shade is required. Frost-tolerant.

C. multicava Cape
One of the quickest to increase and cover shady ground. p.128

Crassula multicava

C. muscosa S Africa
MOSS CYPRESS is an attractive, hardy ground cover.

C. ovata (C. argentea) Cape to Natal
The JADE PLANT, a rounded, winter-flowering shrub (90-150cm), grows wild on mountain slopes. Similar to *Cotyledon orbiculata* (differentiated by pink flower clusters), it harmonizes with formal plantings or pools.

C. perfoliata Cape
Grows to 40-80cm where roots find a cool run among rock. Spectacular sickle-shaped leaves, long-lasting red flower-heads.

C. socialis Cape
Cushion-forming rosettes spread on rock, small white-flowering stems 10cm tall. A recommended ground cover.

Crataegus monogyna

CRATAEGUS Rosaceae

In spring, abundant flowers cover HAWTHORN, cherished by bees. Plentiful red autumn berries feed birds. These wide-spreading trees or shrubs perform best in sun (any soil). They drop their leaves in prolonged summer drought but shoot again with autumn rains (resist the temptation to irrigate). Prune inward-growing branches for a pleasing outline and burn aggressive spines which persist for years on compost heaps. On farms, animals graze under their flowering canopy or behind an unpruned flowering hedge (impenetrable!).

C. azarolus Mediterranean
4-8m. Amber edible fruits follow pretty white bloom.

C. laevigata (C. oxyacantha) Mediterranean, India
The ENGLISH HAWTHORN carries pinkish flowers, red fruit.

C. x lavallei 'Carrierei'
Grows to 6×5m, less thorny. White flowers and long-lasting autumn colour. Large pretty fruits.

C. monogyna Mediterranean
Shrubby 2-6m, best shaped as tree. Fragrant white flowers. Although bacterial fireblight may occur, I have not noticed die-back with native *Crataegus*. p.128

CRINUM Amaryllidaceae

Long leaves shade the ground. Plant giant bulbs in full sun just below surface wherever glorious summer flowers are appreciated (also in containers). To free-draining soil add sand, compost, bonemeal. Although native to streamsides in tropical coastal regions, *Crinum* flourish with Mediterranean winter rain and weekly summer water. Overcrowding ensures best bloom. Propagation: fresh seed, division when dormant. p.69

C. bulbispermum S Africa
White pink-flushed flowers.

C. moorei E Cape
White fragrant flowers on tall stems bloom in woodlands. p.128

C. x powellii
Grown outdoors in protected English gardens, hardy to a short-term frost, this child of the above has clear rosy flower umbels. 'Album' is a breathtaking sight.

CRITHMUM   Umbelliferae
C. maritimum   Mediterranean
Edible SAMPHIRE grow on salt spray-exposed coastal rock. Tasty with salads.

CROCOSMIA   Iridaceae
Light green, sword-like leaves rise from corms, profuse mostly orange flower spikes follow on tall stems (late spring, summer). Plant MONTBRETIA in compost-enriched, well-drained and mulched soil with afternoon shade and they will mature into dense clumps. Water weekly until foliage dries up (together with native vegetation). Propagation: seed, division.

C. x crocosmiiflora
Of garden origin, it flowers when most bulbous plants have died down. Naturalizes freely.

C. masonorum   S Africa, Natal
Native above 1000m, flower spikes rise and arch to 1m.

CROCUS   Iridaceae
Species, flowering earlier than Dutch hybrids, have smaller flowers. When summer is over, plant corms in well-drained porous soil (beware rotting), cover with 5cm soil. Contractile roots pull corms to the right depth. CROCUS adapt to cooler hill gardens, massed under deciduous shrubs, between stepping stones, among rock, wherever the low sun reaches.

C. cancellatus   E Mediterranean
Edible corms grow wild on rocky hills. Leaves follow white to pale lilac autumn flowers.

C. chrysanthus   Balkans
Early in the year, clear orange flowers scent grassy, rocky fields.

C. corsicus   Corsica, Sardinia
Purple spring flowers grace stony pastures.

C. goulimyi   Greece
Exquisite lavender autumn flowers also thrive in southern California.

C. sativus   E Mediterranean
Lilac-purple autumn flowers' large orange stigma produce saffron food dye, requiring a generous supply.

Cussonia paniculata

C. sieberi ssp. **atticus**
'Bowles White' for the White Garden. 'Firefly' lavender- blue, one of the earliest.   p.129

C. speciosus   Near East
Easy to grow, quick to multiply, one of the showiest in autumn (lavender).

C. tommasinianus   Balkans
Purple flowers appear early in woodlands on limestone.

CUPRESSUS   Cupressaceae
C. arizonica var. **glabra**   California
ARIZONA CYPRESS (12×6m), very drought-tolerant, suits hot inland deserts. 'Pyramidalis' has glaucous foliage.

C. macrocarpa   California
MONTEREY CYPRESS (7-12m), a fast-growing coastal windbreak, has a wide-spreading branch structure. Beware cypress canker fungus (cut out and burn diseased growth).

C. sempervirens
     Mediterranean, W Asia
ITALIAN CYPRESS grows wild in the eastern Mediterranean, regionally dying out due to the fungal *Seiridium cardinale*. Replace by Australian *Actinostrobus* and *Callitris,* Californian *Calocedrus,* South African *Widdringtonia* or Mediterranean *Tetraclinis.* 'Stricta' with compact slim growth (12-20m) provides coastal regions with an accent plant.   p.35

Note: Worshipped in Cyprus since antiquity, mentioned in the bible, traditionally planted around cemeteries as a symbol of mourning (said to contain microbia-killing substances).

CUSSONIA   Araliaceae
These spectacular drought-tolerant trees are native to summer rain regions (humid summers, dry winters). In my garden they thrive with Mediterranean winter rain. Plant in well-drained sandy loam in warmest locations and water until established. Maintenance-free cussonias are prominent in waterwise gardens. Use this litter-free accent plant in containers and wherever a large-leaved silhouette is needed. Propagation: seed, cuttings in later years.

Crocus sieberi 'Firefly'

Cyclamen persicum

C. paniculata S Africa
A tuft of greyish green leaves on long stalks tops the bare corky trunk (3m). A single branching may occur. Smaller, suited to most gardens and more drought-tolerant than *C. spicata*. p.129

C. spicata S Africa
3-5m, dark green leaves. Older plants branch.

CYCAS Cycadaceae
C. revoluta SE Asia
The cycad family is a living fossil. Having lived that long, many adaptive qualities have evolved. SAGO PALMS, slow-growing with moderate water demands, suit containers in sun or shade. They are a costly acquisition; once the financial sacrifice is made, propagate by seed or young shoots. p.37, 72, 130

Cycas revoluta

CYCLAMEN Primulaceae
CYCLAMEN are native to stony places. Basal leaves are often attractively blotched. Flower petals, faintly scented, are white, rose or ruby red. Plant tubers half-buried in well-drained humusy soil in open woodlands, thickets or among rock. Cyclamen will come up again if you allow them to die down in summer. Easily propagated by seed.

C. balearicum Balearic Is.
Greyish mottled leaves and minute white flowers thrive in the undergrowth of evergreen woodlands.

C. coum E Mediterranean
Large winter and spring flowers, native to lower mountain sides.

C. graecum Greece
Extremely beautiful leaves, rich pink autumn flowers.

C. hederifolium (C. neapolitanum)
Mediterranean
Summer to autumn flowers rise from limestone-tolerant, hardy tubers.

C. persicum E Mediterranean
The parent of today's large-flowered house plants, heart-shaped leaves frame sweet scented white to pink winter flowers. p.130

CYMBIDIUM Orchidaceae
They are not Mediterranean climate plants, but do well in it, even tolerate snow. Let spill from shaded rock, lean onto gnarled roots, also plant in clay

Cymbidium hybrid

pots (plastic ones topple over) and place under trees such as oak. They soak up winter rain and are refreshed by weekly watering in summer. Oak bark is a good growing medium (collect your own). Feed occasionally with weak fertilizer while in flower or active growth. Move indoors to protect flowers from rain. p.130

CYNARA Compositae
C. cardunculus Mediterranean
Perennial, edible CARDOON grows wild around the Mediterranean.

C. scolymus Mediterranean
The GLOBE ARTICHOKE has elegantly arching grey leaves. Use large flower buds for eating or long-lasting flowers for dry flower arrangements. Grown in vegetable and in flower gardens, plant in rows for formal effects, in groups as drought-tolerant ground cover, on its own for leaf texture. For culinary use, give enriched, well-drained soil and water weekly. Plant offsets in spring or autumn. p.131

• **CYTISUS** Leguminosae/Papilionoideae
BROOMS are a large group of drought-tolerant, sometimes invasive evergreen or deciduous shrubs (further broom include *Spartium, Genista*). Widely used for weeks of spring flower, they grow in full sun in sandy, well-drained soil, are tolerant of salt-laden winds, pollution and thin soil. Cut back or trim for compact growth. *Cytisus* are poisonous and resent root disturbance. Propagation: presoaked or self-sown seed (individual

Cynara scolymus

pots); or cuttings with a heel in summer. Wide tolerance, combined with copious seed, mean they are invasive (beware *Cytisus monspessulanus, racemosus, scoparius*). A more reliable choice is non-aggressive garden hybrids which come in bright shades.

C. battandieri see **Argyrocytisus b.**

C. x **kewensis**
Grown at Kew since 1891, it slowly trails and spreads to 30×100cm. Will cascade over a low wall.

C. x **praecox**
The deciduous, tall WARMINSTER BROOM, lighter coloured than most, is quite hardy. Try 'Albus' or 'Allgold'.

C. purgans   Provence, Mediterranean
A golden splash from spring to summer, reaching 30-70cm.

DAIS   Thymelaeaceae
D. cotinifolia   S Africa
The briefly deciduous DAIS (3-4m) is a native to evergreen forest margins on steep rocky mountain slopes. Its light structure casts little shade. Profuse pale pink spring flowers attract bees. Woody bracts persist like tiny brown stars. This moderately frost-hardy, maintenance-free tree requires a deep, cool root run in compost-enriched, well-drained and mulched soil, with shade from afternoon sun. During hottest summer months water weekly. Irrigation-tolerant. Propagation: seed. Harvested in the wild, the bark provides high quality rope. p.131

DASYLIRION   Agavaceae
D. acrotrichum   Mexico
Endangered in the wild, the SOTOL, a statu-esque *Yucca*-like accent plant with a stout trunk and imposing leaf rosette, slowly reaches 2m. The inflorescence with creamy, bell-shaped flowers shoots up twice that height. *Dasylirion* grows naturally in full sun in well-drained, rocky soil, tolerant of alkalinity, drought and part-shade. Propagation: seed in spring.   p.131

DELAIREA   Compositae
D. odorata (Senecio mikanioides)
                         S Africa
Plant the widely naturalized GERMAN IVY, a 'quick and easy' evergreen trailer, where its invasive habit is an asset. Shoots root where they touch the soil. Without watering and with hard pruning shoot growth is curbed.

DELONIX
            Leguminosae/Caesalpinioideae
D. regia (Poinciana r.)   Madagascar
If yours is a large, very hot garden, grow the deciduous FLAMBOYANT TREE (4-7m). Immense fern-like leaves and showy scarlet summer flowers are a spectacu-lar sight. Fairly tolerant of drought and wind, it needs well-drained and mulched soil. Watch out for water needs during hottest months.

Dasylirion acrotrichum

Dais cotinifolia

DELOSPERMA   Aizoaceae
D. ecklonis   W Cape
A trailing 'ice plant', minute white flowers.

DENDRANTHEMA *pacifica* see **AJANIA p.**

DENDROMECON   Papaveraceae
D. rigida ssp. **harfordii**   California
The ISLAND TREE POPPY (2-5m) is said to be the most beautiful of the subspecies and an outstanding asset to natural gar-dens. This neat rounded shrub (seldom a tree) carries large glaucous leaves and abundant golden spring to summer bloom. Growing demands are rather exacting. The brittle taproot requires sandy, well-drained soil in sun (part shade in hottest locations). No trimming and only little summer watering. Seed germinates after fire (see Propagation) and plants regenerate from root crowns.

DEUTZIA   Saxifragaceae
D. gracilis   Japan
The deciduous DEUTZIA covers its elegantly arching branches in spring with 'snow' and will grow in Mediterranean climates. It likes generously mulched garden soil, dappled shade and weekly watering. Pruning out old canes encourages a fountain-like appearance. Low evergreens hide its bare base. Propagation: cuttings.

DIANELLA   Liliaceae/Phormiaceae
D. intermedia   New Zealand
The evergreen, grass-like FLAX LILY or TURUTU (70-90cm) forms tufts in lowland bush, but is seldom grown in gardens. Blue berries follow small white spring flowers in branched sprays. Fibrous roots require porous garden soil (sun or half-shade), a fertile mulch, water for establishment.

DIANTHUS   Caryophyllaceae
This large genus comprises a wide range of useful border plants. Of characteristic Mediterranean cushion shape, also spreading, carnations flower from spring to autumn. Cutting off spent flowers in-

Dimorphotheca pluvialis (white) and *Felicia heterophylla* (blue), photographed at Kirstenbosch, South Africa

duces second bloom. They do well in light, free-draining garden soil and half-shade in hottest regions. Allow them to spread over paving, tumble from walls or cover rock. Propagation: cuttings, division.

D. deltoides   mostly Mediterranean
The MAIDEN PINK (20-25cm) flowers for months in summer, a reliable ground cover.

DICHELOSTEMMA Liliaceae/Alliaceae
D. pulchellum   California
If you can obtain corms, plant spring-flowering BLUE DICKS (30-50cm) wherever dry poor soils in full sun leave few alternatives. Naturalizes if growing conditions are right. Often listed with *Brodiaea*.

DIETES   Iridaceae
Evergreen *Dietes* (FORTNIGHT LILIES in America) grow from creeping rhizomes into large fan-like clumps. Exquisite flowers on wiry stems open also in winter in favourable climates. Valuable small-scale ground covers, easy in fertile, moisture-retentive sunny ground, they also tolerate poor dry soils. Propagation: seed, division (slow).

D. bicolor (Moraea b.)   E Cape
Breathtaking lemon spring flowers 5cm across. Hardy to a short-term frost.

D. iridioides (D. vegeta)   E Cape
Native along moist forest margins, also in dry bushland to 2000m. Widely grown. White summer bloom; next year's flowers grow from the same stems; so don't cut them off.   p.133
Note: Deciduous *Moraea*, often taken for *Dietes*, grow from corms.

DIGITALIS   Scrophulariaceae
Most FOXGLOVES are perennial, all are drought-tolerant and poisonous. Of easy cultivation, they prefer good garden soil and excellent drainage on northern slopes (southern for southern hemisphere gardeners). As small exclamation marks, they spread on gravel or accompany pine. Seed-propagated.

Digitalis purpurea

D. obscura   W Mediterranean
40-70cm, likes stony pastures.

D. purpurea   Mediterranean
The COMMON FOXGLOVE, the tallest of all, often reaches over 1m. Many pink shades. 'Alba' is striking against shiny, dark green myrtle.   p.132

DIMORPHOTHECA   Compositae
are colourful and fast-growing annuals. For similar plants (all called AFRICAN DAISY) see *Arctotis, Osteospermum*.

D. pluvialis   S Africa
The charming, neat and sturdy WEATHER PROPHET, commonly grown, reaches 30cm.   p.132

D. sinuata   Cape
Multicoloured flowers, 20-30cm tall, enhance for long months the warmest location in your garden.

DIOSPYROS   Ebenaceae
D. kaki   China, Japan
The deciduous, hardy PERSIMMON (5-8m) provides all-year interest. Apple green spring foliage turns copper in autumn. Bright orange fruits remain on trees after leaves have fallen and, once

overripe, squash onto the ground. Plant in well-drained garden soil, mulched deeply, watered weekly. For best fruit, plant varieties which do well in your area. p.133

Note: harvest fruit when firm and astringent and ripen in your kitchen to delicious sweetness.

DIPLACUS see *MIMULUS*

DISTICTIS
D. buccinatoria   Bignoniaceae
    Mexico

As all bignonias, the evergreen BLOOD-RED TRUMPET VINE (5-9m) speedily covers ground and walls. Large flower clusters from summer into autumn are best in warmest regions with fertile, well-drained garden soil and watering until established. Restrain by pruning vigorous growth which is unsuitable for fragile pergolas.

DODONAEA
D. viscosa   Sapindaceae
    widespread

Evergreen NATIVE HOPS grows quickly to 2-4m. Winged creamy-pink seed pods follow insignificant flowers among light-green foliage and remain on plants throughout winter. Tolerant of heat or cold, drought or irrigation, poor alkaline or saline soils, coastal saltspray or wind, *Dodonaea* will grow in most locations. Clips into a tidy hedge. Propagation: seed, cuttings.

DOMBEYA
D. x cayeuxii   Sterculiaceae

This spectacular, evergreen and fast South African shrub (2-4m) carries large, felty leaves. In our unheated conserva-

Dietes iridioides

Dombeya x *cayeuxii*

tory, exquisitely scented pink clusters flower through late winter, a few degrees above freezing, yet heat is appreciated. It requires sheltered, sunny locations, compost-rich garden soil, thick mulching, and watering once or twice a week in summer. It transplants well (cut back) and increases easily from cuttings. Dombeyas should be grown more widely, also in large containers (patio, terrace). Bloom is best appreciated from below. p.133

DORYANTHES
D. palmeri   Agavaceae
    Queensland, Australia

An impressive rosette plant of sculptural outlines, the SPEAR LILY (1.5-2m) has stiff, light green leaves. Flowering stems, 2-3m tall, carry heavy trusses of bright red flowers. Resembling an overgrown *Yucca*, it grows in warmest locations in similar conditions.

DOVYALIS
D. caffra   Flacourtiaceae
    E Cape, Natal

The ornamental evergreen KEI APPLE (2.5-3m) spreads slowly into a tree with a spiny crown. Orange fruits follow nectar-rich spring to summer flowers and serve

as fodder. Use as an easy, drought- and frost-tolerant coastal windbreak or impenetrable hedge. Propagation: seed.

DRACAENA
    Agavaceae

These undemanding drought-tolerant accent plants with creamy flower clusters enjoy warm sheltered locations and grow lusher with water. Prune when too tall. Propagation: insert stem cuttings into soil after allowing them to dry for 24 hours.

Note: *Cordyline* has a creeping rootstock, not so *Dracaena*.

Diospyros kaki in autumn

Echium simplex

Echium candicans

D. draco Canary Is.
The DRAGON TREE (3m, taller after a few centuries) is the only *Dracaena* to grow into a tree. Sword-shaped leaves bunch at the top of branches on a solid trunk.

DROSANTHEMUM Aizoaceae
Members of the so-called 'ice plants', similar to *Lampranthus* (p.13), they are useful ground covers and lawn replacements. Mulched with gravel and kept rather dry, they thrive on hot sunny slopes. After flowering, clip for compactness. Easily propagated by rooted branchlets or cuttings.

D. floribundum Cape, Namibia
In spring sheets of palest pink cover the somewhat straggly grey mass which trails widely, rooting as it goes.

D. hispidum Cape, Namibia
Spreads vigorously or curtains walls. Its shocking-pink flowers require careful attention to colour shades.

D. speciosum W Cape
30cm tall, more difficult to establish than the former. Large orange spring flowers are worth the effort.

DUCHESNEA Rosaceae
D. indica (Fragaria i.) Asia
The perennial MOCK STRAWBERRY has yellow flowers while true strawberries have white flowers. Inedible red berries inside are white and insipid. Propagation: run-

ners, bird-dispersed seed. *Duchesnea* invades with long runners where watered. Less vigorous on poor dry soil, where it becomes a flat ground cover for natural gardens.

DUDLEYA Crassulaceae
D. brittonii California
The best-known of a wide range of Californian coastal cliff succulents, compact flour-dusted rosettes on sturdy stems slowly reach 25-50cm. They like light, air and drought under overhangs. Pull off sections which root readily.

ECHEVERIA Crassulaceae
Succulent green or grey rosette plants, native to cool mountain areas. Small flower bells (yellow, pink, red) on slender arching branches grow on as successive flowers open at their tips. Avoid water on the leaves. Drought-tolerant *Echeveria* grow well in containers or on rocks where graceful flowers are seen to advantage. Increase from easily detached offsets or single leaves.

E. elegans Mexico
Quite common, one of the quickest to grow and spread. Avoid hot sun or confined sites; give sufficient light and air.

E. pulvinata Mexico
Worthwhile for its thick downy leaves, attractive autumn colours and bright flowers.

ECHIUM Boraginaceae
ECHIUM is a striking, undemanding plant, related to kitchen borage. Leaves are large, flowers on tall stems spectacular. Tolerant of poor dry soil, plant on sunny southern slopes with an ample well-drained root run. Water weekly to monthly in hottest summer months. No health problems if well-grown. Remove dead flowerheads. Shrubby echiums are propagated by cuttings, biennial ones by seed (also self-sown), transplanted at seedling stage. Use as tall 'exclamation mark' (*E. simplex, E. wildpretii*) or ground cover (*E. candicans*) and thus help their conservation.

E. candicans (E. fastuosum) Madeira
The perennial PRIDE OF MADEIRA (1-2m) is evergreen. Spectacular spring inflorescences in many blue shades rise from well-branched plants, opening first towards the sun. p.134

E. simplex Canary Is.
The biennial PRIDE OF TENERIFE (1.6-2m) resembles *E. wildpretii*, but bears white inflorescences. p.134

E. wildpretii Canary Is.
Largest of all, long lance-like leaves form a sizeable rosette. In the second year, a tall stem with pink flowers shoots up 2m, resembling an oversized *Eremurus*, a dramatic long-lasting sight, after which the plant dies.

ELAEAGNUS Elaeagnaceae
E. angustifolia Mediterranean, Asia
A sturdy drought-tolerant windbreak, the deciduous RUSSIAN OLIVE (3-5m) likes

full sun, but otherwise is undemanding, tolerating sterile or brackish sandy soils and polluted areas. Outstanding for coastal dune reclamation.

E. x ebbingei

Evergreen vigorous growth (2-4m, same width) reaches into shrubs or trees with short hook-like branchlets. Autumn to winter, tiny cream flowers perfume the air far and wide. Later, small rosy fruit promise tart jellies. Drought-, cold- and heat-tolerant, no special soil or exposure requirements, it needs water until established. Transplants even when older. When cut back, it supplies 'green waste' all year for mulch. Unsuitable for small gardens, use where vigorous growth is an asset, as windbreak or speedy hedge, covering unsightly spots with a mass of shiny leaves.   p.135

E. pungens   Japan

Small scented white flowers, later edible red berries adorn the evergreen often spiny SILVERBERRY (2-4m). Easy to propagate: seed, cuttings.

EPILOBIUM   Onagraceae
E. canum (Zauschneria californica)
                                SW California

Perennial, grey-leaved CALIFORNIA FUCHSIA (40-50cm) prospers on dry, sun-drenched slopes. Plant in natural gardens where its lanky growth does not interfere with more orderly plantings. Red trumpet-shaped flowers attract birds (HUMMINGBIRD FLOWER). Invasive in watered gardens.

Elaeagnus x ebbingei

EREMOPHILA   Myoporaceae

Native to SW Australia mostly in hot, dry inlands, several are known as EMU BUSH. Seldom mentioned (not even by the *Plant Finder*), rarely available, they should be grown widely for drought tolerance, aromatic leaves, long-lasting tubular bloom. Cuttings strike well.

E. alternifolia   Australia

1-2m shrub for warm inland gardens, pink or red flowers.

E. glabra   Australia

Yellow flowers almost all year.

E. longifolia   Australia

A small suckering tree (2-4m), one of the tallest with pink flowers. Emus eat the dark berries.

E. maculata 'Aurea'

The best (1-1.5m), widely grown, golden flowers. Foliage is poisonous to stock.

E. oppositifolia   Australia

An elegant, white- or pink-flowering shrub (3-5m).

ERICA   Ericaceae

Over 600 South African plus several Mediterranean species reach sizes from 5-300cm. Needle-like leaves are an adaptation to summer drought and minute, long-lasting flowers a work of art. A carefully chosen site will ensure success. Acid humusy soil with excellent drainage is part of the 'secret' (humus favours mycorrhizal associations). As they originate in coastal areas or fog-shrouded mountainsides they need high air humidity (avoid dry summer air). Weekly summer watering is normally adequate. Clipping dead flowers improves their looks. Propagation is usually left to professionals.

E. arborea   Mediterranean

The reliable TREE HEATH (2-3m) has low maintenance.   p.135

E. bauera (E. bowienana)   SW Cape

The BRIDAL HEATH reaches (1-1.5m). Small white flower clusters droop gracefully from branch tips.

E. lusitanica   Spain, Portugal

The PORTUGUESE HEATH, more delicate than *E. arborea*, has naturalized in SW England.

E. multiflora   Mediterranean

(60-120cm), heat- and cold-tolerant. Rosy-purple flowers intermittently through the year.   p.135

E. patersonia   SW Cape

Native to hill country, shrubby (30-50cm) with golden waxy winter bloom. South-facing buds open first (north-facing for southern hemisphere gardeners).

Erica arborea

Erica multiflora in the wild

Erigeron karvinskianus

E. japonica   China, Japan
The LOQUAT, closely related to *Photinia*, grows gradually into a shrub/tree (4-6m). Stiff leaf rosettes surround scented flower panicles which produce, at winter's end, yellow 'plums' (deliciously sweet when fully ripe). Plant this frost-hardy, moderately drought-tolerant coastal windbreak in a warm location in deep, well-drained soil over limestone. Loquat naturalizes in unexpected places; grafted varieties bear best fruit.   p.136

Eriocephalus africanus

ERIGERON   Compositae
E. karvinskianus (Vittadinia triloba)
                                Mexico
An easy, trailing ground cover or edging-plant, spilling from fissures with dainty white bloom. Foliage turns brown in dry summers but, lightly clipped, comes back with autumn rains. Drought- and irrigation-tolerant, still best with dappled shade, occasional watering and a cool root run. Propagation: division. p.65, 136

ERIOCEPHALUS   Compositae
E. africanus   S Africa
Native to coastal areas, rosemary-like grey foliage grows into a mounding 60×100cm, looking neat all year. White bloom shines from autumn through winter. The KAPOK BUSH prefers a well-drained sunny southern exposure and tolerates clipping. No special soil or water requirements. Readily increased by cuttings. A mainstay of the drought-tolerant garden, of value whenever a fast and reliable mass of grey foliage is required.   p.136

Erysimum linifolium

ERIOBOTRYA   Rosaceae
E. deflexa 'Bronze Improved'
                                China, Taiwan
The stately BRONZE LOQUAT (6m) has coppery spring growth and requires a cool root run with weekly summer watering.

ERIOGONUM   Polygonaceae
Wild BUCKWHEAT (no wheat) are sturdy perennials and shrubs from coasts, calcareous deserts and mountains. Mounding shapes match cushion-shaped Mediterranean vegetation. Woolly leaves mean they are the choice for a drought-tolerant garden. Plant in perfectly

drained, gritty soil, where deep roots remain undisturbed. Water in hot inland areas. Shaping improves their looks. Easy propagation from ample seed.

E. arborescens   S California
Shrubby SANTA CRUZ ISLAND BUCKWHEAT grows 90-120cm. Pale rose-pink bloom complements dried flower arrangements.

E. crocatum   S California
The perennial coastal SAFFRON BUCKWHEAT (30-50cm) has woolly, almost white foliage. Sunny spring to summer bloom.   p.137

E. fasciculatum   California, Nevada
The CALIFORNIA BUCKWHEAT, 30-70cm tall and much wider, is an undemanding ground cover with pale spring to autumn flower clusters. It controls erosion in desert regions. 'Theodore Payne' is a good lawn substitute.

Eriobotrya japonica

Eriogonum crocatum, Penstemon anguineus and Mimulus aurantiacus at the Yerba Buena Nursery, California

Eriogonum giganteum

E. giganteum   S California
SAINT CATHERINE'S LACE, resembling *E. arborescens*, has longer flowering periods.   p.137

ERYSIMUM   Cruciferae
Perennials or annuals bloom sweetly scented in sunny locations, surviving considerable drought. Try them all.

E. cheiri   Greece
The perennial orange-yellow WALLFLOWER reaches 25-50cm.

E. hieraciifolium   Europe
Brilliant orange spring bloom can be sown *in situ*.

E. linifolium   Spain, Portugal
Adorns rock gardens with lilac flowers from autumn to spring.   p.136

ERYTHRINA
Leguminosae/Papilionoideae
Highly ornamental, often prickly, the CORAL TREE dies back in colder winters; spring shoots resprout from mulch-protected rootstocks. Scarlet summer flowers in dense racemes attract bees. No special soil requirements, well-established trees are drought-tolerant, may occasionally need watering in summer. Propagation: cuttings, seed.

E. caffra   E South Africa
This excellent summer shade tree (5-10m) blooms before leaves come out. Branches may be prickly.

E. corallodendrum   Jamaica, Haiti
This deciduous shrub (2m) for warmest coastal gardens flowers profusely.

E. crista-galli   Brazil
The popular COCKSPUR CORAL TREE (3-5m) has spiny branches and flowers on current season's growth.

E. humeana   S Africa, Natal
This splendid fast-growing tree (3-7m) flowers at an early age. Cutting back after flowering encourages branching.

ESCALLONIA   Saxifragaceae
ESCALLONIA is a benefit in any garden which suffers from drought. A sprawling upright shrub with glossy mostly evergreen leaves, it bears white, rosy or pink flower clusters, sometimes throughout the year. No special requirements for soil, exposure or water (but avoid high alkalinity), it is hardy to -10°C. In hot inland gardens grow in partly shaded deep ground, generously mulched. When well-established, it needs little or no summer watering, depending on exposure and soil conditions. Occasionally remove older stems. No health problems observed. Propagation: cuttings, self-layering, suckers, division of older clumps (cut back). An excellent coastal screen, hedge or specimen on woodland borders; wherever ground needs quick covering in sun or shade, use escallonias.

E. bifida   Brazil, Uruguay
Shrubby or tree-like, gradually reaches 2-5m. Terminal flower clusters among

Eschscholzia californica

large leaves are of pearl-like beauty (summer and autumn).

E. rubra
'Woodside' is a spreading ground-hugging dwarf shrublet (40cm) with red bloom. var. **macrantha** 'Ingramii' a bulky 2-3m with large rose pink flowers over warmer months.   p.137

ESCHSCHOLZIA   Papaveraceae
E. californica   California
The annual or perennial drought-tolerant CALIFORNIA POPPY is a glorious spring sight covering meadows and fields with brilliant bloom for weeks, later turning into seed-loaded, self-seeding straw. Conditions have to be right for such a sight, but even a few plants give pleasure.   p.137

Escallonia rubra (right) with *Fatsia* and *Hebe* (left)

Eucalyptus globulus

EUCALYPTUS   Myrtaceae

The evergreen, drought-tolerant GUM species are legion. IRONBARK refers to hard-barked eucalypts, MALLEE to shrubby ones with beautiful branch structures. If you intend to plant dwarf eucalypts, choose MARLOCK. Juvenile leaves often differ from mature ones. Best in deep sandy soils and full sun with good air circulation. *Eucalyptus* tolerate short-term frost, more so with age. *E. gunnii* and *E. viminalis* are among the hardiest. Protect from sudden temperature fall or drying winds. Cold stress, shallow soil, alkalinity, defective drainage result in chlorosis. Nutrient requirements are low. Initial crown-pruning strengthens weak stems, (stake young trees). When cut to ground, they resprout with several trunks from rootstocks and require thinning. Highly appreciated for fast growth, some trees increase 2m a year. Choose for size, foliage, flowers, nectar, shade or wind protection. Select carefully (debris, invasive roots); little comes up below their canopy. Seed-propagated.

Note: Pungent leaf scent is medicinal against the common cold.

E. citriodora   Queensland, Australia
LEMON-SCENTED GUM (10-30m), tall stately trees with smooth grey trunks, carry creamy flowers at the top, out of sight. Roots do not disturb paving.

E. ficifolia   W Australia
The tender RED-FLOWERING GUM (4-10m), covered for months with brilliant bloom, does better on coasts than inland.

E. globulus   Australia
The quick-growing BLUE GUM (14-30m) reaches tallest heights.   p.138

E. gunnii   Tasmania
The hardy CIDER GUM (10-20m), an excellent windbreak or shade tree, grows as far north as Scotland. Young rounded leaves are silvery, mature pointed ones green.

E. kruseana   W Australia
This highly ornamental MALLEE (2-3m) has silvery blue leaves tipped shell-pink. From autumn to winter powdery white buds precede pale yellow bloom. Although adaptable and suited to arid sandy lands, warmth is required. Shape as ground cover or low tree.

E. nicholii   NSW, Australia
The exquisite WILLOW-LEAVED PEPPERMINT (9-20m) tolerates poor rocky ground. Delicate spring foliage has a silvery purple sheen.

E. torquata   W Australia
The highly desirable cold-tender CORAL or COOLGARDIE GUM (3-8m) flowers at an early age (almost all year), branches often weighed down by bloom.

E. viminalis   S Australia
The quick-growing MANNA GUM (30-40m), appreciated by impatient gardeners, tolerates alkaline soils.

EUONYMUS   Celastraceae
E. japonicus   Japan
Evergreen, spreading shrubs (2-3m) with glossy light green foliage, white summer bloom and attractive orange berries at Christmas. Drought-, heat- and frost-tolerant, they demand no special soil or site. Prone to attack by scale insects, avoid confined shady areas and cut infested branches hard back. An excellent background plant, dense hedge or coastal windbreak. Propagation: seed, cultivars by cuttings.   p.138

Note: *Euonymus*, together with *Abelia*, *Elaeagnus* and *Escallonia*, is used wherever water is scarce and a colourful cover needed.

EUPHORBIA   Euphorbiaceae
2000 species to explore, many are succulent or cactus-like, surviving in arid environments, others are shrubs. A wide range grows happily in Mediterranean climates. SPURGES prefer free-draining garden soil on dry, sunny ground. p.45

A word of caution: The milky sap is often poisonous or skin-irritating. Use protective gloves and glasses. In an emergency rinse with ample water, seek professional help.

E. characias   W Mediterranean
Evergreen woody-based herb (70-100cm), exquisite lime winter bloom, thriving in all conditions (poor, dry soil, shade, frost). Cut dried stalks to ground. Propagation: cuttings.

Euonymus japonicus

Eucalyptus globulus

E. dendroides Mediterranean
In summer dries up to a rounded 50-200cm (summer-deciduous), comes back with autumn rain. Clip for compactness. Weedy in coastal S California. p.19, 25

Note: Suited to grazed gardens or life with animals.

E. ingens S Africa
The CACTUS EUPHORBIA (NABOOM) grows to a succulent tree (2-8m), resembling what most people consider a giant cactus. In hot deserts use as striking silhouette.

E. marginata USA
SNOW ON THE MOUNTAIN is an attractive, easy summer annual, best sown *in situ* and later thinned. p.139

E. myrsinites Mediterranean
An attractive, versatile herb, very slow.

E. pulcherrima Mexico
The deciduous to evergreen CHRISTMAS STAR or POINSETTIA (2-3m) requires hot climates. Tropical-looking scarlet bracts surround small yellow flowers. Cut back for ample bloom. Not really suited to the evergreen, hard-leaved Mediterranean vegetation, but try 'Alba', 'Crema' or 'Rosea' for more restrained effects.

EURYOPS Compositae
Among the best for Mediterranean gardens, these fast-growing evergreen shrubs are mound-forming. Daisy-like yellow bloom rises from autumn to early summer above finely divided often silvery foliage. Will grow in any soil, but require full sun in warm locations (avoid frost), good drainage, ample mulch, monthly deep watering in hottest months. Clip for compactness. Propagation: cuttings.

E. abrotanifolius S Africa
Shrub-like (70-100cm). May seed heavily (pull out surplus).

E. acraeus S Africa
A compact shrub (50-100cm), native to Drakensberg pastureland.

E. pectinatus S Africa
One of the very best for year-round performance (70-150cm). p.38, 139, 173

Euphorbia marginata

E. virgineus S Africa
Upright 100-250cm. Branches with dainty foliage carry myriads of minute flowers, a golden pillow. p.139

X FATSHEDERA Araliaceae
X F. lizei
(*Fatsia japonica* 'Moseri' x *Hedera hibernica*). Evergreen ivy-like leaves, large and shiny, always look neat. Best in shaded soil with weekly watering (surviving with little). Widely used as ground cover or as carefully trained climber.

FATSIA Araliaceae
F. japonica Japan
A shrub (80-270cm), branching with age. Palmate leathery leaves are its chief attraction. The pretty flowers are minute. FATSIA thrives in shade in leafmould- and compost-enriched soil, heavily mulched. When a site suits it, it may reach truly extravagant sizes. Water demands are moderate (more exposure, more water, weekly during hottest months). Frost and poor soil curb vigor. Propagation: self-seeding or basal shoots. Architectural *Fatsia* gives dull corners in shade instant style; several together create a jungle-like appearance. They suit also coastal gardens and containers. p.26, 40

FELICIA Compositae
F. amelloides S Africa
Wide-spreading BLUE MARGUERITE, an outstanding subshrub for year-round bloom, will ramble into nearby shrubs. Cutting back encourages more bloom and compact growth. An undemanding and drought-tolerant choice for sunny, coastal sites, easily propagated by cuttings. 'Jolly' is dwarf.

F. fruticosa S Africa
The evergreen SHRUB ASTER reaches 40-70cm.

Euryops pectinatus

Euryops virgineus

Ficus carica

FERNS

Ferns are usually associated with water. However, a drought-tolerant range will grow in waterwise gardens. Ample mulching protects growing tips from drying out (see *Polypodium*). SPLEEN-WORT (*Asplenium ceterach, A. onopteris*) is occasionally seen in the wild. *A. scolopendrium* grows in cool caves, said to cure liver ailments. Water-demanding ferns come up naturally near dripping taps (*Adiantum capillus-veneris*). p.175

FERRARIA   Iridaceae
F. crispa (F. undulata)   Cape
Sickle-shaped leaves grow over winter. In spring, toad-coloured stars open in

Ferraria crispa

succession over weeks with an unpleasant smell, but who gets so near? Corms summer-bake in well-drained, sandy sunny soil. Propagation: seed.   p.140

FICUS   Moraceae
FICUS are mostly evergreen. Widely known as indoor plants, in the Mediterranean climate in fairly frost-free areas they will thrive outdoors in mulched garden soil with occasional summer watering. Several grow too tall for any but the largest garden. Glossy leaves, when large, give a tropical look.

F. benjamina   India
The evergreen WEEPING FIG (5-8m) gradually grows into a large, spreading tree with drooping leathery foliage. Useful as watered (not over-watered) container plant on wind-protected covered terraces. Somewhat temperamental towards changing living conditions, so give it time.

F. carica   Mediterranean
Deciduous EDIBLE FIG (3-7m), fast-growing and undemanding, thrives in hot sun. Where frost is common, grow with shelter (wall, roof overhang). Drought-tolerant to the point that seedlings grow from stone walls where roots are difficult to remove. Irrigation or fertilizers promote sappy growth and

reduce fruit quality. Plant where fruit and leaf drop are irrelevant. Beautiful foliage patterns (summer shade) and delicious fruits benefit all gardens, young or old, also all generations. Choose from green, yellow, purple figs those which suit your climate.   p.140

F. elastica   Tropical Asia
RUBBER PLANTS, giant spreading trees in hottest regions, require little light. Most reach shrubby 2-9m, drought-tolerant once well-established. In containers best when pot-bound.   p.17

FRAGARIA   Rosaceae
F. chiloensis   Pacific coast
Evergreen BEACH STRAWBERRY, native to different climates, adapts readily to most gardens. Well-shaped leaves are an asset as ground cover, large white flowers a bonus. Annual 'mowing' ensures compactness. Plant in full sun or dappled shade, water when needed depending on location and soil quality (young leaves signal water needs).

F. vesca   Europe
WILD STRAWBERRY, formerly grown in most orchards, is valued for its exquisite fruit (if somebody has time for picking). A single plant came to my garden, now it borders long paths. Detach plantlets, plant shallowly and water until established; later, less water is required.

FRANCOA   Saxifragaceae
F. sonchifolia   Chile
Evergreen leaves in basal clumps look good all year. In summer, pink spike-like flower racemes rise 40cm. This low-

Freesia alba

maintenance perennial has wide tolerances of cold or heat, sun or shade, water or none. Roots thrive in cool, well-mulched, humusy soil. Easy propagation: seed, division.

FRAXINUS — Oleaceae
F. dipetala — California
Attractive shrub or tree (2-5m) with showy spring flowers, native to foothills. Drought-tolerant and easy.

F. ornus — Mediterranean
Deciduous FLOWERING ASH (6-10m) grows quickly. Whitish scented flower panicles are followed by uncomely seed clusters.

F. uhdei — Mexico
Evergreen in mildest areas, fast-growing SHAMEL ASH (7-9m) likes deep soil in full sun or part shade, occasional penetrating summer watering. Resistant to honey fungus, but susceptible to Texas root rot and hot winds.

F. velutina — SW USA
Deciduous ARIZONA ASH (10-15m), a wide-spreading tree, is excellent for 'summer shade and winter sun'. Flowers are inconspicuous, but golden autumn foliage looks like *Acacia* in bloom. After pruning, seal all wounds to avoid heart rot and later breakage. Poorly drained alkaline soils induce iron chlorosis. 'Rio Grande' tolerates some alkalinity.

FREESIA — Iridaceae
F. refracta — SW Cape
Well-known FREESIA (15-35cm) delights passers-by with exquisitely scented spring bloom. Plant corms 5cm deep in porous, well-drained garden soil in a

Fremontodendron 'California Glory', *Ceanothus* 'Frosty Blue' and *Allium haematochiton* (front right). Rancho Santa Ana Botanic Garden.

raised bed in well-aerated, sunny locations to keep flowers dry. Leave to bake in summer. Increased by seed, *Freesia* naturalizes readily. One cannot grow too many.　　　p.140

FREMONTODENDRON — Sterculiaceae
F. californicum — California
The evergreen FLANNEL BUSH (1-5m) is native to dry chaparral slopes and southern oak woodlands with pine and juniper. It grows fast into an accent plant or screen, covered for a month in spring with golden bloom. Plant in loose, very well-drained sunny soil, stake and water in the first year to get it established. Then, no water other than rain to avoid soil-borne fungus diseases. Tip-pinch for compact growth. Ample seed germinates well (expect many variations). Use 'California Glory' for height and hardiness and a glorious flower display. 'Pacific Sunset' (3-4m) espaliers and tolerates garden conditions such as rich irrigated soil. 'Ken Taylor' flowers all year and suits coastal gardens.　　p.141

F. mexicanum — Baja California
Stiff upright and shrubby (3-6m), red-blushed flowers for a longer period than the above. Beware of irritating hairs on the leaves and capsules.　　p.141

FREYLINIA — Scrophulariaceae
F. lanceolata — S Africa
Rarely mentioned, seldom seen, HONEY BELLS reach a shrubby 2-3m. In midwinter, scented orange panicles weigh down willow-leaved branches. Fairly drought-tolerant, this healthy shrub, flowering at a time when few others do, could be used more widely. Propagation: cuttings.　　p.141

Note: Not everybody may like the scent.

FRITILLARIA — Liliaceae/Liliaceae
Fritillaria are coveted by plant enthusiasts. Slender leafy stems (15-50cm) carry delicate nodding bells, often in

Freylinia lanceolata

Fremontodendron mexicanum

purplish tints. Difficult to establish, fritil-
laries like filtered shade in open woodlands, humusy soil (very wet in winter)
and long summer-baking.

F. biflora California
Maroon MISSION BELLS arise 15-35cm
from basal leaves.

F. meleagris E Mediterranean
Among the showiest, the easy
CHEQUERED LILY is bought relatively
cheap. Suited to shade in cooler hill
gardens, watering should replace failing
winter rains.

F. messanensis Mediterranean
Native to open woody underscrub from
sea level to mountain regions.

FUCHSIA Onagraceae

You know FUCHSIA as a house plant. I
wish I could give the name of the one I
planted years ago outdoors. Partly shaded by tall trees, it mixes in with neighbouring *Cestrum, Begonia* and *Canna,* a
flourishing combination. Protected from
wind and hot sun, fuchsias appreciate
air humidity and a cool run in compost-
enriched, well-drained soil, well-mulched.
Take advantage of deep rock-crevices
on northern slopes. Watering once or
twice a week in summer keeps them
happy. In a congenial spot and given
time to settle in, fuchsias become ever
sturdier. They may drop leaves over
driest summers, but well-established
plants come back with autumn rains.
Easy propagation: cuttings. p.26, 142

F. arborescens C America
Shrubby to 3-5m, attractive red flowers
resemble lilac.

F. magellanica Chile
Myriads of red drooping flowers adorn
arching branches of this suckering
'quick and easy' plant. With a shrub's
support, branches reach 2m. Propagation: cuttings, division. 'Alba' has near-
white bloom. Pale-coloured fuchsias
seem less vigorous.

FURCRAEA Agavaceae
F. bedinghausii Mexico
This fleshy rosette plant has sword-
shaped basal leaves (1.5m) which re-
mind me of *Yucca.* The plant dies down
once the bell-shaped flowers on a giant
stem are over. Multiple bulbils root

Furcraea bedinghausii

Furcraea bedinghausii

Fuchsia cv.

where falling to ground or can be stored
dry for years. Plant in well-drained soil
in hottest, sunny locations, exploit its
architectural qualities. p.142

GAILLARDIA Compositae
G. x grandiflora Garden origin
The perennial BLANKET FLOWER
(50-110cm) suits heat. Summer flowers
are buttercup yellow to burnt gold.
Propagation: seed. p.65

GALVEZIA Scrophulariaceae
G. speciosa California
Evergreen GALVEZIA (1-2m) is native to
dry rocky islands. Arching branch tips
mingle with nearby shrubs, bearing
crimson spring flowers. Establish carefully in dappled shade with well-
drained, mulched soil and watch out for
water needs. Trim for compactness.
Propagation: cuttings.

GARRYA Garryaceae
G. elliptica Oregon, California
The evergreen SILK TASSEL (3-7m) is usually a shrub half that size. Shiny leathery leaves and silvery spring tassels
enjoy well-drained, mulched soils,
moderate shade and occasional summer watering.

GAURA Onagraceae
G. lindheimeri Texas, Louisiana
The delicate perennial GAURA
(50-90cm) flowers profusely from spring
to late autumn. Plant in well-drained
and mulched sunny soil, water to establish, cut back to the ground each year.
Propagation: seed, cuttings. p.143

GAZANIA Compositae
TREASURE FLOWERS carpet the ground in
sun. Evergreen or evergrey foliage covers slopes with dense mats, huddles near
rock or spills from crevices. Brilliant,
daisy-like bloom (cream, yellow, orange, copper) open in sun from winter to
summer, also intermittently throughout
the year. Gazanias need good drainage
but accept any soil. In summer, water
once or twice a month, keeping the
foliage dry. Gravel mulch is beneficial.

Propagation: division, cuttings, seed (slower). Larger bloom: 'Gold Rush', 'Royal Gold' and 'Copper King' (winter).

G. krebsiana   S Africa
Grows wild in the drier Karoo. Spectacular golden spring flowers (attractive basal markings) rise from clump-forming, dark leaves, thickly felted beneath. Intolerant of overhead irrigation.   p.38

G. linearis   E Cape to Natal
Golden blotched 'daisies' stand above the foliage from spring to early summer.

G. rigens var. leucolaena   Cape
Native to coastal river areas, TRAILING GAZANIA covers large patches with reasonable speed (lawn substitute). Plain yellow flowers of 'Sunglow' (silvery grey leaves) and 'Sunrise Yellow' (green leaves) are desirable.   p.35

GEIJERA   Rutaceae
G. parviflora   Australia
Evergreen AUSTRALIAN WILLOW (4-6m) are well-behaved, gracefully-foliaged trees which adorn patios and gardens or screen neglected areas. Provide a sunny site, excellent drainage, ample space for penetrating roots which tolerate watered lawns. Mulch improves drought tolerance.

GELSEMIUM   Loganiaceae
G. sempervirens   USA
The evergreen CAROLINA JASMINE in its native South Carolina reaches 6m, with us half that size. Slender-stemmed and twining, it bears glossy lanceolate leaves and clusters of golden flowers from spring to summer. Plant in fertile sunny ground (shade delays flowering) wherever scent is appreciated, but out of children's reach (all parts poisonous). Water until established. Long hot summers ripen wood, promoting cold-hardiness. This vigorous climber, unless controlled, becomes an unsightly tangle. Regularly trimmed, it covers the ground, hangs over walls, climbs into trees.

● **GENISTA** Leguminosae/Papilionoideae
BROOMS, densely branched shrubs with few tiny leaves, are prominent among rocks, less invasive than some of the

Gaura lindheimeri

related *Cytisus*. Showy, often fragrant flowers appear in succession from late winter to summer. Tolerant of poor soils and limited water, they require full sun and excellent drainage. Prune to balance narrow stems with flowering branches. Spiny brooms, avoided by animals, are a good choice for natural gardens.

G. aetnensis   Sardinia, Sicily
MT. ETNA BROOM (2-3m) has fragrant yellow summer flowers.

G. hispanica   Spain
The spiny SPANISH GORSE reaches 50cm. Yellow late spring bloom covers widespreading branches.

G. lydia   Mediterranean
This spreading, prostrate shrublet only 20-40cm high, produces yellow flowers in summer. Quite hardy.

Gladiolus illyricus

G. monosperma see **Retama m.**

G. tinctoria var. **depressa**   Balkan
'Plena', widely grown around Melbourne, low-growing, bears orange-yellow flowers. 'Royal Gold', outstanding when smothered with bloom, needs hard cutting back.

GERBERA   Compositae
G. jamesonii   S Africa
Perennial TRANSVAAL DAISY, widely used in the florist trade, is easily grown. Leaf tufts and scarlet flowers spring from root crowns. Plant crowns level(!) in fertile, well-drained warm soil in full sun (dappled shade in hottest areas). Let them crowd into ever larger clumps. Fresh seed germinates readily. Also divide established crowns; discard woody portions, cut back leaves and replant immediately. Water in but avoid overwatering. Hybrids in cream, yellow, orange, brick.

GINKGO   Ginkgoaceae
G. biloba   SE China
The beauty of the deciduous MAIDENHAIR TREE is well-known, less understood is its drought tolerance. But I hesitate to include it as it seems out of place among evergreen, hard-leaved Mediterranean plants.

GLADIOLUS   Iridaceae
Provides colour when many plants have gone dormant. A mainstay of Mediterranean gardens, they flower in most colours from early winter (*G. dalenii*) to late summer (garden hybrids). Plant corms in rich sandy soil, deeply (!) which keeps flower heads from toppling over. Place bonemeal well below roots. Easy-going species, often daintily elegant, suit natural gardens better than stiff cultivars.

G. carneus   SW Cape
On spring mountain slopes, graceful rosy PAINTED LADIES flower above broad leaves.

G. x **colvillei**
Baby Hybrids, taller than species, suit most Mediterranean gardens. 'Albus' and 'Roseus' are reliable.

G. dalenii S Africa
Provides a striking colour on grey winter days.

G. illyricus Mediterranean
Accompanies *Chamaerops humilis* among rock, naturalizing readily from abundant seed. p.143

G. italicus (G. segetum) Mediterranean
FIELD GLADIOLUS paints spring fields with pale purple hues. Quite hardy, closely related to *G. illyricus*.

G. tristis S Africa
Creamy, scented flower spikes (30-50cm) are exquisite.

Haemanthus albiflos

GRAPTOPETALUM Crassulaceae
G. paraguayense (G. weinbergii) Mexico
The well-behaved MOTHER OF PEARL PLANT (15-25cm) with large-leaved, succulent rosettes likes warm, sheltered locations. Rooted leaves or branch sections, planted in decorative containers, show their advantages best.

GREVILLEA Proteaceae
This large genus of fast-growing evergreen shrubs or trees with finely cut foliage is a drought-tolerant asset for Mediterranean gardens. Showy clusters flower profusely from early winter to late spring (some species nearly all year). Nectar-rich, they attract birds. Grevilleas withstand adverse conditions (poor soil, drought, coastal wind), but deteriorate if watered in summer. Fairly tolerant of alkaline conditions, they prefer acidic soils and pine or oak mulches. Most are half-hardy, others can withstand considerable frost. Hot dry autumns promote wood-ripening and open positions in full sun prevent lankiness. Propagation: seed (easy), or insert small cuttings in sand.

G. robusta E Australia
Summer flowers cover the robust SILKY OAK (15-25m) with gold. Beware shallow, invasive roots.

G. rosmarinifolia E Australia
This undemanding low-growing shrub (1-2m) needs perfectly drained sunny soil but tolerates drought and more cold than most. Spidery crimson flowers from winter to autumn and rosemary-like leaves fit in with natural settings. 'Canberra Gem' with needle-like foliage and long-flowering coral bloom is outstanding and undemanding. p.144

GREYIA Melianthaceae
G. sutherlandii S Africa, Natal
The deciduous, spreading NATAL BOTTLE-BRUSH (1.5-3m) will grow in dry, hot, sunny locations in well- drained sandy soil. Choose for spectacular sealing-wax winter flowers, attractive leathery leaves and reddish autumn colours. Frost-tolerant. Propagation: seed, cuttings, suckers.

GRISELINIA Cornaceae
Outstanding for their waxy, apple-green foliage and sturdy constitution, flowers and fruits are insignificant. Near-hardy, no special soil or water requirements, no health problems. Readily increased by seeds, cuttings. Grow with evergreen New Zealand *Coprosma*, *Hebe*, *Metrosideros* or *Pittosporum*.

G. littoralis New Zealand
Native of lowland and mountain forests in sun and shade, often growing on fallen trees, the KAPUKA is a neat mounding shrub (3-10m), a perfect coastal screen.

G. lucida New Zealand
Epiphytic on coastal rock or on trees (*Metrosideros*), it may reach tree-like proportions (2-4m). Leaves 10-20cm long are superb. p.144

GYPSOPHILA Caryophyllaceae
G. paniculata Europe
The perennial BABY'S BREATH flowers as a white cloud. Thick, fleshy roots mean drought-tolerance. Propagate by stem or root cuttings.

G. repens Mediterranean
Small white summer flower clusters trail over rock.

HAEMANTHUS Amaryllidaceae
Most desirable for Mediterranean gardens, two spectacular large leaves hug the ground in shade or half-shade. Plant in sharply drained, compost-mulched soil, necks just below the surface. Initial watering settles large fleshy roots which like crowded conditions and require a resting period once leaves have died down. Divide before it starts to grow again. Fresh seed (own?), only half covered with soil, will flower after four years.

Grevillea 'Canberra Gem'

Griselinia lucida

H. albiflos   Cape
One of the easiest. Minute white hairs give evergreen, strap-shaped leaves a greyish hue. Golden stamens surrounded by white bracts rise on tall stems. p.144

H. coccineus   Cape
The flower comes up with first signs of autumn (cooler nights). Later, two spectacularly large, shiny leaves 25-60cm long, 15cm wide, spread on the ground.

H. katherinae see *Scadoxus multiflorus*.

HAKEA   Proteaceae
Easy evergreen PINCUSHION TREES (more shrub than tree) with attractive winter or spring flowers suit many difficult conditions. They tolerate poor, dry soils, coastal wind and salt spray, inland heat or cold. Yet they require good drainage, as do most drought-tolerant plants. If conditions suit them too well, several may turn invasive, requiring careful control (see Weeds).

H. laurina   W Australia
Easy to raise, also trained as tree (3-5m), flowers are crimson-cream. Glaucous foliage helps to screen unsightly views. Initially stake.   p.145

H. leucoptera   C & E Australia
NEEDLEWOOD (2-3.5m) bears small white flower clusters, yet the silvery foliage is its main attraction. Its wide-ranging native habitats include sandy soil with lime.

H. multilineata   W Australia
A tall shrub (2-4m) with attractive pink-purple flowers.

H. salicifolia   E Australia
Hardy, quick-growing WILLOW HAKEA (2-4m) suits cooler regions. Handsome creamy flower clusters.

HALIMIUM   Cistaceae
These evergreen shrublets (30-60cm) like hot locations in poor, gravelly, free-draining soil but tolerate short-term frost. They need a close association with soil fungi (mycorrhiza), thus site choice may need a second try. Propagation: seed, summer cuttings.

H. lasianthum   SW Europe
Spreading growth.   p.145

Hakea laurina

H. ocymoides   SW Europe
A more upright growth, golden flowers.

H. umbellatum   Mediterranean
White-flowered, smaller.

HARDENBERGIA
              Leguminosae/Papilionoideae
Evergreen vines (1.5-3m) with dainty violet-blue winter flower racemes mingle with nearby shrubs. Easy-going, they prefer sandy, well-drained loam in full sun or open shade and, if thickly mulched, need only a little summer water. Propagation: seed, cuttings.

H. comptoniana   W Australia
Leaves divided into 3-5 leaflets. Often found under eucalypts.

H. violacea   E Australia, Tasmania
The VINE LILAC, more vigorous than the

Halimium lasianthum

first, has lanceolate leaves. Try also 'Rosea' and 'White Cristal'.

HEBE   Scrophulariaceae
Well-known to gardeners, HEBE is among our best plants for evergreen, mounding masses in part-shade or shade. There is a choice of size (20-300cm), of foliage (small, narrow to large, shiny) and of long-lasting bloom (white, pink, blue, darkest lilac). Very free-draining soils, generous mulching, positions where roots expand into cooler regions, all improve drought tolerance. Water when leaves show stress. Cut back in winter. Cuttings strike well. Transplanting is very easy. Experiment with all hebes whose foliage or bloom pleases you (around 80 species and countless hybrids).

H. buxifolia   New Zealand
Small crowded leaves, white flower clusters. One of the toughest.

H. cupressoides   New Zealand
Slow-growing to 1m, its aromatic foliage mimics cypress.

H. 'Great Orme'
One of the best for. coastal gardens (60-80cm). Attractive pink flowers fade to white.

H. salicifolia   New Zealand
One of the tallest (200-300cm), sweetly scented white flowers.

H. speciosa   New Zealand
Quick growth (100-200cm), purple bloom.   p.60

HEDERA   Araliaceae

Evergreen IVY covers the ground with glossy leaves as a temporary or permanent blanket under trees or on banks. No special demands for soil or position, it thrives on neglect. Extensive roots compete with other plants nearby and vigorous growth may choke tall trees; this requires careful control. Cutting back overgrown areas limits pest or disease problems. Rooted branches increase the stock. Spring pruning encourages light green foliage.

H. canariensis   Canary Is.
Strong-growing with larger leaves, it suits warmer climates.   p.43

H. helix   Mediterranean
ENGLISH IVY (over 55 leaf shapes) is better in cooler regions.   p.39 below

HEDYCHIUM   Zingiberaceae

Spectacular GINGER LILIES (1-2m) are dramatic additions to watered gardens or poolsides, easy to raise from tuberous rootstock. Large leaves and showy fragrant flowers thrive in rich, well-mulched soil in warmest location under a tall open tree canopy. Cut back when new growth shows. Water generously once a week in summer. *Hedychium* tolerates short-term frost. Divide actively growing rhizomes or use fresh seed.

Hedychium coronarium

Hedychium gardnerianum

H. coronarium   India
In hottest locations, the WHITE GINGER flowers late in summer with exotic, far-reaching scent. A tree canopy protects leaves from sunburn.   p.146

H. gardnerianum   India
The KAHILI GINGER spreads vigorously by rhizomes. Summer flowers are scented, spent flowers develop into brilliantly coloured seed which may self-seed.   p.40, 146

H. greenei   Bhutan
Bears brilliant red flowers. Small bulbils develop from spent bloom like miniature plants. Set into good soil, within a year they enrich your stock.   p.147

HELIANTHEMUM   Cistaceae

These evergreen Mediterranean maquis dwarf shrubs thrive on shallow stony soil on sunny dry slopes. SUN ROSES flower profusely in wide colour ranges while sun is out. Planted when small, fibrous roots control erosion efficiently. They respond to trimming and are said to resent summer irrigation once established. No pest problems. Propagation: autumn seed.

HELIANTHUS   Compositae
H. annuus   USA
Quick-growing and easy, SUN FLOWERS are plants for children.

HELICHRYSUM   Compositae

A versatile genus of winter rainfall herbs and dwarf shrubs, EVERLASTINGS like dry, well-drained soils and sunny banks. Most grow close to the ground with greyish velvety leaves. Flowers are insignificant. All resent summer irrigation and respond to trimming in autumn. Easy to propagate with fresh seed (autumn) or cuttings (spring).

H. petiolare   S Africa
Common, easily trimmed into dwarf hedges or formal designs.

H. stoechas   Mediterranean
Gives off a curry-like scent and controls erosion.

Hedychium greenei

HESPERANTHA Iridaceae
H. vaginata Cape
Thrives in Mediterranean climates as do most members of the Iridaceae family. *Sparaxis*-like spring flowers naturalize from seed.

HETEROMELES Rosaceae
H. arbutifolia California
In summer, white flower clusters cover evergreen TOYON (2-5m), followed by a rich show of bright red autumn to winter berries. Shrubs or trees, they prefer deep soils along sunny banks, respond to pruning and trimming once the berries have dropped. Quite drought-tolerant, they survive freezing and prosper under oak. Propagation: fresh autumn-sown seed and semi-ripe summer cuttings.

HIBBERTIA Dilleniaceae
H. scandens Australia
SNAKE VINE (2-3m), lemon flowers resembling single roses, prefers free-draining, mulched sandy loam with a cool root run in sunny or partly shaded coastal regions. Pest-free. Easy propagation: autumn seed, spring cuttings.

HIBISCUS Malvaceae
A large genus of tropical and subtropical annuals, shrubs and subshrubs, grown for their showy flowers. All prefer rich, well-drained, amply-mulched sunny soils, most need water. Hibiscus, when grown correctly, is quite pest-free. Propagation: woody cuttings (winter), semi-hardwood cuttings (spring).

Hemerocallis cv.

HELLEBORUS Ranunculaceae
Evergreen perennial HELLEBORE is valued for its striking foliage and winter to spring flowering. Careful choice of position makes this pest-free plant a success. In the wild, on north-facing slopes cord-like roots creep along under cool rock (also alkaline). Propagation is rather slow: fresh seed, division of crowded clumps.

H. argutifolius W Mediterranean
Native to Corsica and Sardinia, recommended for large-leaved expanding clumps and long-lasting flowers.

Helleborus lividus

H. foetidus C and S Europe
Plant these attractive leaves and white, green or pink flower shades at the foot of trees, rocks or banks. Increase by young vegetative shoots.

H. lividus Majorca
Endemic to Majorca in mountainous woods or undergrowth. The pretty foliage dies down over summer, mulching the ground. p.147

H. orientalis E Mediterranean
The southern LENTEN ROSE, similar to the northern CHRISTMAS ROSE (**H. niger**), flowers somewhat later.

HEMEROCALLIS
Liliaceae/Hemerocallidaceae
The DAYLILY, a fleshy-rooted perennial herb from China, is well-suited to Mediterranean climates. Tolerant of coastal conditions, irrigation or drought, part shade or sun, it provides charming ground cover. Divide frequently, replant in fertile, well-worked ground in large patches. p.147

Hibiscus rosa-sinensis

H. moscheutos　　　　USA
Large-flowered ROSE MALLOW dies down in winter. Deeply mulched, it requires once or twice weekly watering in summer.

H. rosa-sinensis　　Tropical Asia
Rich food ensures countless showy hybrids' best performance. Water as above.　　　　　　　　p.53, 148

H. syriacus　　　　　Asia
Profuse but smaller flowers. Once established, it needs little water.

Hippeastrum 'Appleblossom'

HIPPEASTRUM　　Amaryllidaceae
South American AMARYLLIS, a cold-region house plant, in Mediterranean climates grows outdoors (not to be taken as *Amaryllis belladonna*). In autumn, set summer-dormant bulbs shallowly into rich, free-draining soil, exposed to winter rain and full sun or partial shade. Ash surrounding the pots keeps slugs away. When mulched, all tolerate short-term frost. Fresh seed germinates readily.

H. 'Appleblossom'
A delightful white cultivar, pink-blushed.　　　　　　　　　p.148

H. aulicum　　　　　Brazil
Not as showy as cultivars, but flowers earlier.

H. vittatum　　Peruvian Andes
Leaves appear after white and red striped flowers.

HIPPOPHAË　　　Elaeagnaceae
H. rhamnoides　　Europe, Asia
The deciduous SEA BUCKTHORN (2-5m) requires good drainage and full sun. An effective barrier plant or attractive dune stabilizer, valued for wide soil tolerances, it carries long-lasting, bright orange berries on female plants (where a male pollinator is nearby).

Note: Tart jellies accompany fish.

HOMERIA　　　　　Iridaceae
H. collina (H. breyniana)　　SW Cape
Grow clumps of the sturdy bulbous HOMERIA (40-60cm) where winter-growing strap leaves overhang gracefully. Delicate orange spring flowers on slender stems appear in succession for weeks. Plant small corms 6cm deep in well-drained, porous soil. A sunny position is essential. Grows with winter rain, but tolerates summer irrigation. No health problems observed. Propagation: offsets or seed kept in boxes for 2 years (remember summer dormancy). Poisonous to cattle. In Australia their uncontrolled naturalization is being checked.　　　p.149

H. ochroleuca　　　　SW Cape
Similar to the former, but with yellow flowers.

Note: For 20 years, homerias have not self-sown in my Mediterranean garden.

HOYA　　　　Asclepiadaceae
H. carnosa　　China, Australia
The WAX PLANT's fragrant bloom is worth the trouble you take, mainly patience. Exquisite flower clusters develop on last year's axillary spurs. Shiny-leaved shoots (1-3m) ramble through shrubs. They like rich, well-drained soils in open, frost-free shade, mulch, weekly watering in hottest months. Propagation: cuttings, layering.

HYDRANGEA　　　Saxifragaceae
H. macrophylla　　　　Japan
I hesitate to recommend the well-known HORTENSIA for waterwise gardens, but as it grows beautifully in protected Provence courtyards or under trees with generous weekly watering, I give in. Planted in rich, humusy, well-mulched soil, it grows 1-2m or is pruned back. It tolerates frost and suits containers.　　p.76

H. quercifolia　　　　USA
The deciduous OAKLEAF HYDRANGEA (1-2m) with creamy flowers and colourful autumn foliage, well-suited to Mediterranean summers, stands moderate sun. Propagation: cuttings, suckers.

HYLOTELEPHIUM　　Crassulaceae
H. telephium (Sedum t.)　　Asia
A plant for beginners, the perennial drought-tolerant LIVE-FOREVER (30-50cm) bears exquisite pink summer flowers and goes dormant in winter. Propagation: division, cuttings.　　　　p.62

HYPERICUM　　　　Guttiferae
This large, mostly drought-tolerant genus includes perennial herbs or shrubs of mounding shape. Abundant, often large yolk-coloured flowers with numerous stamens favour sun. Wide tolerance to soil, water, position or temperature. Winter-pruning keeps plants compact. All transplant well (cut back). Propagation: cuttings, seed.

H. balearicum　　　Balearic Is.
This noteworthy evergreen rounded shrub (80-170cm) has small, resinous-scented leaves and flowers for months. A little-known endemic and maintenance-free pioneer on poor stony, disturbed

Hypericum balearicum

Hypericum balearicum in the wild

soil, it should be widely available. Associate with other maquis plants. p.149

Note: Slow to establish in my garden, although native on nearby north-facing mountain slopes, patience was worthwhile.

H. calycinum Balkan
This evergreen quick-spreading ground cover, tolerating sun or shade, flowers on new growth. Cut back to ground in early spring. If watered, it becomes invasive.

H. canariense Canary Islands
A shrub (100-300cm), native to dry scrub. Profuse yellow flowers in large terminal panicles.

H. empetrifolium E Mediterranean
This subshrub (20-40cm) has inward-rolled, heather-like leaves (survival strategy) and star-shaped flowers, pervading rocky maquis with resinous scent.

H. glandulosum Canary Islands
A spreading, profusely flowering shrub (50-180cm), native to forest cliffs and dry, higher zones.

IBERIS Cruciferae
I. saxatilis S Europe
In spring, this evergreen subshrub covers rock in sun or dappled shade with pillows of white bloom.

I. sempervirens S Europe
Evergreen CANDYTUFT (30×30cm), a useful subshrub of characteristic Mediterra-

nean mounding shape, is wonderful in labour-saving gardens. White bloom rises above dark, shiny foliage from winter to spring. Planted in dappled shade in good garden soil, well-mulched, it thrives on a weekly watering. Clipping encourages compact growth. Increase by cuttings. The ground-covering 'Snowflake' (20×80cm) is more compact, has wider leaves and larger flowers.

ICE PLANTS Cape
Several creeping succulents are grouped as so-called ICE PLANTS for the glistening glassy dots covering the leaves of several species. See *Aptenia, Carpobrotus, Delosperma, Drosanthemum, Lampranthus, Mesembryanthemum.*

Homeria collina

ILEX Aquifoliaceae
I. aquifolium China, Europe
HOLLY, best in Atlantic climates, adapts well to Mediterranean regions. In shaded, slightly acid, well-drained garden soil, heavily mulched, it survives with weekly watering, becoming moderately drought-tolerant. Confined conditions induce health problems. Resistant to honey fungus. Plant male and female for bird-attracting, poisonous berries.

I. paraguariensis Argentina, Brazil
MATE, an evergreen tree (10m, less in cultivation) with attractively shiny leaves suits evergreen Mediterranean laurel woods. The same goes for the next.

I. perado Canary Is.
Careful planting encourages drought tolerance.

I. vomitoria Virginia to Texas
YAUPON, large attractive shrubs (4-5m), also pruned into small trees, have long narrow leaves, scarlet berries. They tolerate alkaline soils. Clip as hedge or shape as formal container. 'Nana' and 'Stokes' (40cm, wider than tall) suit formal use.

IMPATIENS Balsaminaceae
I. walleriana Tropical E Africa
The fast-growing BUSY LIZZIE is one of these useful tropical plants which suit Mediterranean summer gardens if watered. In optimum conditions (shade, deep rich soil, ample mulch) watering twice a week may be enough. Cuttings root in water.

Iochroma cyanea

IOCHROMA — Solanaceae

An early South American gift to Europe, together with closely related *Brugmansia, Solanum jasminoides,* potato and tomato, it appreciates fertile garden soil, generous mulch, weekly watering and warm positions (protect from hottest sun). Pruning stimulates vigorous growth. Drooping flower clusters are best appreciated if planted above a path. Propagation: cuttings.

Ipomoea alba

I. cyanea (I. lanceolata) — Columbia
This evergreen shrub with ink-coloured bloom reaches in ideal conditions 2m.
p.150

I. fuchsioides — Andes, Peru
Bright orange flowers are the attraction of this small shrub.

I. grandiflora — Andes
90-120cm, purple flowers.

IPHEION — Liliaceae/Alliaceae

I. uniflorum — S America
Dainty but sturdy SPRING STARFLOWER rises 10-20cm from low-cost bulbs, requiring sun or light shade and summer-baking. 'Wisley Blue' is stronger coloured, best appreciated when massed near a path.

IPOMOEA — Convolvulaceae

MORNING GLORY is a quick pioneer plant. *I. indica* may turn weedy. (See also *Convolvulus*).

I. alba (Calonyction aculeatum) Tropics
Too rampant for the greenhouse (5-8m), the MOON FLOWER vigorously entwines shrub, cypress, fence. White flowers scent summer evenings with bewitching fragrance. Heart-shaped leaves give quick shade or cover. Roots require a cool run in generously mulched soil. They grow with winter rain and a weekly watering in summer. Easy to transplant. Cut back in late winter. Propagation: cuttings; seed often blooms 2 months after germination (hot water treatment). 'Giant White', even larger flowers. p.150

I. horsfalliae — West Indies
The perennial, evergreen STAR GLORY (2-4m) needs warmth. Pendent rosy-red spring flowers, produced on young plants, are worth the effort.

I. quamoclit (Quamoclit vulgaris)
Tropical America
A quick-growing annual vine (3-4m) with scarlet bloom.

IRIS — Iridaceae

Iris was the Greek messenger who descended to earth via the rainbow. Native to most northern hemisphere regions, IRIS is a large genus. Bulbous species (*I. danfordiae, I. reticulata*) prefer cool climates. Rhizomatous *I. germanica* and oncocyclus irises require warmth. Choose the ones suited to your garden, many are very adaptable. They are robust and need little attention nor space. Unequalled for delicate flower beauty from winter (*I. unguicularis*) to summer, they are an unending source of delight. Their wide range attracts bulbous plant enthusiasts.

I. douglasiana — California
Tall spring flowers come up from spreading rhizomes among dark evergreen leaves (30-50cm), drought-tolerant once established. Dappled shade and occasional watering in hotter areas. Seldom available in Europe, the Pacific Coast Hybrids have lovely colours.

I. foetidissima — Europe
Its asset is not dull purplish flowers but the brilliant scarlet autumn seeds. Glossy evergreen foliage (30-40cm) gradually turns into an excellent ground cover in shade, requiring little water.

I. germanica — Mediterranean
This drought-tolerant, easy plant rises from stout rhizomes. Plant just below the surface in sunny, sharply drained soil (neutral or alkaline). Over-crowding reduces flowering. Divide in late summer; autumn rains settle rhizomes into ground. var. **florentina** has smaller, pale bluish-white flowers. p.38, 89

I. japonica — China, Japan
Exquisite flowers are welcome in earliest spring. Creeping stolons with graceful, fan-shaped leaves become a reliable shade ground cover and smother weeds. Plant in autumn in humusy soil, light

Oncocyclus iris

enough for stolons to take hold, water occasionally. It needs no more attention. p.151

I. reticulata   Iran, Iraq
Plant bulbs in autumn in sun near a path, together with grape hyacinths and scillas.

I. susiana   E Mediterranean
One of the loveliest of flowers, it is a member of the exquisite Oncocyclus irises and apparently grew in pharaonic gardens. Easy if given correct growing conditions, namely shallow planting in poor sandy super-drained soil, dry air, ventilation, much light, the hottest, sunniest position in your garden and no summer water, never. Leave undisturbed for years. Tira Nurseries advise: 'Just leave them alone'.   p.150

I. unguicularis (I. stylosa)   Algeria
Native to open oak woodlands in sun or dappled shade, this evergreen undemanding ground cover reaches 30cm. After Christmas, even before, delicately scented lilac flowers grow for weeks through grass-like leaves. To appreciate them better, cut leaves to half height long before buds appear. Divide when you need more.   p.151

I. xiphium   Mediterranean
Bulbous SPANISH IRIS (40-50cm) flower in spring in sunny meadows, preceded by so-called Dutch Iris (larger flowers, taller stems), a colourful, economical infiller. Mark sites for autumn planting.

IXIA   Iridaceae
In spring, lovely flowers in many colours spring from corms among thinnest, grass-like foliage, flower clusters bending the thin stems (30-50cm). Plant in

Iris unguicularis

Iris japonica

full sun 10cm deep, densely where more than a wispy effect is desired. Increase by seed.

I. maculata   SW Cape
Yellow flowers with dark mark.

I. monadelpha   SW Cape
White and pink shades, also darker ones.

I. viridiflora   SW Cape
Taller than the above, startling greenish tints.

JACARANDA   Bignoniaceae
J. mimosifolia   Argentina
The glorious sight of a fully grown JACARANDA (6-10m), covered for months with trumpet-shaped lilac flower clusters, silhouetted against the sky or looked down upon, is remembered by all travellers in South America. Naturally shrubby, *Jacaranda* can be shaped as tree. Deciduous fern-like foliage is semi-evergreen in hottest areas. Heat-demanding, it requires heavily mulched sandy soils, wind protection and deep summer watering every month. Tapering it off towards autumn hardens wood. Spent flowers spread luscious lavender carpets beneath trees.   p.151

Jacaranda mimosifolia

Jasminum odoratissimum

JASMINUM   Oleaceae
Countless long-flowering shrubs and climbers, sometimes difficult to find (except the well-known ones), are water-wise gardeners' delight. Good garden soil in sun, generously mulched, is all JASMINE needs. Several come from forest areas. With a cool root run weekly watering may be sufficient; when well-established, most do without. Propagation: cuttings, layering.   p.152

J. azoricum   Azores
Bushy for years, it gradually grows into a vigorous climber. Shiny evergreen foliage and sweetly-scented white flowers are alluring.

J. fruticans   Mediterranean
Evergreen shrubby (50-90cm), it grows wild in dry hilly scrub with yellow bloom, the only Mediterranean species.

J. humile   Asia
Yellow fragrant flowers cover the evergreen Italian Jasmine in autumn. Arching shoots (3-5m) spill over walls or banks and can take heavy pruning. 'Revolutum' bears larger flowers. p.152

J. mesnyi (J. primulinum)   W China
Use the evergreen PRIMROSE JASMINE (2-3m) as a clipped hedge or, tied to a support, as a climber. Bright yellow late winter to spring bloom resembles J. humile.

J. nudiflorum   N China
The golden bloom of WINTER JASMINE is earlier than the others. Train as an espalier, cut back for fountain-like growth or use as erosion control on banks in sun or shade.

J. officinale   Asia
Native to open mountain woodlands, the deciduous TRUE JASMINE (3-6m) requires training. White scented flowers are attractive from summer onwards. The sturdy f. **grandiflorum** has spectacular flowers, but is evergreen only in warmest regions.

J. polyanthum   China
New growth of this semi-evergreen, fast-growing trailer (3-6m) entwines wire and mesh, rambles over shrubs. White pink-blushed flower panicles and fern-like leaves turn your garden into a scented paradise in spring.   p.152

J. sambac   India
Trained or cut-back as shrub, the evergreen, frost-tender ARABIAN JASMINE (2-3m) with large leaves and heavily-scented white waxy flowers is a superb sight for warmest locations. Many uses (perfume industry, jasmine tea).

J. x stephanense
This robust, twining climber or rambler (2-4m), light pink early summer flowers hidden in apple green foliage, thrives in my sun garden on shallow soil.

Jasminum polyanthum

JUBAEA   Palmae
J. chilensis (J. spectabilis)   Chile
The CHILEAN WINE PALM, one of the hardiest, remotely resembles *Phoenix canariensis*, slowly reaching its final 15m. Water weekly in summer until established.

JUGLANS   Juglandaceae
J. californica   California
CALIFORNIA WALNUT, imposing shrubs or small trees (4-8m), native to southern oak woodlands, bear hard-shelled edible nuts. Will grow in poor soil. Resistant to honey fungus and drought.

Jasminum humile

Kalanchoe 'Tessa'

JUNIPERUS   Cupressaceae

Around 60 species of northern hemisphere trees or shrubs, including many useful low-growing and/or spreading cultivars. In nurseries, only older specimens show ultimate growth habit. Undemanding, sometimes slow to establish, all thrive in well-drained, mulched soil. Damp, humid conditions induce health problems. Patient gardeners propagate juniper by cuttings. Berries, a culinary spice, are used in gin production.

J. californica   California
The light-green CALIFORNIA JUNIPER (7-10m), much-branched from the base, is an asset in desert regions.

Juniperus 'Grey Owl', front right

J. chinensis   China
A bewildering range of cultivars (prostrate, shrubby, tree-like) will tolerate coastal, salt-laden winds.

J. communis   Europe, Asia
This vigorous, tall shrub or tree often outgrows average gardens. Grown in northern Europe, 'Hibernica' the IRISH JUNIPER and 'Suecica' the SWEDISH JUNIPER reach a columnar 5m.

J. conferta   Japan
The versatile SHORE JUNIPER reaches 30cm high by 200cm wide.

J. 'Grey Owl'
This complex hybrid, slow to start, gradually spreads to 2-3m wide and 1-2m tall. Vigorous and quite hardy.   p.153

J. horizontalis   N America
CREEPING JUNIPER forms a low cushion. 'Hugues' inches high; the ground-hugging 'Bar Harbor' 30×300cm wide.

J. occidentalis Washington to California
WESTERN JUNIPER reaches 9-15m, more if the location suits it. Sierra Juniper var. **australis** apparently lives 3000 years.

J. oxycedrus   Mediterranean
PRICKLY JUNIPER (1-12m) has needle-like leaves, useful as hedge. Wood yields the medicinal Oil of Cade. ssp. **oxycedrus**, a prominent maquis member, grows towards mountainous regions while lower ssp. **macrocarp**a favour sandy coasts.

J. phoenicea   Mediterranean
PHOENICIAN JUNIPER (3-5m) suits coastal gardens. Scale-like 'leaves', no spines.

J. sabina   Europe, Asia
The spreading SAVIN. (1.5-3m) prefers sandy alkaline soils. Exposure-tolerant, poisonous.

KALANCHOE   Crassulaceae
K. beharensis   Madagascar
This spectacular succulent produces large, triangular-shaped felty leaves. Yellow bell flowers appear on older plants. Young plants arise readily where fallen leaves touch ground.   p.88

K. blossfeldiana   Madagascar
The succulent FLAMING KATY is sold in Garden Centres as house plant carrying red, pink or yellow flower bunches. In gardens dark green leaves thrive in protected, light shade. Water weekly in summer for best performance.

K. daigremontiana   Madagascar
Flowers with panicles of pink bells. A plant for beginners, small plantlets form along leaf notches.

K. 'Tessa'
Half-shade and weekly summer watering suit this perennial succulent with fleshy green leaves and gracefully drooping orange bells. Insert cuttings.   p.153

KENNEDIA
     Leguminosae/Papilionoideae
K. nigricans   W Australia
The evergreen, woody-based BLACK BEAN (2-4m) twines and scrambles through low eucalypts. Pea-like, near-black spring flowers.

KNIPHOFIA Liliaceae/Asphodelaceae
The flowers of the perennial RED HOT POKER stand torch-like above slender tufted leaves. Tuberous roots like an open sunny aspect, humus-rich soil, excellent drainage and ample mulch. Clumps increase gradually until crowded. Divisions flower the second year. For neat appearance cut dry flower stalks and older leaves. These 'easy plants' give colourful accents in drought-tolerant gardens. Choose from a wide range of dwarf to tall cultivars 40-150cm (white, pink, yellow, red).

K. uvaria   S Africa
Is native to winter-wet, summer-parched places and endures snow (mulch well, tidy up in spring). Introduced early to England, this supposed parent of most garden cultivars reaches half their size (30-40cm).

KOELREUTERIA — Sapindaceae
An ideal proposition for 'summer shade and winter sun', showy flower clusters cover this tree with gold. Bladder-like pods remain on trees for a long time. If that were not enough, autumn foliage is magnificent. *Koelreuteria* likes hot, dry coastal or inland conditions, tolerates wind, alkalinity and smog. Plant in sunny deep, well-drained soils amply mulched, water until established. Deep well-behaved roots allow underplanting.

K. bipinnata (K. integrifolia) — Asia
Papery red pods turn the wide-crowned CHINESE FLAME TREE (6-12m) into fire. Best with occasional deep watering.

K. paniculata — Asia
The GOLDEN RAIN TREE (5-10m) bears brown pods. I have sown a handful of seeds and a forest came up.

KOLKWITZIA — Caprifoliaceae
K. amabilis — China
The deciduous BEAUTY BUSH (150-250cm) in spring carries small pink trumpet flowers on long canes. In cooler mountainous regions plant in sun, dappled shade in lowlands. Mulch generously and water in summer during establishment. Rejuvenate by taking out twiggy branches. No health problems. Propagation: cuttings, suckers.

Note: *The New RHS Dictionary of Gardening* reads '... occurs on the watershed of the Han and Yangtse rivers among rocks at 3000m'. How to duplicate native growing conditions?

Laurus nobilis, pruned into shape

LAGERSTROEMIA — Lythraceae
L. indica — China, Japan
The undemanding, deciduous CRAPE MYRTLE (3-4m), large shrub or small tree, bears profuse, delicately crinkled late summer flowers (purple, rose, white). *Lagerstroemia* thrives in fertile, well-drained soil in hot, dry locations (avoid shade). Almost drought-tolerant, water deeply, but infrequently. Prune for compactness and ample bloom; it flowers on current season's growth. Transplanting is risky. Place where well-shaped trunks, splendidly peeling bark and autumn colours are appreciated. Good container plant, easy from seed. Mildew-resistant cultivars exist.

LAGUNARIA — Malvaceae
L. patersonii — Australia
The evergreen, reasonably fast-growing PYRAMID TREE (5-10m), a stately *Hibiscus* relative for coastal gardens, has greyish leathery foliage and abundant pink bloom. In hot locations *Lagunaria* appreciates a cool, mulch-protected root run (any soil), once established grows with occasional deep summer-soakings, even without. Seed pods contain skin-irritating 'glass wool'. p.154

LAMPRANTHUS — Aizoaceae
In South Africa called MESEMB (abbreviation of *Mesembrianthemum* to which it formerly belonged), this widely-used succulent 'ice plant' is shrubby or trailing, often native to sandy, very summer-dry soil. Daisy-like spring flowers open in sun, carpeting fields with dazzling colour. Carefully match tints, use monochromes or combine with bulbs. It requires hottest, sunny sites, sharply drained. Gravel keeps winter foliage dry, reflects heat. Trim lightly after flowering, take cuttings. Tuck in among sunny rock or between paving. Excellent ground cover for larger areas; stepping stones facilitate maintenance.

L. aureus — Cape
Brilliant orange spring flowers (planted closely) smother this rounded shrublet 30-50cm across.

Lagunaria patersonii

Lantana montevidensis

Lantana camara

L. blandus Cape Town
Last to come out, palest pink flowers cover this spreading shrub 25cm tall, extending earlier species' flowering.

L. roseus Cape
Spreads to 90-150cm. Brilliant pale rosy flowers make a startling show. p.13

L. spectabilis Cape
25cm tall, spreads several times its height. Cyclamen-cerise flowers combine with other 'ice plants' for a long period of spring bloom. p.13

LANTANA Verbenaceae
A successful plant for reliable colour, evergreen in warmest regions with flowers all year. Where deciduous, LANTANA produces summer to late autumn flowers. Provide hottest locations, sunny well-drained soils, mulch-protected roots, deep watering once or twice a month. Spring pruning induces vigorous growth. Propagation: cuttings. Invasive in South Africa.

Lavandula dentata

L. camara Tropical America
Attractive cultivars (50-230cm) are colourful additions to evergreen areas (white, cream, yellow, pink, orange). p.56, 155

L. montevidensis Uruguay
This easy, trailing ground cover rambles over or into anything at hand. Verbena-like lilac bloom covers dull leaves during the warmer season. p.154

LAURUS Lauraceae
L. nobilis Mediterranean
The aromatic SWEET BAY or TRUE LAUREL may reach tree-size, but shrubby 3-6m are more likely. Shiny leathery leaves of kitchen merit are typical of hard-leaved (sclerophyllous) evergreen woodlands. Established by suckers, regrown from stumps, it tolerates coastal conditions, appreciates mulch and well-drained soil in sun or shade. A background for colourful settings, in containers formally clipped, a mainstay of Mediterranean gardens, its merits have been widely sung. p.154

LAVANDULA Labiatae
28 species share specific aromatic scent and 'lavender' flower shades, but differ in leaf and flower shape. Plant generously (the species native to your region) together with Mediterranean rosemary, rock roses, sun roses and broom. Cover banks, line driveways, use several species for extended bloom and scent. Undemanding, lavenders still need full sun and sharp drainage. Summer watering induces 'falling apart', controlled by trimming. Propagation: seed, cuttings. p.27

L. angustifolia (L. officinalis) N Spain
Native to stony fields in mountain regions, ENGLISH LAVENDER (60-120cm) tolerates more cold and drought than most. Flowering extends into summer. Medical and perfume industries use the ethereal oil. Dwarf varieties 'Compacta' 20cm, 'Hidcote' 30cm.

L. dentata W Mediterranean
First to flower, TOOTHED LAVENDER likes chalk. p.155

L. latifolia Mediterranean
SPIKE LAVENDER, more compact than most, cold-hardy as *L. angustifolia*, is similarly sized.

L. multifida Mediterranean
Native to stony garrigue, CUT-LEAVED LAVENDER (70cm) with larger leaves flowers early.

L. stoechas Mediterranean
FRENCH LAVENDER (30-80cm) grows in open maquis and under pine.

LAVATERA Malvaceae
L. arborea W Mediterranean
The easy TREE MALLOW (3-4m) tolerates poor summer-dry soils, may flower the first year from seed.

L. maritima W Mediterranean
Invaluable in coastal gardens and among rock, *Lavatera* (50-100cm) gives accents. Light pink flowers arise from grey felted leaves. Propagation: cuttings, seed.

L. trimestris Mediterranean
The ANNUAL MALLOW (90-150cm) provides colour.

Leucojum aestivum var. *pulchellum*

Libertia formosa

LEONOTIS   Labiatae
L. leonurus   Cape
Orange whorls stand above foliage for months (60-120cm). Shrubby, summer-dormant *Leonotis* suits hottest, well-drained, mulched ground and adorns drought-tolerant gardens. Cut back spent flowers. Quick from cuttings.

LEPTOSPERMUM   Myrtaceae
Adaptable TEA TREES, native to bogs, sandy coasts and forests, carry small solitary flowers among heath-like foliage. They tolerate almost any well-drained, sandy, non-alkaline soil in half-shade. After flowering, take back about one third (no cutting into wood). When established, they are quite drought-tolerant and maintenance-free. Grown in England as screens, low coastal shelter or a small specimen tree, revealing a picturesque trunk. Propagation: semi-hardwood cuttings, seed (slower).

L. laevigatum   Australia
Sturdy and dense (2-4m) with white bloom. Considered weedy in New Zealand, Australia, South Africa.

L. lanigerum   Australia
2-3m, downy young shoots, single white spring flowers.

L. petersonii   Australia
An outstanding small specimen tree with gracefully pendent branches, lemon scented foliage, white flowers.

L. scoparium   New Zealand
MANUKA (2-3m), native to heathlands, sub-alpine regions and riverbeds, has young silky-haired foliage and white winter flowers. Cultivars bloom nearly all year.

LEUCOCORYNE   Liliaceae/Alliaceae
L. ixioides   Chile
GLORY OF THE SUN is an attractive, drought-tolerant Chilean bulb with grass-like foliage and high heat requirements. Plant 15cm deep in full sun in light, sandy, well-drained soil wherever porcelain-blue, exquisitely scented flowers show to best advantage.

LEUCOJUM   Amaryllidaceae
L. aestivum var. **pulchellum**
          Mediterranean
SNOWFLAKE grows wild in nearby countrysides in sun or shade and takes much heat. It summer-bakes in a dry river bed, trampled on by passing sheep, makes do with the little soil rock pockets may hold. I also found a few near the sea where rains had carried them. They favour northern slopes where winter sun does not reach. Their white bells, intermingling with *Brachyglottis greyi*'s grey foliage, are a charming sight.   p.156

LEUCOPHYLLUM   Scrophulariaceae
L. frutescens   Texas
In California called TEXAS RANGER (1-3m), this accomodating slow shrub with evergreen silvery foliage and rosy bells tolerates drought, wind and desert conditions. It needs summer watering until established. Shape for desired volume.

LIBERTIA   Iridaceae
L. formosa   Chile
Rising from rhizomes, evergreen linear leaves (10-30cm) frame white or cream flower stems. Frost-tolerance.   p.156

L. ixioides   New Zealand
NEW ZEALAND IRIS (30-40cm) grow wild in coastal or inland forest clearings and flower from spring to early summer. They spread into spectacular, easily divided clumps. Pretty yellow berries.

LIGUSTRUM   Oleaceae
PRIVET, sturdy 'quick and easy' pioneers for natural gardens, grow in any soil in sun or shade. Invasive roots compete with nearby plants for food and drink. Creamy flowers' far-reaching scent attracts bees. Birds eat, thus distribute poisonous, blackish seed. Vigorous growth may require control. Cut to ground or transplanted, it resprouts and also recovers quickly from drought. Pollution-tolerant. Propagation: cuttings.

L. japonicum   Japan
Slow to 2-4m. Glossy, evergreen leaves are its attraction, suiting formal containers. 'Texanum' smaller, denser.

L. lucidum China, Korea
Resembling *L. japonicum*, the evergreen CHINESE PRIVET, a spreading shrub, may turn into a 9m tree. Often grafted onto common species stock, its large glossy leaves and creamy flower clusters are spectacular. A good coastal windbreak or hedge, best with some summer watering. In South Africa and Australia liable to be invasive.

L. ovalifolium Japan
Semi-deciduous in colder regions, the heat-tolerant CALIFORNIA PRIVET quickly reaches 2-4m, an excellent hedging plant.

LILIUM Liliaceae/Liliaceae
Lilies thrive in well-drained soil, rich in organic matter. Contractile roots, shaded by low vegetation, protected from hottest sun, pull bulbs down to correct depth. Weekly, deep summer watering will do. Lilies are also glorious container plants with prolonged bloom. p.157

L. candidum Mediterranean
MADONNA LILY is different from other lilies. It starts growth with first autumn rains, flowers in late spring, dies down immediately, following the Mediterranean bulbous growth cycle. Plant this lime-tolerant lily shallowly. p.40

L. henryi Asia
Among the tallest (1-1.8m), it naturalizes in suitable sites. p.89

L. longiflorum E Asia
EASTER LILY delights with fragrant, white waxy bloom.

L. washingtonianum California
Adaptable, native to dry woodlands with dappled shade and loamy soil. White, scented summer flowers (1-1.6m) mature into rich rose. Watch water needs before flowering.

LIMONIASTRUM Plumbaginaceae
L. monopetalum Mediterranean
This evergreen, fleshy-leaved shrub (60-90cm), native to sandy beaches or neighbouring saltmarshes, suits coastal gardens. Pink flowers, fragrant once dry, turn violet.

Lilium 'Royal Gold'

LIMONIUM Plumbaginaceae
L. perezii Canary Islands
Ornate lavender flower clusters top stems above large basal leaves. Planted in well-drained sandy soil, mulch-covered, the evergreen perennial SEA LAVENDER is a good fire-retarder, likes coastal gardens and suits dried flower bouquets.

LINUM Linaceae
L. perenne Europe
Perennial BLUE FLAX (40-60cm) should be planted more often. Dainty, it is nevertheless drought-tolerant. Mulched, light sunny soil guarantees best bloom. After flowering trim for compactness. Ample seed will naturalize.

LIPPIA see **ALOYSIA**

LIRIOPE Liliaceae/Convallariaceae
The grass-like foliage of the evergreen perennial LILY TURF makes it a drought-tolerant path borderer or lawn substitute in small areas. Somewhat slow-growing, but easy from seed or from spring-divided clumps, planted in humus-enriched, mulched soil. Try all for their neat foliage and few demands, also the closely related *Ophiopogon*.

L. muscari Asia
Mauve or white spike-like racemes (20-30cm) at summer's end stand for weeks above dark green foliage. p.157

L. spicata Asia
Somewhat lower, it creeps and spreads rapidly by underground rhizomes. Flowers, almost white, show barely among narrow leaves. Cut back before new growth comes.

LITHOCARPUS Fagaceae
L. densiflorus California, Oregon
A member of the coastal oak family, the tall TANBARK OAK (15-20m) appreciates acid soils and infrequent deep summer-watering. Woolly spring shoots and creamy summer flowers are both attractive. An evergreen, broad-leaved tree for cooler regions, an excellent background screen or wind shelter.

Liriope muscari

Lonicera implexa

LITHODORA
Boraginaceae
L. diffusa (L. prostrata)
W Mediterranean
Also sold as *Lithospermum*, this hardy shrublet (20-30cm) with evergreen rosemary-like leaves and gentian blue spring flowers is an asset to any garden. When mulched, it thrives in well-drained, moisture-retentive, limefree soil in full sun or half-shade and appreciates weekly summer watering. Propa-

Lonicera fragrantissima

gation: semi-ripe cuttings. 'Heavenly Blue' is very flat.

L. rosmarinifolia Mediterranean
Less hardy than the first, best among warm rock.

LOBULARIA
Cruciferae
L. maritima Mediterranean
The annual or perennial SWEET ALYSSUM (20cm), white-flowered and trailing, looks best when grown in hot, dry, sandy soil. Trim after flowering. Quick from seed *in situ*, it occasionally escapes. 'Carpet of Snow' with larger bloom spreads scented carpets of snow over rock.

LONICERA
Caprifoliaceae
HONEYSUCKLE are Northern Hemisphere natives (180 species). Mostly undemanding climbers in full sun or half shade (fewer flowers in shade), often scented. All have wide temperature tolerances, varying water demands and transplant readily. Maintenance depends on how plants are meant to grow. Prune unruly ones with hedge clippers. No health problems if well-grown. Berries are poisonous yet attract birds. Propagation: layering, cuttings.

L. etrusca Mediterranean
This drought-tolerant vigorous HONEYSUCKLE (3-4m) is evergreen in warmest regions. Sweetly scented yellowish flowers cover railings along walks, clothe columns, drape walls. A mess of dead twigs may build up beneath; cut to ground for fresh foliage and start anew.

L. fragrantissima China
WINTER HONEYSUCKLE (2-2.5m), a somewhat straggly, bare-based shrub, evergreen in mildest regions, produces delightfully scented creamy winter bloom. p.158

L. hildebrandtiana Asia
The evergreen GIANT BURMESE HONEYSUCKLE in warmest locations climbs 10m, in colder areas 2-3m. Glossy foliage with large cream-orange summer flowers requires mulching, occasional watering and a sturdy support.

L. implexa Mediterranean
This scrambling Mediterranean maquis native (2-4m), once established, toler-

ates drought in driest locations. Train its attractive evergreen foliage and scented flowers, cut back for fresh glaucous spring leaves. p.158

L. japonica Japan
The overpowering evergreen JAPANESE HONEYSUCKLE, deciduous in colder gardens, fast covers room-sized patches. White to yellow flowers like heat. Use as temporary planting where invasiveness is an asset (later pull out or cut heavily back).

L. nitida China
Elegantly arching branches (1-1.6m) carry tiny leaves and minor white spring flowers. For formal uses or containers, the evergreen BOX HONEYSUCKLE takes kindly to trimming.

LOPHOSTEMON
Myrtaceae
L. confertus (Tristania conferta)
E Australia
A well-behaved tree, frost-tender when young, the evergreen BRUSH BOX (10-15m) is closely related to *Eucalyptus*. No special soil requirements, it likes excellent drainage, deep mulch, no summer water once established. Variegated forms divert attention from the beauty of the leaves and the attractively peeling bark.

LOTUS
Leguminosae/Papilionoideae
L. berthelotii Canary Islands
The 'evergrey' perennial PARROT'S BEAK trails 1m, cascades over sunny or half shaded walls. Prolonged pea-like spring and summer bloom (yellow, copper, red) is best with occasional watering. Poor drainage induces root rot.

L. creticus Mediterranean
A pleasing yellow-flowered coastal ground cover 20cm high, it is native to sandy Mediterranean shores and rarely available.

LUPINUS
Leguminosae/Papilionoideae
L. arboreus California
A handsome shrub for beach gardens, the TREE LUPIN (1-2m) bears canary summer flowers. Plant in light, sharply drained soil, mulch, remove spent flower stalks. Increase by seed, give hot water treatment.

Magnolia grandiflora

LYONOTHAMNUS   Rosaceae
L. floribundus   S California Islands
The fast evergreen CATALINA IRONWOOD (6-9m) has variable, oleander-like leaves and white summer flower clusters. It is native to dry slopes, together with *Eriogonum giganteum*. Give a well-drained light soil. Occasional deep summer watering helps their condition, but is not essential. Careful shaping reveals a pleasing trunk structure.

MACFADYENA   Bignoniaceae
M. unguis-cati (Doxantha u.)
    Mexico to Argentina
(See also Bignonia). The glorious, spring-flowering YELLOW TRUMPET VINE fast reaches 3-8m, spills over walls, a golden curtain. Claws hold onto any surface. Evergreen in warmest areas, it requires full sun, stands desert conditions. Drought-tolerant once established, any well-drained, mulched soil will do. For framework prune after flowering. Where invasive, dig up fleshy roots.

MACLURA   Moraceae
M. pomifera   USA
Deciduous OSAGE ORANGE reaches spreading, spiny 10-15m with golden autumn foliage. Male and female plants grown together produce attractive, orange-like fruit. Tough in adverse conditions, resistant to honey fungus, *Maclura* thrives in deserts, is a useful windbreak. Propagation: seed, cuttings.

MAGNOLIA   Magnoliaceae
M. grandiflora   USA
The evergreen SOUTHERN MAGNOLIA (9-15m) with glossy, leathery leaves suits dry regions. Giant cream flowers in my garden are over before the peak of summer heat (England midsummer until frost). Choose a wind-protected location on humusy, well-drained ground. Generous mulch avoids health problems. Seed-propagated plants may take 15 years to flower, grafted ones 2-3 years.   p.159

MAHONIA   Berberidaceae
Evergreen HOLLY GRAPES (70 species), native to dry forest borders, have shiny spiny leaves, attractive bright yellow spring flower clusters, blue autumn berries. Of medium growth rate, they thrive in sun, inland under dappled shade. Once established, they need moderate watering and tolerate heat, wind and drought. American species sucker freely, a useful medium height ground cover.

M. aquifolium   USA
OREGON GRAPE (1-2m) is resistant to honey fungus.

Note: Fruits, used for jellies, also attract birds.

M. x media 'Charity'
This rounded drought-tolerant shrub (2-3m) is a good choice near native oak which would be taxed by summer water. Slender flower racemes scent the air through winter.

M. pinnata   California
CALIFORNIA HOLLY GRAPE is more sun- and drought-tolerant than the former and suits coastal gardens.

MANDEVILLA Apocynaceae
M. laxa (M. suaveolens) Argentina
The deciduous CHILEAN JASMINE (2-3m) goes bare at its base. Sweet-scented spring flowers resemble white oleander (same family) and look best together with foliage plants. *Mandevilla* thrives in organic, moisture-retentive soils, with weekly watering in summer. Although preferring warmest sites, it survives short-term frost. Ample mulch protects tuberous roots, also from disturbance. To induce branching, cut back to ground, but beware of milky sap. Seeds germinate quickly; surplus plants are valued exchanges.

MELALEUCA Myrtaceae
PAPERBARKS (over 150 species) are evergreen, adaptable, undemanding shrubs or trees, cultivated similarly to *Callistemon* from which they differ in small botanical flower details. Bark shreds in thin papery layers, revealing a splendid trunk. Useful in coastal sandy soils.

M. armillaris Australia
Soft, evergreen needle-like leaves and spectacular white spring bloom are an arresting sight. Shaped as tree (3-6m) or kept low, it performs as hedge, windbreak or background to your plantings. It tolerates alkaline soils and salt spray.

Melianthus major

M. cordata Australia
1m, one of the lowest, native to swampy winter soil on rock, it suits hottest, driest summer regions. Pinkish flowers.

M. hypericifolia Australia
This shrub or small tree (2-4m) with bright red bottle brushes adapts to most locations and transplants even when older.

M. microphylla Australia
Spreading to 3m with tiny leaves and small creamy flower clusters. Very drought-tolerant.

M. nesophila Australia
The large, shrubby WESTERN TEA MYRTLE (5-8m) is used as coastal hedge or trained into a tree with striking branch structures. Pale green foliage contrasts with small, purple summer flower 'balls' and suits clipping.

M. styphelioides E Australia
A truly magnificent shrub or tree, the PRICKLY PAPERBARK (6-12m) will tolerate swampy brackish to hot, dry soils. Deep roots do not compete with nearby plants.

MELIA Meliaceae
M. azederach SW Asia
The deciduous CHINABERRY is a fast-growing pioneer tree. Fragrant lilac spring flowers appear with leaves. In winter, mustard seed bunches hang on bare branches, used to fashion rosaries. Well worth planting in difficult sites, tolerant of alkaline soils, drought and cold, it needs little care. Few disadvantages other than a tendency to sucker and seed itself. Fruit bats eat the seed, toxic to other animals and humans. Brittle branches may break in wind. Widely used street tree in southern Europe, attractive shade for larger gardens.

MELIANTHUS Melianthaceae
M. major S Africa
The HONEY FLOWER (1.5-2m) is easily grown, a waterwise eye catcher and striking accent plant. Showy nectar-filled flower racemes, dark burgundy-red, contrast with bluish-grey foliage. Few needs: best drainage as all drought-tolerant plants, fertile, mulched sunny soil, occasional summer watering in hottest months. Easy propagation: seed, cuttings. p.17, 35, 160

MELISSA Labiatae
M. officinalis S Europe
LEMON BALM of culinary fame is a perennial herb (50cm) with light green, lemono-scented leaves which are its chief attraction. Cream, late summer flowers are often cut back which keeps the plant compact. It grows best in rich humid soil but tolerates some drought in shade. Dripping taps make it invasive. Propagation is quick and easy by root division. p.161

MESEMBRYANTHEMUM Aizoaceae
M. crystallinum Cape
A succulent annual on creeping spreading stems and excellent lawn replacement in coastal areas. Minute white daisies open in sun. Leaves are edible and fragile, thus sow *in situ*. See also 'Ice Plants'.

MESPILUS Rosaceae
M. germanica Europe, Asia Minor
MEDLAR are deciduous shrubs or small trees (2-4m), already mentioned in Charlemagne's fruit list around 800 AC. Creamy spring flowers resemble single roses on felty leaf beds. Drought-tolerant medlar grow in most sunny, well-

Mespilus germanica

Melissa officinalis

Mirabilis jalapa

draining soils. Graft onto hawthorn, pear or quince. Once inward-growing branches have been cut out, they require no attention other than harvesting their mushy, tart autumn fruits. Leaving them to mature in a cool place is called 'bletting'. Before exotic pineapple or banana were on everybody's plate, medlar were welcome additions to apple and walnut. Medlar sweetmeats, served with port, are an acquired taste, today liked by few.   p.161

METROSIDEROS   Myrtaceae
M. excelsa   New Zealand
The evergreen, spreading POHUTUKAWA or CHRISTMAS TREE (8-18m) grows fast, a magnificent specimen. Large shiny leaves are tomentose beneath. Scarlet 'Christmas flowers' mean summer bloom for northern hemisphere gardens. Native to coasts, extremely wind-resistant, on deep, well-drained soils they withstand almost any exposure, also moderate frost. Cut back after a particularly dry summer, new growth resprouts readily. Vigorous roots lift terrace floors. Propagation: cuttings, seed. 'Aurea' yellow-flowered. Bushmen use an inner bark decoction against dysentery.

MIMOSA see **ACACIA**

MIMULUS   Scrophulariaceae
MONKEY FLOWERS, small evergreen shrubs with narrow, often sticky leaves, flower from spring to late summer in delicate white, pink, yellow or red shades. Loose rocky soil, sharp drainage, ample mulch suit these plants. Dry locations in shady woodlands accommodate chaparral natives, said to be drought-tolerant. Hybrids need weekly watering. Prune in spring for compact appearance before growth resumes, also after flowering. Propagation: seed, cuttings. Although considered undemanding, I find their establishment challenging.

M. aurantiacus (Diplacus a.)   California
Native to rocky coasts, foothills and redwood forests, the BUSH MONKEY FLOWER reaches 1m. Graceful orange flowers, also in lovely pastel hybrids.   p.137, 161

M. bifidus   California
Largest flowers in yellow to pink shades dislike overhead irrigation.

M. longiflorus   S California
A well-branched shrub (90cm) from coastal foothills.

MIRABILIS   Nyctaginaceae
M. jalapa   Tropical America
Drop a few seeds and perennial MARVEL OF PERU (70×70cm) will come up with white, yellow or shocking-pink flowers. Also called FOUR O'CLOCK, flowers open in afternoon, close towards morning. Reject inferior colours by pulling out tuberous roots. It appreciates hot sun, grows in any soil and tolerates drought. These easy marvels thrive among rubble on dusty by-roads, looking from a distance like giant balloons.   p.161

MORAEA   Iridaceae
Delicate, beautifully shaded spring flowers on 30-50cm stems come up in succession week long. The species below keep each iris-like flower open for several days, others are fleeting. Plant small corms 10cm deep in well-drained light soil, sand and compost added. They appreciate open sun or, where

Mimulus aurantiacus

Myoporum laetum

springs are very hot and dry, half-shade. *Moraea* thrives with natural winter rain but, without needing it, tolerates summer irrigation. Seed sown in moist shade germinates after a month, transferred after two years into individual pots.

M. neopavonia · Cape
Similar to *M. villosa*, but has orange flowers with dark blue markings, today rare in nature.

M. tripetala SW Cape
Pale blue flowers among long slender leaves.

M. villosa SW Cape
PEACOCK FLOWER from hill country is exquisitely marked. After having lost one of these dainty treasures, I first establish moraeas in pots.

Muscari armeniacum

MORUS Moraceae
Deciduous MULBERRY (8-12m) were grown in Egypt and Mesopotamia in times past. Attractive autumn foliage turns golden. They favour cool winters, wind protection and alkaline soils. Shape carefully. To avoid health problems, don't cultivate the ground beneath trees. Resistant to Texas root rot. These quick pioneers for marginal areas tolerate other plants beneath their canopy.

M. alba China
Leaves of the WHITE MULBERRY fed silk worms in China thousands of years ago. Weeping 'Chaparral' or quick-growing 'Fruitless' are recommended.

M. nigra Iran
Enjoyed by humans and birds alike, the BLACK MULBERRY has sweet fruits which ripen from green and red to black.

MUSCARI Liliaceae/Hyacinthaceae
M. armeniacum Mediterranean
GRAPE HYACINTH (15-25cm) with slender, shiny leaves has cheerful gentian-blue spring bloom. Plant bulbs in loamy soil in full sun near a path or between stepping-stones (if not stepped on). Rapid naturalization. p.162

MYOPORUM Myoporaceae
Quick and easy, no demands for soil and position, frost-hardy MYOPORUM is drought-tolerant. Small, pretty white flowers attract bees. Unless size and location are well-matched, its vigorous growth will need control. *Myoporum*

Myrsine africana

transplants well. Easy propagation by cuttings. Use as bulky screen, windbreak or versatile pioneer plant.

M. debile Australia
The SPRAWLING MYOPORUM (30×90cm) covers hot inland banks.

M. insulare Australia
Of highway fame, BOOBYALLA, more drought-tolerant than most, suits brackish or saline soils, controls driftsand.

M. laetum New Zealand
The evergreen rounded NGAIO (2-7m), a vigorous hedge and coastal plant, requires trimming. p.40, 53, 162

M. parvifolium Australia
The CREEPING MYOPORUM hugs the ground 2-3m wide, a flat lawn replacement. Rooting branches require light soil, minimal watering. Established plants in half-shade are drought-tolerant.

MYRICA Myricaceae
M. californica California
Shaped into low mounds by coastal winds, the handsome evergreen CALIFORNIA WAX MYRTLE (3-8m) appreciates dappled shade, ocean fog and, drought-tolerant, grows into a reliable shiny-leaved hedge.

MYRSINE Myrsinaceae
M. africana Africa, Asia
Native to mountain regions, the evergreen AFRICAN BOXWOOD (50-90cm) has shiny foliage and insignificant flowers. Tolerant of drought and frost, undemanding on soil and location, it likes well-mulched, humusy soil in sun or half shade. One of the best, easily controlled by clipping, it is outstanding for formal shapes in containers or as low hedge. Propagation: cuttings. p.162

Myrtus communis

MYRTUS   Myrtaceae
M. communis   Mediterranean
Sometimes sold as *Myrtus boetica*, the hardy evergreen MYRTLE (1-3m) is widely grown in temperate and tropical regions. var. **italica** and var. **romana** both refer to Mediterranean locations. White scented flowers are profuse in summer, crushed leaves are pleasantly aromatic, black berries edible. Likes well-drained, humusy soil in sun or shade. Transplanting requires care. Allow it to grow untrimmed or clip into formal designs. Propagation: seed, cuttings. 'Microphylla' dwarf. 'Tarentina' small leaves and compact rounded habit. p.53, 163

M. ugni see **Ugni molinae**

NARCISSUS   Amaryllidaceae
Northern hemisphere bulbs mostly from the Mediterranean, several from Asia. Plant DAFFODIL for cheerful spring bloom in places where dying leaves can be hidden. Remember good garden soil, sand, bonemeal, drainage and sunny sites. In the natural garden among lavender and rosemary or at the foot of old olive trees, species may look best. When they like the growing conditions, they naturalize. Spring rains batter taller garden hybrids but, near the house, indulge in clumps of the dependable 'King Alfred'.   p.163

N. bulbocodium   Mediterranean
PETTICOAT DAFFODIL shines in early spring among low grass, a jewel in lemon and gold.

N. elegans   W Mediterranean
Exquisitely fragrant flowers among dark green foliage (10-20cm) for hottest regions.

N. jonquilla   W Mediterranean
JONQUIL bears late, scented flower clusters.

N. tazetta   Mediterranean to Iran
Native to meadows and pasture lands (30-40cm), glaucous leaves and creamy fragrant flowers often naturalize. Their widespread distribution indicates wide tolerances. 'Paper White', taller than the species, in cold weather lasts weeks, but may be knocked over by rain. Around Christmas, richly scented flowers shine 'white as paper' on a dark green foil and promise spring.

N. triandrus   NW Mediterranean
Delicate, minute ANGEL'S TEARS, pale yellow or cream, require excellent drainage – as do all bulbs.

NEOMARICA   Iridaceae
Leaves and flowers are tall, elegant, iris-like. This herbaceous perennial with creeping rhizomes likes hot locations with fertile soil and weekly watering in summer. Propagation: seed, also plantlets forming in plant axils.

N. gracilis   Mexico to Brazil
Creamy white and blue summer flowers on 40cm stems.   p.163

N. northiana   Brazil
Fragrant creamy spotted flowers on 80cm stems.

NEPETA   Labiatae
N. x faassenii
A perennial ground cover on sloping terrain with attractive blue summer flowers among grey foliage. Clip for compact

Narcissus species

growth. Low water requirements. Propagation: division.

NERINE   Amaryllidaceae
N. sarniensis   SW Cape
The hardy GUERNSEY LILY (25-45cm), native to mountainous crevices with poor soils in sun or half-shade, flowers with iridescent sparkle through winter. Plant in late summer in perfectly drained sandy loam, 'necks' level with surrounding ground. Later provide a long summer dormancy; bulbs rot easily. Leave undisturbed for years. Seeds fall off and, pressed lightly into the ground, root almost instantly, flowering the third year.

Neomarica gracilis

Olea europaea var. *oleaster*

NERIUM Apocynaceae
N. oleander Mediterranean
Evergreen OLEANDER, a mainstay of Mediterranean gardens, grows naturally in rocky ravines in North African deserts. Branches quickly spread 2-3m, giving instant cover. Leathery leaves cope with driest air, roots search deeply for moisture. Plant in any well-drained and mulched soil, even brackish or saline, in hottest sun. Water to establish. Unfavourable conditions such as shade, shallow ground, overhead irrigation or poor air circulation mean health problems. Control: cut back hard and transplant to suitable locations. Annual pruning of some older wood to base improves air circulation. Cuttings, standing in water, grow roots. Restraining this vigorous grower to below natural height involves extra work. Low-growing cultivars retard fires. This ornamental pioneer with showy terminal flower heads from summer to autumn furnishes driveways, protects from sea breeze or street noise, beautifies grazing grounds. All parts are poisonous and animals don't touch it. For cooler regions: the rosy 'Dr. Golfin', peachy pink 'Monsieur Belaguier', salmon cheeked 'Mrs. Roeding' – a choice company. p.10, 88, 95

Beware: Oleander is potentially invasive near water courses in eastern South Africa which, however, has no Mediterranean climate.

NIGELLA Ranunculaceae
N. damascena Mediterranean
The annual LOVE-IN-A-MIST (30-50cm) gives quick colour with charming light-blue spring flowers. It dies down in summer drought but pretty seed heads assure its return each year. Combine with the equally easy *Calendula*.

Olearia insignis

OENOTHERA Onagraceae
A useful companion in waterwise gardens, the EVENING PRIMROSE likes a poor dry soil in sun or half-shade, rots with summer irrigation.

O. drummondii Texas, Mexico
Taproots efficiently stabilize dunes.

O. fruticosa ssp. **glauca** Appalachians
The SUNDROP opens during early summer days.

O. macrocarpa (O. missouriensis)
 Missouri to Texas
A prostrate spreader with giant lemon summer flowers.

O. speciosa Mexico
From spring to autumn it paints summer gardens pink (20-30cm). Flowers open at nightfall, close 24 hours later. Trim this robust, perennial bank cover occasionally. Water until established (beware invasiveness).

OLEA Oleaceae
O. europaea var. **europaea**
 Mediterranean
The EDIBLE OLIVE, rarely reaching 8m, still grows widely on terraced land, often many centuries old. Poets praise trees' silvery foliage, their gnarled trunks and spreading crowns. Missionaries introduced this main Mediterranean crop to California. Olives tolerate any soil and short-term frost. When cut hard back, they will transplant bare rooted ('quite easily', it is said), its southern side again planted south – if you have a crane at hand. Or carefully shape those on your land, removing badly placed branches and basal suckers. Irrigation or fertilizer weaken trees. Scale insects (*Saissetia oleae*) and black soot occur in confined locations, controlled by better air circulation. Vigorous pruning encourages new growth. Trunks and above-ground roots should remain exposed to the sun, but underplant with spring bulbs. Fruits, first green, later near black, are soaked in water, preserved in brine. 'Mission' very cold-hardy, 'Little Ollie' dwarf, bushy habit. p.20

See 'Homemade Olive Oil', leaflet 2789, Division of Agricultural Sciences, University of California.

O. europaea var. **oleaster**
WILD OLIVE occurs in rocky Mediterranean maquis wherever birds have dropped the seed. They grow reasonably fast but when grazed develop a dwarfer, spinier character, leaves becoming minute (a reversible process, similar to oak). Once fenced and shaped, branches develop from a strong rootstock, slowly at first, then quicker with larger leaves. Small fruits, enjoyed by birds, cause a black mess as do all olives. Pollen may cause allergies. p.19, 30, 89, 164

OLEARIA Asteraceae/Compositae
A bloom-covered DAISY BUSH is a striking early summer sight and should be grown widely. Chalk-tolerant, grow in full sun and mulch sensitive surface roots (no digging). Clipped for compact growth, the trimmings can be used for cuttings.

O. ciliata Australia, Tasmania
Rich blue flowers and heath-like leaves cover this globe (30cm).

O. x haastii New Zealand
100-150cm tall with small leathery leaves and floriferous white flower-heads. Pollution-tolerant. 'Waikariensis' (150-200cm), a white-flowering pyramid. p.165

O. insignis (Pachystegia i.) New Zealand
Evergreen *Pachystegia* (60-80cm), native to cliffs from sea level to 1200m, spreads 150cm with large leathery leaves and daisy-like summer flowers. It prefers poor, limed soils. Mulch keeps roots cool, weeds under control. One of the most attractive shrubs New Zealand has given to the garden world, seldom available. p.72, 164

OPHIOPOGON Liliaceae/Convallariaceae
Closely related to Liriope with the same requirements and uses.

O. japonicus Japan, China
Lilac flowers in short upright racemes grow from large stolons and tuberous roots. 'Albus' white. 'Kyoto Dwarf' dense, 3-5cm tall.

Olearia × haastii 'Waikariensis'

Opuntia ficus-indica

O. planiscapus Japan
20-30cm, quite hardy. Pretty lilac or white flowers grow from thickened roots and resemble *Convallaria* (same family).

OPUNTIA Cactaceae
PRICKLY PEAR, a large genus of varied appearance, native from northern USA to South America's southern tip, have widely differing requirements such as daylength, light levels, altitude, temperature. The ones sold at local nurseries are probably easiest. Plant in gritty soil and remember drainage. Several, introduced to Australia and South Africa as forage, have become a weed problem.

O. ficus-indica Mexico
The BARBARY FIG (1.5-3m) grows next to Mediterranean farmsteads, reaching tree-like proportions. Juicy 'leaves' (flat stem joints) and plum-sized fruits are fodder. Juicy golden fruit are tasty, once peeled. A well-grown plant shows magnificent outlines against an evening sky. Planted close together, they gradually become an impenetrable hedge. A fallen leaf takes root, often quicker than when carefully planted. Beware bristles: use gloves, folded paper or tool – plant away from path or pool. p.165

ORIGANUM Labiatae
O. majorana Mediterranean
SWEET MARJORAM, a perennial habitué in orchards and widespread escape, likes

sunny rocks in well-drained garden soil. Trim and water if necessary.

ORNITHOGALUM Liliaceae/Hyacinthaceae
Easy in Mediterranean climates, native to stony fields, roadsides or grassy pastures, this delightful flower flourishes in any free-draining soil.

O. arabicum Mediterranean
One of the tallest (50cm) it has fragrant, white waxy flowers among fleshy leaves and prefers warmer regions. Bulblets naturalize. p.165

O. longibracteatum (O. caudatum) S Africa
amuses children. In California called PREGNANT ONION, small bulblets swell between fleshy tunics, fall off and take root when touching soil. Seeds germinate easily and may get out of hand.

Ornithogalum arabicum

O. montanum E Mediterranean
White clustered stars arise among leaves (10-20cm).

O. narbonense Mediterranean
Loose, upright racemes (25-40cm) carry milk-white spring flowers. Leaves die down shortly after.

O. thyrsoides Cape
CHINCHERINCHEE (20-30cm) carry long-lasting white flower racemes. 'Aureum' golden flowers.

O. umbellatum Mediterranean
Snow-white spring flower clusters grow among grass-like foliage in places where bulbs do not dry out. Very hardy, suiting colder regions or north-facing ground (south-facing for southern hemisphere gardeners), the easy-going STAR OF BETHLEHEM may naturalize, also escape.

Paeonia cambessedesii, from red turning pale pink

OSMANTHUS Oleaceae
Neat, evergreen SWEET OLIVE are desirable shrubs or trees. Leathery leaves resemble the Mediterranean sclerophyllous foliage and respond to clipping. If carefully chosen, creamy white flowers scent gardens from spring to autumn. These vigorous but slow-growing plants like organic soil in part-shade and, once established, are tolerant of drought and sun exposure. Propagation: fresh seeds, cuttings, layering.

O. x burkwoodii
Refined, rounded (1.5×1.5m), good on chalky soils.

O. delavayi W China
Although smaller than most (1-2m), in spring flower size and mass excel. Likes chalky soils.

O. fragrans Asia
FRAGRANT OLIVE (2-6m) tender in colder regions, is outstanding for larger leaves and sweetest summer fragrance (all year in mild climates).

Paeonia cambessedesii

O. heterophyllus (O. aquifolium) Japan
Wind-tolerant CHINESE HOLLY (2-4m), hardier than most, scents the air in late summer.

OSTEOSPERMUM Compositae
From the gardener's point of view, Osteospermum is unnecessarily separated from Arctotis and Dimorphotheca (which see). All are called AFRICAN DAISY and are mostly raised as prolific many-coloured hybrids. Well-drained soils in full sun and mulch-protected roots are all they need.

O. barberiae S Africa
Rhizomatous, spreading 40cm with magenta winter flowers.

O. ecklonis S Africa
Shrubby 50-80cm, white flowers with dark blue centres.

O. fruticosum S Africa, SE coast
This fast-growing perennial ground cover 25-45cm tall, grows from cuttings in situ. Watch for water or shade requirements until established. Summer heat checks winter to spring bloom. 'White Cloud' and 'Snow White' spread fresh carpets, less flat: 'African Queen' darkest purple. p.42

OTANTHUS Compositae
O. maritimus Mediterranean
COTTONWEED, a succulent creeper with yellow summer flowers, effectively stabilizes its native dry, coastal sand. White felt protects foliage against drying-out, against salt-laden winds and the heat generated by hot sand.

OTHONNA Compositae
O. cheirifolia (Othonnopsis c.)
 Algeria, Tunesia
Leathery glaucous leaves on spreading branches (15-25cm) grow wild on coastal rock. A quick-growing drought-tolerant plant with golden summer bloom, easy to propagate from cuttings in situ.

OXALIS Oxalidaceae
Comprise many (beautiful) species which, once nursed into strong individuals, may go out of control. O. pes-caprae with cheerful lemon spring bloom covers Mediterranean fields to the horizon. OXALIS originate from the Cape, Chile, Mexico, America, Asia. Many are obnoxious weeds, impossible to eradicate. They propagate themselves by seed (ejected in all directions) and offsets so tiny no sieve will select them. Discard Oxalis-contaminated soil.

PACHYSTEGIA see **OLEARIA**

PAEONIA Paeoniaceae
PEONIES are legion. From Asia come deciduous tree peonies, woody-stemmed shrubs, the glory of watered gardens. Mediterranean herbaceous peonies highlight natural gardens. Terminal flowers with numerous yellow stamens come in shades of rose, red, white. Even out of flower, their foliage (often red-veined) is worthwhile. Mediterranean lime- and cold-tolerant peonies thrive on winter rain. Plant on north-facing slopes, protected from afternoon sun by a shrub; large holes accomodate rhizomatous or tuberous roots, buds not more than 3cm below soil level. Mix bone-meal and compost into the planting hole and mulch well. Transplanting demands care; cord-like roots establish slowly. Perfect drainage and ventilation prevent fungal peony wilt (*Botrytis paeoniae*). Propagation: fresh seed or roots (3 buds per section).

P. broteri Iberian Peninsula
30-40cm, shiny leaves divided into narrow leaflets, carmine flowers. Common in southern Spain.

P. californica S California
A herbaceous perennial (50cm) with brownish-purple, cup-shaped spring flowers 3cm across.

P. cambessedesii Balearic Is.
Red-veined leaves reach 30cm. Bright flowers 10cm across are followed by intriguing fruits (carpels). Pitch-black seeds rest on shocking-pink beds, germinating readily. p.86, 166

P. clusii Crete
Endemic to Crete and **P. rhodia** to Rhodes, both bear white flowers.

P. mascula Mediterranean
Native to deciduous woods from NW Africa to Israel. One of the tallest (50-90cm), multi-stemmed, large-leaved with solitary purple flowers 10cm across. In medieval times their medicinal properties were appreciated. A yellow variety occurs in Sicily.

P. officinalis S France to Albania
Often cultivated, it is native to meadows or scrub. Much-divided leaves (bluish beneath), red flowers 8-20cm.

Parkinsonia aculeata

PANCRATIUM Amaryllidaceae
Bulbous perennial herbs with exquisite, white scented flower umbels grow naturally in coastal sand. In the garden only the best drainage is good enough and summer-baking vital. Propagation: seed, offsets.

P. illyricum Corsica, Sardinia
Leaves around 40cm long, early summer flowers.

P. maritimum W Mediterranean
Along sandy beaches among drying foliage, the SEA DAFFODIL produces flower stalks at the end of summer from long-necked bulbs. Their scent is worth the trip. Digging bulbs on the beach would destroy this lovely sight. p.167

PANDOREA Bignoniaceae
P. jasminoides (Bignonia j.) Australia
The evergreen BOWER PLANT will cover a house wall if there is wire to support it. From summer to autumn, white flower clusters adorn glossy dark foliage. Well-drained fertile, sunny ground suits it, roots established under a cool mulch. This healthy drought-tolerant climber requires little maintenance. However, train the first shoots carefully. Increase by cuttings. Choose from 'Alba' or 'Rosea', both are good.

P. pandorana (P. australis) Australia
Where speed is essential, the evergreen WONGA-WONGA VINE, hardier than the first, covers with shiny foliage and creamy winter bloom unsightly objects. A dead tree is an ideal support.

PARKINSONIA
Leguminosae/Caesalpinioideae
P. aculeata California
The deciduous JERUSALEM THORN (5-8m) bears attractive yellow spring flowers. Feathery foliage allows light through all year. It tolerates alkaline soil but resents irrigation. Prune crossing shoots. Sow into individual pots after having used hot water treatment (see Propagation). This pioneer shrub/tree becomes weedy in near-desert conditions. p.167

Pancratium maritimum

Passiflora × allardii

Passiflora cinnabarina

PARTHENOCISSUS Vitaceae
P. tricuspidata (Ampelopsis t.) China
The well-known BOSTON IVY covers fast whatever you want to hide (clings by tendrils). It is kept within bounds by careful pruning. Increase by layering.

PASSIFLORA Passifloraceae
Among the most delightful climbers for Mediterranean climates, PASSIFLORA come in many sizes from potted plants to all-embracing vines. Shapes of lower leaves differ often from tip growth. Flowers, from minute and exquisite to 12cm across, are of many colours. Flowering is best once hot summer is over and lasts nearly all year. Fruits are exquisite or insipid. *P. coccinea* is tender, others tolerate short-term snow or frost. Passifloras require minimal care. Plant in humusy soil, head in sun, roots in shade. Widespreading roots rot in confined, soggy conditions. Passifloras can be grown in containers or trained on walls, but to ramble through shrubs and up into trees is their delight. Your problem will be to keep flowers (and fruits!) within sight. Cut half back for vigorous spring growth. Seeds, sent by friends from the Americas or obtained from fruits at specialty shops, germinate easily (surplus plants are cherished gifts). Common names differ from country to country but botanical names ensure that you get what you mean to order. *Passion Flowers* by Vanderplank gives reliable details (see Bibliography). p.92

P. caerulea Brazil, Argentina
The hardy BLUE PASSION FLOWER is a 'weed' which is best kept out of the garden. Even root fragments left behind grow into vigorous plants, as I learned to regret. If you feel you must have one, grow in a container and enjoy its flowers and bright orange fruits (insipid unless cooked).

P. x caeruleoracemosa
(*P. caerulea* x *racemosa*) grown in England since the 19th century, is a showy vine with large, purple flowers.

P. cinnabarina SE Australia
A slender climber (2-3m), in early spring graceful globular green fruits follow choice cinnabar flowers. p.168

P. edulis Brazil, Paraguay
PASSION FRUIT (5-7m) bears purple fruits which fall to ground when ripe. Juice is mildly somniferous. f. **flavicarpa** has yellow fruit.

P. ligularis C America
Vigorous SWEET GRANADILLA (4-6m) is best in warm regions above 1000m. An orange brittle shell, cut open, reveals a delicious, exotic jelly. In our Mediterranean garden it is a shy bloomer. In the Andes at 1.700m, it climbed into nearby eucalypts, bearing ample fruit.

P. manicata South America
Grows in many Mediterranean gardens. Profuse, fire engine red flowers open in early summer and again once autumn rains refresh the air.

P. mollissima Venezuela to Bolivia
Native at 2-3000m it has large pink flowers and small edible, banana-shaped fruit.

PAULOWNIA Scrophulariaceae
P. tomentosa China
The very ornamental EMPRESS TREE (6-15m) carries fragrant lilac spring flowers in impressive panicles before giant leaves come out. Very tolerant of frost, reasonably so of drought and pollution, *Paulownia* likes well-drained, fertile soil in sun. Brittle wood and large leaves require wind protection. In summer, a wide crown shades large areas. Surface roots discourage other plantings. Native to deciduous higher altitude woodlands, *Paulownia* tolerates the shade of taller trees.

PAVONIA Malvaceae
P. hastata Brazil
This undemanding small shrub (60-100cm) carries pale pink autumn flowers which resemble small *Hibiscus*. Plant in sun or half-shade. Propagation: cuttings, seed. p.169

Passiflora amethystina covering a *Pistacia lentiscus*

PELARGONIUM   Geraniaceae

We have grown GERANIUM all our lives, but may not realize that they are natives of the Cape, which has a Mediterranean climate and nobody to water them in the wild. Try to simulate native conditions such as light well-drained soil in warm, sunny positions (intermittent shade in hottest areas). Thick mulch under their well-established leaf canopies keeps roots cool. Water only when needed. Pampering with rich soil, irrigation or fertilizer shortens their life, full shade encourages lank growth. Sprinter and Carefree series grow naturally compact. Tip-pinch others. Remove spent flowers and yellowing leaves regularly. Propagation: cuttings, dried 24 hours in shade. *Pelargonium* (their correct name) and true *Geranium* have small differences in flower anatomy.

Pelargonium includes subshrubs (*P.* x *domesticum, P.* x *hortorum*) and climbers (*P. peltatum*) with long spring to autumn flowering periods. Scented-leaved *P. graveolens* and *P. tomentosum* are excellent drought-tolerant greenery with insignificant flowers. Passers-by brush leaves, releasing their aromatic oils. Tuberous-rooted succulent *P. carnosum* covers driest ground, delighting plant enthusiasts.

P. carnosum   South Africa
Dormant in summer, bonsai-like succulent stems carry small creamy flowers in spring.

P. x domesticum
REGAL GERANIUM (50-80cm) carries compact leaves with splendid bloom, in time turning straggly. Prune judiciously or start anew.   p.27

Pavonia hastata

P. graveolens   S Africa
The ROSE GERANIUM (70-100cm) with edible leaves and small white flowers yields geranium oil.

P. x hortorum
GARDEN GERANIUM (ZONAL *PELARGONIUM*) is best grown compact, its roots shaded. Many flower colours; mixing all, copies the Andean women's multi-coloured skirts, a startling sight, best framed by a unifying evergreen background.   p.52

P. peltatum   S Africa
The fleshy-leaved IVY GERANIUM trails along beds, hangs over walls, climbs into shrubs, an asset to young gardens. Variegated leaves look chlorotic.   p.53

P. tomentosum   SW Cape
Soft velvety, peppermint-scented leaves quickly cover the ground in sun or dappled shade. Tiny white flowers are pretty.

PENSTEMON   Scrophulariaceae
Evergreen and widely used in England, PENSTEMON flowers in many colours from spring into autumn. It enjoys sun (light shade in hottest areas). Drought-tolerant, easily transplanted, species are killed by kindness which would mean rich soil with regular irrigation. Cultivars do well in garden conditions. Propagation: division, seed.   p.17, 137, 169

P. barbatus   W USA
Excellent for cold mountain regions, red flower panicles rise from fresh green leaves (60-90cm).

P. heterophyllus ssp. purdyi   California
Brilliant blue flowers (30-50cm) among dark green leaves are best in full sun (spring, summer). They tolerate heat, salt spray, wind and suit coastal gardens.

P. pinifolius   New Mexico
The common name of the PINE-LEAVED PENSTEMON tells what waterwise gardeners like to hear: narrow, pine-like leaves mean drought survival, turning this spreading shrublet into a useful ground cover or lawn replacement. Not all common names are so helpful.

P. spectabilis   California
Upright stems with green or glaucous leaves and early summer flowers reach 50-90cm.   p.169

Penstemon 'Hidcote Pink'

Penstemon spectabilis in front of *Yucca whipplei* and scrub oak in the San Jacinto mountains. Courtesy Santa Ana Botanic Garden, California.

PEROVSKIA   Labiatae
P. atriplicifolia   Pakistan
An open shrublet, the deciduous RUSSIAN SAGE (50-90cm) is an asset to sunny gardens, dry or not. Slender powder-blue panicles stand above feathery grey

Persea americana

areas shade from afternoon sun. Undemanding and almost drought-tolerant, at the end of summer, watering weekly or twice monthly may be required. Drought-stressed but well-planted specimens recuperate with autumn rains (cut back). Propagation: cuttings, division.
p.171

P. coronarius   S Europe
Vigorous deciduous growth (2-3m), very fragrant flowers.

P. lewisii   California
The deciduous WILD MOCK ORANGE (2-3m) is native to rocky slopes in mixed woodlands.

P. mexicanus   Mexico
Tender and evergreen (4-6m), it covers banks or walls with drooping branches.

PHILLYREA   Oleaceae
Evergreen MOCK PRIVET, closely related to *Osmanthus*, is a glossy-leaved, densely-branched shrub. Tiny fragrant flowers call out from dry rocky ground (limestone). Use both for formal shapes or reliable, yearlong cover.

P. angustifolia   Mediterranean
Clip small leaves for box-like compactness to 2m.   p.30

P. latifolia   Mediterranean
This shrub or small tree (4-6m) carries larger, rounder leaves.

PHLOMIS   Labiatae
These shrubby perennials, usually cut back for neat appearance, are grown with other drought-tolerant Mediterranean natives. Easy in any well-drained sunny ground. Mulch encourages establishment. Increased by cuttings.

foliage. Removing spent flowers prolongs bloom into autumn. *Perovskia* tolerates chalky soils, colder mountain regions or coastal areas, but demands excellent drainage as do all drought-tolerant plants. Increased by summer cuttings. 'Blue Spire' has larger flowers.

PERSEA   Lauraceae
P. americana   Mexico, S America
AVOCADOS, evergreen tall rounded trees, are today bred as spreading shrubs to 7×7m. Large leaves are shiny, flowers insignificant, fruits delicious. Wind and sun 'burn' young stems (wrap in straw). Later, lower branches shield stems and shade the ground. Only the best drainage is adequate. Check, for example, on groundwater; can winter rain flow away? Working the soil beneath trees harms shallow roots which are best protected by fallen leaves. Cut out dry wood, lift lower branches barely off the ground so that low-hanging fruits remain dry. Heavy pruning encourages water shoots which would require more pruning. Avocados tolerate short frost and are resistant to honey fungus.
Avocados come in many sizes. Their evergreen shiny volume reasonably fast blocks an undesirable view. 'Wurtz' (also known as 'Dwarf') suits tubs. Gua-

temala varieties bear large fruit, smaller-fruited Mexican ones tolerate more cold. You need 3-4 plants to harvest fruit. Nurseries will recommend those suited to your garden.   p.170

PETUNIA   Solanaceae
Native to Argentina, PETUNIAS today sell as long-flowering hybrids. They grow in sun and light shade wherever sandy soils or drought are problems. Pinch back.

PHILADELPHUS   Saxifragaceae
Choose MOCK ORANGES wherever creamy spring flowers' scent is wanted and bare bases are hidden. Plant in deep, well-mulched soil. In hot inland

Phlomis fruticosa

Phygelius aequalis 'Yellow Trumpet'

P. fruticosa   Mediterranean
The rugged JERUSALEM SAGE (80-100cm)
carries yellow summer flowers.   p.170

P. italica   Balearic Is.
Pink flowers, grey felty leaves, refined
appearance (30cm).

PHLOX   Polemoniaceae
P. subulata   USA
The evergreen, colourful MOSS PHLOX
likes well-drained, poor sunny soils on
the dry side. Mat-forming, it creeps and
roots 50cm wide. Confined locations
predispose it to powdery mildew. Propagation: cuttings, division, seed.

PHOENIX   Palmae
P. canariensis   Canary Is.
The magnificent wide-spreading CAN-
ARY DATE PALM (9-12m), drought-tolerant
once established, although slow, assumes its architectural role the moment
it is planted. I remember the fronds'
graceful movements in a snowstorm.
frontcover, p.13, 45

P. dactylifera   Mediterranean
Grown in arid regions for the last 5000
years, the DATE is a vital crop from Morocco to Pakistan. Towering and clump-
forming, suckering from the base, it may
rise 20m, suiting large gardens. In hot regions, grow your own date. It requires
deep watering or ground water and tolerates saline water and coastal conditions.   p.104

P. theophrasti   Cyprus
If planted more often, it would be saved
from extinction.

PHORMIUM   Agavaceae
P. colensoi   New Zealand
Smaller than the next, it is ideal for
reduced areas.

P. tenax   New Zealand
An easy plant, the evergreen, perennial
NEW ZEALAND FLAX (1.5-2m) is appreciated for its giant, sword-like leaves.
Towering flower stalks, magnificent
silhouettes against a blue Mediterranean
sky, carry red to yellow flower clusters.
Any mulched soil will suit it. If carefully
chosen, variegated leaves create harmonious colour blends, still green usually
seems best.   p.171

PHOTINIA   Rosaceae
P. serratifolia (P. serrulata)   China
PHOTINIA is an evergreen spreading
shrub or small tree (3-10m). Glossy new
leaves are coppery, early flower clusters
cream, later berries red. Generously
mulched sunny ground suits this sturdy
screen or hedge, which is drought- and
wind-tolerant once established. Cutting
back to 1m rejuvenates older plants.

PHYGELIUS   Scrophulariaceae
P. aequalis   E Cape
Evergreen in mild areas, it grows gradually into a rounded bush to 1m. Older
stems become woody. Greyish-rose
flowers are best when summer is over
and cooler days prevail. Easy in half-
shaded, well-drained fertile soil. In be-
low-freezing temperatures cut back and
cover with mulch; spring regrowth is
vigorous. Semi-ripe autumn cuttings are
quicker than seed. 'Yellow Trumpet'
bears wider leaves.   p.170

PHYLA   Verbenaceae
P. nodiflora (Lippia n.)   USA
Creeps along with rooting shoots 1cm
high, growing happily into other plants,
difficult to eradicate. Charming tiny
white buttony flowers require sun. For
an excellent summer ground cover
prepare rooted sections, around 25-50
per square metre, and water until
established. This deciduous lawn
replacement looks somewhat poor in
winter.

PHYLICA   Rhamnaceae
P. ericoides   Cape
Evergreen and rounded (40-60cm), it
resembles *Erica* (tiny leaves, white
flowerheads). Use widely as reliable,
maintenance-free cover, multiplied by
cuttings.   p.171

P. plumosa (P. pubescens)   Cape
This evergreen shrub (60-150cm) with
tufted, feathery plumes, native to lower
mountain slopes, is best in humusy acid
soil and likes sunny seacoast gardens.
Annual trimming after flowering keeps
both compact. Propagation: autumn
cuttings, seed in sand.

Philadelphus 'Lemoinei', *with Quercus ilex*

Phormium tenax, right

Phylica ericoides, left

PIMELEA Thymelaeaceae
P. ferruginea W Australia
This desirable evergreen shrub, related to *Daphne*, grows into a rounded 80-150cm, in spring topped with pink 'pincushions'. It tolerates limy coastal ground, preferably light, and likes full sun (shade in hottest areas). Perfect drainage is vital. For compact growth, trim after flowering; flowers develop on previous year's growth. Transplanting is sometimes difficult. Pimelea is relatively short-lived but easily propagated by seed.

PINUS Pinaceae
Evergreen trees (shrubs in unfavourable conditions), PINES grow in sun, sometimes in pure stands or lonely on steep cliffs. Several are extremely drought-tolerant. All need excellent drainage. Shape for attractive outlines. Where naturally-growing pine interfere with other trees, trim back to keep low or transplant young specimens. Pine are pioneers in difficult, dry terrain, sensitive to pollution and invasive in South Africa. Procession Caterpillars occasionally attack *P. halepensis* and *P. canariensis* (see Plant Health). Propagation: seed. See also p.20.

Pittosporum tobira

P. halepensis Mediterranean
In driest Mediterranean locations, the ALEPPO PINE (10-15m) covers large tracts on limestone hills to the water's edge. This pioneer with upright growth (tortured in trying conditions) often takes over abandoned farm ground or overtakes slow oak. Resin flavours Greek retsina wine. p.14, 173

P. pinaster (P. maritima)
W Mediterranean
The MARITIME PINE (18-25m) grows very fast in forest formation on siliceous sandy or rocky coastal soils. It controls erosion at the Golden Gate Park, San Francisco.

P. pinea Mediterranean
Planted since Roman times, the elegant STONE (UMBRELLA) PINE (10-25m) characterizes Mediterranean landscapes and likes sandy coasts. Cones yield the edible pinyon. 'Correvoniana' prostrate miniature growth for containers, 'Fragilis' thin-shelled seeds.

P. radiata C California
The very fast-growing MONTEREY PINE (20-25m) prefers deep soils in cooler areas, tolerates coastal winds. For large gardens.

P. torreyana California
Rare and fast-growing TORREY PINE (9-20m) occurs naturally on Santa Rosa Island and on eroded coastal bluffs in San Diego County. It likes coastal conditions and tolerates heat or drought. It responds to summer irrigation but requires sharp drainage. Growing in gardens could prevent its extinction.

PISTACIA Anacardiaceae
Native to the maquis, to open woods or mountain regions, LENTISC does well on parched, calcareous soils under hot summer sun. Shrubs or trees, mostly slow, they are grown for their evergreen foliage (*P. lentiscus*), autumn-colouring (*P. chinensis*) or pretty fruits and edible nuts (*P. vera*). Deciduous species (*P. chinensis, P. terebinthus*) suit cooler regions. Plant in sharply drained, humusy soil. Mulch liberally. Fungal root rot threatens lentisc in poor drainage; avoid summer-watering, compacted soils and poorly ventilated or deeply shaded locations. Propagation: seed (remove pulp, soak overnight).

P. atlantica Mt. Atlas, N Africa
Evergreen in mild climates, deciduous in colder areas, the BETOUM (10-15m) is useful in hot, windy inland regions, an excellent rootstock for *P. vera*.

P. chinensis China
A deciduous round-crowned tree (10-20m), it is appreciated for drought tolerance and striking autumn colour.

P. lentiscus Mediterranean
Evergreen shrubs (1-4m), LENTISC cover large tracts on well-drained, often rocky ground, looking best in hot, dry summers. Very old specimens can be shaped as trees. Leathery leaves clip well. Since ancient times, stems yield resin for medicine and varnish, drupes provide oil for sweetmeat or liqueur. Carbon was esteemed for ironing, lasting longer than any other. Shepherds place cooling leaves into their shoes. p.17, 21, 35, 83

P. terebinthus Mediterranean
Deciduous, it differs from *P. lentiscus* by terminal leaflet.

P. vera Greece, Syria, Mesopotamia
Native to mountainous regions on poor soil, PISTACHIO develops into a deciduous tree (3-7m), larger-leaved than others. Widely cultivated (Greece, California), grow 1 male and 5 female plants to harvest edible pistachio nuts.

PITTOSPORUM   Pittosporaceae
Useful evergreen foliage plants (shrubs, trees). Small clustered flowers among glossy leathery leaves are often sweetly scented. Easy in deep, humusy soil in sun or intermittent shade. Perfect drainage is vital. All benefit from heavy mulching. Cutting back rejuvenates overgrown specimens. Increased by cuttings. Excellent shelter belts, they also provide beautiful backdrops.

P. crassifolium   New Zealand
The CARO grows almost columnar. Leaves are dark green above, downy white below, flowers crimson.

P. eugenioides   New Zealand
The handsome TARATA (6-8m) grows as a densely branched tree. Pale green leaves frame large trusses of greenish, honey-scented summer flowers.

P. phillyreoides   Australia
The graceful DESERT WILLOW (3-8m) is a useful, very drought-tolerant small inland tree with showy red seed capsules.

P. tenuifolium   New Zealand
Called TAWHIWHI (or easier KOHUHU), this graceful, slender-trunked tree is most attractive. Small leaves when young are near black. Many cultivars.

P. tobira   China, Japan
In the Mediterranean, the TOBIRA (3-6m) is widely grown for its large glossy leaves, sweetly scented cream flowers and sturdy constitution. Shaped carefully for an interesting branch formation or grown as it will, it suits coastal areas.   p.172, 173

P. undulatum   E Australia
The attractive VICTORIAN BOX (4-10m, similar width) bears fragrant creamy spring flowers and showy orange fruit.

Note: Golf clubs are made from this wood.

Platanus orientalis

Pittosporum tobira in front of *Pinus halepensis* with *Euryops pectinatus* at its feet.

PLATANUS   Platanaceae
Widely used in Mediterranean regions, deciduous PLANE grow best in hot regions and are indifferent to drought, compacted soil or air pollution. Their attractive bark flakes in patches. Imposing, they suit avenues or city parks. Long-lived, they shade a spring or on gravelly riverbanks draw from groundwater. Where you see an isolated plane, it means water is there. Napoleon planted planes to shade the roads where his armies marched along. Increased by cuttings.

P. x acerifolia
The LONDON PLANE (10-25m), widely abused as a street tree, cut up and cut down, still perseveres. 'Tremonia' very fast-growing.

P. occidentalis   N USA
The AMERICAN PLANE is susceptible to fungal diseases which thrive in cooler regions with humid summers. Today it is often replaced by *P. orientalis*.

P. orientalis
     Mediterranean to Himalaya
The ORIENTAL PLANE (10-18m), somewhat slower-growing, with finely cut leaves. Branches stretch near horizontal.   p.173

Plectranthus arabicus

Polygala myrtifolia var. grandiflora

PLECTRANTHUS Labiatae
Excellent quick-growing ground covers in sun or shade, *Plectranthus* flower in blue shades, prefer light rich humusy soil, initially need summer watering. When established, they become quite drought-tolerant. Easy to propagate: cuttings (rooted in water), rooting sidebranches, seed.

P. arabicus (Coleus a.) Arabia
Within a year it grows to a rounded evergreen 30-50cm, kept compact by clipping. Clear blue flowers top firm apple green foliage from autumn to spring. This sturdy pioneer thrives in full sun or moderate shade. It tolerates scarce soil, water and heat. Best of all, it increases freely from cuttings, stuck into ground at any time in almost any place. Planted widely, it covers all ground. p.174

P. neochilus S Africa
A trailing ground cover with aromatic leaves, navy flowers.

PLUMBAGO Plumbaginaceae
P. auriculata (P. capensis) S Africa
Evergreen in warmest locations, freezing back in cold ones, the exuberant PLUMBAGO spreads 3m. It enjoys hot, sharply drained sites. From summer onwards, its phlox-like bloom rambles into trees, covers banks and fences and is kept within bounds by spring pruning. White gardens use 'Alba'. Propagation: cuttings, suckers. p.57, 174

PODRANEA Bignoniaceae
P. ricasoliana S Africa
The deciduous PINK TRUMPET VINE comes into its own from late summer into early winter. Pink flower clusters on thin trailing branches reach out wide. Tie or let grow into a supporting tree. Cutting back in winter keeps it within bounds. Humusy well-drained soil in sun or half shade and occasional summer watering suit it. p.41, 175

POLYGALA Polygalaceae
Purple, pea-like flowers on evergreen shoots appear all year, except over hottest months. Easy in humusy soil in sun or half shade with occasional summer watering. Experiment with all species for their reliability.

P. myrtifolia E Cape, Natal
Planted in dry sunny areas it withstands considerable frost. var. **grandiflora** has larger flowers. p.174

P. virgata Cape
This upright somewhat stiff shrub (1-2m) goes bare at its base.

POLYGONUM Polygonaceae
P. aubertii (Fallopia a.) Asia
The rampant SILVER LACE VINE, evergreen in warmer areas, covers terrace roofs or tree stumps in a season, a house in a few years. Creamy bloom in frothy billowing masses is open from spring to autumn. Give mulched sunny soil and monthly summer waterings. Control by cutting to ground.

P. capitatum Himalaya
Creeping stems take root as they expand. Pink flower buttons are out most months. Irreplaceable as a flat, quick-growing, undemanding ground cover. Trim for compact growth. 'Magic Carpet' compact, slightly taller.

POLYPODIUM Polypodiaceae
Drought-tolerant, these clump-forming ferns with delicate fronds grow wild in shady cracks or stony walls, established by creeping rhizomes, increased by division.

P. cambricum (P. australe) Europe
The low, creeping WELSH POLYPODY suits small corners. p.175

P. glycyrrhiza Alaska to California
LICORICE FERN (30cm) has large fronds.

Plumbago auriculata

P. scouleri   NW USA
with even longer fronds, also grows on tree trunks.

POMADERRIS   Rhamnaceae
P. grandis   Australia
The evergreen POMADERRIS shrub (1-4m) enhances coastal shade gardens with its white flower clusters.

PONCIRUS   Rutaceae
P. trifoliata   Asia
This deciduous thorny mass with white scented bloom and small orange-like fruits is ideal for 'Life with Animals'. Thorns protect nesting birds. Drought-tolerant, its demands are minimal. Increased by seed.

Podranea ricasoliana

POPULUS   Salicaceae
P. alba   Europe, Mediterranean
The WHITE POPLAR (9-15m), an excellent windbreak, suits sunny natural gardens and tolerates salt air and drought. Roots invade house foundations.

P. nigra   Mediterranean
'Italica' (LOMBARDY POPLAR), intolerant of coastal conditions, has a neat cypress-like outline.

PORTULACA   Portulacaceae
P. grandiflora   S America
The delightful ROSE MOSS, a succulent ground-covering summer annual for hottest areas, self-sows in gravelly mulch. Drought-tolerant, but best with infrequent summer watering; plant in any soil.   p.175

PORTULACARIA   Portulacaceae
P. afra   S Africa
The succulent SPEKBOOM (its South African name) may grow to minitree-like proportions. Delicate pink flower clusters occur in hottest regions. No special soil requirements. Drought-tolerant and fire-retardant, it needs excellent drainage. The similar Jade Plant (*Crassula argentea*) tolerates less heat.

POTENTILLA   Rosaceae
P. fruticosa   widespread
A deciduous, drought-tolerant shrub (30-100cm) with slight bloom, CINQUE-FOIL tolerates poorest soils. Best in sunny sites with occasional watering. var. **mandschurica** can stand more drought than others.

PROSOPIS Leguminosae/Mimosoideae
P. glandulosa   California, Mexico
The deciduous to evergreen HONEY MES-QUITE (5-7m) is a thorny spreading shrub or tree. Characteristic of desert trees, its sparse feathery foliage gives little shade. It likes deep soils for the taproot to search for water way down, tolerates saline conditions, drought or irrigation. It controls erosion and provides shelter from winds. Fragrant flowers attract bees, ample seedpods provide fodder. Easy seed propagation. Beware the invasive *P. juliiflora!*

PROSTANTHERA   Labiatae
Grow in sun or semi-shade for its delightfully scented foliage and a splash of spring colour. Cutting back after flowering keeps these evergreen shrubs in good shape. Water when needed. Most species are short-lived.

P. cuneata   SE Australia
Dense and rounded (50-80cm) with white summer bloom. Frost-tolerant.

P. rotundifolia   S Australia
The MINT BUSH (100-180cm) has smallest leaves, blue spring flowers.

Polypodium cambricum

Portulaca grandiflora

Protea susannae

Prunus armeniaca 'Flora Pleno'

PROTEA   Proteaceae
Superb but tricky, they require sharply drained, slightly acid soil (pH 6.5), a sunny slope, much light, air circulation yet no wind, occasional summer watering until established. Fine roots resent disturbance. Proteas are sensitive to nitrates and phosphates, and soils and mulches should be low in nutrients, but a pinch of magnesium sulphate seems beneficial. Established plants tolerate short-term frost. Propagation: summer cuttings, autumn seed. Other protea family members are sturdier (*Hakea*, *Grevillea*) and their smaller flowers seem to suit Mediterranean plant communities best.

P. susannae   Cape
Reaching 2-3m, evergreen, silvery grey foliage with pink artichoke-like flowers are both splendid. I tried several proteas. Only this one, received pot-bound, succeeded.   p.176

PRUNUS   Rosaceae
Deciduous *Prunus* provide glorious spring bloom and delicious fruits. If evergreen, their rounded, glossy mass provides ground cover and screens. A fast-growing framework for our gardens, all thrive in sunny calcareous, well-aerated and -drained soils and are trouble-free. Occasional slow summer watering may

be beneficial. Where shade encroaches and drainage or ventilation is poor, there may be health problems. Thinning improves air circulation. Evergreen *P. ilicifolia* and *P. lyonii* (sturdy, but elegant hedges, resistant to honey fungus) tolerate hard cutting back, but prune deciduous species with restraint. In frosty areas, use late-flowering varieties.

P. armeniaca   N China
The small, deciduous APRICOT tree, cultivated in China since 3000 BC, provides flowers and fruits. Sharp drainage (best on terraces) is essential. Thinning produces larger, healthier fruits. 'Flora Pleno' looks exquisite.   p.176

P. x domestica   S Europe, Eurasia
Grow the deciduous, easy COMMON PLUM (3-6m) for flowers and fruits. Nurseries will advise on cultivars.

P. dulcis (P. amygdalus)   Mediterranean, Asia
ALMOND, ablaze with late winter bloom, sets fruits on young trees (3-6m). Harvest at the end of summer, spreading a net below the tree. Beat the nuts down with long canes. Eat fresh; stored, they last into a second year. Almonds will grow on poor soils.   p.19, 23, 176

P. ilicifolia   California
The evergreen rounded ISLAY soon reaches 3m, eventually 5-7m. Shiny leaves are less prickly than the true holly. White spring flowers come in thick racemes and the red fruits are edible. Drought-tolerant.

P. lusitanica   W Mediterranean
The evergreen PORTUGAL LAUREL, a shiny dark green mass, slow at first, reaches 3-5m, eventually 8m. Clipping keeps it at desired height. Formal shapes need attention.

P. lyonii   California Islands
The attractive evergreen CATALINA CHERRY, shrub or small tree, is native to the chaparral. Blackish, edible but insipid fruits follow creamy spring flowers.

P. serotina   USA
The deciduous RUM CHERRY (10m), shrub or tree, is a good windbreak and assists dune reclamation. Black fruits follow white flower racemes.

P. serrulata   Japan, China
The tall deciduous ORIENTAL CHERRY has many splendid cultivars and growth

Prunus dulcis

Punica granatum (flower)

Punica granatum (fruit)

Punica granatum (autumn foliage)

forms (columnar, spreading, arching, rounded). Single or double spring flowers come in white or pink.

P. spinosa Mediterranean
In early spring the deciduous SLOE (2-5m) is covered with snowy bloom. Vitamin-rich miniature plums taste best after chilling. Prune wild-growing sloes into shape. p.58

PSIDIUM Myrtaceae
Ornamental evergreen GUAVA are spring-flowering shrubs, closely related to *Acca*. Low to medium growth rates. They enjoy rich and deep well-drained soils in hot sun. Moderately drought-tolerant once established, they appreciate weekly to monthly summer watering until fruits ripen. Guavas suit coastal gardens and are desirable container plants.

P. guajava Tropical America
Semi-deciduous GUAVA (3-6m) has pear-shaped fruits, eaten as jellies. Fruit colour varies: 'Beaumont' pink, 'Detwiler' yellow, 'Pear' creamy.

P. littorale var. **littorale** Brazil
The smaller, evergreen LEMON GUAVA (2-5m) with yellow somewhat acid fruit tolerates short-term frost. PURPLE GUAVA var. **longipes** has purple, sweet fruit.

PUNICA Punicaceae
P. granatum Mediterranean
The deciduous, spiny-branched POME-GRANATE (2-4m) has many assets. Grow

early bulbs beneath its bare branches, enjoy its magnificent coppery spring foliage, golden in autumn, and bright orange flowers. Tart, leather-skinned fruits, a food since ancient times, can be stored for refreshing drinks. Drought-tolerant, it requires alkaline soil, sharp drainage, hot sun. Transplants at any age (but cut back). Propagation: cuttings, suckers. Allow it to grow as it will, shape into a small tree or clip as dense hedge. An undemanding container plant for hot terraces, an excellent candidate for life with animals (sheep won't touch it) or a mainstay of dry gardens. 'Alba Plena' (2m) has creamy double flowers, rarely bears fruit. 'Plena' orange double flowers. 'Nana' and 'Nana Plena' evergreen in mild areas, are slow-growing formal container plants with pulpless mini-fruits. p.177

PYRACANTHA Rosaceae
Drought-tolerant FIRETHORNS, closely related to *Cotoneaster and Crataegus*, are evergreen hardy shrubs (2-5m, similar spread). Abundant fruits stand out from afar (yellow, orange, red). No candidate for small gardens, they suit dry stony places in sun where little else will grow. Shape over first years, but as a defensive hedge allow it to grow as it will; animals respect formidable thorns. Susceptible to fireblight (cut back hard, burn infected branches, raise your own plants from seed). Ideal for absentee owners.

P. angustifolia SW China
Yellow winter berries adorn abandoned coastal gardens.

P. coccinea Mediterranean
Coral-red berries provide winter colour. 'Lalandei' for coldest regions. American nurseries sell 'Monrovia' brilliant orange berries; 'Santa Cruz' prostrate, large red berries; 'Shawnee' immune to fireblight.

PYROSTEGIA Bignoniaceae
P. venusta (P. ignea) Brazil, Paraguay
The evergreen ORANGE TRUMPET CREEPER (4-6m), appreciated for prolific flowering, prefers ordinary soil in hot sheltered locations, ample mulch and little water (once established).

QUERCUS Fagaceae
OAKS (sacred to Zeus and Hecate) are native to California and the Mediterranean where, in times past, they covered large tracts and today occur in reduced stands. Evergreen leaves, blown down by winds, are partly shed when summer drought sets in, carpeting the ground with grey silver. Oaks reach their tallest size with warm summers. They regrow from stumps after browsing or burning. Excessive pruning stimulates water shoots which may be prone to mildew (*Q. robur* in midsummer). The fungus *Armillaria mellea*, more serious, occurs in any oak population. It does not naturally reach epidemic proportions, but where delicate interactions are upset by summer watering, honey fungus (also called oak root fungus) may soon kill branches or fully-grown trees. The most delicate area extends from the trunk to

the drip line, but chief danger zones are the root crown, the trunk itself and the area next to it. Old trees are particularly susceptible. Dry-gardening under and near oak is the only long-term answer. Oak are undemanding, but remember a few don'ts:

– Don't water beneath oak, thus no lawns.

– Don't use soil amendments.

– Don't change grading or drainage patterns nearby.

– Don't compact the soil with paving, heavy equipment or traffic.

– Don't trench or cut roots.

Which, summing up, means 'leave the place as is'.

From: *Oak Woodland Preservation*, by Hardesty Ass. See Bibliography.

Space permitting, plant oak. Try to simulate natural habitats. Plant fresh healthy acorns in autumn. Remove caps and lay on their sides, covered with soil a finger deep. Plant more than you need to allow for those eaten by rodents, thin later. Acorns germinate in early winter. Before growing surface shoots, they establish a taproot which resents disturbance. For planting in pots choose deep containers. A wide range of oak species suits varying terrains. Leaves may be leathery or hairy, shiny or dull, lobed, spiny or soft-edged while acorns are narrow, pointed, large or globular. But an oak's outline, if allowed to grow, is always imposing.

Q. agrifolia
S California

In valleys or alluvial sites evergreen spreading CALIFORNIA LIVE OAK (12-19m) grows occasionally in pure stands, tolerating dry sandy soils and shade.

Quercus ilex

Quercus ilex

Q. coccifera
Mediterranean

The evergreen slow-growing KERMES OAK (0.5-3m) colonizes poor ground (dry limestone, siliceous soils). Twiggy growth and small *Ilex*-like leaves, heavily browsed, shape into low mounds. Roots reach wide. Kermes oaks resprout after fire, cutting to ground or browsing. When fenced and allowed to grow, leaves gradually lose their defensive features, branches reach out. Host to a scale insect (*Coccus ilicis*) which yields a fine scarlet dye. ssp. **calliprinos** (PALESTINE OAK 10m) may live 700 years. Leaves are larger, acorns nearly covered by caps.

Q. douglasii
California

The deciduous BLUE OAK, native to steeper slopes on shallow soils, flourishes in dry, hot areas, slowly reaching a wide-spreading, low-branching 5-15m. Its light shade and deep roots allow drought-tolerant vegetation to grow beneath it.

Q. dumosa
California

Evergreen shiny-leaved CALIFORNIA SCRUB OAK (1-2.5m, same width) is very slow-growing. Most tolerant of poor rocky soils, half-shade and drought, it requires good drainage and resprouts after fire. Acorns are eaten by livestock. Use as slow-growing hedge or clip into cushion shapes where reduced space inhibits natural growth (see p.83).

Q. ilex
W Mediterranean

The evergreen HOLM OAK in times past covered most Mediterranean lands. Hard, durable wood was used for house- and ship-building (keels). Charcoal-making needed a never-ending supply. Pigs fed on the acorns. The bark yields tannin. So it is little wonder that so few oaks are left. They grow in small stands on northern slopes, with age spreading 15-20m, wider than tall. Near-horizontal branches on oldest trees (800 years were estimated) carry an enormous weight. Roots go deep (10m has been measured) and spread widely. Holm oaks grow on poor even rocky soil, gradually enriching it with decaying foliage (a mild acidifier). var. **ballota** has sweet, edible acorns, eaten like chestnuts.

p.19, 21, 57, 171, 178

Q. ithaburensis ssp. macrolepis
Greece, Palestine

Deciduous VALLONEA OAK (6-17m), often growing singly, is valued for its beautifully large leaves, silvery beneath. Cups yield a dark dye. Acorns have been eaten in times of famine.

Q. libani
Near East

Slender, deciduous LEBANON OAK (5-6m), densely branched shrubs or trees, prefer mountain areas.

Q. lobata
California

A prominent member of the Californian hardwood community, the deciduous, fast-growing VALLEY OAK (10-25m) is native to fertile valley bottoms or stream banks in deep soil. Roots spread beyond the dripline. Summer watering induces health problems.

Q. pubescens   S Europe, Turkey
The DOWNY OAK (15-18m) is a magnificent specimen tree with a large rounded crown and blackish bark.

Q. rotundifolia see **Q. ilex** var. **ballota**

Q. suber   W Mediterranean
Favouring hot regions, the evergreen CORK OAK (6-15m or less) grows on siliceous soil and rock. Barked every 7-10 years, it supports an important industry. In open forests, it encourages rich undergrowth.

RANUNCULUS   Ranunculaceae
R. asiaticus   Mediterranean
The exquisite tuberous PERSIAN BUTTERCUP likes sharply drained sunny ground. Overwatered tubers rot. After soaking, plant tubers 5cm deep, less in heavy soils, best where they can be watched.   p.179

• **RETAMA**   Leguminosae/Papilionoideae
R. monosperma (Genista m.)
          Mediterranean
The excellent BRIDAL VEIL BROOM reaches 4×2m, a white curtain from late winter to spring.

RHAMNUS   Rhamnaceae
R. alaternus   Mediterranean
A maquis native, the evergreen BUCKTHORN (3-5m), large shrub or tree, grows fast where birds drop its seed. Abundant jet-black seeds may be invasive but

plantlets are easily pulled out. Shiny leaves are often variable, early spring flowers inconspicuous. Quite cold-hardy, it tolerates drought as well as most other unfavourable conditions. Vigorous growth can be trimmed into size. Useful pioneer, evergreen framework or quick cover for woodland gardens.   p.19, 40

R. californica   California
The evergreen COFFEEBERRY (2-4m), a variable widely grown shrub, likes full sun to light shade. No special needs for soil or water. 'Seaview' 0.5×2m, lower but wider.

R. ludovici-salvatoris   Balearic Is.
A drought-tolerant Balearic Island gift to gardens with a similar climate, it looks box-like, as if trimmed by the gardener and, once discovered, will be used widely. A small rounded shrub, at first upright, it grows slowly to an evergreen rounded 60-90cm (gradually 150cm). Small serrate leaves are brown beneath, flowers are insignificant. Grow in humus-enriched, sharply-drained soil, simulating its wild home. Highly localized, it is found in oak woods together with *Phillyrea latifolia,* in places where *Clematis flammula* and *Lonicera implexa* climb into *Pistacia lentiscus*, with *Cyclamen balearicum* and *Ruscus aculeatus* at its feet. No health problems. Propagation: seed.   p.179

RHAPHIOLEPIS   Rosaceae
These splendid shrubs (1-2m) with evergreen leathery foliage, hardy and drought-tolerant, grow in moisture-retentive, humusy and well-drained soil in sun or half-shade, well-mulched. They transplant readily. A neat appear-

Ranunculus Bloomingdale hybrid

Rhaphiolepis × delacourii

ance balances slow growth. Propagation: cuttings, seed.

R. × **delacourii**
(*R. indica* x *R. umbellata*) is of garden origin. Smaller-leaved than its parents, it carries flowers in upright clusters.   p.179

R. indica   China
The desirable, narrow-leaved INDIA HAWTHORN bears white pink-tinged flowers in terminal clusters (no thorns). 'Enchantress' smaller, faster, pink.

R. umbellata (R. japonica)   Japan
Roundish leaves, white scented flowers.

Rhamnus ludovici-salvatoris

Rhamnus ludovici-salvatoris, photographed in the mountains of Mallorca

Rhamnus ludovici-salvatoris, cropped for garden use, mimicking box

Robinia hispida 'Macrophylla'

RHIGOZUM Bignoniaceae
R. obovatum South Africa
Evergreen KAROO GOLD (1-3m) is very drought-tolerant and quite frost-hardy. Beautiful flower masses on previous season's growth cover this sparsely-leaved shrub from spring onwards. Native to semi-deserts, thus plant in sunny, hot locations in gravelly soil, add compost, sand, mulch and check on drainage. Easy from seed.

RHUS Anacardiaceae
A prominent genus among the drought-tolerant plants, SUMAC are excellent slope stabilizers and fire-preventers. Taproots help their survival in dry summers if planting sites are carefully chosen. Best in warm, dry places, tolerant of poor soils. Propagation: suckers, cuttings, seed (soaked). Avoid rash-inducing Poison Oak (*R. diversiloba*) or Poison Ivy (*R. radicans*). Tempted by pretty leaves, never plant either.

R. integrifolia S California
The shrubby LEMONADE BERRY (1-3m, same width) with roundish leathery leaves and white to pink flower clusters grows into a useful evergreen mass (hedge). Edible berries taste like bitter lemon. Best on coast; inland provide deep monthly summer watering or replace by *R. ovata*.

R. lancea South Africa
The evergreen AFRICAN SUMAC (3-6m), a spreading Cape tree, has sparse, dark green foliage, greenish flowers from winter to spring. An excellent windbreak, very drought-resistant and hardy, it tolerates brakish or saline soils. Transplants well, even when older. Propagation: cuttings, seed.

R. ovata California
The evergreen aromatic SUGAR BUSH (1-3m), a rounded, densely branched shrub, grows wild on dry southern chaparral slopes. Attractive all year, red buds open into white flowers. Susceptible to honey fungus. Protect from afternoon sun. Drought-tolerant if well-established.

RIBES Saxifragaceae
A spineless *Ribes* is called CURRANT and GOOSEBERRY when spiny. Excellent drought-tolerant garden plants once established, they will grow in many soils. Protect from afternoon sun. Shrubs may become deciduous in summer but resprout. Normally, pests and diseases are no problem. Propagation: seed, cutting, division.

R. speciosum California
The shrubby FUCHSIA-FLOWERED GOOSEBERRY (1-2m) grows wild in the southern California coastal chaparral. Plant where rich bloom is enjoyed and bristles are an asset.

R. viburnifolium California
Native to chaparral canyons, the evergreen shrubby CATALINA CURRANT (1m) spreads slowly 2-3m. Over winter, low-lying, scented-leaved branches take root in soft humid soil. Spring brings tiny rose flowers, autumn red berries. On the coast, light shade may suffice, inland plant in full shade. This is an excellent ground cover under oak as it does not require summer-watering.

RICINUS Euphorbiaceae
R. communis widespread
Evergreen in warmest regions, the deciduous drought-tolerant CASTOR BEAN (1-3m) tolerates poor soil. In fertile, irrigated ground in full sun it reaches tree-like proportions and staking may be required. Sown in spring *in situ*, seeds sprout quickly. Site this outstanding, undemanding plant where leaf beauty is appreciated (against the sky, a white-washed wall, in containers). Excellent garden qualities are counteracted by potential invasiveness. Discard seeds which contain the highly toxic ricin.
p.26, 180

Tip: Pot small surplus plants for later filling in.

ROBINIA Leguminosae/Papilionoideae
Deciduous, sun-requiring ROBINIA grow equally well in mountain areas or at the coast, in dry poor soil or with irrigation, but do not transplant. Propagation: seed.

R. hispida 'Macrophylla'
The shrubby ROSE ACACIA (1.5-2m) carries rich racemes from spring onwards.

Ricinus communis

Attractive reddish bristles cover branches (no spines). It suffers less from wind breakage than the species which is native to dry hillsides from Virginia to Alabama and bears aggressive spines.   p.180

R. pseudoacacia   USA
BLACK LOCUST (12-22m) bears enticing creamy white flowers in spring. It grows naturally in the Appalachians on well-drained calcareous soil and today colonizes wastegrounds in Europe. Plant where its invasive character is desirable such as on poor, dry soil in difficult areas, also in containers for a quick-growing drought-tolerant screen.   p.181

ROMNEYA   Papaveraceae
R. coulteri   Mexico, California
The spectacular perennial MATILIJA POPPY (120-250cm) is native to dry canyons. From creeping rootstocks rise fragrant early summer flowers on woody-based stems. *Romneya* prefers light, well-drained sunny ground, but tolerates many soil and moisture conditions, including drought, heat and wind. In dry summers, leaves and stems may dry up, returning with autumn rains. Annual pruning encourages vigorous growth. A striking plant for dry, warm coastal gardens or inland. Although difficult to get started, once established it can become rampant. Propagation: seed or root cuttings in shaded humid sand. var. **trichocalyx,** compact growth, larger flowers.   p.12

ROMULEA   Iridaceae
The charming ROMULEA (10cm) has thin rush-like leaves. Bright crocus-like

Robinia pseudoacacia

spring flowers open in sunlight. Native to many regions which all share the Mediterranean climate such as Lebanese mountain slopes beneath melting snow, the South African Drakensberg at still higher altitudes, but also coastal sand. Plant the pea-sized corms in a well-drained sandy soil which is wettest in winter and bakes hard in summer, imitating its native habitat. Seeds germinate in a month and flower by the third year.

R. bulbocodium   Mediterranean
Mimics lilac spring crocus with new buds opening continuously.

R. citrina   Namaqualand, S Africa
Delicate yellow starry flowers.

ROSA   Rosaceae
All visitors ask about them, but hot sun often scorches their fragile petals and I planted few. Several roses however have found their way into our garden and I plan to experiment with low-growing landscaping roses developed in Mediterranean regions. The shiny-leaved branches of 'New Dawn' cover column and terrace with overflowing spring bloom. 'Queen Elizabeth', raised from cuttings, grows very tall, flowering all year. 'Iceberg', summer-dormant, returns with autumn rains' refreshing air, its pale white flowers striking against the

dark luminous foliage. 'Mermaid' certainly does climb and reaches the roof. Shiny leaves are less susceptible to fungal diseases which are often fostered by poor drainage and inadequate ventilation.   p.59

R. banksiae   China
Evergreen, drought-tolerant and reliable. Once you have found an area large enough to suit its long, fountain-like shoots, this spineless rose (3-6m) will delight you with scented bloom and apple green spring foliage. Careful pruning prevents dead growth building up beneath (fire hazard). var. **banksiae** carries single or double white flowers; var. **normalis** 'Lutea' small yellow pompons in fat clusters.

R. phoenicia   E Mediterranean
Deciduous (2-4m), white flower clusters cover slender stems.

R. rugosa   Asia
Called SEA TOMATO in California for its edible red hips, it will grow in poor sandy soils in salty coastal air and is useful in dune reclamation. Single pink flowers. 'Alba' single white.

R. sempervirens   Mediterranean
In maquis and open woods, this charming evergreen climber (5-8m) covers hedges and shrubs with white spring bloom and exquisite scent.   p.181

Rosa sempervirens in habitat

181

Rosmarinus officinalis, prostrate, photographed on the Spanish coast

Rosmarinus officinalis

ROSMARINUS Labiatae
R. officinalis Mediterranean
An often-used Mediterranean native, the aromatic ROSEMARY is variable. From autumn to early spring in the wild you will find many flower shades, also pink or white. Plants reach 60-150cm and growth is prostrate, pendent or upright. Keep at desired height or clip for compact growth, but not into wood. Rosemary is never a problem, if planted on hot sunny ground, sharply drained. Fertilizer and summer watering do more harm than good. Propagation: layering or cuttings from selected plants. Plant in all places where drought tolerance is an asset, also near the kitchen. At nurseries, select the growth form you want. p.182

RUDBECKIA Compositae
R. fulgida var. **deamii** USA
Perennial CONEFLOWER (50-80cm) with yellow bloom from summer to autumn has minimal water requirements. Poor dry soil inhibits a somewhat aggressive growth.

RUSCUS Liliaceae/Asparagaceae
R. aculeatus Mediterranean
Undemanding, the evergreen BUTCHER'S BROOM (30-80cm) has prickly-leaved stems. Red berries stand out in shaded ground in time for Christmas. Provide humusy, well-mulched soil, water until established. Totally drought-tolerant, one of the best for 'dry shade'. p.183

R. hypoglossum Italy, Turkey
Unbranched (30-60cm), this faster and denser ground cover forms with time a uniform evergreen mass in shade. Watering accelerates establishment. Increase by division.

RUSSELIA Scrophulariaceae
R. equisetiformis (R. juncea) Mexico
Half-hardy, evergreen *Russelia* (60-100cm) arches with rush-like, almost leafless branches over walls and banks. In full sun scarlet flowers are a spectacular sight from spring onwards. Drought-tolerant and no special soil requirements. Propagated by cuttings. p.183

RUTA Rutaceae
R. graveolens SE Europe
The drought-tolerant, perennial RUE grows in any sunny, well-drained soil among limestone, on dry slopes or near the kitchen. Barely brushed, glaucous leaves give off aromatic scent. Clip annually for compactness. Propagation: seeds, cuttings. Maintenance-free and well-suited to absentee gardeners.

SALVIA Labiatae
The name derives from the latin *salvare* (heal), referring to its medicinal properties. This large, widely distributed genus, flourishing in Mediterranean climates and well-represented in California, flowers all summer. SAGE relishes well-drained sunny ground. Perennials may need some summer-watering (depending on sites) but once established are longer-lived with little. Corrective trimming helps them to look good. Cuttings strike well and serve as inexpensive, temporary fill-in. All have additional qualities: fire retardance, erosion control, bee pasture. One species scents the air as if a thousand beeswax candles were lit.

S. apiana California
A shrubby chaparral member at lower altitudes, the BEE SAGE (1-2m) carries white summer bloom on willow-like stems.

S. clevelandii California
One of the best, this rounded shrub (60-100cm) grows naturally on dry coastal slopes. In inland gardens protect from hottest afternoon sun. Leaves are polished grey, lavender summer flowers delightfully fragrant.

S. elegans Mexico
The perennial PINEAPPLE SAGE (50-90cm) carries scarlet autumn bloom. Delightfully scented leaves enrich cooking.

Russelia equisetiformis

S. fruticosa (S. triloba) Mediterranean
This felty shrub (30-100cm) scents its native maquis with aromatic fragrance. Blue, pink, rarely white bloom from spring to summer. Choose a warm spot.

S. greggii Texas
The rounded evergreen AUTUMN SAGE (70-100cm) in inland gardens needs watered shade over hottest months. Pink flowers.

S. involucrata Mexico
A delightful perennial to 1m, flowering in late summer. Summer-watering. p.183

S. lavandulifolia Spain
This upright, aromatic subshrub (30-60cm), frost-hardy, grows naturally on stony mountain pastures, an asset to

Ruscus aculeatus

hillside gardens. Neat grey foliage, pale violet flowers.

S. leucantha Mexico
Cutting back hard improves the looks of the drought-tolerant, tender MEXICAN BUSH SAGE.

S. leucophylla California
The spring-flowering PURPLE SAGE (60-90cm) is a first-rate mounding ground cover on dry coastal hillsides. Aromatic leaves turn near white in heat.

S. mellifera California
The BLACK SAGE (50-150cm), an excellent pioneer for unsettled areas (slopes), has aromatic dark leaves, pale blue spring flowers.

S. microphylla Mexico
This discreet, shrubby herb (60-110cm), flowering late summer to spring, suits sheltered woodlands.

S. officinalis Mediterranean
The strongly aromatic GARDEN SAGE (30-60cm) grows wild on stony pastures. Quite hardy, it dies back where drainage is poor. Leaves contain a natural antibiotic against sore throats.

S. patens Mexico
The evergreen GENTIAN SAGE is best in part shade.

S. sonomensis California
The fire-retardant CREEPING SAGE (barely 15-25cm) spreads profusely. Blue-purple flowers.

S. splendens S America
The tender, annual SCARLET SAGE calls for careful colour combinations. A white variety is available. Provide weekly summer watering.

SANSEVIERIA Agavaceae
S. trifasciata Tropical Africa
The evergreen SNAKE PLANT (30-100cm) provides useful accents. Sword-like leaves and insignificant but scented flowers grow from a sturdy rhizome, surviving almost total neglect. Gravel protects leaf bases from rotting in winter. Propagation: leaf-cuttings, division.

SANTOLINA Compositae
S. chamaecyparissus Mediterranean
The aromatic LAVENDER COTTON

Santolina chamaecyparissus

(20-40cm), although undemanding, requires good drainage. After flowering, trim grey, finely toothed foliage for compactness. Increased by cuttings. Try 'Pretty Carol' for compact growth. p.183

S. rosmarinifolia Spain
ssp. **canescens** is taller, faster-growing, fire-retardant. Its neat grey mound requires less trimming.

SARCOCOCCA Buxaceae
SWEET BOX, an evergreen dense shrub (1-2m), tolerates chalk and thrives even in deep dry shade. Insignificant white winter flowers hide among dark, shiny leaves, their sweet scent noticed from

Salvia involucrata

Scadoxus puniceus

afar. Underground runners slowly spread 2m; humusy moisture-retentive soil benefits growth and establishment. Propagation: seed, cuttings, division. *Aucuba* and *Ruscus* have similar tolerance of drought, frost and shade.

S. hookeriana　　　　　Himalaya
var. **humilis** (30cm) a spreading ground cover. Black berries.

S. ruscifolia　　　　　China
Distinguished by red berries.

SATUREJA　　　　　Labiatae
S. hortensis　　　　　Mediterranean
A traditional kitchen herb, aromatic SUMMER SAVORY accompanies string beans.

S. thymbra　　　　　Mediterranean
Early spring flowers resemble those of thyme and grow on dry stony hillsides.

Schefflera actinophylla

SCABIOSA　　　　　Dipsacaceae
S. columbaria　　　　　Widespread
Perennial PINCUSHION FLOWERS (40-60cm) with great potential in sunny Mediterranean gardens, have finely-cut grey leaves and summer to winter lavender flowers.

SCADOXUS　　　　　Amaryllidaceae
S. multiflorus ssp. **katherinae**
　　　　　S Africa, Natal
The BLOOD LILY, easy to grow, is spectacular. Several basal leaves join in an elongated succulent 'stem' (distinguished from the two ground-hugging leaves of *Haemanthus* to which it once belonged). Plant dormant fleshy bulbs with their necks just below surface in well-drained humusy soil, richly mulched, partly shaded (no midday sun). Surrounding wood ashes keep snails away. Once leaves have died down, bulbs rest. *Scadoxus* tolerate and even like crowded roots and thus suit containers, charming where grouped under trees. Propagation: fresh seed, division.

S. puniceus　　　　　S Africa, Natal
The ROYAL PAINT BRUSH, a gem for the botanical enthusiast, carries spectacular scarlet flower heads weeklong. Native to summer rain regions (no Mediterranean climate), replace with weekly summer watering until leaves die down.　p.184

SCHEFFLERA　　　　　Araliaceae
S. actinophylla　　　　　Taiwan
The evergreen *Schefflera* has spectacular tropical-looking leaves, in warmest regions reaches 5-7m, much less in cooler gardens. Purple berries follow pink flowers. Give dappled shade in frost-free coastal areas, rich soil, moderate watering when dry. Transplants well, tolerates heavy pruning (cut material can be used for propagation).　p.184

SCHINUS　　　　　Anacardiaceae
Schinus, evergreen drought-tolerant pioneer trees, are useful where little else will grow, however beware their invasive habit. If well-watered, they are fire-retardant. Roots uplift paving. Pruning promotes vigorous growth. Plant from containers or seed.

S. molle　　　　　Mexico, S America
Used worldwide, the spreading PEPPER TREE (6-10m) has willow-like, pendulous branches and pepper-like berries. In sun, this frost-tender coastal tree tolerates any soil, even brackish.

S. terebinthifolius　　　　　Brazil
The magnificent rare BRAZILIAN PEPPER TREE (5-8m) is less drought-tolerant than *S. molle*. *Pistacia*-like leaves and red berries are well worth growing it (hedge or wind-break).

SCHOTIA
　　　　Leguminosae/Caesalpinioideae
Highly ornamental slow spreading trees, native to forest margins, briefly drop their leaves during their spectacular spring flower show. Use as drought-tolerant coastal windbreaks in warm regions. They attract bees. Easy propagation from seed.

S. afra　　　　　S Africa
The evergreen HOTTENTOT'S BEAN (3m) bears cerise bloom.

S. brachypetala　　　　　S Africa
Or choose the TREE FUCHSIA (5-10m) with spectacular crimson flowers.

SCILLA　　　　Liliaceae/Hyacinthaceae
S. peruviana　　　　　W Mediterranean
Native to the Mediterranean, not Peru. Larger than most scillas, a few bulbs with blue-mauve flowers make quite a show. Readily increased by seed.

S. siberica　　　　　S Russia
As spring approaches, these dainty bulbous plants (10-15cm), totally undemanding, are waterwise gardens' delight. They will naturalize in fertile sandy soil.

SEDUM　　　　　Crassulaceae
Succulent SEDUM are easily grown in sun or part-shade, tolerate drought, poor stony soils and colder regions but need excellent drainage. Star-like flower clusters attract butterflies. Try any of these outstanding lawn substitutes. Increased from small sections, beg a piece whenever you see new ones.

S. album Europe, Asia
Evergreen, mat-forming, with pinkish-white flowers.

S. rubrotinctum Origin obscure
Very drought-tolerant, gradually growing into dense mats. p.185

S. sediforme (S. altissimum)
Mediterranean
Branching stems (15-40cm), summer-flowering.

S. telephium see ***Hylotelephium t.***

SEMPERVIVUM Crassulaceae
From the latin *semper* (forever) and *vivere* (live). The succulent HOUSE LEEK grows wild from Caucasus to Atlas mountains in widely varied growing conditions. Fleshy leaf rosettes spread by short stolons and suit sunny spots as small-scale ground covers. Star-shaped flowers rise from rosettes which die down once seed has set. Quite hardy, with no special requirements except for drainage, offsets can be detached for easy propagation. Tuck into fissures or let them grow over rock.

S. arachnoideum
Pyrenees to Carpathians
Small purple flowers over rosettes 5cm across.

S. ciliosum Bulgaria
Summer flowers rise to 10cm above compact rosettes.

S. tectorum C Europe
HOUSE LEEK protects houses and their owners from the dangers of daily life, it is believed. Insert offsets with some soil between tiles.

Note: Leaf juice treats skin burns.

SENECIO Compositae
This largest genus of useful, often drought-tolerant plants with widely different growth habits includes also succulents. Variously-sized flowers are mostly daisy-like. No special soil requirements, all like excellent drainage and full sun. Mulch controls weeds and avoids digging around plants as with all surface rooters. Over winter, cut back for shape. Increase by cuttings.

S. cineraria Mediterranean
A reliable drought-tolerant grey mass (30-70cm high and wider), it likes well-drained areas. The compact 'Silverdust' (25cm) is appreciated for its finely-lobed silvery leaves. p.15, 185

S. glastifolius S Africa
This perennial sturdy subshrub (60-100cm) provides brilliant long-lasting colour in spring. Easy from seed. p.53

S. grandifolius see ***Telanthophora grandifolia***

S. greyi see ***Brachyglottis g.***

S. mikanioides see ***Delairea odorata***

S. radicans S Africa
The succulent CREEPING BERRIES with time form mats with pretty white flowers.

SENNA
Leguminosae/Caesalpinioideae
Many SENNA formerly belonged to *Cassia*. Evergreen or deciduous shrubs or trees with showy golden flower racemes, they are mostly native to tropical regions (high heat requirements). They die back in colder climates, but if protected by mulch, may resprout from base. They require poor, light, well-drained soils in full sun and infrequent, deep waterings in midsummer. Most are benefitted by cutting back. Propagation: seeds, cuttings.

S. alata (Cassia a.) Tropical regions
This attractive winter-flowering shrub or tree reaches 3×3m.

S. armata California
An asset to all desert gardens, this drought-tolerant shrub bears long-lasting bloom.

S. artemisioides W Australia
Wispy, evergreen and drought-hardy to 1m. Spring to summer flowering.

S. didymobotrya Tropical Africa
Flowers in candle-like formation, leaf scent is peanut-like.

S. multiglandulosa Widespread
2-3m, flowers all winter in small clusters.

S. sturtii Australia
This widespread, low shrub thrives in inland regions. Short flower sprays adorn woolly, fern-like foliage.

Senecio cineraria

SISYRINCHIUM Iridaceae
Grow readily into evergreen sword-leaved clumps. In light shade, they survive some drought. Easily raised from seed or divided; try them all.

S. bellum California
The spring-flowering BLUE-EYED GRASS (15cm) with patience and sufficient plants grows into small-scale ground cover.

S. californicum California
Somewhat taller than the first, follows it closely in bloom (yellow). It tolerates damp, poorly drained ground.

S. striatum Argentina, Chile
Creamy flower clusters on slender spikes (30-60cm) stand above glaucous foliage which blackens with age. Seed self-sows freely.

Sedum rubrotinctum

Solandra maxima

SMILACINA Liliaceae/Convallariaceae
S. racemosa   N America
Related to *Aspidistra, Liriope* and *Ophiopogon*, this perennial likes humusy soil, a cool root run, mulch and shade and appreciates some summer-watering. Red berries follow creamy fragrant flowers. It slowly spreads as a ground cover under trees. Propagation: seed, division.

SOLANDRA   Solanaceae
S. maxima   Mexico
Large, tropical-looking leaves of the CHALICE VINE are evergreen in warmer locations. Left to their own devices, shoots reach out wide, blooming on tips (often out of sight). But cut back, the green glossy foliage is a perfect foil for the giant scented cups which flower in winter and summer. Provide richly drained and mulched soil in sun, weekly summer watering. Later, monthly watering may suffice (watch for wilting tip growth). Over-watering encourages vegetative growth at the expense of flowers. Propagation: cuttings, layering.   p.186

SOLANUM   Solanaceae
S. crispum   Chile
This vigorous evergreen shrub, given a support, climbs to 2-3m and tolerates neglect. Lilac blue flowers.

S. jasminoides   S America
The deciduous POTATO VINE (2-4m) is evergreen in mildest regions. It straggles over rock and up into trees with lavender flowers almost all year. With few cultural requirements, almost drought- and wind-tolerant, it flourishes in sun or shade. Hard cutting back is beneficial. Propagation: cuttings, layering. 'Album' pretty white flowers.   p.187

SOLLYA   Pittosporaceae
S. heterophylla   SW Australia
The evergreen, twining BLUEBELL CREEPER has many uses. Delicate foliage and graceful summer bloom hang over walls, hide fences or fill containers. Choose full sun or dappled shade, a moisture-retentive, well-drained soil, generous mulch. Trim for compactness. Propagation: cuttings.   p.187

Note: Planted at the foot of a wild olive, with sun for part of the day, occasionally watered, it soon reached 2.5m.

SOPHORA
                Leguminosae/Papilionoideae
S. japonica   Asia
The deciduous, very ornamental JAPANESE PAGODA TREE has cream late summer flowers and golden autumn foliage. Frost hardy, moderately drought tolerant, it grows in any soil and resists honey fungus. In full sun as a spreading specimen or windbreak, it slowly reaches 6m, gradually increasing speed. Flowers, said to appear 30 years after planting, are worth the wait. In hottest climates, seedlings may become invasive.

S. secundiflora   Texas, Mexico
The evergreen MESCAL BEAN (3-6m), a well-behaved, slow-growing background shrub or specimen tree, has violet-blue, highly scented spring flowers, followed by large pods with poisonous brilliant red seed. Enjoys hot spots, well-drained alkaline soil, weekly to monthly summer watering (quantities depend, among other factors, on soil quality).

SPARAXIS   Iridaceae
S. tricolor   Cape
Easy bulbs for Mediterranean gardens. Plant 5cm deep in full sun before September 15th (southern hemisphere: March 15th). A few weeks later, apple green leaf tips show above ground, grow through winter until many-coloured spring flowers appear. Easily propagated by seed as are most Iridaceae family members, naturalizing even in rock clefts. Many hybrids.

SPARMANNIA   Tiliaceae
S. africana   South Africa
Known as a house plant, this attractive shrub/tree, discovered during Captain Cook's second voyage, shoots up to 3-5m. White flower clusters appear at branch ends, appreciated by bees. Plant in good soil in sun or filtered shade. *Sparmannia* is not a plant of the Mediterranean climate although thriving in it and requires weekly summer watering. Over-watering induces sappy growth and health problems. Aim for a solid, well-ripened branch structure. Transplants well (cut back). Easily increased by cuttings.

● *SPARTIUM*
Leguminosae/Papilionoideae
S. junceum Mediterranean
The SPANISH BROOM (1.5-3m) with almost leafless green stems and golden
spring bloom tolerates poor rocky soil,
drought, pollution, fire. It may become
invasive where conditions are too
favourable. See also *Genista.* p.30

SPATHODEA Bignoniaceae
S. campanulata Tropical Africa
Glorious orange flowers cover almost all
year the spreading, dark green canopy of
the AFRICAN TULIP TREE (9-12m). Drought-
tolerant in favourable conditions
(moisture-retentive soil, rich mulch, all
ground covered), it requires hot, frost-
free locations. Use as specimen tree to
shade widespread paving or as coastal
windbreak. Propagation: cuttings, seed;
but acquiring a potted plant would be
best.

SPIRAEA Rosaceae
Plant these deciduous shrubs, underplanted with spring bulbs, for their profuse flowering. Easily propagated by cuttings or division, try all at little expense.
If planted in dappled shade in fertile
mulched ground, weekly summer watering may be adequate. Cut out some
older branches each year for rejuvena-
tion. No health problems observed.

S. cantoniensis China
Spring bloom covers the gracefully arching branches with snow.

S. douglasii W USA
(1-2m), carries deep pink flowers a
month later. Suckering freely, it suits
large gardens where 'covering the
ground' is a problem.

STACHYS Labiatae
S. byzantina Near East
Perennial LAMB'S EARS, more prominent
for evergrey furry leaves than for mauve
flower stalks, is a dependable flat ground
cover on sunny raised ground. On a bed
of gravel felty leaves remain dry. Divide
mats before new growth starts. 'Silver
Carpet' is a good choice.

Solanum jasminoides 'Album'

Sollya heterophylla

STERNBERGIA Amaryllidaceae
S. lutea Mediterranean
The herald of autumn, often believed to
be a 'yellow autumn crocus', it is an
amaryllid, not a crocus (Iridaceae), and
one of the easiest for spectacular displays. Plant before first autumn rains in
warm sunny sites, bulbs barely covered
(no flowers in shade). No special soil requirements, they may grow on dry walls
which give them the excellent drainage
they need. Leaves die down with summer drought. Divide over-crowded
patches. p.58, 187

STRELITZIA Musaceae
S. reginae Cape
Intriguing flowers among evergreen
banana-like leaves give the BIRD OF

PARADISE an exotic look. Pampered and
allowed to become crowded, this is an
excellent choice for hot locations: litter-
free near the pool or grown in a container on a terrace. Propagation: seed, division.

STREPTOCARPUS Gesneriaceae
S. rexii Cape
CAPE PRIMROSE, usually a perennial
house plant, does well planted out in the
garden. First acclimatize and propagate
for an ample supply (division, leaf cuttings). It requires humusy, free-draining
mulched soil, a cool run near rock, protection from taxing summer sun, weekly
watering. Flowers will be smaller but
growth is healthy which counts more
than size.

Sternbergia lutea

STREPTOSOLEN   Solanaceae
S. jamesonii   Columbia, Peru
A South American gift to drought-tolerant gardens, the evergreen MARMA-LADE BUSH flowers almost all year with cheerful orange bloom, suitably framed by *Brachyglottis greyi* and *Coprosma repens*. A southern aspect (protected from midday sun), a moisture-holding, well-drained soil, mulch and weekly summer watering are its only requirements.
      p.188

STYRAX   Styracaceae
S. officinale var. **californicum**
      N California
The deciduous shrubby CALIFORNIA SNOWBELL (2-5m) establishes more quickly in reasonably fertile, mulched ground than in its native rocky soil. Scented white flower clusters are delightful.

SUCCULENTS

See *Aloe, Carpobrotus, Cotyledon, Crassula, Drosanthemum, Echeveria, Euphorbia, Graptopetalum, Kalanchoe, Lampranthus, Mesembryanthemum, Sedum, Sempervivum, Senecio.*

All cacti belong to the Cactaceae family and are succulents (latin for 'juicy'). But not all succulents are cacti. They may belong to such families as Apocynaceae, Asclepiadaceae, Crassulaceae, Euphorbiaceae or Liliaceae, which are partly native to more or less arid regions.

Succulents have an enormous potential to survive long droughts due to their ability to store water in fleshy leaves and

Streptosolen jamesonii

A collection of succulents

stems. Further adaptations for water conservation include sun-reflecting hairs, reduced surfaces and compact growth. Thick hairy mats create a layer of still air on plant surfaces and so reduce transpiration.

Many are slow-growing, requiring patience, others grow rapidly. Remember their origins when choosing a site (light and hours of sunshine). Mostly tolerant of dry, poor ground, they prefer excellent drainage. All benefit from dry mulch (gravel). The least juicy tolerate temperatures to freezing. Succulents need a dry resting period. The only maintenance they require is an occasional clean-up. Ideal for beginners, most are easily propagated. Break small sections off mother plants, allow cuts to dry for several hours before inserting into well-drained sandy soil. Water sparingly until first roots develop.

Their glorious flowers are often out of season, lasting for weeks. Consider your garden's design and plants' architectural merits. Observe their ultimate height,

Syringa microphylla 'Superba'

width and volume, texture and colour shade, the same as with other plants. Carefully chosen sites allow leaves and flowers to stand out, complementing other plantings or each other. Succulents cloak rock, spring from soil-filled cracks or hang from walls, wherever leaves remain dry. They spread carpets over gravel, suit terraces, come to our rescue for difficult, dry sites. Left to grow on their own, they develop their full potential.   p.59, 64, 71, 188

Note: Succulents could also be used in large patches of a single species, not dotted about.

SUTHERLANDIA
      Leguminosae/Papilionoideae
S. frutescens   Cape
The highly ornamental evergreen BALLOON PEA (1m) is a fast-growing shrublet with scarlet spring flowers. Very tolerant of drought and frost, it grows in poor, even brackish, saline soils in full sun. Prune to rejuvenate. Propagation: cuttings or seeds in individual pots.

SYRINGA   Oleaceae
Deciduous LILAC does well in Mediterranean gardens, prefers north-facing sites in dappled shade and generously mulched fertile soil (neutral to alkaline loam). Good air circulation prevents health problems. Keep an eye on it until established. Syringas are frequently grafted onto the common privet.

S. x chinensis
2-4m, more graceful than the common lilac, tolerates hot summers. Pink flowers, 'Alba' white.

S. microphylla 'Superba'
An open shrub around 1.5m which suits woodlands. Sweetly-fragrant pink flowers disappear in hot summers, return in autumn.   p.188

S. vulgaris   SE Europe
The COMMON LILAC will in time reach 5×3m. California Descanso Hybrids prefer mild winters.

TAGETES   Compositae
Tough, colourful, easy to grow, the annual MARIGOLD does best in full sun with weekly watering.

TAMARIX — Tamaricaceae

TAMARISK, native to coastal regions, suits windy coastal gardens and makes a graceful shelterbelt. Natural growth is shrubby, but well-shaped, slender weeping branches in flower are a sight to behold. Flowers (white, mostly pink) are on current or previous year's growth, according to species. Long hot summers ensure spectacular autumn flower displays. Plant in sunny, deep sandy soil. *Tamarix* use soil salts to help to reduce transpiration, thus drought tolerance is best in saline ground. Taproots, searching for moisture, deprive neighbours of water (the competitive *T. aphylla* is not listed below). Cutting hard back encourages vigorous new growth. Woody cuttings with occasional summer watering strike readily (potentially invasive in California). Irrigation boosts its fire-retardant characteristics.

T. africana — N Africa
2-4m tall, pale pink spring flowers.

T. chinensis — E Asia
The variable SALT CEDAR (2-8m), also shrub-like, embellishes waterwise gardens with summer bloom. A dry soil keeps vigorous roots within bounds.

T. gallica — Mediterranean
One of the tallest, hardier than most, the spring-flowering MANNA PLANT (5-7m) turns golden in autumn.

T. ramosissima — Europe, Asia
Hardy dune erosion controller (4-5m). Try 'Pink Cascade'.

Tecomaria capensis

Telanthophora grandifolia

TANACETUM — Compositae
T. parthenium — SE Europe
The aromatic perennial FEVERFEW (20-40cm), considered a weed, may grow wild in your garden. I find it an asset and transplant self-sown seedlings to problem areas. Their white bloom shines for weeks with minimal care. 'Ball's Double White' scores 40cm; 'Golden Ball' 20cm dwarf compact; 'Golden Moss' a flat carpet. p.31

TAXUS — Taxaceae
T. baccata — Europe, Asia
The very slow YEW (6-10m) is long-lived to 1000 years. It likes high air humidity and a somewhat alkaline soil. Highly tolerant of heat or cold, sun or shade, dry or wet conditions, it survives transplanting, clipping, pruning, cutting (even into old wood). All parts are poisonous. Propagation: stratified seed. 'Fastigiata', the Irish Yew, may replace cypress which has a similar growth habit.

TECOMA — Bignoniaceae
T. stans — US to Argentina
Evergreen spreading, the glorious TRUMPET BUSH grows rapidly to 3-5m. Carefully planted in moisture retentive soil with generous mulching and a cool root run, this drought-tolerant climber is an excellent bulky windbreak for coastal gardens, tolerating some frost.

TECOMARIA — Bignoniaceae
T. capensis — South Africa
The evergreen CAPE HONEYSUCKLE (deciduous in colder regions) is closely related to *Tecoma*. From autumn into winter, its flower clusters glow deep orange. Rampant shoots will ramble through shrubs, be trained up walls, tumble over fences. A good choice for coastal conditions, a sunny heat-reflecting slope suits it best. Mulched cool roots tolerate dry summers in any well-drained soil. Cut back before transplanting. Cuttings or layering augment your stock. p.189

TELANTHOPHORA — Compositae
T. grandifolia (Senecio grandifolius) — Mexico
Over winter, largest yellow flower clusters top this dramatic shrub (2-4m). Plant sheltered so that winds cannot damage its outsized leaves. Grows well from cuttings. p.189

Teucrium fruticans (right)

Teucrium fruticans

TEMPLETONIA
Leguminosae/Papilionoideae
T. retusa   S and W Australia
Staked, the drought-tolerant COCKIES TONGUE (1-2m) is an ideal plant for drained, limy or sandy soils at water's edge (beach gardens). Brilliant coral-red winter to spring flowers bring glaucous, leathery foliage to life. Moderate growth requires little shaping. Propagation: seed, cuttings.   p.190

TETRACLINIS   Cupressaceae
T. articulata   W Mediterranean
The evergreen ARAR (8-12m) is closely related to *Callitris*, *Calocedrus*, *Thuja* and *Widdringtonia*. It replaces cypress which is threatened by health problems in many areas. Native to hot dry zones, it suits low altitudes in similar regions. Propagation by seed is easy.   p.191

TETRASTIGMA   Vitaceae
T. voinierianum (Cissus voinieriana)
      Laos
The vigorous, undemanding LIZARD PLANT grows quickly along any support reached by its long tendrils. Giant leaves bestow a tropical look. A quick summer shade for your terrace or conservatory, your only problem will be to keep it within bounds (cut hard back in winter). Give light soil and weekly summer watering (or experiment with less once established). Easily increased by cuttings.

Note: Although considered tropical and tender, it remained evergreen in our conservatory at short-term 4° C.

TEUCRIUM   Labiatae
T. chamaedrys   Widespread
This evergreen spreading ground cover (25×50cm) has dark green leaves and purple or white flowers which attract bees. Fire-retardant if well-watered.

T. flavum   Mediterranean
This evergreen subshrub (30-50cm) with creamy summer flowers is an easy plant for covering the ground. Sun or shade, water or none, fertile or poor rocky soil, all will do. Cut back after flowering. Propagation: seed (self-sown), cuttings.

T. fruticans   Mediterranean
A sturdy Mediterranean pioneer, very easy, GERMANDER (100-200cm) in time will become an impenetrable wildlife haven. Inconspicuous pale blue flowers are delightful. Helped by generous mulching, *Teucrium* covers all areas where soil is poor or scarce, requiring sun and sharp drainage. Allow it to grow freely, control by clipping or cut to ground each year. Propagation: cuttings, division.   p.190, 193/below

THRYPTOMENE   Myrtaceae
T. saxicola   W Australia
A collector's item, the evergreen *Thryptomene* (70-90cm) carries exquisite pale rose winter flowers among tiny leaves. Reasonably hardy, it is said to require sandy, slightly acid soil. Transplanting is difficult, so is propagation; try small autumn cuttings. If you have fresh seed, sow it.

THUNBERGIA   Acanthaceae
T. grandiflora   Bengal
The exquisite, tender SKY VINE climbs fast 3-5m. Warm sites, rich soil, mulch and watering once or twice a week are required.

T. gregorii   Tropical Africa
Drought-tolerant, it is common in California and twines to 2m with softly hairy leaves and solitary, bright orange flowers. Establish with twice monthly summer water.   p.190

Note: I planted mine with its roots shaded by a scented *Pelargonium*, over and through which it rambles.

THYMELAEA   Thymelaeaceae
T. hirsuta   Mediterranean
A sturdy shrub (40-90cm) with minute, stem-hugging leaves, native to dry, rocky or sandy coastal sites.

T. tartonraira   Mediterranean
20-50cm, found in dry sandy or rocky places near the sea. I hope that both will soon be widely available.

Thunbergia gregorii

Templetonia retusa

Tetraclinis articulata, 2 years old

Tradescantia fluminensis

THYMUS Labiatae

The aromatic kitchen THYME, a creeping or upright ground cover, is easy. Frost- and drought-tolerant, it prefers light sandy, well-drained soils in sun. Gravel keeps foliage dry in winter. Clip to keep compact; lawn mowers may handle larger patches (cutting blades high). Attracts bees. Propagation: cuttings.

Note: 'The Garden', March 1992, lists many thymes.

T. serpyllum Mediterranean
The CREEPING THYME (6-10cm) fills in between stepping stones, a flat ground cover.

T. vulgaris Mediterranean
The COMMON THYME (20-30cm) grows well in containers, a candidate for the minigarden, as are all thyme.

TIPUANA Leguminosae/Papilionaceae
T. tipu Bolivia
The ornamental evergreen TIPU TREE (deciduous in colder regions) is a moderately fast-growing street tree (7-10m). Showy yellow spring flowers feed bees. Provide a mulched cool root run, occasional watering and avoid planting near the coast.

TITHONIA Compositae
T. rotundifolia Mexico
This perennial with abundant orange summer to autumn bloom grows fast to your own height. A cheerful, drought-tolerant cover for poor soils under hot sun, it naturalizes if happy. Low-growing varieties suit exposed sites.

TRACHELIUM Campanulaceae
T. caeruleum Mediterranean
An exquisite and easy perennial (30-80cm), drought-tolerant, it lines walks, springs from walls, suits natural gardens with clustered lilac flower heads. Sow in well-drained, moisture-retentive calcareous cracks in sun or shade, insert cuttings or plant naturalized seedlings. Cut back in winter. Try 'White Veil' or 'Blue Veil'. p.191

TRACHELOSPERMUM Apocynaceae
T. asiaticum (Rhynchospermum a.)
Japan
Leaves are darker and smaller than the below. Early cream bloom.

T. jasminoides Japan, China
The taller evergreen STAR JASMINE (3-6m), a perfect twining climber or dense, woody-stemmed ground cover, has fragrant white flower clusters, glossy leaves, vividly bronze red winter foliage. Hardy and tolerant of heat, it grows in sun and shade, with water or without. Summer watering accelerates growth which initially is slow. Tips root in mulched humusy soil. Trim where needed. Propagation: layering, cuttings, seed (your own slender pods).

TRADESCANTIA Commelinaceae
Carefully positioned succulent leaves shade the ground which they cover in sun or shade. Each node takes root, encouraged by humusy soil and weekly summer watering. Reputedly tender, hard-working *Tradescantia* will survive a short-term frost.

T. fluminensis Brazil
Shoots with small white flowers among apple green leaves extend widely. p.191

Note: Children place cuttings into a glass, watch over winter root growth, plant out in spring.

T. sillamontana Mexico
Covered with pretty purple summer flowers, ground-hugging woolly grey stems reach a foot. Branches will break off in winter but resprout in spring.

TRICHOSTEMA Lamiaceae
T. lanatum California
Summer-flowering WOOLLY BLUE CURLS (70-120cm), profusely branching shrubs, bear aromatic rosemary-like foliage. Best in free-draining soil on sun-drenched coastal slopes without summer watering. Increased by seed.

Trachelium caeruleum

Tulipa saxatilis

TRITELEIA Liliaceae/Tricyrtidaceae
California bulbous plants, rarer than
Cape bulbs, include heat- and drought-
tolerant *Triteleia*, differing in small details in the flower from *Brodiaea*. Tall
flower stalks (50cm) appear in summer
sun once slender leaves have almost
died down.

T. ixioides California
The GOLDEN BRODIAEA.

T. laxa California
Commonly called GRASSNUT, grape-
violet flowers rise from grass-like
foliage. 'Queen Fabiola' pale violet.

Tropaeolum majus

TRITONIA Iridaceae
T. crocata South Africa
This useful Cape bulb resembling
Sparaxis, naturalizes as readily. Over
winter spear-shaped leaves (25cm) push
through well-drained, sunny ground,
followed by spring flowers in many orange shades. In unusually dry winters
one or two waterings are needed to
replace the rain, otherwise growth will
be stunted. Summer-baking is essential.

TROPAEOLUM Tropaeolaceae
T. majus Columbia to Peru
Did the traveller who brought drought-
tolerant NASTURTIUM 1684 to Holland
know what a boon it would be to our gardens? A few seeds tucked into sunny soil
soon cover bare ground among newly
planted specimens, self-seeding only
months later. Rarely are better results
met with less expense. p.76/left, 192

Note: This pioneer adorns Canary Island
waste grounds.

TULBAGHIA Liliaceae/Alliaceae
Perennial WILD GARLIC (20-30cm) is
characterized by narrow foliage and
pale lilac flower umbels. From a few
bulbs or rhizomes, raised from ample
seed and planted 5cm deep in sun or
dappled shade, sizeable clumps will
form, naturalizing into a small-scale
ground cover. Divide when flowering
decreases.

T. fragrans Cape
SWEET GARLIC has richly scented winter
flowers.

T. violacea Natal, South Africa
Thrives on neglect. Use leaves in the
kitchen. p.193

TULIPA Liliaceae/Liliaceae
Tall large-flowered garden tulips, known
to all, are easily damaged by rain. More
suitable are smaller botanical species,
native to the mountains of Turkestan. All
thrive in well-drained fertile soil among
low cushion plants or bordering paths in
the natural garden. Winter cold is essential.
Do not accept from nurserymen bulbs
from the wild. Or take cultivars as re-

placements, so protecting the species
from extinction.

T. clusiana Iran
The rosy-white LADY TULIP is reliable in
warmer climates.

T. greigii C Asia
Grows wild on fertile sunny mountain
slopes.

T. praestans C Asia
Native to light woodlands and to the
steep earthy slopes of the southern Pamir
Alai, this scarlet tulip is one of the
earliest.

T. saxatilis Mediterranean
The graceful stoloniferous CANDIA TULIP
(25cm), native to stony Cretan fields,
carries perfect pale lilac flowers and
used to be grown widely in Mediterranean gardens. p.192

Note: I would love to grow the pale pink
T. cretica, native to Cretan mountains
and naturalizing freely by stolons, if only
I knew where to obtain it.

T. sylvestris Unknown origin
Growing wild in vineyards, English
gardeners naturalize this stoloniferous
yellow tulip in meadows and woodlands.

UGNI Myrtaceae
U. molinae (Myrtus ugni) Chile
A desirable garden plant, the evergreen
CHILEAN GUAVA (1-2m) carries shiny
leaves, white, fragrant flower brushes
and small, edible fruits. It requires sunny
neutral or acid soil (inland part-shade)
and weekly watering in hottest summers.
Easily shaped, it suits formal plantings
and containers.

UMBELLULARIA Lauraceae
U. californica Oregon, California
In moist rich soil, the evergreen deep-
rooted CALIFORNIA BAY (17-20m) is a
stately tree. Glossy strongly aromatic
leaves, used for cooking, suggest the
Mediterranean bay (*Laurus nobilis*).
With shallow dry soil or drying winds it
remains a neat, bulky 5m screen. Flowers are minute, fruits inedible. Initial
shading encourages establishment. Can
be pruned and shaped.

URGINEA Liliaceae/Hyacinthaceae
U. maritima W Mediterranean
The spectacular SEA SQUILL is the queen of Mediterranean bulbs. Giant, they show half above ground. In autumn, large, fleshy leaves are preceded by tall white flower spikes. Easily grown (summer-baking), somewhat slow to establish, increased by seed, this stately autumn flower would be widely planted if better known. p.69

VELTHEIMIA Liliaceae/Hyacinthaceae
V. capensis W Cape
A pale pink flower raceme delights us in early spring above shiny, wavy-edged leaves. Plants dry off when summer arrives and bulbs are then baked. Plant in well-drained humusy soil in half shade. Readily increased from own seed.

VERBASCUM Scrophulariaceae
V. olympicum Turkey
Bright golden flowers rise on tall stems (140cm) above largest, near-white felty leaves. MULLEIN is to your sunny, drought-tolerant garden the exclamation mark all gardens need. Easy to grow from seed. p.25

Tulbaghia violacea

Vinca difformis

VERBENA Verbenaceae
V. peruviana S America
grows into a flat, scarlet carpet on sunny poor dry ground (no treading). Increased by cuttings.

V. rigida (V. venosa) Brazil, Argentina
This undemanding spreading perennial herb (20-40cm) flowers in a few months from seed. Many colours.

VIBURNUM Caprifoliaceae
These evergreen or deciduous shrubs, valued for deliciously fragrant flowers or dependable mass of greenery, grow in humusy, slightly shaded ground with acidic pine or oak leaf mulches and weekly summer watering. Prune right after flowering or next year's display will be lost. Propagation: seed, cuttings, suckers, layering (depending on species). With careful choice the flowering season may be long.

V. x burkwoodii
Evergreen, straggly (2×1m), outstanding for waxy white late winter bloom.

V. plicatum 'Mariesii'
Deciduous, it lights up gardens with dazzling white spring bloom, best on horizontal growth (cut out vertical shoots).

V. suspensum (V. sandankwa) Japan
This evergreen shiny shrub (2-3m) bears pendulous white flower clusters in late winter, followed by red berries. Give deep soil enriched with leafmold in dappled shade and occasional watering in hottest summer months.

V. tinus Mediterranean
The evergreen drought-tolerant LAURUSTINUS (2-6m) grows wild in open sunny thickets or coastal oak woodlands. An only Mediterranean species, it has other requirements than the above and tolerates alkaline soils. Although a fully grown winter-flowering laurustinus is a glorious sight, vigorous growth may also be pruned for desired height and shape. There may be health problems in poorly aerated shade. Cutting to ground helps only for a time; better to transplant it into sun and replace by another, more suitable plant. Naturalizes in favourable conditions. p.80, 193

Viburnum tinus

VINCA Apocynaceae
V. difformis Mediterranean
The evergreen PERIWINKLE, left to its own devices, covers bare ground speedily, climbs into nearby shrubs or, if cut down, assumes nicely rounded shapes. No special soil requirements, it grows quickest in good half-shaded soil with weekly summer watering. Drought-tolerant once established. Propagation: cuttings, division, layering. p.193

V. minor Mediterranean
A smaller, flatter version, less aggressive, even slow to start (depending on plants obtained). The pure white form is a dense ground cover for the White Garden.

VIOLA Violaceae
V. odorata Mediterranean
The scented drought-tolerant SWEET VIOLET is a delightful ground cover in dappled shade. Extend patches by seed, dividing older plants or rooted runners.

Viburnum odoratissimum

VITEX Verbenaceae
V. agnus-castus Mediterranean
Usually a multi-trunked shrub with deciduous, gracefully divided foliage and mauve-blue flower panicles from midsummer to autumn, the spreading MEDITERRANEAN CHASTE TREE (2-3m, more in hottest regions) suits dry sites near oak and is resistant to honey fungus. 'Alba' is charming.

VITIS Vitaceae
V. vinifera Mediterranean
The deciduous GRAPE VINE soon covers an arbour. Locals will gladly help you to choose suitable varieties and sites, also with pruning. Tender leaves enrich Greek cooking. p.53/centre, 194

WASHINGTONIA Palmae
W. filifera California
The CALIFORNIAN WASHINGTONIA (15-18m) likes hot, well-drained locations where roots reach ground water. Old leaves form a 'skirt'. Wind-hardy and sprinkler-tolerant. Roots gradually lift paving.

W. robusta Mexico
The MEXICAN WASHINGTONIA (25-30m) carries its fan-like foliage in a crown, its slender trunk curving with age. This fast grower with no special soil or water requirements tolerates short-lived frost.

Yucca gloriosa

Vitis vinifera

WATSONIA Iridaceae
W. borbonica (W. pyramidata) SW Cape
The tall, sword-leaved *Watsonia* (90-150cm), native to mountain slopes, thrives in well-drained, sunny positions with ample winter rain. Leave it undisturbed. Spring flowers come in pink shades. ssp. **ardernei** mostly white.

W. fourcadei SW Cape
Salmon red, many-flowered spikes (70-140cm). For the vase, burn stem bases.

WESTRINGIA Labiatae
W. fruticosa (W. rosmariniformis) Australia
This evergreen, rounded shrub (60-150cm) enjoys a well-drained and mulched sunny soil. Where rosemary falls apart with age, *Westringia* remains compact. Where box takes time to reach a reasonable size, *Westringia* grows well from the start. Where other plantings wilt in drought, *Westringia* looks better than during any other period. This relia-

Westringia fruticosa

ble pioneer, low coastal hedge or clipped container plant readily strikes from cuttings. p.194

WIDDRINGTONIA Cupressaceae
W. nodiflora S Africa
The AFRICAN CYPRESS (2-7m) has a narrow crown and glaucous foliage. An alternative to cypress, an ornamental windbreak or clipped hedge, it is best on well-drained soil in warm areas and takes some drought. Propagation: seed, cuttings. p.194

WISTERIA Leguminosae/Papilionoideae
W. floribunda Japan
The scented JAPANESE WISTERIA twines clockwise. Long flower clusters open from the base, together with the foliage, adorning house, archway or arbour in sun.

W. sinensis China
The CHINESE WISTERIA twines anti-clockwise. Flowers appear before leaves, at once opening almost full-length. Everybody knows this spectacular spring-bloomer, not all are aware of its easy character. Best in cooler regions, any well-drained soil will suit it. Carefully prune in winter, cutting shoots which grow towards the wall; in summer shorten new shoots to avoid tangling. As wood matures, branches arch gracefully

Widdringtonia nodiflora, 3 years old

Zantedeschia aethiopica

into space while clusters hang free. Re-move suckers or train as multi-trunked shrub, low tree or bank cover. Well-trained plants may fill several functions. Cuttings and grafted plants are better than seedlings. p.90

XANTHORRHOEA Xanthorrhoeaceae
X. quadrangulata S Australia
Slowly reaching 2m, its flower spikes double that height. The fully drought-tolerant AUSTRALIAN GRASSTREE grows readily from seed. Add plenty of sand to sharply drained, loose soil in full sun (as for *Yucca*).

YUCCA Agavaceae
YUCCAS are undemanding evergreen perennials with sword-shaped, succu-lent leaves. Some with time turn into shrubs, even trees. The presence of spines varies. Essential in Mediterranean gardens, they are at their best where their architectural outlines and startling flowers stand out. Even young plants confer instant style to a dull area. Toler-ant of shallow ground, coastal and des-ert conditions or wind, they like sunny aspects. Fire-retardant if well-groomed. Easy propagation: seed, suckers.

Y. aloifolia USA
'SPANISH BAYONET' well describes its aggressive leaf tips.

Y. elephantipes (Y. gigantea) Mexico
The branched GIANT YUCCA (4-8m) suits tropical settings in protected locations and likes rich irrigated ground. p.80

Y. filamentosa USA
Freely used, very hardy.

Y. gloriosa Carolina to Florida
The multi-trunked SPANISH DAGGER reaches 3m (without its glorious flower stem). Soft tips suit swimming pools and walks. p.194

Y. whipplei S California
OUR LORD'S CANDLE is stemless and agressively tipped. Inflorescences grow to an impressive 2-4m. Parent plants die after flowering. p.22, 169

ZANTEDESCHIA Araceae
Z. aethiopica Cape
The easy CALLA LILY (50-120cm) grows and flowers with no demands other than natural winter rain and a reasonably light, mulched soil in dappled shade. Dying down with summer drought, it is restored by autumn rains, producing lush foliage which frames magnificent 'flowers' in early spring. From ample

seed grow flowering plants within a year. p.68, 195

Z. elliotiana Origin unknown
The summer-flowering GOLDEN CALLA (30-50cm) has spotted leaves. Weekly summer water, also for the next.

Z. rehmannii S Africa, Natal
Narrow leaves come out in spring, fol-lowed by lovely pink summer bloom. Needs more heat than the others.

ZAUSCHNERIA see **EPILOBIUM**

ZINNIA Compositae
The annual Mexican ZINNIA provides in-stant summer colour in young gardens. Easy to grow in hot sun and good soil. Overhead water encourages mildew; better to soak the soil. p.81

ZIZIPHUS Rhamnaceae
Z. jujuba Mediterranean, Asia
The deciduous, spiny COMMON JUJUBE (5-8m) grows slowly. Deep rooted and hardy, it is suited to natural or desert gar-dens. Olive-sized edible fruit are sweet-est in hot dry regions. Shape for pleasing trunk lines.

Glossary

acid (soils) in solution have a pH of less than 7

aerobic process taking place with oxygen and not possible without it

alkaline soil as opposed to acid soil, with a pH in solution superior to 7

anaerobic a process occurring without oxygen

annual plants complete their life cycle in one growing season

baking a bulb spends the summer underground without irrigation

bulbil bulb-like structure developing in the leaf axil on above ground stems (*Lilium lancifolium*)

bulblet offset of a bulb or corm which does not yet flower (*Crocus*)

bulbous plants have underground storage organs:

bulb – stores food in scales

corm – thickened underground stem with food stored in the centre from which it produces a whole plant each year (*Gladiolus*)

rhizome – a creeping stem (above or just below ground), storing food (*Iris germanica*)

tuber – a thickened fleshy underground stem which does not extend as rhizomes do (potato)

tuberous root – a thickened, food-storing root (not a stem as with tubers)

chlorophyll the green pigment of plant cells which is the receptor of light energy in photosynthesis

chlorosis reduced development of chlorophyll

contractile (roots) by shortening, pull or push a seedling or bulb to its adequate depth

corm see bulbous plants

cuticle the protective layer that covers the epidermis

cv. (cultivar) cultivated variety

deciduous plants shed their leaves yearly (summer- or winter-deciduous)

disintegrating decomposing bodies

drainage refers to the passage of water and air in the soil. Sandy soils with larger granules let water drain through quickly, replaced by air which is vital for roots. Heavy clay soils with small granules allow water to drain away only slowly

drip line runs around the plant's outer perimeter, often indicating how far its roots reach

ecology the study of relationships between living things and the environment

endemic confined to a particular region, often very reduced

endosperm-rich seed stores ample food

epiphyte grows on or holds onto another plant (or rock) without feeding on it

evaporation the loss of water from the soil

evergreen an evergreen plant seems to keep its leaves year-round, but actually sheds part of these (but never all at once) while new leaves grow

f. (form) growing stronger than the type

genus grouping different species

geophyte any plant which copes with summer drought by shedding its above ground body and survives via its underground storage organs (bulb, corm, rhizome, tuber)

herbaceous (plants) die annually down to the ground to grow again with the following season

humus a decomposing, extremely water-retentive, dark brown organic matter in the soil, an ideal medium for an active soil life and congenial to roots

hybrid a plant which results from a cross between genetically unlike individuals, usually sterile

in situ in the natural, final position

layering a branch making roots while placed in close contact with the soil surface

life cycle means plants' developing and dying down, occurring at fixed seasons

organic (matter) derives from a once living organism

perennial (plants) live for more than 2 years

pH indicates the concentration of hydrogen ions in a (soil) solution. Below 7 is acidic, 7 is neutral and above 7 is alkaline

photosynthesis means the conversion of carbon dioxide and water into carbohydrates, taking the energy from light (helped by chlorophyll)

phraeatophyllous reaching for ground water

rhizome see bulbous plants

sclerophyllous hard-leaved

soil life see Chapter One, The Soil

sp. (species) individuals with the same character and which can breed with each other

ssp. (subspecies) a subdivision of a species

stolon stem that creeps along the ground, taking root at intervals, forming new plants

stoloniferous producing stolons

stoma, stomata (pl) minute openings mostly on the underside of leaves

stratification exposes seeds for a certain time to cold (to simulate a cold winter period) with the intention that an ensuing warm period induces seeds to germinate

stress any situation which goes against a plant's growing needs

sucker arises from the plant's roots, sometimes distant from the mother plant and with time will develop into an identical plant. Severed from the root with sufficient fine roots, it will grow on

summer dormancy as opposed to winter dormancy, is one of the survival strategies plants choose to cope with long hot and dry summers

taproot goes strait down into the ground from the embryonic root

tender sensitive to frost, as opposed to hardy

transpiration loss of water vapour through plants' leaves via their pores (stomata)

tuber see bulbous plants

var. (variety) a plant whose distinct character does not justify classification as a separate species

xerophytes have adapted to arid regions and are among the most drought-tolerant plants

Useful Addresses

All gave delight, from all
I learned, to all goes gratitude.

ENGLAND

RHS The Royal Horticultural Society,
80 Vincent Square, London, SW1P 2PE.
Members receive monthly 'The Garden', annually a seed list and enjoy
free entry to the RHS Gardens Wisley, Surrey (plant sale; the largest
botanical book store in Europe). Visit the Mediterranean Bank.

The Royal Botanic Gardens Kew (visit the Mediterranean section),
Richmond, Surrey

Beth Chatto (sells Mediterranean plants),
White Barn House, Elmstead Market, Colchester CO7 7DB

Burncoose & Southdown Nurseries,
Gwenapp, Redruth, Cornwall TR16 6BJ

Thompson & Morgan (seeds),
London Road, Ipswich IP2 0BA

HDRA (Sales) Ltd. (seeds of Green Manure),
Ryton Gardens, Ryton-on-Dunsmore, Coventry, CV8 3LG

Henry Doubleday Research Association,
(organic gardening advice, also a branch in Australia),
Ryton Gardens, Ryton-on-Dunsmore, Coventry CV8 3LG

Soil Association (organic gardening advice),
86 Colston Street, Bristol BS1 5BB

The Plant Finder, 40.000 Plants and Where to Buy,
Headmain, Whitbourne 1995

Wheldon & Wesley (books old and new, quarterly catalogue)
Codicote, Hitchin, Herts. SG4 TE

FRANCE

Jardin Exotique de Monaco (succulents)

Jardin des Plantes (Botanic Garden)
163 rue Auguste Broussonnet, Montpellier

Jardin Villa Thuret (Botanic Garden)
chemin G. Raymond, Antibes

Villa Val Rahmeh, av. Saint-Jacques, Menton-Gavarre

20.000 Plantes - Ou et comment les acheter?
Cordier, F. et J., La Maison Rustique, Paris 1992

Journées des Plantes de Courson (spring, autumn)
Courson Monteloup, 91680 Bruyères-le-Chatel

Pépinières Michèle Dental (rare plants),
1569 Route de la Mer, 06410 Biot/Cannes

Bonaut Elie (rare Mediterranean climate plants),
566 chemin des Maures, 06600 Antibes

Pépinières La Mayrale (wide plant choice)
Route de Marcôrignan, 11100 Narbonne

Pépinières de Kerisnel (wide plant choice)
29250 Saint-Pol-de-Léon

Société Nationale d'Horticulture de France
84 rue de Grenelle, 75007 Paris

GERMANY

Insel Mainau, Bodensee (in summer Mediterranean
vegetation on display)

Pflanzeneinkaufsfuehrer, Bezugsquellen fuer 13.000 Pflanzenarten
A. Erhardt, Eugen Ulmer Verlag, Stuttgart 1992

Albert Schenkel, Exotische Saemereien,
Postfach 550927, 2000 Hamburg 55

Horst Gewiehs (bulbs),
Postfach 1270, 2720 Rotenburg/Wuemme

Walter Daunicht Gaertnerei (Australian natives),
Gaertner Strasse 5, 2957 Westoverledingen- Voellen

Flora Mediterranea (excellent catalogue DM 10),
Kirchweg 10, 8053 Heigenhausen

Koeltz Books
P.O. Box 1360, 6240 Koenigstein

GREECE

Sparoza (garden with Mediterranean plants),
Box 14, Peania, 19002 Greece

HOLLAND, BELGIUM

Arboretum Waasland Nurseries (trees, shrubs, climbers)
Kriekelaarstraat 29, B-9100 Nieuwkerken

Pieter Zwijnenburg (trees, shrubs, climbers),
Halve Raak 18, Boskoop/Holland

ITALY

Villa Taranto, 28048 Pallanza, Lago Maggiore (17 ha)

Hanbury Gardens, La Mortola, 18030 Latte (18 ha)

Orto Botanico, 35123 Padua (founded 1545, 2 ha)

Istituto Botanico, Via Lincoln 2, 90133 Palermo (10 ha)

Patrucco (roses for Mediterranean gardens),
Via Privata delle Rose 1, 18010 Diano S. Pietro

SPAIN

Mar y Murta, Blanes, Costa Brava (15 ha)

Parque de Ruben Dario (a cliff garden above the port
planted almost solely with succulents), Barcelona

Gardens of the Generalife (moorish style), Granada

Real Jardin Botanico, Madrid (founded 1755)

The Alcazar's moorish gardens, Sevilla

The Canary Islands give inspiration although
theirs is not a Mediterranean type climate

Adena Forestal (native trees for reafforestation),
calle Sol 7, 02270 Villamalea/Albacete

Garden Center Los Peñotes,
Ctra de Burgos (salida 13), La Moraleja

Hortus Vivero, Santa Maria, Mallorca

Viveros Orero (fruit trees),
Apartado 9, Segorbe (Castellón)

Viveros Vallgorguina,
Ctra de San Celoni a Arenys km 13.5 (nr. Barcelona)

SWITZERLAND
Isola di Brissago, Ticino
(Botanic Garden, Mediterranean climate plants)

ISRAEL
University Botanical Garden, Jerusalem

Tira Nurseries (Oncyclus irises only)
Tirat Tsvi, D.N. Emek Beit Shean, 10815

AUSTRALIA, NEW ZEALAND
King's Park Botanic Garden, Perth

Mount Lofty Botanic Garden, near Adelaide

The National Botanic Gardens, Canberra (40 ha)

Burrendong Arboretum near Wellington, NZ (l50 ha)

Bower Bird Books (reduced prices)
PO Box 104, Winmalee 2777, Australia

The Australian Garden Journal (quarterly),
PO Box 588, Bowral NSW 2576

The Society for Growing Australian Plants (South Australian Region)
PO Box 410, Padstow, NSW 2211

Western Australian Wildflower Society
(sells seed together with *Hints on Growing Native Plants*)
PO Box 64, Nedlands, 6009, WA

The Australian Plant Finder
Frances Hutchison, Simon & Schuster

Nindethana Seed Service (native trees, shrubs, books)
939 Woogenilup, 6324, WA

CALIFORNIA
Rancho Santa Ana Botanic Garden (native plants),
1500 North College Avenue, Claremont CA 91711

Santa Barbara Botanic Garden (native plants, bookshop)
1212 Mission Canyon Rd., Santa Barbara CA 93105

Strybing Arboretum and Botanical Gardens (native plants)
Ninth Avenue at Lincoln Way, San Francisco CA 94122

Tilden National Park, Berkeley CA (native plants)

City of Santa Barbara Firescapes Demonstration Garden,
Corner Mission Ridge and Stanwood Drive

International Bulb Society (publishes 'Herbertia')
UCI Arboretum, University of California, Irvine CA 92717

Source List of Plants and Seeds, Andersen Horticultural Library,
3675 Arboretum Drive, Chanhassen MN 55317- 0039

S & S Seeds
PO Box 1275, Carpinteria CA

Theodore Payne Foundation (seeds)
10459 Tuxford St., Sun Valley CA 91352

Frosty Hollow Nursery
PO Box 53, Washington 98260

Yerba Buena Nursery (California native plants)
19500 Skyline Blvd., Woodside Ca 94062,
Highway 35 south of San Francisco

Saratoga Horticultural Foundation (useful addresses)
PO Box 308, Saratoga CA 95071

VLT Gardner Books,
625 E. Victoria Street, Santa Barbara CA 93103
fax (805) 969-4787

'Pacific Horticulture' (quarterly)
PO Box 485, Berkeley CA 94701

SOUTH AFRICA
Consult *A Visitor's Guide to Gardens in South Africa*,
N. Gardiner, Struik, Cape Town 1988

The Botanical Society of South Africa (members receive monthly
'Veld & Flora', annual seed list. Excellent bookshop),
Kirstenbosch Botanical Garden, Claremont 7735, RSA

IBSA Indigenous Bulb Growers Association of South Africa
(annual seed list to members, newsletter),
PO Box 12265, N1 City 7463, RSA

Cape Seed & Bulb, (indigenous bulbous plants)
Box 4063, Stellenbosch, 7609

Sunburst Nursery (indigenous bulbous plants)
PO Box 183, Howard Place 7450

Honingklip Book Sales (catalogue)
402 CPOA, 231 Main Road, Rondebosch 7700

Importing plants may require a phytosanitary certificate.

Note: A well developed root system is vital in a Mediterranean climate. Look for plants in adequately sized pots and reject roots which curl or grow through the drainage hole. Buying bare-root is always a risk. Avoid a purchase at a place showing health problems or pernicious weeds such as *Oxalis*, as tempting as the plant may be!

Addresses are the ones available to me. I made every effort to ensure that factual details were accurate at the time this book went into press.

Bibliography

BATTEN, A. (1986)
Flowers of Southern Africa
Frandsen, Sandton RSA

BEARD, J.S. (1990)
Plant Life of Western Australia
Kangaroo Press, Kenthurst NSW

BECKETT, E. (1993)
Illustrated Flora of Mallorca
Editorial Moll, Palma de Mallorca

* BRICKELL, C., Editor-in-Chief. (1992)
The RHS Encyclopedia of Gardening
Dorling Kindersley, London

* BRICKELL, C., Editor-in-Chief. (1994)
*The RHS Gardeners' Encyclopedia of
Plants and Flowers*
Dorling Kindersley, London

CAPON, B. (1994)
Plant Survival
Timber Press, Portland Oregon

CARLQUIST, S. (1985)
*Vasicentric Tracheids as a Drought Survival
Mechanism in the Woody Flora of Southern
California and Similar Regions*
Aliso 11(1), p. 37-68

CASTRI di, F. (1981)
Ecosystems of the World
Elsevier, Amsterdam

CHALK, D. (1988)
Hebes and Parahebes
Christopher Helm, London

* CHATTO, B. (1988)
The Dry Garden
Dent, London

COLLENETTE, S. (1985)
Flowers of Saudi Arabia
Scorpion, London

CORDIER, F. et J. (1992)
20.000 Plantes, Où et comment les acheter?
S.N.H.F. et La Maison Rustique

COURTRIGHT, G. (1988)
Trees and Shrubs for Temperate Climates
Timber Press, Portland Oregon

DALLMAN, P. (1998)
*Plant Life in the World's Mediterranean
Climates*
University of California Press, Berkeley

DEPARTMENT of WATER RESOURCES
(1981)
*Plants for California Landscapes, A Catalog
of Drought-Tolerant Plants*, Bulletin 209,
PO Box 388, Sacramento CA 95802

* DUFFIELD M.R. & JONES W.D. (1992)
Plants for Dry Climates
HP Books, Los Angeles

ELLEFSON C. et al. (1992)
*Xeriscape Gardening, Water Conservation
for the American Landscape*
Macmillan New York

* ELIOVSON, S. (1987)
Wild Flowers of Southern Africa
Macmillan South Africa

EMERY, D. (1988)
*Seed Propagation of Native California
Plants*
Santa Barbara Botanic Garden,
Santa Barbara CA

FOURIE, D.M.
*A Preliminary List of Plants for Water
Conservation Gardening in South Africa*
Department of Agriculture and Water
Supply, Pretoria, RSA

GOMEZ-CAMPO, C. Editor (1985)
*Plant conservation in the Mediterranean
area*
Dr. W. Junk Publishers, Dordrecht

* GRACE, J. General Editor (1983, revised)
Climbers and Trailers
Reed, Wellington New Zealand

* GRACE, J. General Editor (1984)
Handbook of Trees and Shrubs
(Southern Hemisphere)
Reed, Wellington New Zealand

GRAF, A. (1986)
Tropica,
Color Cyclopedia of Exotic Plants and Trees
Roehrs Company, East Rutherford, N.J.

HARDESTY, N. (1984)
*Oak Woodland Preservation and Land
Planning.* Hardesty Ass., Palo Alto CA

HOFFMANN, A. (1979)
Flora Silvestre de Chile, Zona Central
Ediciones Fundacion Claudio Gay,
Santiago de Chile

* HUXLEY, A. & TAYLOR, W. (1984)
Flowers of Greece and the Aegean
Chatto and Windus, London

HUXLEY, A. editor in chief. (1992)
*The New Royal Horticultural Society
Dictionary of Gardening*
Macmillan, London

INNES, C. (1985)
The World of Iridaceae
Holly Gate International, Ashington UK

JACKSON, W. (1982, revised)
Wild Flowers of Table Mountain
Howard Timmins, Cape Town

* JEPPE, B. (1989)
*Spring and Winter Flowering Bulbs of the
Cape.* Oxford University Press, Cape Town

JOFFE, P. (1994)
*The Gardener's Guide to
South African Plants*

JOHNSON E. et al. (1993)
The Low-Water Flower Gardener
Millard Publishing, Tucson Arizona

JOHNSON, H. (1984)
Encyclopaedia of Trees
Mitchell Beazley, London

JONES, L. (1992)
Gardens in Provence
Flammarion, Paris

KEATOR, G. (1998)
The Life of an Oak
Heyday Books, Berkeley

KUMMEROW, J. (1981)
Structure of Roots and Root Systems
Ecosystems of the World,
vol. 11, p. 269-288, Amsterdam

KUMMEROW, J. and ALEXANDER, J.
(1978)
Chaparral Plants under Water Stress
Environment Southwest, San Diego
Society of Natural History, No. 483

KUMMEROW J. et al. (1978)
*Seasonal Changes of Fine Root Density in
the Southern California Chaparral*
Oecologia (Berl.) 37, p. 201-212

KUMMEROW, J. and LANTZ, R. (1983)
*Effect of Fire on Fine Root Density in
Red Shank Chaparral*
Plant and Soil 70, p. 347-352, The Hague.

LATYMER, H. (1990)
The Mediterranean Gardener
Windward, London

LENZ, L. & DOURLEY, J. (1981)
California Native Trees & Shrubs
Rancho Santa Ana Botanic Garden,
Claremont, CA

LOPEZ GONZALEZ, G. (1982)
*La Guia de INCAFO de los Arboles y
Arbustos de la Peninsula Iberica*
Incafo, Madrid

LORD, E. and WILLIS, J. (1984)
Shrubs and Trees for Australian Gardens
Lothian, Melbourne

MARCHANT, N.G. et al. (1987)
Flora of the Perth Region
Western Australian Herbarium,
Dept. of Agriculture

* MAXWELL, V.S. (1986)
*A Simple Guide to Gardening
on the Costa del Sol.* Malaga,
Club de Jardinería de la Costa del Sol

METCALF, L.J. (1987 revised)
*The Cultivation of New Zealand Trees
and Shrubs*
Reed Methuen, Auckland

MILLARD, S. (1989)
Gardening in Dry Climates
Ortho Books, Chevron Chemical Co.,
San Ramon CA

MOORE, E. (1986)
Gardening in the Middle East
Stacey International, London

MULLER, K. (1974)
Trees of Santa Barbara
Santa Barbara Botanic Garden,
Santa Barbara CA

MUNZ, P.A. (1974)
A Flora of Southern California
University of California Press, Berkeley

NABIL el-HADIDI, M. (1988 revised)
The Street Trees of Egypt
The American University in Cairo Press

NEHRLING, A. and I. (1960)
*Easy Gardening with Drought-resistant
Plants.* Hearthside Press, New York

* NOAILLES, Vicomte de and
LANCASTER, R. (1977)
Plantes de Jardins Méditerranéens
Editions Floraisse, Antony

* PENDLETON S. (1989)
Absentee Gardener Spain
Anaya Publishers, London

PERRY B. (1992)
Landscape Plants for Western Regions.
An illustrated guide to plants for water
conservation
Land Design Publishing, Claremont CA

PERRY B. (1989 reprint)
*Trees and Shrubs for Dry California
Landscapes*
Land Design Publishing, Claremont CA

* PHILLIPS, R. and RIX, M. (1983)
The Bulb Book
Pan Books, London

* PHILLIPS, R. and RIX, M. (1989)
Shrubs
Pan Books, London

PIENAAR, K. (1988, second ed.)
Grow South African Plants
Struik, Cape Town

PLESSIS, N. du & DUNCAN, G. (1989)
Bulbous Plants of Southern Africa
Tafelberg, Cape Town

* POLUNIN, O. & SMYTHIES, B. (1973)
Flowers of south-west Europe
Oxford University Press

POYNTON, R.J. (1984)
Trees and Shrubs cultivated in South Africa
Directorate of Forestry, Pretoria

* POLUNIN, O. & HUXLEY, A. (1972)
Flowers of the Mediterranean
Chatto and Windus, London

QUEST-RITSON, C. (1992)
The English Garden Abroad
Viking, London

RACINE, M., et al. (1987)
*Jardins de Provence,
Jardins de la Côte d'Azur.*
Edisud, Aix-en-Provence

RAUH, W. (1979)
Die grossartige Welt der Sukkulenten
Paul Parey, Berlin, Hamburg

RAVEN, P., (1986 reprint)
Biology of Plants
Worth Publishers, New York

* READMAN, J. (1991)
Soil Care and Management
HDRA/Search Press, Tunbridge Wells, Kent

* READMAN, J. (1991)
Weeds: How to Control and Love Them
HDRA/Search Press, Tunbridge Wells, Kent

RIKLI, M. (1943)
Das Pflanzenkleid der Mittelmeerlaender
Verlag Hans Huber, Bern

SALMON, J.T. (1982 reprint)
New Zealand Flowers and Plants
Reed, Wellington NZ

SARATOGA HORTICULTURAL
FOUNDATION (1983)
Success List of Water-Conserving Plants
PO Box 308, Saratoga CA

SCHMIDT, M. (1980)
Growing California Native Plants
University of California Press, Berkeley

* SCHOENFELDER I. & P. (1984)
Wild Flowers of the Mediterranean
Collins, London

STEARN, W. and DAVIS, P. (1984)
Peonies of Greece
The Goulandris Natural History Museum
Kifissia Greece

STRID, A. (1980)
Wild Flowers of Mount Olympus
The Goulandris Natural History Museum
Kifissia Greece

* SUNSET editors. (1992)
Western Garden Book
Lane Publishing, Menlo Park CA

* SUNSET editors. (1989)
Waterwise Gardening
Lane Publishing, Menlo Park CA

TAYLOR, J. (1993)
Plants for Dry Gardens
Lincoln, London

TAYLOR'S GUIDE (1990) to
Water-saving Gardening
Houghton Mifflin, Boston

THOMAS, A. (1965)
Gardening in Hot Countries
Faber & Faber, London

THOMPSON, H. (1914)
Flowering Plants of the Riviera
Longmans, London

VAN-OLLENBACH, A.W. (1978)
Planting Guide to the Middle East
The Architectural Press, London

VANDERPLANK, J. (1991)
Passion Flowers
Cassell, London

VOGTS, M. (1982)
*South Africa's Proteaceae
Know them and Grow them*
Struik, Cape Town

WATERS, G. and HARLOW N. (1990)
*The Pacific Horticulture Book of Western
Gardening.* David Godine, Boston

WELSH, P. (2000)
Southern California Gardening
Chronicle Books, San Francisco

* Recommended to beginners

Index

Page numbers in *italic* refer to illustrations,
bold numbers to main entries,
normal print to short references

Abelia *101,***101**,22,52
  floribunda **101**
  x grandiflora *101,***101**,99
  schumannii **101**
Abies **101**,20
  bracteata **101**
  cephalonica **101**,20
  pinsapo **101**
Abutilon **101**,22,52,88,97,99
  x hybridum **101**
  megapotamicum **101**
Acacia *13,101,***101**,42,59,85,97-99
  baileyana **101**
  cultriformis **102**
  cyclops **102**
  dealbata *13,***102**
  glaucoptera **102**
  longifolia *102,***102**
  melanoxylon **102**,97
  podalyriifolia **102**
  saligna **102**
  verticillata **102**
Acanthus *102,***102**,85,88
  mollis *102,***102**,96
Acca **102**
  sellowiana **102**,97,98
Achillea **102**,51,98
  millefolium **102**,50
Acokanthera **103**
  oblongifolia **103**
Actinidia **103**
  deliciosa **103**
Actinostrobus **103**
  pyramidalis **103**
Aeonium *103,***103**,22,58,88
  arboreum *103,***103**
  canariense **103**
  simsii **103**
Aesculus **103**
  californica **103**,97,98
Agapanthus
    *103,***103**,49,51,59,96,99
  africanus **103**
  praecox **103**,97
African boxwood /Myrsine
African cypress /Widdringtonia
African daisy /Arctotis,
    Dimorphotheca
African tulip tree /Spathodea
Agathosma **104**
  foetidissima *104,***104**
  ovata **104**
Agave *25,53,104,***104**,98
  americana *104,183,190,***104**
  attenuata *25,53,***104**
Agonis **104**
  flexuosa **104**
Ailanthus **104**,85

altissima *104,***104**
Ajania *25,***104**
  pacifica *25,***104**,25
Ajuga **104**
  reptans *104,*51
Albizia **105**,85
  julibrissin **105**
Alcea **105**
  rosea **105**
Allium *31,105,141,***105**,21,85,89
  caeruleum **105**
  cepa **105**
  giganteum **105**
  haematochiton *141,***105**
  neapolitanum **105**
  roseum *105,***105**
  triquetrum *31,105,***105**
Allocasuarina see Casuarina
Almond /Prunus dulcis
Alocasia *53,***105**
  macrorrhiza *53,***105**,96
Aloe *59,64,71,105,***105**,94,98
  arborescens *59,***105**,96-99
  ciliaris *105,***105**
  ferox **105**
  thraskii **105**
  variegata **105**
  vera **105**
Aloysia **106**
  triphylla **106**
Alstroemeria *12,106,***106**,31
  aurea **106**
  ligtu **106**
Alyogyne **106**
  huegelii **106**
Alyssum **106**
  montanum **106**
  wulfenianum **106**
X Amarine *106,***106**,58
  tubergenii *106,***106**
Amaryllis *87,***106**,23,86,100
  belladonna *87,***106**,23,59
Amorpha **106**,85
  californica **106**
Anemone **106**,21,98
  blanda **106**
  coronaria *106,*87
  hupehensis *106,*22,88
Angel's hair /Artemisia
Angel's tears /Narcissus
Angel's trumpet /Brugmansia
Anigozanthos *107,***107**
  flavidus **107**
  viridis **107**
Anisodontea *107,***107**,88,97
  capensis *107,***107**,97,99
Antigonon **107**
  leptopus **107**,99

Antirrhinum **107**
  majus **107**
Apricot /Prunus armeniaca
Aptenia *107,***107**
  cordifolia *107,***107**,50,69,98
Aquilegia *107,*87
  formosa **107**
  vulgaris **107**
Arabis **107**
  caucasica **107**
Arar /Tetraclinis
Arbutus *108,***108**,20,95,96
  andrachne **108**
  menziesii **108**
  unedo *108,***108**,64,94,98
Arctostaphylos **108**,64,95,98
  densiflora **108**
  edmundsii 'Carmel Sur' **108**
  franciscana **108**
  glandulosa *81,***108**
  'Green Sphere' **108**
  hookeri **108**,51
  pumila **108**
  uva-ursi *108,*98
Arctotheca **108**,95
  calendula **108**,50,85,98
Arctotis *109,***109**,97,98
  acaulis *109,***109**
  fastuosa **109**
  venusta **109**,51
Argyranthemum
    *27,***109**,25,88,97-99
  frutescens *27,***109**,47,59
Argyrocytisus **109**
  battandieri **109**,97
Arisarum *109,***109**
  vulgare *109,***109**
Aristea *109,*87
  ecklonii **109**
  macrocarpa **109**
  major **109**
Armeria **109**
  maritima **109**,98
Artemisia
    *110,***110**,25,88,94,98,99
  abrotanum **110**
  absinthium **110**,79
  arborescens *110,***110**
  schmidtiana **110**,80
Arthropodium *110,***110**,87
  cirrhatum *110,***110**
Artichoke /Cynara
Arum *111,***110**
  dioscoridis **110**
  italicum *111,***110**,96
  pictum *66,***110**
Ash /Fraxinus
Asparagus **110**,25

acutifolius **110**
albus **110**
Asphodeline **110**
  lutea **110**
Asphodelus *111,***111**,31
  aestivus *111,***111**
  fistulosus **111**
Aspidistra *111,*89
  elatior **111**,96
Aster **111**
  amellus **111**
  dumosus **111**
Asteriscus **111**
  maritimus **111**
Atriplex **111**,98
  canescens **111**
  halimus **111**
  semibaccata **111**,98
Aubrieta **111**
  deltoidea **111**
Aucuba **111**
  japonica **111**,98
Aurinia **111**
  saxatilis **111**,51,98
Australian fuchsia /Correa
Australian willow /Geijera
Avocado /Persea

Babiana *111,*23,99
  stricta **111**
  villosa **111**
Baby's breath /Gypsophila
Baccharis **112**,64
  pilularis **112**,51,98
Balloon pea /Sutherlandia
Ballota *112,***112**,51,79,88
  acetabulosa *112,***112**
Banksia **112**
  ericifolia **112**
  integrifolia **112**
Barbados pride /Caesalpinia
Barbary fig /Opuntia
Barleria *112,***112**,83
  obtusa *112,***112**
Barosma see Agathosma
Bartlettina **112**
  sordida **112**
Basket-of-gold /Aurinia
Bauhinia *112,***112**
  galpinii **113**
  variegata *112,***113**
Bear's Breeches /Acanthus
Bearberry /Arctostaphylos
Beaumontia **113**,77,96
  grandiflora **113**,97
Beauty bush /Kolkwitzia
Beefwood /Casuarina

number in *italic* – illustration
bold number – main entry
normal print – short reference

Begonia 53,**113**,52
Belamcanda **113**,87
  chinensis **113**
Belladonna lily /*Amaryllis*
Bellflower /*Campanula*
Bergenia **113**,96
  ciliata **113**
  crassifolia **113**
Beschorneria **113**,*113*
  yuccoides **113**,*113*
Bignonia **113**,58,59
  capreolata **113**
Billardiera **113**
  longiflora **113**
Bindweed /*Convolvulus*
Bird-of-paradise /*Caesalpinia,*
  Strelitzia
Black bean /*Kennedia*
Black locust /*Robinia*
Blackwood /*Acacia melanoxylon*
Bladder senna /*Colutea*
Blanket flower /*Gaillardia*
Bletilla **113**
  striata **113**
Blood lily /*Scadoxus*
Bloomeria **113**
  crocea **113**
Blue dicks /*Dichelostemma*
Blue fan palm /*Brahea*
Blue marguerite /*Felicia*
Blue stars /*Aristea*
Blue-eyed grass /*Sisyrinchium*
Bluebeard /*Caryopteris*
Bluebell creeper /*Sollya*
Blueblossom /*Ceanothus*
Bolusanthus **113**
  speciosus **113**
Boobyalla /*Myoporum*
Boronia **114**,83
  heterophylla **114**,97
  megastigma **114**
Boston ivy /*Parthenocissus*
Bottlebrush /*Callistemon*
Bougainvillea 4,57,59,**114**,*114*,
  37,49,65,83,98
  glabra 43,**114**,99
  spectabilis 4,57,59,**114**,*114*,99
Bower plant /*Pandorea*
Boxwood /*Buxus*
Brachyglottis **136**,*114*
  greyi **136**,*114*
Brahea **114**
  armata **114**,99
  edulis **114**
Bridal veil broom /*Retama*
Broom /*Cytisus, Genista*
Brugmansia
  115,*114*,77,97,99,100
  arborea **114**
  aurea *115*,**114**
  sanguinea **114**
  suaveolens **114**
Brush box /*Lophostemon*
Buchu /*Agathosma*
Buckthorn /*Rhamnus*
Buckwheat /*Eriogonum*

Buddleja *114*,**114**,22,88,99
  alternifolia **115**
  davidii **115**,98
  madagascariensis **115**,22
  officinalis **115**,97
  x weyeriana *114*,**115**
Bugle /*Ajuga*
Bulbine **115**
  frutescens **115**
Bulbinella *115*,**115**,23
  cauda-felis **115**
  floribunda *115*,**115**
Bupleurum *115*,**115**,97-99
  fruticosum *115*,**115**,43,87
Bush anemone /*Carpenteria*
Busy Lizzie /*Impatiens*
Butcher's broom /*Ruscus*
Butia **115**
  capitata *13*,**115**,99
Butterfly bush /*Buddleja*
Buxus **116**,*116*,59,62,87,94
  balearica **116**,*116*,99
  microphylla 46,**116**,99
  sempervirens **116**,96

Cabbage tree /*Cussonia*
Cactus /*Succulents*
Caesalpinia **116**,*116*,86
  gilliesii *116*,**116**
  pulcherrima **116**
Calendula **116**,81,87
  officinalis **116**,98,99
California bay /*Umbellularia*
California buckeye /*Aesculus*
California fuchsia /*Epilobium*
California lilac /*Ceanothus*
California poppy /*Eschscholzia*
California snowbell /*Styrax*
California walnut /*Juglans*
California wax myrtle /*Myrica*
Calla /*Zantedeschia*
Callistemon **116**,95,97-99
  citrinus **116**,97,98
  rigidus **116**
  viminalis **116**,98
Callitris **116**,83
  columellaris **116**
  preissii **116**
Calocedrus **116**
  decurrens **116**,97
Calochortus **116**,96
  albus **117**
  luteus **117**
  venustus **117**
Calonyction see *Ipomoea*
Calothamnus **117**
  quadrifidus **117**
  villosus **117**
Camellia **117**,*117*,30,52
  japonica *117*,**117**
Campanula **117**
  carpatica **117**
  isophylla **117**
  rapunculoides **117**
Camphor tree /*Cinnamomum*
Campsis **117**,*117*
  grandiflora **117**
  radicans *117*,**117**,49,98,99
  x tagliabuana 'Mme Galen' **117**

Canary date palm /
  Phoenix canariensis
Candytuft /*Iberis*
Canna 53,75,**118**,52,77,89,99
  indica 53,75,**118**,96,97
Cape honeysuckle /*Tecomaria*
Cape primrose /*Streptocarpus*
Cape weed /*Arctotheca*
Caper /*Capparis*
Capparis **118**,*118*
  spinosa **118**,*118*
Caragana **118**
  arborescens **118**
Cardoon /*Cynara*
Carissa **118**,*118*,65
  bispinosa **118**
  macrocarpa **118**,*118*,97
Caro /*Pittosporum crassifolium*
Carob /*Ceratonia*
Carolina jasmine /*Gelsemium*
Carpenteria **118**,*118*,45,77
  californica **118**,*118*,97
Carpobrotus 48,**118**
  edulis 48,**118**,50
Carya **118**
  illinoinensis **118**,80
Caryopteris **119**
  x clandonensis **119**
Cassia see *Senna*
Cast-iron plant /*Aspidistra*
Castanea **119**
  sativa **119**,80
Castor bean /*Ricinus*
Casuarina **119**,97,99
  cunninghamiana **119**
  equisetifolia **119**
  verticillata **119**
Catalina currant /*Ribes*
Catalina ironwood /
  Lyonothamnus
Catalina mountain lilac /
  Ceanothus arboreus
Catha **119**
  edulis **119**
Catharanthus **119**,*119*
  roseus **119**,*119*
Ceanothus
  77,*119*,*141*,**119**,64,65,98
  arboreus **119**,99
  'Concha' **119**
  'Frosty Blue' *141*,**119**
  'Joyce Coulter' **119**
  leucodermis **119**
  maritimus **119**
  'Ray Hartmann' **119**
  rigidus 'Snow Flurries' *119*,**119**
  thyrsiflorus **119**,51
Cedar /*Cedrus*
Cedrus **120**,20,37
  deodara **120**,97
  libani **120**
Celtis **120**,*120*,94,98
  australis **120**,*120*
  occidentalis **120**
Centaurea **120**,21
  cineraria **120**,98
Centranthus **120**,*120*,85
  ruber **120**,*120*
Century plant /*Agave*
Cerastium **120**,*120*,88,98

tomentosum **120**,*120*,51,97,99
Ceratonia **121**,*120*,20,94,98
  siliqua **121**,*120*,58,82,96,99
Ceratostigma **121**,*121*
  griffithii **121**
  plumbaginoides **121**
  willmottianum *121*,**121**
Cercis **121**,*121*,95,98
  occidentalis **121**,98
  siliquastrum
    121,*121*,49,59,64,82
Cestrum **122**,*122*
  aurantiacum **122**
  elegans **122**
  nocturnum **122**,97
  parqui **122**
Chalice vine /*Solandra*
Chamaerops
  13,53,**122**,*122*,21,87
  humilis **122**,*122*,97-99
Chaparral whitethorn /*Ceanothus*
Chasmanthe **122**,*122*,58,87
  floribunda **122**,*122*
Chaste tree /*Vitex*
Chequered lily /*Fritillaria*
Cherry /*Prunus*
Chilean guava /*Ugni*
Chilean jasmine /*Mandevilla*
Chilean wine palm /*Jubaea*
Chinaberry /*Melia*
Chincherinchee /*Ornithogalum*
Chinese flame tree /*Koelreuteria*
Chinese ground orchid /*Bletilla*
Chinese holly /*Osmanthus*
Choisya *123*,**122**,88,94
  ternata *123*,**122**,96-99
Chorisia **122**
  speciosa **122**
Christmas star /*Euphorbia*
Christmas tree /*Metrosideros*
Chrysanthemum 22,**123**
  coronarium 22,**123**
  frutescens see *Argyranthemum*
Cinnamomum **123**
  camphora **123**
Cinquefoil /*Potentilla*
Cistus 21,44,55,**123**,20,88,95-99
  x aguilarii **123**
  albidus 21,**123**,99
  ladanifer 44,*123*,**123**
  laurifolius **123**
  monspeliensis **123**,20
  populifolius **123**
  x purpureus **123**
  salviifolius **123**,20
Citrus **123**,*123*,21,81,97-99
  limon **123**,*123*
Clematis 21,101,**124**,*124*,20
  armandii **124**,97
  cirrhosa **124**,*124*,97
  flammula 21,101,**124**
  montana **124**
  orientalis **124**
  texensis **124**
Clianthus **124**
  puniceus **124**
Clivia 32,**124**,86,89,97,99
  miniata 32,**124**,96,99,100
Clytostoma **125**
  callistigioides **125**

Cneorum 124,**125**,24,96
  tricoccon 124,**125**,39
Cockies tongue /Templetonia
Coffeeberry /
    Rhamnus californica
Colchicum **125**,22,31,58
  cupanii **125**
  longiflorum **125**
  stevenii **125**
Coleonema **125**,**125**,65,83
  pulchrum 125,**125**,97
Columbine /Aquilegia
Colutea **125**
  arborescens **125**
Coneflower /Rudbeckia
Convolvulus **125**,**125**,85
  althaeoides **125**
  cneorum **125**,39,98
  sabatius 125,**125**,99
Coolgardie gum /Eucalyptus
Coprosma **125**,**125**
  x kirkii 125,**125**,51,98
  lucida **125**
  repens 125,**125**,98,99
Coral tree /Erythrina
Coral vine /Antigonon
Cordyline **126**
  australis **126**,97,98
Coreopsis 126,**126**,22,59,89,99
  gigantea 126,**126**
  maritima **126**
  verticillata **126**
Corokia **126**,98
  buddleioides **126**
  cotoneaster **126**
  macrocarpa **126**
Coronilla 126,**126**,43,59,72,87,97
  emerus **126**
  valentina 126,**126**,98,99
Correa **127**,**126**
  alba **127**
  backhousiana **127**
  pulchella **127**
  reflexa 127,**127**
Corynocarpus **127**
  laevigata **127**,99
Cosmos **127**
Cotinus **127**
  coggygria **127**
Cotoneaster 127,**127**,98,99
  buxifolius **127**
  congestus **127**,98
  dammeri **127**,51,98
  lacteus **127**
  microphyllus **127**
Cottonweed /Otanthus
Cotyledon 127,**127**
  orbiculata 127,**127**
Crape myrtle /Lagerstroemia
Crassula 128,**128**,50,88
  coccinea **128**
  multicava 128,**128**
  muscosa **128**
  ovata **128**
  perfoliata **128**
  socialis **128**
Crataegus 128,**128**,59
  azarolus **128**
  laevigata **128**
  x lavallei 'Carrierei' **128**

monogyna 128,**128**
Creeping berries /Senecio
Crinum 69,128,**128**,23,79,86,
    97-100
  bulbispermum 69,**128**
  moorei 128,**128**
  x powellii **128**,96
Crithmum **129**
  maritimum **129**
Crocosmia **129**,87
  x crocosmiiflora **129**
  masonorum **129**
Crocus 129,**129**,21,22,23,31,59
  cancellatus **129**
  chrysanthus **129**
  corsicus **129**
  goulimyi **129**
  sativus **129**
  sieberi 129,**129**
  speciosus **129**
  tommasinianus **129**
Cross vine /Bignonia
Crown daisy /Chrysanthemum
Crown vetch /Coronilla
Cupressus
    35,39,41,58,**129**,83,87
  arizonica **129**,97
  macrocarpa **129**,98
  sempervirens
    35,39,41,58,**129**,99
Currant /Ribes
Cussonia 129,**129**,94,97
  paniculata 129,**130**
  spicata **130**
Cycas 37,72,130,**130**,99
  revoluta 130,**130**
Cyclamen
    130,**130**,31,45,87,96,99
  balearicum 130,**130**
  coum **130**
  graecum **130**
  hederifolium **130**
  persicum 130,**130**
Cymbidium 130,**130**
Cynara 131,**130**,47
  cardunculus **130**
  scolymus 131,**130**,96,97
Cypress /Cupressus
Cypress pine /Callitris
Cytisus 130,45,85,96-99
  battandieri see Argyrocytisus
  x kewensis **131**
  x praecox **131**,97
  purgans **131**

Daffodil /Narcissus
Dais **131**,**131**
  cotinifolia 131,**131**
Daisy bush /Olearia
Dasylirion 131,**131**
  acrotrichum 131,**131**
Date /Phoenix dactylifera
Datura /Brugmansia
Daylily /Hemerocallis
Delairea **131**
  odorata **131**
Delonix **131**,86
  regia **131**
Delosperma **131**

ecklonis **131**
Dendranthema see Ajania
Dendromecon **131**,**131**,44
  rigida **131**
Deodar /Cedrus deodara
Desert willow /Pittosporum
Deutzia **132**
  gracilis **132**
Dianella **132**
  intermedia **132**
Dianthus **132**
  deltoides **132**,51
Dichelostemma **132**
  pulchellum **132**
Dietes 133,**132**,87,89,97-99
  bicolor **132**
  iridioides 133,**132**,99
Digitalis 132,**132**,39,87
  obscura **132**
  purpurea 132,**132**
Dimorphotheca
    132,**132**,50,88,97
  pluvialis 132,**132**
  sinuata **132**
Diospyros 133,**132**
  kaki 133,**132**,80
Diplacus see Mimulus
Distictis **133**
  buccinatoria **133**
Dodonaea **133**
  viscosa 133,97
Dombeya 133,**133**,99
  x cayeuxii 133,**133**
Doryanthes **133**
  palmeri **133**
Dovyalis **133**
  caffra **133**
Doxantha see Macfadyena
Dracaena **133**
  draco **133**
Dragon tree /Dracaena
Drosanthemum **134**
  floribundum **134**
  hispidum **134**
  speciosum **134**
Duchesnea **134**
  indica **134**,51,85
Dudleya **134**
  brittonii **134**
Dwarf chaparral broom /
    Baccharis pilularis

Easter lily /Lilium
Echeveria **134**
  elegans **134**
  pulvinata **134**
Echium 134,**134**,87,97
  candicans 134,**134**
  simplex 134,**134**
  wildpretii **134**
Elaeagnus 135,**134**,65,87,97-99
  angustifolia 134,**134**
  x ebbingei 135,**135**,97,99
  pungens **135**,99
Elephant's ear /Alocasia
Empress tree /Paulownia
Emu bush /Eremophila
Epilobium **135**
  canum **135**

Eremophila **135**,83
  alternifolia **135**
  glabra **135**
  longifolia **135**
  maculata 'Aurea' **135**
  oppositifolia **135**
Erica 135,**135**,31,39,62,96
  arborea 135,**135**,20
  bauera **135**
  lusitanica **135**
  multiflora 135,**135**,20
  patersonia **135**
Erigeron 65,136,**136**,97-99
  karvinskianus 136,**136**,48,51
Eriobotrya 136,**136**,94
  deflexa 136,97
  japonica 136,**136**,96,99
Eriocephalus 136,**136**,56,88
  africanus 136,**136**,47,98,99
Eriogonum 137,**136**,98
  arborescens **136**
  crocatum 137,**136**
  fasciculatum **136**,98
  giganteum 137,**137**
Erysimum 136,**137**
  cheiri **137**
  hieraciifolium **137**
  linifolium 136,**137**
Erythrina **137**,86
  caffra **137**
  corallodendrum **137**
  crista-galli **137**
  humeana **137**
Escallonia 137,**137**,52,89,97
  bifida **137**
  rubra 137,**137**,98,99
Eschscholzia 137,**137**
  californica 137,**137**,98
Eucalyptus 138,**138**,64,85,97-99
  citriodora **138**
  ficifolia **138**,98
  globulus 138,**138**
  gunnii **138**
  kruseana **138**
  nicholii **138**
  torquata **138**
  viminalis **138**
Euonymus 138,**138**,88,97-99
  japonicus 138,**138**,49,82,98
Euphorbia 19,25,45,138,**138**,21,94
  characias **138**
  dendroides 19,25,**139**,22,23
  ingens **139**
  marginata 139,**139**
  myrsinites **139**
  pulcherrima **139**
Euryops 38,139,173 **139**,45,88
  abrotanifolius **139**
  acraeus **139**
  pectinatus 139,**139**,22,47,95,97
  virgineus 139,**139**,59
Evening primrose /Oenothera
Everlasting flower /Helichrysum

F
X Fatshedera **139**
  lizei **139**,51,96
Fatsia 26,40,63,**139**,26,52
  japonica 26,40,63,**139**,96-99

number in *italic* – illustration
bold number – main entry
normal print – short reference

Feijoa see *Acca*
Felicia 132,**139**,22,88
  amelloides **139**,51,97,98
  fruticosa 139
Ferns 175,**140**,96
Ferraria 140,**140**
  crispa 140,**140**
Feverfew /*Tanacetum*
Ficus 140,**140**,31,96,99
  benjamina **140**
  carica 140,**140**,81
  elastica 17,**140**
Fig /*Ficus carica*
Fir /*Abies*
Firethorn /*Pyracantha*
Flamboyant /*Delonix*
Flaming Katy /*Kalanchoe*
Flannel bush /*Fremontodendron*
Flax /*Linum*
Flax lily /*Dianella*
Flowering Maple /*Abutilon*
Fortnight lily /*Dietes*
Four o'clock /*Mirabilis*
Foxglove /*Digitalis*
Fragaria **140**
  chiloensis **140**,51
  vesca **140**,51
Fragrant olive /*Osmanthus*
Francoa **140**
  sonchifolia **140**
Fraxinus **141**,20,43,87,98,99
  dipetala **141**
  ornus **141**
  uhdei **141**
  velutina **141**
Freesia 140,**141**,87,89,96-99
  refracta **141**,98
Fremontodendron
  141,**141**,44,64,80
  californicum 141,**141**
  mexicanum 141,**141**
Freylinia 141,**141**,22
  lanceolata 141,**141**,22,97
Friar's cowl /*Arisarum*
Fritillaria **141**,59
  biflora **142**
  meleagris **142**
  messanensis **142**
Fuchsia 26,142,**142**,88
  arborescens **142**
  magellanica **142**
Furcràea 142,**142**
  bedinghausii 142,**142**

Gaillardia 65,**142**,59
  x grandiflora 65,**142**
Galvezia **142**
  speciosa **142**,98
Garlic /*Allium, Tulbaghia*
Garrya **142**
  elliptica **142**
Gaura 143,**142**
  lindheimeri 143,**142**
Gazania 35,38 **142**,43,47,51,
  89,97

krebsiana 38 **143**
linearis **143**
rigens 35 **143**,98
Geijera **143**
  parviflora **143**
Gelsemium **143**
  sempervirens **143**,97
Genista **143**,31,85,98
  aetnensis **143**,97
  hispanica **143**,99
  lydia **143**
  monosperma see *Retama*
  tinctoria **143**
Geranium /*Pelargonium*
Gerbera **143**
  jamesonii **143**,97
German ivy /*Delairea*
Germander /*Teucrium*
Giant taro /*Alocasia*
Ginger lily /*Hedychium*
Ginkgo **143**
  biloba **143**,80
Gladiolus 143,**143**,21
  x colvillei **143**
  dalenii **144**,97
  illyricus 143,**144**
  italicus **144**
  tristis **144**
Glory of the sun /*Leucocoryne*
Golden rain tree /*Koelreuteria*
Gooseberry /*Ribes*
Grape /*Vitis*
Grape hyacinth /*Muscari*
Grapefruit /*Citrus*
Graptopetalum **144**
  paraguayense **144**
Grass tree /*Xanthorrhoea*
Grassnut /*Triteleia*
Grevillea 144,**144**,50,59,94,97
  robusta **144**,98
  rosmarinifolia 144,**144**,51
Greyia **144**
  sutherlandii **144**
Griselinia 144,**144**,96-99
  littoralis 144,97,98
  lucida 144,**144**,96,97
  paniculata **144**
  repens **144**
Guadalupe palm /*Brahea*
Guava /*Psidium*
Guernsey lily /*Nerine*
Gum tree /*Eucalyptus*

Hackberry /*Celtis*
Haemanthus 144,**144**,86,89,99
  albiflos 144,**145**,96,97
  coccineus **145**
Hakea 145,**145**,25,85,97
  laurina 145,**145**,97,99
  leucoptera **145**
  multilineata **145**
  salicifolia **145**
Halimium 145,**145**,52
  lasianthum 145,**145**
  ocymoides **145**
  umbellatum **145**
Hardenbergia **145**,86
  comptoniana **145**
  violacea **145**,51

Hawthorn /*Crataegus*
Heath /*Erica*
Hebe 60,63,137,**145**,22,52,97,99
  buxifolia **145**
  cupressoides **145**
  'Great Orme' **145**
  salicifolia **145**
  speciosa 60,**145**,96
Hedera 39,43, **146**,51,98
  canariensis 43,**146**
  helix 39,**146**,85,99
Hedge thorn /*Carissa*
Hedychium
  40,146,147,**146**,31,96
  coronarium 146,**146**,97
  gardnerianum 146,**146**
  greenei 147,**146**
Helianthemum **146**,51
Helianthus **146**
  annuus **146**
Helichrysum **146**,50,52
  petiolare **146**
  stoechas **146**
Helleborus 147,**147**,39,62,97
  argutifolius **147**
  foetidus **147**
  lividus 147,**147**
  orientalis **147**
Hemerocallis 147,**147**,89,99
Herald's trumpet /*Beaumontia*
Hesperantha **147**,23
  vaginata **147**
Heteromeles **147**,44
  arbutifolia **147**,64,97,98
Hibbertia **147**
  scandens **147**
Hibiscus 148,**147**,30,37,97,99
  moscheutos **148**
  rosa-sinensis 148,**148**,52,77
  syriacus **148**
Hippeastrum 148,**148**,79,89,99
  'Appleblossom' 148,**148**
  aulicum **148**
  vittatum **148**
Hippophaë **148**
  rhamnoides **148**,98
Holly /*Ilex*
Holly grape /*Mahonia*
Hollyhock /*Alcea*
Homeria 149,**148**,89
  collina 149,**148**
Honey bells /*Freylinia*
Honey flower /*Melianthus*
Honey mesquite /*Prosopis*
Honeysuckle /*Lonicera*
Horsetail tree /*Casuarina*
Hortensia /*Hydrangea*
Hottentot bean /*Schotia*
Hottentot fig /*Carpobrotus*
House leek /*Sempervivum*
Hoya **148**
  carnosa **148**
Hummingbird flower /*Epilobium*
Hydrangea 76,**148**,77,100
  macrophylla 76,**148**,52
  quercifolia **148**,82
Hylotelephium 62,**148**
  telephium 62,**148**
Hypericum 149,**148**,21,39,48,52
  balearicum 149,**148**,56

calycinum **149**,51,98,99
canariense **149**
empetrifolium **149**
glandulosum **149**

Iberis **149**
  saxatilis 44,**149**,51
  sempervirens **149**,51
Ice Plants **149**
Ilex **149**
  aquifolium **149**,80
  paraguariensis **149**
  perado **149**
  vomitoria **149**
Impatiens **149**,79,88
  walleriana **149**,79
Incense cedar /*Calocedrus*
India hawthorn /*Rhaphiolepis*
Indigobush /*Amorpha*
Iochroma 150,**150**
  cyanea 150,**150**
  fuchsioides **150**
  grandiflora **150**
Ipheion **150**
  uniflorum **150**
Ipomoea 150,**150**
  alba 150,**150**
  horsfalliae **150**
  quamoclit **150**
Iris 38,89,150,**150**,89,99
  douglasiana **150**
  foetidissima **150**,47
  germanica 38,89,**150**,89,91
  japonica 151,**150**,47,51,96
  reticulata **151**
  susiana 150,**151**
  unguicularis 151,**151**,47,51,97
  xiphium **151**
Islay /*Prunus ilicifolia*
Ivy /*Hedera*
Ixia **151**,45
  maculata **151**
  monadelpha **151**
  viridiflora **151**

Jacaranda 151,**151**,43
  mimosifolia 151,**151**,43,80
Jade plant /*Crassula*
Japanese anemone /*Anemone*
Japanese pagoda tree /*Sophora*
Jasminum
  152,**152**,47,49,83,97-99
  azoricum **152**
  fruticans **152**,98
  humile 152,**152**
  mesnyi 152,**152**
  nudiflorum **152**,98
  officinale **152**
  polyanthum 152,**152**,98
  sambac **152**
  x stephanense **152**,98
Jerusalem sage /*Phlomis*
Jerusalem thorn /*Parkinsonia*
Jessamine /*Cestrum, Jasminum*
Jonquil /*Narcissus jonquilla*
Jubaea **152**
  chilensis **152**
Judas tree /*Cercis*

Juglans **152**,98
  californica **152**
Juniperus *153*,**153**,20,21,25,97-99
  californica **153**
  chinensis **153**
  communis **153**,99
  conferta **153**
  'Grey Owl' *153*,**153**
  horizontalis **153**,98
  occidentalis **153**
  oxycedrus **153**
  phoenicea **153**,20
  sabina **153**

*K*alanchoe *88*,*153*,**153**
  beharensis *88*,**153**,88
  blossfeldiana **153**
  daigremontiana **153**
  'Tessa' *153*,**153**
Kangaroo paw /*Anigozanthos*
Kapuka /*Griselinia*
Karoo gold /*Rhigozum*
Kei apple /*Dovyalis*
Kennedia **153**
  nigricans **153**
Khat /*Catha*
Kiwi Vine /*Actinidia*
Kniphofia **153**,89,98,99
  uvaria **153**,97
Koelreuteria **154**,87
  bipinnata **154**
  paniculata **154**,98
Kohuhu /*Pittosporum*
Kolkwitzia **154**
  amabilis **154**

*L*adanum /*Cistus*
Lagerstroemia **154**
  indica **154**,97,99
Lagunaria **154**,**154**
  patersonii *154*,**154**,97,98
Lamb's ears /*Stachys*
Lampranthus *13*,**154**,99
  aureus **154**
  blandus **155**
  roseus *13*,**155**
  spectabilis *13*,**155**
Lantana *154*,*155*,**155**,50,99
  camara **155**,**155**,85,97-99
  montevidensis
    154,**155**,48,51,98
Laurel /*Laurus*
Laurus *154*,**155**,65,20,94,96-100
  nobilis *154*,**155**,49,64,94,100
Laurustinus /*Viburnum tinus*
Lavandula
    27,*155*,**155**,20,47,97-99
  angustifolia **155**,64,98
  dentata *155*,**155**,64
  latifolia **155**,99
  multifida **155**,88
  stoechas **155**,98,51
Lavatera **155**
  arborea **155**
  maritima **155**,98
Lavender /*Lavandula*
Lavender cotton /*Santolina*
Lemon /*Citrus limon*

Lemon verbena /*Aloysia*
Lemonade berry /*Rhus*
Lenten rose /*Helleborus*
Lentisc /
  Pistacia lentiscus
Leonotis **156**
  leonurus **156**,22,59
Leopard lily /*Belamcanda*
Leptospermum **156**,98
  laevigatum **156**,97
  lanigerum **156**
  petersonii **156**
  scoparium **156**
Leucocoryne **156**
  ixioides **156**
Leucojum *156*,**156**
  aestivum *156*,**156**,64
Leucophyllum **156**
  frutescens **156**
Libertia *63*,*156*,**156**,87
  formosa *156*,**156**
  ixioides **156**
Libocedrus see *Calocedrus*
Licorice fern /*Polypodium*
Ligustrum *156*,**156**,99
  japonicum **156**
  lucidum **156**,47,97
  ovalifolium **156**
Lilac /*Syringa*
Lilac hibiscus /*Alyogyne*
Lilium *40*,*89*,*157*,**157**,87,89,99
  candidum *40*,**157**
  henryi *89*,**157**
  longiflorum **157**
  washingtonianum **157**
Lily of the Incas /*Alstroemeria*
Lily turf /*Liriope*
Limoniastrum **157**
  monopetalum **157**
Limonium **157**
  perezii **157**,96,98
Linum **157**
  perenne **157**
Lippia see *Aloysia*
Liriope *157*,**157**,51,89,97
  muscari *157*,**157**
  spicata **157**,51
Lithocarpus **157**
  densiflorus **157**
Lithodora **158**,51
  diffusa **158**,51
  rosmarinifolia **158**
Live-forever /*Hylotelephium*
Lizard plant /*Tetrastigma*
Lobularia **158**
  maritima **158**
Lonicera *158*,**158**,43,85,89,97-100
  etrusca **158**,98
  fragrantissima *158*,**158**,100,97
  hildebrandtiana **158**
  implexa *158*,**158**
  japonica **158**,98
  nitida **158**
Loquat /*Eriobotrya*
Lotus **158**,88
  berthelotii **158**
  creticus **158**
Love-in-a-mist /*Nigella*
Lupinus **158**
  arboreus **158**

Lyonothamnus **159**
  floribundus **159**

*M*acfadyena **159**,51,94
  unguis-cati **159**,51
Maclura **159**
  pomifera **159**,80
Madonna lily /*Lilium*
Madrone /*Arbutus menziesii*
Magnolia *159*,**159**
  grandiflora *159*,**159**,80,96,99
Mahonia *159*,**159**,87
  aquifolium **159**,80
  x *media* 'Charity' **159**
  pinnata **159**
Maiden pink /*Dianthus*
Maidenhair tree /*Ginkgo*
Mallee /*Eucalyptus*
Mandevilla **160**
  laxa **160**,97
Manna plant /*Tamarix*
Manuka /*Leptospermum*
Manzanita /*Arctostaphylos*
Marigold /*Calendula, Tagetes*
Mariposa lily /*Calochortus*
Marjoram /*Origanum*
Marlock /*Eucalyptus*
Marmalade bush /*Streptosolen*
Marvel of Peru /*Mirabilis*
Maté /*Ilex*
Matilija poppy /*Romneya*
Mediterranean fan palm /
  Chamaerops
Medlar /*Mespilus*
Melaleuca **160**,45,97,98
  armillaris **160**,87
  cordata **160**
  hypericifolia **160**
  microphylla **160**
  nesophila **160**
  styphelioides **160**
Melia **160**
  azederach **160**,64,98
Melianthus *17*,*35*,*160*,**160**,25,95
  major *17*,*35*,*160*,**160**,96,99
Melissa *161*,**160**
  officinalis *161*,**160**
Mescal bean /*Sophora*
Mesemb /*Lampranthus*
Mesembryanthemum **160**
  crystallinum **160**
Mespilus *161*,**160**,52
  germanica *161*,**160**
Metrosideros **161**
  excelsa **161**,98,99
Mexican orange /*Choisya*
Mimosa /*Acacia*
Mimulus *161*,**161**,77
  aurantiacus *161*,**161**
  bifidus **161**
  longiflorus **161**
Mint /*Mentha*
Mint bush /*Prostanthera*
Mirabilis *161*,**161**,87
  jalapa *161*,**161**,99
Mirror plant /*Coprosma*
Mission bells /*Fritillaria*
Mock orange /*Philadelphus*

Mock privet /*Phillyrea*
Mock strawberry /*Duchesnea*
Monkey flower /*Mimulus*
Montbretia /*Crocosmia*
Moraea **161**,23
  neopavonia **162**
  tripetala **162**
  villosa **162**
Morning glory /*Ipomoea*
Moroccan broom /*Argyrocytisus*
Morus **162**
  alba **162**,99
  nigra **162**,98
Moss cypress /*Crassula*
Mother of pearl plant/
  Graptopetalum
Mt. Etna broom /*Genista*
Mulberry /*Morus*
Mullein /*Verbascum*
Muscari *162*,**162**,23,59
  armeniacum *162*,**162**
Myoporum *162*,**162**,85,88,96-99
  debile **162**
  insulare **162**,99
  laetum *40*,*53*,*162*,**162**,97,98
  parvifolium **162**,98
Myrica **162**,94
  californica **162**
Myrsine *162*,**162**,88,94
  africana *162*,**162**,97-99
Myrtle /*Myrtus*
Myrtus *53*,*163*,**163**,59,88,95,96
  communis *53*,*163*,**163**,20,
    94-97,99
  ugni see *Ugni molinae*

*N*aboom /*Euphorbia*
Narcissus *163*,**163**,21,23,97
  bulbocodium **163**
  elegans **163**
  jonquilla **163**
  tazetta **163**,97
  triandrus **163**
Nasturtium /*Tropaeolum*
Natal bottlebrush /*Greyia*
Natal plum /*Carissa*
Native hops /*Dodonaea*
Needlewood /*Hakea*
Neomarica *163*,**163**
  gracilis *163*,**163**,97
  northiana **163**
Nepeta **163**
  x *faassenii* **163**
Nerine **163**,31,99
  sarniensis **163**,97
Nerium
    10,*88*,*95*,**164**,50,88,94,98
  oleander
    10,*88*,*95*,**164**,47,97-100
Net bush /*Calothamnus*
New Zealand flax /*Phormium*
New Zealand iris /*Libertia*
New Zealand laurel /*Corynocarpus*
Ngaio /*Myoporum*
Nigella **164**,87
  damascena **164**

*O*ak /*Quercus*

number in *italic* – illustration
bold number – main entry
normal print – short reference

Oenothera **164**
  drummondii **164**
  fruticosa **164**
  macrocarpa **164**
  speciosa **164**
Olea 19,20,30,89,**164**,20,87,99
  europaea var. *europaea*
    20,**164**,83
  europaea var. *oleaster*
    30,89,164,**164**,78,94
Oleander /*Nerium*
Olearia 164,165,**165**
  ciliata **165**
  x *haastii* 165,**165**
  insignis 72,164,**165**
Olive /*Olea*
Ophiopogon **165**,89,97
  japonicus **165**,51
  planiscapus **165**
Opuntia 165,**165**,85,94
  ficus-indica 165,**165**
Orach /*Atriplex*
Orange /*Citrus*
Orchid tree /*Bauhinia*
Oregon grape /*Mahonia*
Origanum **165**
  majorana **165**
Ornithogalum 165,**165**,21,23
  arabicum 165,**165**
  longibracteatum **165**,85
  montanum **166**
  narbonense **166**
  thyrsoides **166**
  umbellatum **166**
Osage orange /*Maclura*
Osmanthus **166**
  x *burkwoodii* **166**
  delavayi **166**
  fragrans **166**
  heterophyllus **166**,97
Osteospermum 42,**166**,70,98,99
  barberiae **166**
  ecklonis **166**
  fruticosum 42,**166**,51,97,99
Otanthus **166**
  maritimus **166**
Othonna **166**
  cheirifolia **166**
Our Lord's candle /*Yucca*
Oxalis **166**,85

Pachystegia see *Olearia*
Paeonia 87,166,**167**,31,62,87
  broteri **167**
  californica **167**
  cambessedesii 86,166,**167**
  clusii **167**
  mascula **167**
  officinalis **167**
Painted lady /*Gladiolus*
Palm /*Brahea, Butia, Chamaerops,*
  Jubaea, Phoenix, Washingtonia
Pancratium 167,**167**,23
  illyricum **167**
  maritimum 167,**167**,98

Pandorea **167**,86,94
  jasminoides **167**,99
  pandorana **167**
Paperbark /*Melaleuca*
Parkinsonia 167,**167**
  aculeata 167,**167**
Parrot's beak /*Clianthus, Lotus*
Parthenocissus **168**
  tricuspidata 168,98,99
Passiflora 92,168,**168**,58,97
  caerulea **168**
  x *caeruleoracemosa* **168**
  cinnabarina 168,**168**
  edulis **168**
  ligularis **168**
  manicata **168**
  mollissima **168**
Passion flower /*Passiflora*
Paulownia **168**
  tomentosa **168**
Pavonia 169,**168**,22
  hastata 169,**168**
Peacock flower /*Moraea*
Pecan /*Carya*
Pelargonium 27,52,53,**169**,
  44,49,65,88,96,100
  carnosum **169**
  x *domesticum* 27,**169**,99
  graveolens **169**
  x *hortorum* 52,**169**,99
  peltatum 53,**169**,51,97,98
  tomentosum **169**,51
Penstemon 17,137,169,**169**,45
  barbatus **169**
  heterophyllus **169**,98
  pinifolius **169**
  spectabilis 169,**169**
Peony /*Paeonia*
Pepper tree /*Schinus*
Periwinkle /*Catharanthus, Vinca*
Perovskia **169**
  atriplicifolia **169**
Persea 170,**170**
  americana 170,**170**,83
Persian buttercup /*Ranunculus*
Persimmon /*Diospyros*
Petunia **170**,81
Philadelphus 171,**170**,94,97
  coronarius **170**
  lewisii **170**
  mexicanus **170**
Phillyrea 30,**170**,20,43
  angustifolia 30,**170**
  latifolia **170**
Phlomis 170,**170**,21,88,95
  fruticosa 170,**171**,43
  italica **171**
Phlox **171**
  subulata **171**
Phoenix 2,13,45,104,**171**,49,97-99
  canariensis 13,39,45,**171**,95
  dactylifera 104,**171**
  theophrastii **171**
Phormium 171,**171**,89
  colensoi **171**
  tenax 171,**171**,47,96,98,99
Photinia **171**
  serratifolia **171**
Phygelius 170,**171**,52
  aequalis 170,**171**

Phyla **171**
  nodiflora **171**,51
Phylica 171,**171**
  ericoides 171,**171**,47,51
  plumosa **171**
Pimelea **172**,64
  ferruginea **172**
Pincushion flower /*Scabiosa*
Pincushion tree /*Hakea*
Pine /*Pinus*
Pineapple Guava /*Acca*
Pinus 14,173,**172**,31,79,87,97-99
  halepensis 14,173,**172**,20
  pinaster **172**,20
  pinea **172**,20
  radiata **172**
  torreyana **172**
Pistachio /*Pistacia*
Pistacia 17,21,35,83,**172**,22,31
  atlantica **172**
  chinensis **172**,98
  lentiscus 17,19,21,35,38,40,
    63,83,**172**,20,94,
  terebinthus **172**
  vera **172**
Pittosporum 172,173,**173**,88,97-99
  crassifolium **173**
  eugenioides **173**
  phillyreoides **173**
  tenuifolium **173**
  tobira 172,173,**173**,96,98,99
  undulatum **173**,85
Plane /*Platanus*
Platanus 173,**173**,52
  x *acerifolia* **173**
  occidentalis **173**
  orientalis 173,**173**
Plectranthus 174,**174**,88,99
  arabicus 174,**174**,99
Plum /*Prunus* x *domestica*
Plumbago 57,174,**174**,50,58,88
  auriculata 57,174,**174**,83,99
Podranea 41,175,**174**,83,94
  ricasoliana 41,174,**174**,99
Pohutukawa /*Metrosideros*
Poinciana see *Caesalpinia*
Poinsettia /*Euphorbia*
Polygala 174,**174**,88
  myrtifolia 174,**174**,97
  virgata **174**
Polygonum **174**,99
  aubertii **174**,99
  capitatum **174**,51
Polypodium 175,**175**
  cambricum 175,**175**
  glycyrrhiza **175**
  scouleri **175**
Pomaderris **175**
  grandis **175**
Pomegranate /*Punica*
Poncirus **175**
  trifoliata **175**
Poplar /*Populus*
Populus **175**,54
  alba **175**,98
  nigra **175**,99
Portugal laurel /*Prunus*
Portulaca 175,**175**
  grandiflora 175,**175**
Portulacaria **175**

  afra **175**
Potato vine /*Solanum*
Potentilla **175**
  fruticosa **175**
Prickly Moses /*Acacia*
Prickly pear /*Opuntia*
Pride of de Kaap /*Bauhinia*
Pride of Madeira /*Echium*
Pride of Tenerife /*Echium*
Privet /*Ligustrum*
Prosopis **175**
  glandulosa **175**
Prostanthera **175**
  cuneata **175**
  rotundifolia **175**
Protea 176,**176**,31,96
  susannae 176,**176**
Prunus 19,23,58,176,**176**,59,88
  armeniaca 176,**176**,82
  x *domestica* **176**
  dulcis 19,23,176,**176**,43,81,97
  ilicifolia **176**,64
  lusitanica **176**,96,99
  lyonii **176**
  serotina **176**
  serrulata **176**
  spinosa 58,**177**
Psidium **177**,97
  guajava **177**
  littorale **177**,80
Punica 177,**177**,43,52
  granatum 177,**177**,98,99
Pyracantha 50,**177**,97,98
  angustifolia **177**
  coccinea 50,**177**,98
Pyramid tree /*Lagunaria*
Pyrostegia **177**
  venusta **177**,99

Quercus **177**,24,31,87,97-99
  agrifolia **178**
  coccifera **178**,20
  douglasii **178**
  dumosa **178**
  ilex 19,21,57,171,178,**178**,20,98
  ithaburensis **178**
  libani **178**
  lobata **178**
  pubescens **178**
  suber **178**,24

Ranunculus 179,**179**
  asiaticus 179,**179**
Red valerian /*Centranthus*
Red-hot poker /*Kniphofia*
Red-skinned onion /*Allium*
Redbud /*Cercis*
Rengarenga /*Arthropodium*
Retama **179**,26
  monosperma **179**,26
Rhamnus
  19,40,179,**179**,87,94,96-99
  alaternus 19,40,**179**,20,49,96-98
  californica **179**,64,96
  ludovici-salvatoris 179 **179**,49
Rhaphiolepis 179,**179**
  x *delacourii* 179,**179**
  indica **179**,97,98

umbellata **179**
Rhigozum **180**
    obovatum **180**
Rhus **180**,86
    integrifolia **180**,98
    lancea **180**,95,98
    ovata **180**,97
Ribes **180**
    speciosum **180**
    viburnifolium **180**,98
Ricinus 26,*180*,**180**,26
    communis
        26,*180*,**180**,26,96,99
Robinia 180,181,**180**,94
    hispida 'Macrophylla' *180*,**180**
    pseudoacacia
        181,*181*,85,97,99
Rock lily /*Arthropodium*
Rock rose /*Cistus*
Rockcress /*Arabis*
Romneya 12,**181**,44,86
    coulteri *12*,**181**
Romulea **181**
    bulbocodium **181**
    citrina **181**
Rosa 59,181,**181**,83,89
    banksiae **181**,83,98
    phoenicia **181**
    rugosa **181**,98
    sempervirens **181**,*181*
Rose acacia /*Robinia*
Rose mallow /*Hibiscus*
Rose moss /*Portulaca*
Rosemary /*Rosmarinus*
Rosmarinus **182**,*182*,20,88,89
    officinalis **182**,*182*,47,51,97-99
Royal paint brush /*Scadoxus*
Rubber plant /*Ficus elastica*
Rudbeckia **182**
    fulgida **182**
Rue /*Ruta*
Ruscus 183,**182**,89
    aculeatus **183**,*182*,51
    hypoglossum **182**,51,96
Russelia 183,**182**
    equisetiformis **183**,*182*
Russian olive /*Elaeagnus*
Russian sage /*Perovskia*
Ruta **182**,52,87
    graveolens **182**

Sage /*Salvia*
Sago palm /*Cycas*
Salt cedar /*Tamarix*
Saltbush /*Atriplex*
Salvia 183,**182**,22,88,99
    apiana **182**
    clevelandii **182**
    elegans **182**
    fruticosa **183**
    greggii **183**
    involucrata 183,**183**
    lavandulifolia **183**
    leucantha **183**,83
    leucophylla **183**
    mellifera **183**
    microphylla **183**,97
    officinalis **183**,99
    patens **183**

sonomensis **183**,98
    splendens **183**
Samphire /*Crithmum*
Sansevieria **183**
    trifasciata **183**
Santolina 183,**183**,51,98
    chamaecyparissus *183*,**183**,98
    rosmarinifolia **183**
Sarcococca **183**,65
    hookeriana **184**
    ruscifolia **184**
Satureja **184**
    hortensis **184**
    thymbra **184**
Savin /*Juniperus sabina*
Scabiosa **184**
    columbaria **184**
Scadoxus 184,**184**,31,79,99
    multiflorus **184**
    puniceus 184,**184**
Schefflera 184,**184**
    actinophylla 184,**184**,96
Schinus **184**,100
    molle **184**,97-99
    terebinthifolius **184**,97
Schotia **184**
    afra **184**,98
    brachypetala **184**
Scilla **184**,21
    peruviana **184**
    siberica **184**
Scorpion senna /*Coronilla*
Sea buckthorn /*Hippophaë*
Sea daffodil /*Pancratium*
Sea dahlia /*Coreopsis*
Sea lavender /*Limonium*
Sea pink /*Armeria*
Sea squill /*Urginea*
Sea tomato /*Rosa rugosa*
Sedum 185,*184*,50,88
    album **185**
    rubrotinctum 185,**185**
    sediforme **185**
Sempervivum **185**,89
    arachnoideum **185**
    ciliosum **185**
    tectorum **185**
Senecio 15,53,185,**185**,83,97
    cineraria 15,185,**185**,98
    glastifolius 53,**185**
    greyi see *Brachyglottis*
    mikanioides see *Delairea*
Senna 185,86
    alata **185**
    armata **185**
    artemisioides **185**
    didymobotrya **185**
    multiglandulosa **185**
    sturtii **185**
She oak /*Casuarina*
Siberian pea tree /*Caragana*
Silk tassel /*Garrya*
Silk tree /*Albizia*
Silky oak /*Grevillea*
Silver lace vine /*Polygonum*
Silverberry /*Elaeagnus*
Silverbush /*Convolvulus*
Sisyrinchium **185**,87
    bellum 185,51
    californicum **185**

striatum **185**
Sky vine /*Thunbergia*
Sloe /*Prunus spinosa*
Smilacina **186**
    racemosa **186**
Smoke tree /*Cotinus*
Snake plant /*Sansevieria*
Snake vine /*Hibbertia*
Snapdragon /*Antirrhinum*
Snow on the mountain /*Euphorbia*
Snow-in-summer /*Cerastium*
Snowflake /*Leucojum*
Solandra 186,**186**,88,89
    maxima 186,**186**,83,96,97
Solanum 187,**186**,47,88
    crispum **186**
    jasminoides 187,**186**,58,98,99
Sollya 187,**186**
    heterophylla 187,**186**
Sophora **186**
    japonica **186**,80
    secundiflora **186**,97
Sotol /*Dasylirion*
South African wisteria /
    Bolusanthus
Southernwood /*Artemisia*
Southsea ironwood /*Casuarina*
Spanish bayonet /*Yucca*
Spanish broom /*Spartium*
Spanish chestnut /*Castanea*
Spanish dagger /*Yucca*
Spanish gorse /*Genista*
Sparaxis **186**,45
    tricolor **186**,98
Sparmannia **186**,95,99
    africana **186**,99
Spartium 30,**187**,20,79
    junceum **187**,20,26,85,97
Spathodea **187**
    campanulata **187**
Spear lily /*Doryanthes*
Spekboom /*Portulacaria*
Spiraea **187**,59,88,94
    cantoniensis **187**
    douglasii 187,54
Spring starflower /*Ipheion*
Spurge /*Euphorbia*
Spurge olive /*Cneorum*
St. Catherine's lace /*Eriogonum*
Stachys **187**
    byzantina **187**
Star glory /*Ipomoea*
Star jasmine /*Trachelospermum*
Star of Bethlehem /*Ornithogalum*
Sternbergia 58,187,**187**,22,58
    lutea 58,187,**187**,22,99
Strawberry /*Fragaria*
Strawberry tree /*Arbutus unedo*
Strelitzia **187**,99
    reginae 187,96,97
Streptocarpus **187**,88
    rexii **187**
Streptosolen 188,**188**
    jamesonii 188,**188**
Styrax **188**
    officinale **188**,59
Succulents 56,**188**,98,99
Sugar bush /*Rhus*
Sumac /*Rhus*
Sun flower /*Helianthus*

Sun rose /*Helianthemum*
Sundrop /*Oenothera*
Sutherlandia **188**
    frutescens **188**
Sweet alyssum /*Lobularia*
Sweet bay /*Laurus*
Sweet box /*Sarcococca*
Sweet granadilla /*Passiflora*
Sweet olive /*Osmanthus*
Syringa 188,**188**,37,59
    x *chinensis* **188**
    microphylla 188,**188**, 97
    vulgaris **188**

Tagetes **188**
Tamarix **189**,47,85,88,97-99
    africana **189**
    chinensis **189**
    gallica **189**
    ramosissima **189**
Tanacetum 31,**189**
    parthenium 31,**189**,85
Tanbark oak /*Lithocarpus*
Tarata /*Pittosporum*
Taupata /*Coprosma*
Tawhiwhi /*Pittosporum*
Taxus **189**,59
    baccata **189**,97
Tea tree /*Leptospermum*
Tecoma **189**
    stans **189**
Tecomaria 189,**189**,83
    capensis 189,**189**,47,98,99
Telanthophora 189,**189**
    grandifolia 189,**189**
Templetonia 190,**190**
    retusa 190,**190**,97
Tetraclinis 191,**190**,83
    articulata 191,**190**
Tetrastigma **190**
    voinierianum 190,**190**,98,99
Teucrium 190,**190**,43,72,83,88
    chamaedrys **190**,51
    flavum **190**
    fruticans 190,**190**,43,83,97-99
Texas ranger /*Leucophyllum*
Thryptomene **190**,65
    saxicola **190**
Thunbergia 190,**190**,99
    grandiflora **190**
    gregorii 190,**190**,97
Thymelaea **190**
    hirsuta **190**
    tartonraira **190**
Thymus **191**,47,50,88
    serpyllum **191**,99
    vulgaris **191**,99
Tipu tree /*Tipuana*
Tipuana **191**
    tipu **191**,43,98,99
Tithonia **191**
    rotundifolia **191**
Tobira /*Pittosporum*
Trachelium **191**,*191*,39
    caeruleum 191,**191**
Trachelospermum
    191,49,51,94,96
    asiaticum **191**,98,99
    jasminoides **191**,98,99

number in *italic* – illustration
bold number – main entry
normal print – short reference

Tradescantia *191,***191**,88
  *fluminensis 191,***191**
  sillamontana **191**
Transvaal daisy /*Gerbera*
Treasure flower /*Gazania*
Tree fuchsia /*Schotia*
Tree Mallow /*Lavatera*
Tree of heaven /*Ailanthus*
Tree poppy /*Dendromecon*
Trichostema **191**,44
  lanatum **191**
Triteleia **192**
  ixioides **192**
  laxa **192**
Tritonia **192**
  crocata **192**
Tropaeolum **192**,***192**,43,99
  majus
    *192,***192**,43,47,50,51,86
Trumpet bush /*Tecoma*
Trumpet creeper /*Campsis,
    Pyrostegia*
Trumpet vine /*Bignonia, Distictis,
    Macfadyena, Podranea*
Tulbaghia **193**,***192**,87
  fragrans **192**
  *violacea 193,***192**,98
Tulipa **192**,***192**,31,59
  clusiana **192**

  greigii **192**
  praestans **192**
  *saxatilis 192,***192**
  sylvestris **192**
Turutu /*Dianella*

Ugni **192**
  molinae **192**
Umbellularia **192**
  californica **192**,64,97
Urginea 69,**193**,22,58
  *maritima 69,***193**,98

Veltheimia **193**,99
  capensis **193**
Venidium see *Arctotis*
Verbascum 25,**193**
  olympicum **193**
Verbena **193**,51
  peruviana **193**,51,98
  rigida **193**
Viburnum 80,**193**,***193**,97
  x *burkwoodii* **193**
  plicatum 'Mariesii' **193**
  suspensum **193**,96
  tinus 80,**193**,***193**,20,
    42,47,58,87,89,96-99
Victorian box /*Pittosporum*
Vinca **193**,***193**,47,89,96-100
  *difformis 193,***193**,51,96-99
  minor **193**,51

Vine lilac /*Hardenbergia*
Viola **193**,51
  odorata **193**,97
Violet /*Viola*
Violet mist /*Bartlettina*
Vitex **194**
  agnus-castus **194**,80
Vitis 53,194,**194**,49
  *vinifera 53,194,***194**,81

Wallflower /*Erysimum*
Washingtonia 194,49,98
  filifera **194**
  robusta **194**
Watsonia **194**,45
  borbonica **194**
  fourcadei **194**
Wattle /*Acacia*
Wax plant /*Hoya*
Weather prophet /*Dimorphotheca*
Welsh polypody /*Polypodium*
Western tea myrtle /*Melaleuca*
Westringia 194,**194**,45,59,88,94
  *fruticosa 194,***194**,47,97-99
Widdringtonia 194,**194**
  nodiflora 194,**194**
Willow myrtle /*Agonis*
Willow-leaved peppermint/
    Eucalyptus
Wintersweet /*Acokanthera*
Wisteria 90,**194**,47,98
  floribunda **194**

  sinensis 90,**194**,97
Wonga-wonga vine /*Pandorea*
Woolly blue curls /*Trichostema*
Wormwood /*Artemisia*

Xanthorrhoea **195**
  quadrangulata **195**

Yarrow /*Achillea*
Yatay palm /*Butia*
Yaupon /*Ilex vomitoria*
Yew /*Taxus*
Yucca 22,80,194,**195**,
    22,47,88,99
  aloifolia **195**
  elephantipes 80,**195**
  filamentosa **195**
  gloriosa 194,**195**,97,100,
  whipplei 22,169,**195**,98

Zantedeschia 68,195,**195**,96,99
  aethiopica 68,195,**195**,22,64
  elliotiana **195**
  rehmannii **195**
Zauschneria see *Epilobium*
Zinnia 81,**195**,81
Ziziphus **195**
  jujuba **195**

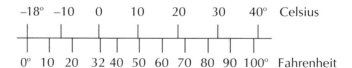

Temperature Conversion   °C = 5/9 (°F−32)   °F = 9/5°C+32

| −18° | −10 | 0 | 10 | 20 | 30 | 40° | Celsius |

| 0° | 10 | 20 | 32 | 40 | 50 | 60 | 70 | 80 | 90 | 100° | Fahrenheit |

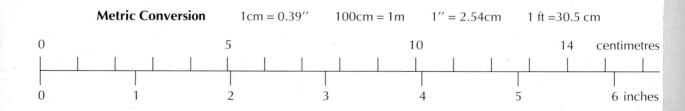

Metric Conversion   1cm = 0.39"   100cm = 1m   1" = 2.54cm   1 ft =30.5 cm

| 0 | 5 | 10 | 14 | centimetres |
| 0 | 1 | 2 | 3 | 4 | 5 | 6 inches |